Reimagining Criminal Justice, Search for Truth and Human Rights

Salah H. Khaled Jr.

Reimagining Criminal Justice, Search for Truth and Human Rights

Moving Beyond Objectifying Inquisitorial Procedures

palgrave
macmillan

Salah H. Khaled Jr.
Faculty of Law
Universidade Federal do Rio Grande
- FURG
Rio Grande, Rio Grande do Sul
Brazil

ISBN 978-3-032-27226-3 ISBN 978-3-032-27227-0 (eBook)
https://doi.org/10.1007/978-3-032-27227-0

The original submitted manuscript has been translated into English. The translation was done using artificial intelligence. A subsequent revision was performed by the author(s) to further refine the work and to ensure that the translation is appropriate concerning content and scientific correctness. It may, however, read stylistically different from a conventional translation.

Cover credit: Ricardo Takamura

This Palgrave Macmillan imprint is published by the registered company Springer Nature Switzerland AG
The registered company address is: Gewerbestrasse 11, 6330 Cham, Switzerland

Contents

CHAPTER 1

Reimagining Criminal Justice and Confronting the Search for Truth in Criminal Proceedings

This book provides a critical analysis of the "ambition for truth" in criminal proceedings, highlighting how this perspective continues to shape current practices and may, in some cases, contribute to the objectification of defendants and the infringement of human rights. Furthermore, it contends that evidential inquisitorialism, evidentiary positivism, and evidentiary rationalism are distinct epistemologies united by an underlying authoritarian political agenda: the pursuit of truth. Adopting a radically different perspective, this study is based on the principle that contemporary criminal justice systems should prioritise the safeguarding of human rights. Instead of perceiving defendants as societal enemies, it is crucial to establish epistemological frameworks that critically examine and resist the inheriting selectivity of the penal system—a phenomenon where particular social groups, such as those who are economically disadvantaged, marginalised, or racialised, are disproportionately subject to targeting, arrest, and conviction.

History shows that rather than functioning as a mechanism for the underprivileged to challenge authoritarian power, criminal justice appears to reinforce police selectivity and contribute to the widespread incarceration of the same populations, perpetuating existing hierarchies related to class, race, gender, sexuality, and spirituality.

S. H. Khaled Jr., *Reimagining Criminal Justice, Search for Truth and Human Rights*, https://doi.org/10.1007/978-3-032-27227-0_1

Contemporary criminal proceedings are guided by an ideology focused on the pursuit of truth, which may result in practices that risk infringing upon human rights and the dignity of individuals facing charges.

A transition towards prioritising human rights is therefore essential. Achieving this objective necessitates a departure from the persistently dominant inquisitorial approach centred on the "search for truth" within criminal proceedings and requires political, cultural and epistemological transformation. Consequently, it is imperative to reconceptualise criminal justice, the pursuit of truth, and human rights, to prevent the objectification of accused individuals.

The pursuit of truth is widely regarded as the primary objective within the criminal justice system, often considered superior to other objectives such as the protection of human rights and the assurance of due process. This interpretation prevails in current studies of evidentiary rationalism, where the judge is assigned an "epistemic function" (Taruffo 2010) focused on truth-seeking, which encompasses the management of evidence and compromises the impartiality required by the accusatory model of criminal proceedings. History shows that when the search for truth is elevated to a central place, the accused's safeguards are invariably relegated to the margins.

The perspective presented here departs significantly from rationalist approaches. While frequently characterised as a mechanism for achieving justice, this inquisitorial-inspired rationalist epistemology—with its emphasis on truth-seeking—operates within an authoritative framework that tends to overlook the possibility that criminal proceedings can potentially confirm outcomes already anticipated by the judge (Coutinho 2023). Notably, this rationalist model is distinguished by its tendency to privilege hypotheses over empirical evidence, which can have detrimental implications for the defendant and increases the likelihood of wrongful convictions.

Advocates of evidentiary rationalism often question the necessity of rules designed to protect human rights and support their removal in pursuit of a comprehensive search for truth (Laudan 2013; Beltrán 2021).

Despite these concerns, the dominance of the search for truth ideology within the criminal justice system persists, supported by a longstanding authoritarian tradition that is rarely acknowledged by its proponents. Contemporary criminal justice systems governed by civil law frameworks primarily adhere to the principle of truth-seeking, a core tenet rooted in the inquisitorial model established in Continental Europe during the twelfth and thirteenth centuries.

Throughout the ensuing centuries, the convergence of truth-seeking with the objectification of the accused remained a consistent feature. Neither the advent of penal modernity nor the process of secularisation produced significant political or epistemological shifts in this regard. The implementation of the French "mixed" criminal procedure system in the nineteenth century, together with advancements in scientific methodologies and the adoption of legal positivist epistemology based on the subject-object framework, reinforced a focus on truth-seeking. This system was designed to enhance mechanisms for social control rather than to promote civil liberties and was widely adopted in Continental Europe and Latin America.

Modern procedural systems underpinned by legal positivist epistemology continued inquisitorial "lovelessness for adversarial proceedings" (Martins 2010), positioning the judge and prosecution as collaborators within a "scientific" framework. Rather than advancing adversarial structures, the Cartesian philosophy of consciousness, which underpins this renewed orientation towards uncovering truth, reinforced the cognitive authority of the judge by centralising evidentiary management, ultimately serving mechanisms of social control (Streck 2016).

In the early twentieth century, criminal procedure principles established in Fascist Italy gained significant prominence and were widely adopted as models for authoritarian governance centred on truth-seeking. These principles notably impacted Brazil by shaping judicial practices related to mass and selective incarceration, and they also influenced emerging forms of authoritarian social control in other Western countries that follow the civil law tradition.

Over time, an objectification-centred approach to criminal procedure has become prevalent, forming a key element within systems that may infringe upon human rights and contribute to elevated incarceration rates among populations made vulnerable by global capitalism. A key element of this dynamic is the conceptualisation of truth and the view of criminal proceedings as mechanisms for its determination—a perspective that remains prominent in civil law systems. In these jurisdictions, judges play a pivotal role in managing evidence and, in accordance with contemporary rationalist evidentiary law frameworks, fulfil an "epistemic function" (Taruffo 2010) centred on truth-seeking—one that potentially leads to human rights violations and the objectification of the accused.

This matter transcends theoretical considerations, underscoring the critical necessity to reassess criminal justice systems and reflect on the influence of prevailing rationalist epistemological frameworks—particularly those articulated by Michelle Taruffo and Jordi Ferrer Beltrán, that are highly influential in continental Europe and Latin America.

These frameworks have subtly reimplemented inquisitorial approaches to truth-seeking and promoted the adoption of Alfred Tarski's correspondence theory of truth. However, the uncritical adoption of Tarski's theory within procedural epistemologies is problematic; originally intended for different purposes, it does not adequately account for the specific contextual factors inherent in evidentiary practices within criminal proceedings and favours authoritarian tendencies.

In contrast to the static perspective offered by rationalism, criminal procedure is more accurately understood as a political, cultural, social, and fundamentally human phenomenon. It involves individuals who are not merely executors of legal mandates but actors guided by intent and interpretation, responding with agency and adaptability to varied contexts. Each criminal proceeding emerges from a distinctive interplay between the broad application of primary criminalisation (criminal law), an event that results in a criminalised action, and a pattern of social interaction that encompasses secondary criminalisation by law enforcement and charges initiated by the Public Prosecutor's Office. It is only after these developments that the judicial process commences, wherein the judge, prosecutor, and defence counsel assume their respective roles to determine the outcome for the accused within an environment characterised by complexity and uncertainty.

As discussed throughout this book, both the ideology of truth-seeking and the conceptualisation of truth within criminal proceedings substantially influence outcomes for the accused. Employing a correspondence theory of truth and establishing truth-seeking as the primary objective of judicial proceedings may lead to practices that objectify individuals and lead to judicial errors.

This indicates the need for a revised perspective on truth and human rights protection to support effective harm reduction strategies. Based on this premise, this study seeks to examine the production of truth in criminal proceedings, going beyond the epistemic excesses associated with correspondence-based concepts of truth. It aims to challenge dominant notions by proposing an approach that prioritises respect for the human rights of the accused and rejects objectification.

Rather than simply documenting the prevailing penal authoritarianism in Western contexts, this study offers an epistemology of restraint intended to encourage containment, minimalism, and moderation—a programme of minimal intervention as advocated by Bosworth (Bosworth 2010: 252). The goal is to curtail authoritarian practices and mitigate adverse effects arising from the exercise, whether excessive or not, of state power—a genuine policy focused on harm reduction (Lopes Jr 2007: 56).

Examining criminal justice from a harm reduction perspective facilitates an analysis focused on safeguarding human rights and addressing the ongoing objectification of individuals accused of crimes—an issue prevalent worldwide and stemming from inquisitorial traditions that continue to influence civil law systems.

Building on this foundational premise, the discussion will address the cognitive framework of criminal procedure, emphasising its inherent complexity. This methodology facilitates a critical analysis of conventional monological and coercive standards in the construction and enforcement of truth within Western criminal justice, thereby opening possibilities for reimagining judicial practices.

This study acknowledges the urgency of advancing models of criminal procedure that may offer viable alternatives to Western criminal justice, which faces well-documented challenges. These include the reinforcement of social hierarchies defined by class, race, gender, sexuality, and spirituality (Khaled Jr and Gloecker 2026), as well as its tendency to perpetuate power imbalances and marginalisation, rather than safeguarding the rights of individuals made vulnerable by global capitalism. Recognising these realities, the proposed approach aims to develop a harm reduction programme firmly dedicated to the promotion and defence of human rights within existing structures.

This perspective acknowledges that, while the eventual elimination of criminal justice and the prison complex may be an aspirational goal, it is not feasible under current historical circumstances. Consequently, critiques are directed towards resistance and potential restructuring of the existing system, informed by a sense of urgency.

Against this backdrop, it becomes imperative to interrogate the relationship between criminal procedure and the broader socio-political context in which it operates. By exposing the limitations inherent in systems that privilege the search for truth over the safeguarding of individual rights, this study recognises the urgent need for judicial practices that are responsive to the realities of marginalisation and social inequality.

A reimagined criminal justice system must therefore adopt frameworks that foreground procedural fairness, transparency, and the dignity of all participants. Such an approach requires moving beyond rationalist models and embracing pluralistic and interdisciplinary methodologies capable of challenging entrenched power structures and providing meaningful protection to those most at risk of injustice—something that criminal justice systems have failed to properly address.

Reimagining criminal justice involves revising the epistemological foundations of criminal procedure. This process is comparable to how international law addressed the realities of war, ultimately leading to the establishment of international humanitarian law. The latter does not serve to legitimise conflict; rather, it aims to prevent or alleviate its most severe consequences.

The integration of global political mechanisms with regional judicial oversight illustrates that international humanitarian law aims to establish an initial framework for planetary citizenship and protection of human rights. This approach ensures that, in principle, every individual is recognised as a person entitled to a basic set of rights, which must be upheld irrespective of nationality, belief, race, gender, sexual orientation, ethnicity, culture, financial standing, health, age, or any other grounds that could potentially serve as justification for denial or violation (Zaffaroni 2022: 6).

It is imperative to recognise that the genuine legality regarding punitive and military power lies not in their application, but rather in ensuring their measured and reasonable moderation. Such restraint is essential to uphold the credibility of legal scholarship and to prevent future disregard for legal principles. Maintaining this ontological respect within the law is required both ethically and, most importantly, legally, as it concerns the effective enforcement of constitutional and international norms (Zaffaroni 2026).

However, despite the existence of international human rights treaties, the persistent application of inquisitorial, positivist and rationalist epistemologies in Western criminal justice systems—especially those based on civil law traditions—remains a significant concern. This framework can be associated with repeated human rights infringements by State actors, including law enforcement officials, prosecutors, and judges. Consequently, effectively incorporating human rights principles into criminal justice processes and penal institutions continues to present substantial challenges, as authoritarian and selective mechanisms of social control often take precedence over humanitarian considerations.

In capitalist societies, the operation of penal systems is guided by an underlying structural logic that extends beyond isolated actions. This framework encompasses both covert selectivity and overt arbitrariness, resulting in violations of human rights that contravene not only the normative principles—such as constitutional commitments to the rule of law and liberal criminal procedure—but also the intended purposes of criminal law and punishment. At a fundamental level, this system is characterised by a reversed instrumental effectiveness underpinned by symbolic legitimisation (Andrade 2012: 2022).

A thorough analysis of the societal effects of criminal laws and prohibitions is essential, especially considering their social costs. The penal system, traditionally perceived as an instrument for combating crime, has progressively broadened its definitions of criminal behaviour, thereby criminalising increasing facets of human activity in pursuit of an elusive ideal of societal security. This ongoing expansion reinforces the penal system's punitive character and legitimises its authority by positioning security as an overriding principle. As a result, this dynamic tends to weaken horizontal social bonds within communities, while simultaneously consolidating vertical structures of authority (Zaffaroni et al., 2003: 59).

In practice, the system demonstrates a pronounced selectivity when transitioning from primary criminalisation (criminal law) to secondary criminalisation (police enforcement). The ostensibly "egalitarian" legislative agenda often becomes in practice a mechanism for targeting socially vulnerable groups, reflecting certain underlying conditions that enable this outcome (Zaffaroni et al., 2003: 59). As Zaffaroni notes, the exercise of power within all penal systems tends to reproduce violence, selectivity, institutionalised corruption, power concentration, social hierarchy, and the erosion of communal relationships. These are not merely situational features but rather structural in nature (Zaffaroni et al., 2003: 15). Ultimately, the system predominantly targets individuals accused of street-level criminal acts, who typically lack access to political or economic influence or mass communication, thus presenting fewer obstacles to such selective enforcement (Zaffaroni et al., 2003: 46).

In this context, the criminal justice system reinforces selective policing practices, rather than serving as a safeguard against authoritarianism that upholds opportunities for the accused to exercise resistance and have their rights protected. More specifically, the dominant emphasis on uncovering the truth can potentially diminish the accused's capacity to challenge charges and may influence the judge's role away from strict impartiality towards an orientation more closely associated with the prosecution.

There is a need to challenge this paradigm and consider alternative approaches to criminal justice: as it has been argued, the subject of Western knowledge does not seek the truth, but only the truth that grants him power; for this reason, he forces the object to respond, even under torture, both in the inquisitorial procedure and in the scientific method (Zaffaroni 2022: 174).

Contrary to conventional assumptions, there exists a continuity rather than an opposition between inquisitorial epistemology and modern rationality. The philosophy of conscience has, in its unique manner, enhanced the cognitive privilege of the judge inherent to the inquisitorial system.

As will be examined throughout this book, the "search for truth in criminal proceedings" ideology represents a complex intersection of knowledge and power that facilitates the continuation of objectifying approaches toward the accused. This dynamic can lead to violations of human rights, despite being routinely presented as serving noble objectives such as the "common good" and "social peace".

This ideology also facilitates viewing the accused as less than fully human. Within this framework, any leniency extended towards the offender is perceived as demonstrating disregard for the victim's suffering (Garland 2008). Contrary to this trend, it is important to state that all individuals are human beings and, as such, possess inalienable rights that exist independently of state recognition or concession.

The perspective adopted in this book does not regard human rights as benefits granted by the State, but as historical constructs arising from the struggles of peoples against oppression. Therefore, it does not settle for the traditional theory of human rights, which assumes that their legal codification and safeguards are sufficient to limit State abuses (Carvalho 2022: 216), something that has historically proven insufficient—despite the enshrinement of human rights at the international normative level, their effectiveness remains relative, as atrocities continue to be committed (Zaffaroni 2022: 8). Rather than being satisfied with mere rhetorical appeals, the task now is to defend the discourse of human rights from any imperial hegemonic pretensions and to reaffirm them as instruments of popular struggle and resistance (Zaffaroni 2022: 19–20) within a reimagined criminal justice system.

This context necessitates a critical evaluation of the procedural cognitive framework. Achieving meaningful reform requires abandoning the pursuit of truth, in all its forms—whether real, material, substantial, relative, or approximate—as such approaches contribute to the objectification of defendants and facilitate systematic violations of human rights.

For the purposes of the analysis proposed here, the reader will notice the recurrence of certain arguments throughout the chapters. This approach aims both to clarify the topics of each section and to consolidate these arguments through the issues, themes, and problems discussed in each chapter, which collectively converge towards the goal of reimagining criminal justice that underpins the writing of this book.

The issue of truth in criminal proceedings still requires significant discussion, especially considering the many abuses enabled by relying on the concept of corresponding truth and the judge's presumed ability to uncover it. Luigi Ferrajoli asserts that "without an adequate theory of truth, verifiability, and procedural verification, the entire construction of Enlightenment criminal law [...] ends up resting on sand; the political and civil functions associated with it are rendered purely ideological and thus disqualified" (Ferrajoli 2002: 39).

Ferrajoli reviewed the discourse on "real truth" and moved beyond conventional criminal procedure methodologies. But he did not fully move past the boundaries of corresponding truth, retaining it in a relativised form. Similarly, Michele Taruffo, within the framework of contemporary rationalist thought, adopted a comparable approach (Taruffo 2010: 95), though he emphasised the judge's responsibility to actively seek truth, distinguishing his view from Ferrajoli's.

Taruffo's approach grounds the judge's epistemic role in a theory of corresponding truth. Although Taruffo (2010) and Beltrán (2007) have updated the criterion of correspondence in legal procedure, their revisions remain insufficient to address the complexities specific to criminal proceedings. Notably, these frameworks do not effectively enable the necessary discursive transformation to re-examine established views on criminal justice, and in several respects, they introduce additional challenges rather than resolving existing issues.

Ultimately, both Taruffo and Beltrán utilise Alfred Tarski's correspondence theory of truth in a relative and approximate sense. They maintain, rather than abandon, the rational pursuit of truth, offering only nuanced modifications—an approach that doesn't fully support the implementation of an accusatorial system capable of appropriately limiting punitive power. Thus, reliance on the concept of relative corresponding truth continues to underpin the judge's search for truth—an "ambition for truth" which can lead to forms of judicial activism not aligned with the accusatorial model of due process and may perpetuate the objectification of the accused.

The ambition of truth can be characterised as an intentional effort to confirm a predetermined accusatory hypothesis selected by the judge. This pursuit is unrestrained, often resulting in the disregard of procedural norms; due process is overshadowed by the discretionary decision-making of a judge who acknowledges no boundaries in his search for the truth. All actions are justified in the name of the search for truth, which becomes central to the structure of criminal procedure, with its perceived sanctity legitimising methods that may exceed legal constraints. A criminal procedure driven by the ambition for truth inherently risks becoming objectifying—truth does not serve as a limitation but rather as justification for punitive practices of an authoritarian nature.

Drawing on Plato's analogy of *pharmakon* and language, truth can function as either remedy or poison based on its application. Distinctions between remedy and poison may depend on dosage or, pertinently in this context, the role assigned to truth within the criminal procedural framework. When truth is elevated as the primary objective, criminal proceedings may succumb to persecutory inclinations. Consequently, it is imperative to (re)define truth's position within a revitalised criminal justice system, informed by constitutional principles and dedicated to the protection of human rights—which does not simply mean adhering to a model of exiled truth, but rather redefining the concept of truth and abandoning the search for a mythical corresponding truth, be it absolute or relative.

Rui Cunha Martins observes that this subject demands a more sophisticated strategy than simply dismissing the concept of truth (Martins 2010: 39), arguing that the longstanding challenge of truth in criminal cases fundamentally requires a change in perspective (Martins 2010: 81). As Gauer remarks, it is imperative to consider knowledge as surpassing the straightforward determination and application of a truth criterion (Gauer 1998: 25).

The alternative to evidentiary rationalism presented here reflects an epistemological shift designed to address a longstanding limitation within legal-criminal theory: the emphasis on correspondence-based truth as the cornerstone of criminal procedure, which may inadvertently legitimise authoritarian punitive practices—an outcome misaligned with the foundational principles of a democratic state governed by the rule of law. This broader approach instead advocates for a framework in which truth production transcends mere correspondence, drawing upon an epistemology grounded in the pastness of the past (Ricoeur 1997). This epistemology recognises the inherent complexity of events, evidence, and traces of the past, and underscores the importance of constructing frameworks that aim to accurately reconstruct past occurrences but emphasise protecting the rights of the accused.

It should be noted that this study neither proposes a comprehensive theory of procedural criminal truth nor establishes a definitive standard of truth for events under judicial review. Additionally, it does not define the criteria for determining truth across various crimes or procedural mechanisms within civil or common law systems. The analysis is restricted to the examination of truth production within the jurisdiction of a single judge operating under the civil law tradition, specifically within European continental and Latin American contexts, which continue to exhibit punitive practices characteristic of the inquisitorial model.

Building on Ruth Gauer's assertion that "perhaps we are living in a moment in which the analyst is, above all, a creator of meaning, rather than a respondent to questions" (Gauer 1998: 24), this study employs an analytical framework. This approach rigorously examines and restores the importance of the theme of truth within criminal proceedings. By centring analysis on the pastness of the past, the study aims to transcend the epistemic excesses linked to the pursuit of truth and to reaffirm the ritualised constraints on punitive authority, consistent with the requirement that contemporary criminal procedure upholds the human rights of the accused.

Gadamer contends that the philosopher's role is to highlight what is problematic and intellectually provocative, presenting issues for contemplation rather than universally accepted conclusions (Gadamer 1992: 43). Ricoeur similarly asserts that an eminent philosopher introduces new forms of inquiry (Ricoeur 1968: 65).

Although not intended to generate major philosophical breakthroughs, this study aims to establish a suitable epistemological framework for criminal proceedings by raising questions regarding truth production that are frequently overlooked by advocates of nineteenth-century scientism and contemporary evidentiary rationalism. It demonstrates that their dependence on methodological rationality is fundamentally unsuited to criminal proceedings and potentially harmful for the accused.

With this premise in mind, it is important to address the significant challenge posed by the temporal distance from the event being examined in criminal proceedings. Key considerations include identifying the factual foundation for judicial decisions and evaluating the lived experience of criminal proceedings—the presence of competing narratives designed to persuade the judge adds further complexity to this evaluation. Moreover, it is necessary to assess the extent to which narrative forms within judgements represent truth, as these constitute a reconstruction of past events influenced by the historical context of human experience.

Answers to these complex questions cannot overlook their inherent difficulty; instead, they must acknowledge it as an essential foundation. It's widely recognised that the notion of truth has been a persistent challenge for philosophers since Ancient Greece. The debate over truth remains active and continues to be significant within much of modern philosophical discussion. As Gil points out, "Many schools of contemporary philosophy—despite opposing views—share a lasting uncertainty about truth" (Martins 2002: 16). According to him, "There is no clear-cut answer about truth [...] Simply put, truth remains completely problematic" (Martins 2002: 16).

While it might not occupy such a preeminent space as in philosophy, the relationship between criminal procedure and the search for truth is a highly complex and continually debated issue. Traditional approaches have historically emphasised establishing truth through correspondence-based frameworks; however, contemporary discussions, especially within Brazilian socio-legal studies, increasingly acknowledge the limitations of these models. Over recent decades, numerous studies have critiqued the persistent authoritarian and inquisitorial characteristics of Brazilian criminal justice, advocating for a more regulated limitation of punitive powers and emphasising procedural safeguards over a pursuit of absolute truth.

A comprehensive understanding of truth recognises its inherent complexity, a perspective that epistemologies rooted in correspondence theory do not fully accommodate, despite their continued dominance in studies of criminal proceedings. The rationale for upholding correspondence-based truth regarding historical events relies upon maintaining the law's separation from other fields of knowledge.

This isolation creates substantial obstacles; interdisciplinary communication is increasingly vital, especially when addressing critical points that question fundamental assumptions within various knowledge domains. Progress in knowledge is facilitated by cross-disciplinary engagement. Considering contemporary challenges facing science, traditional compartmentalisation is proving insufficient for addressing the multifaceted nature of reality. Scientific research has advanced through specialisation but now underscores the importance of integration to tackle complex issues and shifting contexts. Strict, dogmatic frameworks ultimately diminish and overlook the realities they aim to interpret (Coutinho 2002: 176).

Following Coutinho's insight, this study seeks to provide a critical overview of the production of truth within criminal proceedings, examining how procedural norms, evidentiary practices, and philosophical perspectives have shaped the current theoretical and judicial landscape. The continued isolation of legal discourse is untenable; fostering openness to insights from other disciplines should be actively promoted (Lopes Jr 2005: 55). By drawing on interdisciplinary insights and acknowledging the risks of objectification and authoritarian tendencies, the analysis underscores the necessity of reimagining the concept of truth as a construct that serves both justice and the protection of human rights.

Evidentiary rationalism acknowledges the value of interdisciplinary perspectives; however, its integrative approach is fundamentally limited. Rather than engaging with philosophical and historical theories that address the nature of the past, it relies on epistemological frameworks developed for other disciplines, such as Tarski's correspondence theory of truth. Additionally, evidentiary rationalism utilises reasoning and evaluation models that confer excessive trust in the judge's cognitive authority, often without adequately considering exclusionary rules governing evidence management.

Ferrer Beltrán argues that legal proof isn't as distinct from other evidence domains as often suggested, since uncertainty and regulation do not preclude applying general epistemological rationality (Beltrán 2007: 29). Taruffo adds that, despite different roles for judges and scientists, their methods of handling evidence are similar, and scientific reasoning can benefit legal evidence studies (Taruffo 2005: 331).

This approach tends to generalise and overlooks the particular requirements of legal evidence management, which must be conducted within the framework of due process. Such a context imposes specific limitations on punitive authority to uphold human rights.

The analytical methodology utilised in this work incorporates multidisciplinary theoretical frameworks, distinguishing itself from rationalist research through its foundational premises and acknowledgement of the distinct nature of evidence management within legal proceedings—a topic that received limited consideration from Taruffo and Ferrer Beltrán. Following Gauer, I agree that rejecting entrenched legal knowledge requires adopting new languages, echoing Bachelard's concept of the "epistemological obstacle" (Gauer 2009: 113).

The analysis will explore the historical development of procedural models, highlighting the transition from inquisitorial to accusatorial systems and the emergence of mixed frameworks. It will also address the epistemological challenges posed by temporal distance, evidentiary uncertainty, and the influence of narrative in judicial decision-making. Ultimately, the study aims to contribute to ongoing debates about truth production in criminal procedure, advocating for a model that balances the demands of accuracy with the imperative to safeguard the rights of the accused.

Following the introductory discussion presented herein, Chapter 2 offers a comprehensive historical examination of accusatorial and inquisitorial criminal procedural frameworks. The analysis includes the development of the concept of "truth" within legal proceedings, tracing its historical evolution from a limitation on authority to a mechanism for legitimising arbitrariness under the pretext of truth-seeking.

The third chapter details the inquisitorial nature of mixed procedural systems, emphasising the transitions between inquisitorial and accusatorial systems in Europe and the subsequent development of the mixed model. The chapter concludes by evaluating the current Brazilian procedural system, including a concise case study that illustrates the ongoing influence of objectifying practices in shaping a criminal procedure focused on the pursuit of truth.

The fourth chapter examines correspondence theory of truth, scientificity and legal positivism, discussing the political and epistemological factors influencing the pursuit of truth and the development of modern thought—both pivotal for understanding how inquisitorial discourse has shifted towards arguments based on scientific reasoning. It presents concepts that challenge the conventional limits of modern rationality, an important step in revitalising the notion of truth within criminal proceedings.

Chapter 5 builds upon these principles, discussing the dynamics involved in framing past events as legal facts. The discussion addresses selective criminalisation, evidentiary positivism, the intricacies of social contexts and reevaluates the frequently simplistic approach to factual determinations prevalent in legal practice. The chapter also provides initial insights regarding the respective roles of judge and historian, establishing a foundation for the subsequent chapter.

Chapter 6 examines the analogical nature of the traces of the past and the hallucinatory character of evidence, undertaking a comprehensive analysis of the "pastness of the past" and the analogical construction of truth within criminal proceedings, focusing on the complexities involved in safeguarding the human rights of the accused. The discussion further considers the inherent uncertainties associated with evidence production, highlighting its potentially hallucinatory aspects. Key topics addressed include the duality embedded within the concept of "pastness", representance and the analogical production of truth, as well as the role of the judge in evidentiary activity.

Chapter 7 provides an in-depth analysis of the lived experience of criminal proceedings. It discusses the significance of evidentiary processes, the complex interaction among certainty, belief, and conviction, and examines narrative representations as they intersect with the inherent uncertainty present in procedural legal contexts. Additionally, it addresses dialogical adversarial proceedings as a framework for constraining the hallucinatory character of evidence.

Chapter 8 examines criminal procedure and the complexities of the late modern era, providing an analytical perspective on the challenges posed by speed and risk within and beyond criminal procedure. It discusses the evolution of criminal procedure as a cultural phenomenon and investigates the boundaries of perception, memory, and testimony. Additionally, the chapter critically assesses the concept of truth-seeking, suggesting it is a myth that merits thoughtful reconsideration.

Chapter 9 offers a nuanced examination of the role of the judge, portraying the judge as an individual influenced by personal experience, and evaluates how judicial narratives function as instruments for the production of truth. The discussion includes: the judge's role as a being-in-the-world; the hermeneutic circle and interpretive processes; a hermeneutical reconsideration of the subject-object framework; the concept of free motivated conviction, addressing decisionism and the regulation of subjective domains; and the pivotal moment of truth construction, wherein judgement functions as a narrative analogous of past events, arguing that the prevailing uncertainty of the past justifies the priority of procedural safeguards over the ambition of discovering the truth, this being the most solid way to contain punitive power and promote social justice.

In conclusion, Chapter 10 brings a final analysis that revisits the arguments previously outlined and will aim to clarify the status of truth in criminal proceedings and consider its significance within an accusatorial system characterised by party-driven evidence management and a commitment to uphold the rights of the accused. This discussion will demonstrate that the impetus to restrain punitive authority and uphold human rights necessitates moving beyond a criminal justice model centred on the pursuit of truth. Moreover, it is the inherent impossibility of achieving an absolute or even approximate truth that most compellingly supports prioritising procedural safeguards over the ambition for truth.

CHAPTER 2

Accusatorial and Inquisitorial Procedural Systems

The Role of Criminal Procedures in Producing the Truth

This section will focus on examining how various procedural systems have historically addressed the production of truth. This inquiry aims to analyse and characterise these systems and their respective methods for establishing truth. Accordingly, the approach intends to situate the issue of truth production within its historical context by systematically studying specific criminal procedural frameworks.

Armenta Deu notes that criminal procedure has alternated between accusatorial and inquisitorial systems, with neither ever fully realised (Armenta Deu 1995: 11). Contemporary studies largely agree that pure systems no longer exist; instead, opinions differ over how to classify current mixed systems. Lopes Jr. argues it is essential to determine each system's guiding principle, rather than simply label them as mixed (Lopes Jr 2010: 56). Aragoneses Alonso describes historical moments of pure systems but highlights their mutual influence over time (Aragoneses Alonso 1986: 39). Badaró observes that contemporary procedures combine elements from both systems, varying in predominance (Badaró 2003: 102). Thus, discussion about the structure and guiding principles of these systems remains central to analysing criminal procedural frameworks.

S. H. Khaled Jr., *Reimagining Criminal Justice, Search for Truth and Human Rights*, https://doi.org/10.1007/978-3-032-27227-0_2

This represents the traditional perspective, which is seldom disregarded in legal studies; therefore, Montero Aroca's viewpoint is noteworthy. According to Aroca, only the accusatorial procedure qualifies as a genuine criminal procedure, while the inquisitorial method does not warrant this classification. He contends that an inquisitorial procedure does not actually exist, as it was never, nor can it be, regarded as a proper procedural model (Aroca 1997: 28).

While Montero Aroca argues that only the accusatorial model aligns with the definition of legal procedure, Bachmaier-Winter challenges whether limiting the concept solely to this framework is productive or relevant. If that were the case, inquisitorial procedures would be reduced to mere methods. Bachmaier-Winter asserts that such a position disrupts established procedural theory—a viewpoint I share. I prefer to examine the production of truth in legal systems by analysing their historical development, noting that the distinction between inquisitorial and accusatorial models remains significant for interpreting current criminal justice practices and understanding the ongoing pursuit of truth within them. The inquisitorial model has not been relegated to history. Instead, its influence endures, primarily through the discourse of truth-seeking and the judge's role in that pursuit.

The pursuit of truth in criminal cases stems from political, legal, and scientific traditions. Historically, this ideal has persisted and adapted, often linked to authoritarian regimes that enforced "truths" through persecution. The search for truth began to take shape in the Roman Empire, gained importance during religious inquisitions, and later shaped secular legal systems in Continental Europe. As modern legal practices evolved, a mixed but mainly inquisitorial system emerged, influenced by seventeenth- to nineteenth-century shifts towards scientific methods for uncovering presumed objective truths.

To analyse the production of truth in criminal proceedings, one must examine how different procedural systems have addressed this issue, which informs their classification as accusatorial or inquisitorial. According to Garapon and Papapoulos (2008: 12), each system has distinct methods for producing truth, though these are ideal types rather than realities; contemporary legal systems blend elements from both models. Thus, classification hinges on identifying which guiding principle is most prominent in each system. Defining these legal systems goes beyond academic debate or doctrinal differences; a genuine effort to reimagine criminal justice requires re-examining the core meaning of accusatorial and inquisitorial models.

My analysis assumes that the inquisitorial framework has historically dominated, especially in continental law. The issue is not whether it exists, but how much inquisitorialism is present (Carvalho 2008: 77; Martins 2010: 32; Lopes Jr 2010: 506). Although there have been attempts at substantial reform, the contemporary criminal justice system continues to reflect many inquisitorial practices. Analysing the methods by which truth is determined in these systems is fundamental to developing a genuinely democratic accusatorial procedure—a goal that remains unfulfilled due to an ongoing emphasis on factual discovery and the correspondence theory that underlies persistent inquisitorial dominance.

The enduring presence of inquisitorial practices throughout centuries is closely associated with power dynamics and the political framework of the state. Within the ongoing interplay between legal and political domains, the latter has consistently demonstrated an ability to exert influence over the regulated limitation of punitive authority that should guide the purpose of criminal proceedings. Historically, whether through actions of state representatives or intellectuals aligned with authoritarian agendas, technical and rhetorical justifications have frequently been advanced to broaden punitive powers, thereby favouring a persecutory approach over checks on such authority. This underscores the intricate relationship between knowledge and power, as well as the inherently political nature of criminal justice systems rooted in modernity.

Maier contends that criminal procedural law is closely shaped by the political system, more so than other legal areas (Maier 2006: 260). Badaró argues that choosing a procedural model is a political decision reflecting how the State relates to its citizens, stating it mirrors the balance between authority and liberty (Badaró 2003: 106). Goldschmidt maintains that procedural principles are part of broader state policy, and a country's criminal procedure reflects whether its Constitution is democratic or authoritarian (Goldschmidt 2010: 778).

The normative dimension is only part of the issue. Brazilian scholars have argued that due process safeguards in the accusatorial system established by the 1988 Constitution conflict with inquisitorial elements from the 1941 Code of Criminal Procedure. Despite these critiques, the Code—created during the Vargas dictatorship—is still widely used. While proposals for a new code are being considered, judges remain reluctant to give up powers they see as crucial for establishing truth, which they equate with reality (Martins 2010: 37).

These observations indicate that legal culture, including the understanding of the criminal procedural system, extends beyond normative components. Normative elements are influenced by political beliefs as well as the prevailing perspectives on science and knowledge within specific historical contexts. In this sense, Foucault points out that there are various sites in society where truth is formed, where a set of rules of the game are defined, based on domains of knowledge, as is the case, in particular, with judicial practices (Foucault 2003: 11). For Foucault, "there can only be certain types of subject of knowledge, certain orders of truth, certain domains of knowledge, based on political conditions which are the ground upon which the subject, the domains of knowledge, and the relations of truth are formed" (Foucault 2003: 27).

Regarding the concept of truth that has become dominant in modernity, specific political conditions played an essential role in shaping this form of knowledge. Rather than emerging abruptly, such knowledge develops progressively, becoming increasingly structured and interconnected with prevailing power dynamics. This relationship operates dialectically, enabling knowledge to sustain its own advancement while concurrently reinforcing the continuity and influence of power. As Foucault states, the truth-power relationship is essential to all mechanisms of punishment, including contemporary penal practices (Foucault 2008: 47). For the author, "we are forced to produce the truth by the power which demands this truth and which needs it in order to function; we must tell the truth, we are coerced, we are condemned to confess the truth or to find it" (Foucault 2005: 29).

The mechanisms underlying the development of this relationship merit thorough examination. As Foucault suggests, "to the solemnity of origins, one must oppose, in good historical method, the meticulous and unavowable smallness of these fabrications, these inventions" (Foucault 2003: 12). Accordingly, it is essential to commence the narrative with a historical analysis of procedural systems to accurately determine their foundational components in the context of truth production.

Badaró (2003: 101) explains that criminal procedure has evolved through accusatorial and inquisitorial models, highlighting a "mixed system" formed by the 1808 *Code d'instruction criminelle*. This analysis follows that approach, focusing on often-overlooked aspects—particularly truth production and the rights of the accused.

Before proceeding with the historical analysis, it is important to note that "accusatorial" and "inquisitorial" stem from Romano-canonical traditions during the Middle Ages, distinct from Ancient practices in Greece and Rome, which should not be seen as direct predecessors. Rather than existing in isolation, accusatorial and inquisitorial models overlapped and influenced each other. I must also highlight that references to the "Inquisition" should be interpreted broadly, as different forms existed—references to the "Inquisition" should be interpreted in epistemological and not institutional terms.

Truth as a Limitation on Authority in the Greek Criminal Procedural System

A historical review of Antiquity reveals the widespread presence of what may be termed "archaic forms of punitive authority" across different societies. During this period, corporal punishment and the frequent use of the death penalty were common, with little regard for individualising penalties—punishments could extend to the relatives of the accused. The determination of suffering often hinged more on the accused's social status and affiliations than on objective assessments of truth.

Ancient Greece marked a pivotal departure from these practices; in Athens, the integration of truth into punitive procedures emerged to limit the exercise of punitive power, rather than serving as justification for authoritarian enforcement.

However, we should avoid considering this as the starting point for European accusatorial legal systems. A rigorous historical interpretation is necessary to prevent recurring misconceptions in criminal procedure literature, such as the tendency to classify Greek culture as Western exemplified by Ferrajoli (Ferrajoli 2002: 111). Dussel critiques the ideological framework that constructs a linear and progressive account of history, presenting Greek culture as exclusively European and Western. This perspective creates a narrative fiction, suggesting that since Greek and Roman times these cultures have been central to world history. The traditional sequence—Greek World/Pagan and Christian Roman World/Medieval Christian World/Modern European World—is widely accepted but represents an ideological construct. According to Dussel (2005), this form of historical diachrony emerged from late eighteenth-century German Romanticism and constitutes a retrospective conceptual manipulation of the "Aryan model", which he identifies as inherently racist.

Consequently, "Greece" should not be conflated with "Europe" or "modernity"; its cultural heritage warrants recognition as a distinct chapter within the history of criminal procedural systems. Notably, the Athenian procedural system introduced mechanisms for resisting punitive authority. When discussing this tradition in relation to the broader history of criminal procedural systems, a study is engaging with a legacy that encompasses Christian-Byzantine and Arab-Muslim influences, rather than modernity alone. With this critical distinction in view, the analysis can proceed.

Foucault observes that in Ancient Greece, political struggles and disputes gave rise to a novel form of juridical and judicial discovery of truth (Foucault 2003: 55). According to Foucault, the production of "truth" functioned not as reinforcement of power, but as a collective achievement by Greek citizens standing against authoritarianism. Within this framework, truth was conceptualised as a limitation on power, rather than as a tool for repression or prevention; it was intrinsically linked to proof and the demonstration of arguments through rhetoric—the right to present a truth without power against a power lacking truth (Foucault 2003: 54). Cordero further notes that criminal procedure operates as a verbal apparatus, where the accusatorial approach inherently generates controversy, and classical rhetoric flourished in such an environment (Cordero 2000: 319).

Consequently, truth operated not as a rationale or instrument for the imposition of punitive authority, but rather as a constraint upon it, serving as an essential criterion for establishing a robust evidentiary foundation before any penalty could be imposed. This approach positioned truth as a methodical framework for knowledge, centred on the demonstration and persuasion of factual accuracy. Traces of the accusatorial system can be seen in Greek law, which was distinguished by the active involvement of citizens both in initiating accusations and in rendering judgements (Lopes Jr 2009: 56; Ferrajoli 2002: 111). Legal proceedings during this period were conducted orally, publicly, and followed a strongly adversarial format (Maier 2006: 269). The criminal procedure in Greece—from the sixth to the fourth centuries BC, and specifically in Athens—is often described as a purely accusatorial model, since any Athenian citizen (circa 399 BC) was entitled to present accusations before the relevant authorities, amounting to genuine popular prosecution (Ambos 2008: 40).

The Greek legal system divided offences into public and private categories. Any citizen could prosecute public offences, using procedures similar to modern criminal law, while private matters resembled civil proceedings (Aragoneses Alonso 1986: 39). Aristotle highlighted popular accusation as central to Solon's judicial reforms. Trials had admissibility requirements and scheduled dates; prosecutors bore costs and posted security deposits against false claims. Others could replace the original accuser, and defendants, though required to represent themselves, sometimes received help from fellow citizens.

The Greek judicial system upheld parity between the accuser and accused, allowing the latter to remain free before trial if three citizens vouched for their attendance, except in cases like treason or conspiracy (Maier 2006: 270). This reflected a strong presumption of innocence and ensured fair defence opportunities with procedural checks on punitive authority. Courts consisted of 501 to 6,000 judges depending on the offence, with verdicts representing popular sovereignty. Athenian justice was noted for its democratised legal proceedings (Ambos 2008: 51).

While procedural aspects of the system deserve mention, Greek punitive practices often involved harsh sanctions that overlooked individual rights for state interests. Ferrajoli notes that early Greek law imposed punishment without regard for guilt or voluntariness, sometimes affecting an offender's family (Ferrajoli 2002: 390). He also highlights an authoritarian utilitarian approach in Thrasymachus's definition of justice in Plato's Republic (Ferrajoli 2002: 210).

Zaffaroni notes that the idea of justifying different punishments for perceived enemies dates to Antiquity, especially Protagoras and Plato. Plato argued that offenders are inferior due to their lack of access to pure ideas and suggested elimination if this incapacity cannot be fixed (Zaffaroni 2007: 83). Greek philosophers, except Aristotle—who favoured retributive punishment—rarely considered punishment from the perspective of those punished. Although Aristotle did not directly discuss the State's right to punish, his view of suicide as an unjust act against the city deserving penalty suggests he accepted the State's authority to impose sanctions (Aristotle 2002: 126; Bar 2007: 386).

Despite these problems, prosecution and judgement remained distinct, parties provided evidence, and trials took place publicly and orally. The system relied on adversarial debate to produce the truth, with judges assessing only the information presented by each side and issuing their verdict (Orbaneja 1997: 124).

The system developed by the Greeks marks a significant period characterised by openness and opposition to authoritarian power. It stands as a noteworthy example in history where the production of truth did not serve as a tool or justification for arbitrary institutional power, a point that will be further examined subsequently.

Roman Systems: Truth Shifts Between Restraint and Objectification

Rome exemplifies how legal and political factors shape criminal procedure over time. Its evolving political systems influenced different procedural models: from *cognitio* in the Monarchy, to the *accusatio* system of the Republic, and back to *cognitio* under the Empire (Maier 2006; Aragoneses Alonso 1986).

In the *cognitio* system of public criminal procedure, State officials, mainly magistrates, handled all roles for social defence (Manzini 1951: 5). Magistrates had centralised authority to clarify facts, start proceedings on their own, and use discretion in investigations (Maier 2006: 275). With no procedural limits, they could investigate and decide freely as they saw fit (Manzini 1951: 5).

The judge could act independently of provocation, with no fixed procedures or evidence regulations, nor a guaranteed right for the accused to intervene. After the *vocatio* summons, preventive detention could be imposed indefinitely, especially for repeat disobedience, though this was not intended as punishment (Maier 2006: 275). Adult male convicts could seek annulment through *provocatio*, requiring the magistrate to present the case for reconsideration to the people.

The *cognitio* system combined prosecution and judgement, enabling judges to collect evidence independently and giving them unchecked punitive authority. This approach made procedures highly punitive and lacked safeguards, especially for women and non-citizens who couldn't appeal (Lopes Jr 2009: 57). These issues led to the eventual replacement of *cognitio* with *accusatio*.

Similar to Greece, Rome's social structure incorporated aspects of both authoritarian and democratic systems; however, the authoritarian characteristics tended to dominate. Foucault ties Rome's sovereign power over life and death to *patria potestas*, the father's authority over his household, which extended to state power through Roman law (Foucault 1998: 127). This legal framework introduced the distinction between personal (*inimicus*) and political enemies (*hostis*), with the latter deprived of rights and seen as a threat to the community (Zaffaroni 2007). The Senate could declare someone a *hostis judicatus*—a public enemy—under exceptional circumstances, such as treason. Foreigners (*hostis alienigena*) and others who challenged authority were similarly marginalised, not by their own choice but by imposition from those in power.

Major reforms in Roman criminal prosecution occurred in the final century of the Republic. These changes shifted the criminal procedure from objectifying treatment of the accused, similar to Greek developments that curbed arbitrary punishments by limiting punitive power. In Rome, the magistrate's role during *accusatio* was purely judicial, issuing verdicts without prosecutorial involvement (Manzini 1951: 6). According to Lopes Jr., any citizen could bring charges for *delicta publica*; prosecution was handled not by the state but by voluntary community representatives (*accusator*) (Lopes Jr 2009: 57).

The system mirrored the Athenian approach: no one could be tried without a formal accusation (*nemo in judicium tradetur sine accusatione*). By separating prosecutorial and judicial roles and assigning evidence management to the parties, it moved away from *cognitio*'s truth-seeking methods. This introduced safeguards against harsh penalties and spurred reforms leading to the adoption of *accusatio* and popular courts. Jurors needed only to be citizens aged 30 or above. Any citizen could start proceedings before a popular assembly, which took over criminal jurisdiction from magistrates. The centuriate assemblies mostly handled capital offences but could review other cases as needed (Maier 2006: 276).

The *accusatio* was governed by laws tailored to different offences, with prosecutors acting as community representatives seeking justice for societal harm (Manzini 1951: 6). They gained legal and public speaking experience, but few other benefits, and faced criminal liability for abuses like false accusations (Maier 2006: 281).

In the *accusatio*, citizens became prosecutors, viewing crime as a threat to community coexistence. Despite this shift, impunity did not occur—many citizens competed to prosecute, and disputes were resolved by procedure (Maier 2006: 278–279). Prosecutors could not appeal or reopen cases due to their public status. State prosecution relied on private action, making the process adversarial and balanced, rather than dominated by one authority. Roman *accusatio* involved oral, public debates that guided tribunal decisions and restricted court influence over case matters (Maier 2006: 282).

The *accusatio* system is defined by instructions from the investigating party, who also must prove the case, overseen by a passive judge (Aragoneses Alonso 1986: 40). The *iudices* serve as impartial arbiters between prosecutor and accused, with both sides presenting their cases and the judge deciding based solely on provided evidence (Cordero 2000: 322). Proceedings centre on whether the accused committed the alleged act and what legal consequences should result (Cordero 2000: 320).

The Roman system valued factual accuracy but relied on adversarial debate, where an independent party brought accusations and magistrates acted as passive arbiters, voting at the end of public proceedings without deliberation (Aragoneses Alonso 1986: 39). This approach, resembling the Greek model, kept judicial and prosecutorial roles separate and tasked parties with managing evidence within a public, oral, and dialogical process (Prado 2006: 75–76). Defendants typically remained free before sentencing, judges did not initiate investigations, and the system emphasised transparency—at one point banning pre-trial detention entirely (Ferrajoli 2002: 443).

This model showed benefits over *cognitio* and proved to be more democratic, especially as it moved away from monarchy-era truth-seeking. However, the possibility of resistance to power was soon lost with the Republic's fall and Empire's rise. Sovereignty shifted to the emperor, centralising justice and placing criminal prosecution under state officials (Maier 2006: 284–285). Early on, state agents handled judicial policing for cases lacking an *accusatio* (Maier 2006: 76). Eventually, imperial justice became completely dominant.

The Republic's system of criminal prosecution eventually collapsed, partly due to a rise in unfounded and revenge-driven accusations (Maier 2006: 285). Manzini argued that the accusatorial model failed to control growing crime rates and had significant drawbacks, as many accusations were motivated by personal vendettas (Manzini 1951: 7). However, it should be noted that Manzini was one of the architects of the Italian fascist regime and an adherent of the Italian inquisitorial tradition, which largely explains his interpretation of several significant shifts in the history of procedural systems. According to Cordero, the author is xenophobic, a supporter of repression, a defender of the "glorious" inquisitorial past, and opposed to comparative law studies. In his limited, opaque, and phobic mental universe, philosophy means a subversive virus (Cordero 2000: 85).

In the Empire, *cognitio extra ordinem* emerged as a centralised judicial process, shifting some prosecutions from private citizens to official prosecutors acting on rumours or their own initiative (Maier 2006: 286). The initial phase became secret, with public hearings before a judge representing higher authority (Aragoneses Alonso 1986: 4). Over time, judges combined investigative and adjudicative roles, leading to confidential proceedings where they investigated, judged, and sentenced. These legal changes mirrored Rome's evolving political structure and authoritarian methods of exercising punitive power.

The shift away from *accusatio* assumptions was evident, as judges took an active, prosecutorial role throughout investigations and proceedings, motivated by a relentless search for truth. This method aimed to suppress dissent against those in authority.

Cognitio extra ordinem became the standard criminal procedure, concentrating prosecution and judgement in one person to support the new political system (Maier 2006: 287). This method replaced *accusatio*, ending procedural transparency (Manzini 1951: 8–9), and favoured greater social control as political structures changed.

After private crimes became state matters, government control over punishment increased and accusation limits vanished. Prado notes that secret written procedures introduced by the state paved the way for the Inquisition in Continental Europe (Prado 2006:77). Lopes Jr., Carvalho, and Ferrajoli trace the inquisitorial system to Imperial Rome's handling of offences against the emperor (Lopes Jr 2009:58; Carvalho 2003:7; Ferrajoli 2002:453), with torture allowed during these proceedings (Prado 2006:77; Moura 1994:8). Coutinho adds that such hierarchical methods predate the Inquisition, originating from ancient Rome and early legal systems (Coutinho 2001:18).

While the *accusatio* was rendered largely obsolete, it remained in existence as a marginal and minor aspect of legal proceedings. Conversely, *cognitio* became the principal legal tradition passed down from Roman law to later generations. Preserved first within canon law and academic institutions, *cognitio's* epistemology was subsequently reintroduced across continental Europe in the thirteenth century (Maier 2006: 286), eventually replacing the formerly prevailing accusatorial models. Centuries later, *cognitio's* legacy continued to shape legal practices across Europe, influencing subsequent developments in both ecclesiastical and secular contexts.

Accusatorial System and "Irrational" Ordeals

Following the dissolution of the Roman Empire's centralised structures, the resulting decentralisation of political authority facilitated the rise of Germanic law and the emergence of accusatorial procedures (Ferrajoli 2002: 453). Taruffo notes that with the Germanic invasions of Europe, their legal traditions were applied to both criminal and civil cases—a distinction not clearly defined for an extended period (Taruffo 2010: 15).

The accusatorial procedure rooted in Germanic practice functioned as an adversarial system wherein the parties engaged directly, including the issuance of summons, opportunities for response, challenges, and presentation of evidence (Manzini 1951: 11). Social control over conduct deemed harmful was exercised collectively by community members, who provided sworn statements to establish the accused's culpability or innocence (Winter 2008: 18). Formal judicial procedures, meanwhile, held a secondary role and were pursued principally when private, extrajudicial resolutions proved unsuccessful, thereby initiating proceedings with clear accusatorial features (Maier 2006: 265).

After the collapse of the Roman Empire, its legal tradition was preserved by the Catholic Church, which remained the only lasting institution during the gradual decline and eventual dissolution caused by the barbarian invasions. The preservation of the Roman legal legacy facilitated the subsequent development of inquisitorial procedures from the twelfth and thirteenth centuries onwards, when they were no longer restricted mainly to internal ecclesiastical disciplinary processes.

The spread of inquisitorial procedure in Continental Europe stemmed from the growth of ecclesiastical and secular courts, which led to the decline of the accusatorial and ordeal systems that became prevalent in the Middle Ages after the fall of the Roman Empire.

Before moving forward with an analysis of inquisitorial procedure, it is important to clarify common misunderstandings about medieval accusatory practices and the role of ordeals. This excerpt does not provide a full analysis but addresses several such errors in the following sections.

The ordeal system, known as *iudicium* in ancient Latin and later as the "judgement of God", is often dismissed as irrational, with its abandonment viewed as legal progress. Critics assert modern practices are more rational, but this assumption ignores ongoing issues like selectivity, police violence, judicial misconduct, and mass incarceration. Such idealised views fail under real-world examination and overlook the political nature of legal procedures and their connection to power and knowledge.

The belief that the past can be reconstructed and told as a narrative substantiated by proof is deeply intertwined with the development of criminal procedure throughout history. This idea is also linked to the enduring perspective of truth-seeking, which often shapes how these systems are understood. According to Lévy-Bruhl, ordeals represent a renewal of the present moment (Lévi-Bruhl 1964). Unlike modern and contemporary procedures, ordeals should not be evaluated as if they were methods of factual verification; instead, they should be considered according to their own unique logic.

Rudimentary analyses of ordeal procedures are often supported by the evolutionist perspective, which regards history as "evolution" or "progress"—a perspective that can be linked to the portrayal of all "premodern" knowledge as lacking reason or meaning. Ordeals have very peculiar epistemological implications—and should be understood as such. They should not simply be measured by criteria foreign to them.

The interpretation of these practices must be contextualised within the socio-political frameworks dominant during their respective periods. Patetta offers a foundational definition of an ordeal: "we call ordeal any procedure, of whatever kind, by which it is believed possible to induce supernatural beings to manifest in some way their decision on a matter producing legal effects" (Patetta 1890: 2). Similarly, Cordero describes ordeals as decision-making processes premised on the belief that the physical order of the world can respond to moral inquiries, or alternatively, that a deity may intervene in the causal chain, altering outcomes in circumstances where justice necessitates it: "since water, a pure element, rejects the guilty just as considered; immersed or bound, floats" (Cordero 1981: 768).

The year 1215 is often seen as the end of the ordeal system, since the Fourth Lateran Council's Canon 18 forbade clergy from blessing ordeals by hot or cold water or red-hot iron: "nor may anyone confer a rite of blessing or consecration upon purgation by ordeal of hot or cold water or of red-hot iron, while preserving, however, the previously promulgated prohibitions on individual combats and duels". This decision set in motion the gradual abandonment of ordeals, making way for a new process for determining criminal responsibility and punishments. On the continent, the ordeal was replaced by the legal or tariffed proofs system. Still, it's important to note that both systems often relied on similar reasoning: courts demanded conclusions they saw as certain (not just likely), as pointed out by Ferrajoli (2004: 135).

The first and major error in accusing the ordeals of being an "irrational" system lies in understanding it as if it were based on factual evidence. Ordeals were, in a sense, "reverse oracles", considered capable of revealing hidden truths from the past. They were not, as the simplistic critique suggests, systems of "magical attribution" of facts.

A distinct interpretative reasoning, represented by Robert Bartlett, views ordeals as a mechanism for resolving cases in the face of factual uncertainty. According to Bartlett, "ordeals were intended to reveal a specific fact; they developed to address specific allegations when other evidence was lacking" (Bartlett 1986: 79). Following this line of reasoning, it can be said that the decline of ordeals was due to the emergence of a new epistemology and new forms of rationality.

A second approach to understanding the phenomenon of ordeals is presented by Whitman, who argues that this procedure should not be regarded as an oracular or magical method for divining the resolution of a case in the face of evidentiary uncertainty. Whitman asserts that it is a mistake to treat the decline of ordeals as merely an episode in the history of fact-finding (Whitman 2008: 56). The author's thesis, which coincides with the emergence of the jury, centres on the issue of moral responsibility for judgement. In other words, in his view, there was no epistemological revolution, but rather other changes connected to governmental practice. Ordeals had the effect of "sparing" humans from responsibility for judgement and, above all, for judicial error.

This perception makes perfect sense within a worldview in which there was a perceived "natural" order of things. Outside the modern framework, people defined themselves in terms of personal identity, self-image, and self-awareness, based on what was perceived as the "natural" order of the world, on incorporation into tradition and local customs which, ultimately, provided some level of integration of the self and the cosmos—that the world and the place of humans within it were part of God's creation or of an equivalent force (Khaled Jr and Morrison 2024).

Throughout Europe during the High Middle Ages and into the Late Middle Ages, judgements of God—such as ordeals—were employed in various forms. The simplest type was the duel, which was only available to people considered "honourable", while other methods were reserved for those seen as socially inferior. Despite common claims in procedural studies, ordeals were never standard practices within criminal justice; they did not regularly serve as a typical system of evaluating evidence or determining criminal responsibility. Instead, ordeals acted as a supplementary process alongside existing criminal procedures, mainly used when the accusatorial system reached its limits. Ordeals could be used only if four conditions were met: no formal accusation had been made; there were no witnesses; the accused had not confessed; and the case could not be settled by the sworn word of an honourable person—a privilege reserved for the elite. Clearly, ordeals functioned as secondary measures rather than independent systems. The gradual development of autonomous criminal procedures—especially with the rise of the inquisitorial system and its comprehensive rules—eventually led to the decline and abandonment of ordeals.

Ordeals could only be used in criminal cases without a formal accusation, when accusations were still considered private matters. According to Bartlett, criminal proceedings at this time began with a private accusation—meaning the accuser was responsible for officially bringing charges, presenting evidence, and accepting the consequences if their claim failed (Bartlett 1986: 29). This process was risky, as the punishment intended for the defendant could instead fall upon the accuser if they failed. The accusatorial system started with a solemn oath, called the *juramentum de calumniae*, in which the accuser swore to honestly charge the accused, knowing they would face the same penalties if proven wrong.

Ordeals were typically utilised when accusations arose from anonymous sources within society (*fama*—a concept of significant importance) without direct witnesses or when no individual was willing to formally charge the accused. The ordeal process could be circumvented if a formal accuser or a sworn witness was present. Similarly, if a confession was obtained, the ordeal was unnecessary; thus, it is accurate to state the procedure also served as leverage to elicit confessions. Further exceptions included the purgation oath, wherein noblemen provided testimony. This legal provision was exclusively available to the privileged class, thereby exempting them from undergoing ordeals.

Morris observes that the ordeal procedure enabled members of vulnerable social groups to benefit from trials substantiated by testimony (Morris 1975: 96). In cases where a purgation witness was unavailable, these individuals could present their own testimony, with God serving as the ultimate witness. Consequently, the central focus of the ordeal was on testing the truthfulness of the individual's statement, rather than verifying correspondence between the statement and the actual event. As

Gaudemet notes, the primary aim of ordeals was "to verify the reliability of a person's testimony" (Gaudemet 1965: 100). Thus, such rituals did not involve the examination or proof of factual elements. Ordeals were typically administered to those from lower social classes who were accused of crimes, providing, as Whitman suggests, a means for acquittal (Whitman 2008: 102). Accordingly, they fulfilled a specific social function aligned with prevailing worldviews and social hierarchies. While only research into primary sources can determine the effectiveness of this practice as a check on punitive authority, it constituted the sole form of resistance accessible to the marginalised at that time.

If this viewpoint holds merit—which appears likely—it challenges the common narrative that monopolising punitive practices represents a process of progressive rationalisation and the abolishment of private vengeance. Instead, it shows that "pre-modern" conflict resolution methods could help reduce harm or at least demonstrate an intent to do so, without constituting what Zaffaroni (2003) refers to as the State's sequestration of conflict. Additionally, analyses that overlook the hierarchical structure of the society in question miss a key element concerning ordeals: the existence of varying levels and forms of evidence depending on the accused's social status. The necessity to validate the accused's statement and invoke God's witness for those from lower social ranks are central aspects of ordeals. As noted, noble defendants could call witnesses, but their testimony served not to establish facts, but rather to confirm the defendant's word.

Ordeals were not systems for assessing evidence or investigative methods leading to procedures for determining criminal responsibility, despite common beliefs. The prevailing view in legal studies suggests that ordeals occurred when there was no official accuser or witnesses to a crime. As a result, some have argued that ordeals were used as alternatives when evidence was lacking. It is clear, however, that medieval evidence extended beyond just witness testimony. Ordeals sought to reveal the "truth" rather than facts. They typically took place when public suspicion (*fama*) existed but there were neither accusers, witnesses, nor confessions available. In this way, ordeals functioned as rituals intended to confirm the credibility of an account. This is underscored by the fact that those with privilege could avoid ordeals by taking a purgation oath from another nobleman. Whitman (2008: 96) notes that the function of ordeals—even when guilt could be determined through other means—was to remove the moral burden from making the judgement.

The ordeal system did not function as the standard model of criminal procedure; rather, it operated as an auxiliary mechanism intended to corroborate statements, serving as a veracity test primarily for individuals lacking privileged social status. The presence of numerous exceptions to the application of ordeals lends credence to Whitman's hypothesis that this method was not primarily designed to assign criminal responsibility amidst evidentiary uncertainty.

Starting in the thirteenth century, major shifts in the criminal justice system brought about noteworthy consequences, including the abandonment of ordeals and the prohibition introduced by Canon 18 of the Fourth Lateran Council in 1215. In England, this shift away from ordeals resulted in a new system featuring formal public accusations, which differed from continental practices at the time. As the English jury system gradually evolved, regions on the continent turned to torture following the end of ordeals. The introduction of testimony was crucial in the early development of the English judicial system; initially, jurors acted as witnesses, marking a significant transformation.

Beginning in the thirteenth century, the inquisitorial system emerged with a distinct approach to assigning criminal responsibility, differing from that of ordeals. Nonetheless, both systems shared a foundational aim: exercising punitive power when a crime was widely recognised within the community (*fama*, *notorium*, *manifesta*) (Fraher 1984). The shift from ordeal-based justice to the inquisitorial model across Continental Europe reflected changing attitudes towards crime; specifically, the belief that "no crime should go unpunished" became an issue of public importance (Fraher 1989: 24). Consequently, this transformation was not just about rationalising or implementing an "epistemological revolution" in a narrow sense but must also be understood as part of a broader political change in how the state and society administer punishment.

The imperative to punish all crimes played a critical role in shaping the inquisitorial system, which evolved differently from the English jury system. Across continental Europe, the resurgence of Justinian Roman law and its dissemination were instrumental in establishing the use of torture as a defining component of the inquisitorial procedure. The early development of institutions that would later underpin contemporary criminal justice systems also prompted reforms in medieval punitive practices as procedures shifted towards more public forms. This transition, which included mandatory witness attendance and the transformation of testimony into a civic responsibility, ultimately led to the abolition of ordeals throughout both England and continental Europe.

While the English jury did not employ torture, as indicated by Langbein's influential research, jurors historically functioned as witnesses responsible for evaluating factual matters (Langbein 2006). Consequently, there was no restriction preventing jurors from rendering judgements based on information obtained outside official proceedings. The progressive distinction between jurors and witnesses contributed to the establishment of guidelines regarding judicial conviction derived from case documentation (*Iudex iuxta alligata et probata iudicare debet*), which forbids judges from relying on personal knowledge. It is notable that similar prohibitions developed in continental jurisdictions, motivated by comparable factors such as the potential for judges to also serve as witnesses to criminal acts or, specifically, to act as confessors.

The adoption of public procedures partly explains the decline of ordeals and the rise of new legal forms. In England, witnesses became judges, while in continental Europe, the accused became a witness, leading to the use of torture (Marchetti 1994).

As Sbriccoli highlights, the strong move towards making criminal proceedings public was key to the major changes seen between the thirteenth and fourteenth centuries. This period saw activities become more centralised and hierarchical, judicial actions increasingly shaped by law, and the judiciary grow into a professional class (Sbriccoli 2011: 461). Whitman's argument—that reforms in how knowledge is approached did not lead to shifts in evidentiary practices—should be considered carefully. The modern approach to evidence, with its "rationalist" branches, developed alongside the emergence of probability as an objective concept, which differed from the medieval view that saw probability as based on opinion. Adopting probabilistic reasoning played a role in ending ordeal-based systems, which relied on rhetorical tradition (Giuliani 1971: 136). In truth, ordeal methods were not about determining uncertain facts. Meanwhile, the renewed interest in Roman law and the introduction of torture partly stemmed from the adoption of a new adjudication system: legal proof. This system, linked to developing inquisitorial models, gradually replaced the formerly dominant accusatorial elements—a shift explored further below.

The Inquisitorial Procedure and the Ambition for Truth

A pivotal development in the transformation of criminal justice during the twelfth-century transition was the methodological shift and increasing focus on truth. The emerging inquisitorial procedure, characterised by its automatisation, led to the displacement of adversarial proceedings—an integral feature of the earlier accusatorial model.

Given the existence of different "inquisitions"—ancient and modern, as well as different tribunals—it is important to stress that any reference to the "Inquisition" can only be made at a certain level of generality. In this section, a detailed analysis of these particularities will not be undertaken—the focus will be on the epistemological and political aspects that define the inquisitorial "search for truth". As Zaffaroni points out, the *inquisitio* should not be identified nor limited to the Roman Inquisition, which was an institution that centralised the power of the Pope, nor with the Iberian Inquisition in the service of royal power, but rather with what was practised as a way of establishing truth in all secular courts, this being [...] the common practice of justice that accompanied the mercantile revolution and colonialism (Zaffaroni 2007: 39).

Continental Europe maintained Imperial Roman canon law through universities, Italian glossators, and the Church's influence (Maier 2006: 289). Inquisitorial procedures emerged in the twelfth and thirteenth centuries from Bologna and Paris scholars, shaped by Roman law and Church authority (Winter 2008: 16). Medieval canon law incorporated aspects of secular institutions to form the inquisitorial system, replacing ancient Germanic law except in England. The Church adopted inquisitorial methods before secular authorities followed suit (Orbaneja and Quemada 1997: 124).

The inquisitorial revolution met the needs of church and state: the church sought to combat heresy, while civil authorities needed stronger crime control amid economic growth. Private accusations proved insufficient, prompting adoption of Roman legal traditions for technical judgements and official interrogations—practices dating back to Carolingian *iudicia synodalia* (Cordero 2000: 16).

The inquisitorial procedure, developed to serve church or royal interests, became a foundational system in criminal law by emphasising interrogation of the accused as a means of uncovering truth—a method still seen today. This approach treated the accused as an object of knowledge, shaping both religious and secular investigations.

The Inquisition started taking shape in 1215—the same year as England's Magna Carta—when the Lateran Council decided that only suspects were necessary for legal proceedings, and accusers weren't required (Cordero 1986: 46). That year, all liturgical endorsement of ordeals ended, and papal decrees rejected all *purgatio vulgaris*. Once clergy were banned from participating in ordeals, inquisitorial methods gained ground (Winter 2008: 18–19). The Church didn't just ban clerical participation; because objects used in ordeals—like swords or water—had to be blessed by a priest, this ban made holding ordeals nearly impossible (Taruffo 2010: 14).

Inquisitorial procedures became dominant during the thirteenth and fourteenth centuries. As the Church entered the secular realm, clergy broadened their authority to judge any offence that might affect religion, regardless of who committed it (Moura 1994: 12). This led to steadily broader ecclesiastical jurisdiction.

The inquisitorial procedure originated within the Church and broadened as ecclesiastical authority expanded, encompassing a range of criminal offences deemed contrary to church interests (Prado 2006: 82). Although the original goal focused narrowly on persecuting those with differing views of Christianity, over the following centuries, the Inquisition's reach kept growing, eventually targeting Jews, Muslims, and others in an expanding campaign against difference.

Territorial jurisdiction was rigorously defined, and responsibility for prosecuting offences was shared between secular and ecclesiastical authorities, with disputes typically resolved according to established customs (Manzini 1951: 32). While primarily intended for religious matters such as heresy, ecclesiastical jurisdiction ultimately served to reinforce state authority and absolutist governance (Maier 2006: 302). The Inquisition had a profound impact through its anti-heresy initiatives and remained in force until its abolition in 1834 (Zaffaroni et al. 2002: 236).

In response to challenges that threatened the prevailing dominant worldview—including ideas contrary to the established religious and civic order—Inquisition Tribunals were formally instituted. They received legal sanction under the *Constitutio Excomuniamus* (1231) issued by Pope Gregory IX, later reinforced with Innocent IV's bull *Ad extirpanda* in 1252 (Coutinho 2001: 23). The institution developed incrementally: initial investigations were conducted by papal delegates, followed by the involvement of the Dominicans; its presence was noted as early as 1227 in Florence. The issuance of "*Ad extirpanda*" in 1252 marked the definitive establishment of this mechanism (Cordero 1986: 46). While punitive measures against dissent existed prior to this period, it is generally accepted that from 1252 forward, a formal process for regulating "heretical" beliefs commenced, particularly supported by the Church's *consigli* (Carvalho 2003: 11).

Punitive power first served to reinforce papal authority, targeting dissident sects with severe measures. After these groups were largely eliminated, its focus shifted to women and was soon adopted by secular courts. During the Counter-Reformation, the Inquisition restructured and began targeting Lutheran heretics. Throughout the pre-modern era, punitive power remained highly selective (Zaffaroni 2007: 88). Zaffaroni notes that "pre-modern doctrine not only admitted the selectivity of punitive power but sought to legitimise it, implicitly accepting that impunity prevails for friends and punishment for enemies" (Zaffaroni 2007: 88).

The Inquisition, rooted in intolerance and absolute religious truths, treated heresy as a threat and justified torture (Lopes Jr 2009: 62–63). Only divine order was considered true with opposing views dismissed (Gössel 2007: 104). Although initially against torture, the Church expanded its use to heresy trials and secular courts in the thirteenth century (Winter 2008: 19), making criminal prosecution especially harsh. The Inquisition enforced strict principles to preserve political and social stability (Maier 2006: 89). These ecclesiastical methods, later adopted across Europe, reached new heights of sophistication and cruelty, traces of which remain today.

The inquisitorial system, influenced by religious dogma, used specialised methods as described in Eymerich's *Directorium Inquisitorum* (published in 1376, expanded in 1578 by La Peña) and Kramer and Spengler's *Malleus Maleficarum* (published in 1487). Zaffaroni observes that *Malleus* built upon established punitive practices and justified witch persecution, even labelling doubters of the existence of witches as heretics (Zaffaroni et al. 2003: 510–511).

Carvalho describes this body of knowledge as logical, cohesive, and influential in shaping many modern and contemporary authoritarian legal models (Carvalho 2003: 6). It is considered trans-historical, supporting the legitimation of authoritarian judicial systems based on social defence

(Carvalho 2003: 12). Cordero adds that the Inquisition fostered apologetic rhetoric with arguments that continue to echo in various eras and regions (Cordero 2000: 19). According to Coutinho,

> it is, without doubt, the greatest legal contrivance the world has known; and knows. Despite its source, the Church, it is diabolical in its structure (which demonstrates that it is, at times and ironically, populated by agents of hell!), persisting for more than 700 years. This was not in vain: it arose for a specific purpose and, because it serves—and will continue to serve, if we do not awaken—it remains intact. (Coutinho 2001: 18)

The inquisitorial apparatus was conceived as a tool for the persecution and eradication of otherness, labelled as an enemy to be fought for the sake of the kingdom of heaven. Zaffaroni, Alagia, and Slokar highlight that "the Church—as the depository of the imperial Roman legal tradition, acquired through its Romanisation—practised *inquisitio* to elicit confession, which was the means of revealing the state of sin, understood as a personal characteristic that the offence merely revealed" (Zaffaroni et al. 2002: 236).

The new model's repressive origins can be traced to the ancient Roman *cognitio extraordinem*. Taruffo (2010: 38) notes that, unlike England's shift to jury trials, Continental Europe relied on evidentiary practices from Roman tradition.

The inquisitorial procedure, rooted in Roman tradition, was fully developed during the Inquisition. Unlike earlier systems, the Inquisition enforced conformity to Church dogma, punishing any beliefs deemed heretical rather than crimes against people or property (Carvalho 2008: 58). Absolutist European states later adopted this approach as an instrument for social control, establishing a procedural framework focused on uncovering "real truth" that continues to influence legal systems today (Carvalho 2003: 12).

The inquisitorial system is defined by its search for truth and served as a tool of authoritarian power. Judges held extensive authority, often resulting in proceedings without clear legal limits or adversarial debate. According to Cordero, this led to secret hearings instead of open contest (Cordero 1986: 9). Goldschmidt notes that Germanic procedures were oral, but criminal cases shifted towards written records under Roman-canonical law. This change persisted until the French Revolution returned oral trials to prominence (Goldschmidt 2010: 789).

The role of the judge is transformed, as he previously remained impassive in the face of a dispute; he becomes a militant organ. A mystique is born; he discovers and eliminates heresies or crimes, combats evil forces in a daily crusade; it is by his merit that the world is not devoured by the devil; if he were neutral, he would be complicit with the devil; ultimately, scruples are equated with cowardice (Cordero 2000: 21). As Zaffaroni explains, the subject of knowledge—*inquisitor* (interrogator or investigator)—questions the object of knowledge—*inquired* (interrogated or investigated)—and thus obtains the truth. If the object does not respond sufficiently or does so without the clarity or precision demanded by the subject, he is coerced until the answer is obtained (by means of torture). The inquisitor or interrogator ceases to be an *arbitrator* and becomes an *investigator*; virtue is on his side because he exercises sovereign power, since he considers himself the *victim* (usurping or confiscating the role of the victim). God no longer decides between two equals as parties, but is instead held hostage by the lord, the *dominus* (Zaffaroni 2007: 38).

Nicholas Eymerich systematised inquisitorial knowledge by writing the *Directorium Inquisitorum*, the Manual of the Inquisitors. This foundational work established principles that still influence a prosecutorial approach in legal procedures today. Its enduring significance warrants examination of its key aspects.

The Inquisition targeted anyone considered a threat to its authority, labelling them as heretics. According to Eymerich, a heretic is someone who rejects true doctrine for a false and misguided one (Eymerich 1993: 31).

The inquisitorial system divides human experience into strict binaries, enforcing social control by allowing no compromise. Those not fully aligned with Church doctrine are labelled heretics and targeted for persecution. The *Directorium Inquisitorum* serves as a tool to intervene in reality according to Church guidelines. Zaffaroni notes that this framework legitimises inquisitorial power, assuming it always pursues good and authorising violence against obstacles to such knowledge. Both torture and vivisection are justified by the premise of saving humanity from threats like Satan or disease. Any resistance to inquisitorial knowledge is seen as opposing the good and supporting evil (Zaffaroni 2007: 41).

Eymerich's work follows canon law, providing a systematic overview of substantive and procedural issues. His manual classifies types of sacred transgressions and identifies groups he considers enemies—such as blasphemers, heretics, excommunicates, apostates, converts to Judaism or

Islam, non-believers, and others opposing the Christian faith (Eymerich 1993: 36–74). He argues for extending the Inquisition's authority to include Jews and Muslims, justifying this broad scope as necessary for targeting perceived threats to established power.

Eymerich broadened the definition of heretics to include anyone who opposed the Inquisition, directly or indirectly (Eymerich 1993: 75). Francisco de La Peña further categorised those who threatened the Inquisition as enemies (Eymerich 1993: 76). Any deviation was seen as hostility needing elimination. Zaffaroni notes that power's desire for knowledge leads to violent interrogation and social hierarchy, allowing it to define "good" label "evil" and designate enemies (Zaffaroni 2007: 41).

The system aimed to control society by eliminating differences and categorising individuals based on suspicion of heresy: weak, strong, or grave. Weak suspicion arises from secret meetings or unusual behaviour; strong suspicion involves frequenting heretics' homes or hiding them; grave suspicion is directed at those who honour, seek communion with, or imitate heretical rituals (Eymerich 1993: 77).

Sanctions follow similar rules: individuals suspected of heresy face canonical penalties such as a year of penance and potential excommunication, after which they may be condemned. Strongly suspected persons risk harsher consequences for repeat offences. Those refusing to abjure are handed to secular authorities for execution. Grave suspicion alone can result in conviction without defence; non-confession leads to secular punishment, while confession grants pardon but retains condemnation. Even rumours (fama) can suffice for grave heresy charges. Eymerich lists thirteen verdicts, applying also to those aiding heretics (Eymerich 1993).

Eymerich's method aimed to enforce hierarchy and suppress diversity by punishing those suspected of heresy. The focus was not on the harm caused but on perceived threats to the system. Inquisitorial epistemology emphasised judging individuals as inherently dangerous or wicked, rather than their specific acts, viewing immoral actions as evidence of personal corruption (Carvalho 2003: 14–16).

Procedural decisionism is a central element of inquisitorial epistemology, influencing both judgements and sentence enforcement (Carvalho 2003: 16). Eymerich's manual details these procedures, which could start by accusation, denunciation, or investigation. If initiated by accusation, the accuser risked penalties if unable to prove guilt—a method Eymerich notes was rarely used in practice (Eymerich 1993: 106).

Once accusations were nearly eliminated, judges began to investigate cases independently and secretly, taking on roles as both accuser and investigator. This blurred the line between judge and prosecutor, turning the accused into the central subject of prosecution rather than a party in the proceedings (Alonso 1986: 41). Judges adopted inquisitorial duties, compelling confessions through coercion (Lopes Jr 2005: 157). In the pure inquisitorial procedure, only the judge—inquisitor—and the object of investigation participate (Roxin 2003: 86). As Coutinho notes,

> the direct control of criminal proceedings by the clergy conveniently excludes a prosecuting body: the *actus trium personarum* is no longer sustainable. The inquisitor is tasked with both prosecution and judgement, transforming the accused into a mere *object of verification*, which is why the notion of *party* is entirely meaningless. The superiority of the judge is, evidently, clear (but logical, within the system's structure), not least because the initiation and momentum of the proceedings are his responsibility, as can be seen, among other things, from the fact that he determines both the *thema probandum* and the *thema decidendum*. Thus, a feature of utmost importance is established, marking the system as *pure*, that is, the *absence of parties* in the sense we attribute to the term today. (Coutinho 2001: 23)

The inquisitorial procedure usually started when an informant reported heresy. The inquisitor acted independently rather than advocating for either side (Eymerich 1993: 107). Proceedings could also begin with the judge's own investigation, reflecting a system designed to thoroughly examine society and eliminate dissent.

> If there is neither a spontaneous confession nor an accusation or denunciation but rather rumours in a given city or region that someone has said or done something against the faith or in favour of heretics, in this case the inquisitor must investigate, not at the behest of any party, but according to his own prerogatives. This is a very common way of "proceeding". And if the rumours reach the inquisitor's ears from honest and well-behaved people, the procedure will always begin, in the presence of the notary and two witnesses, with the drafting of the record, in which the content of these rumours is transcribed. (Eymerich 1993: 108)

Rumours were enough to prompt criminal prosecution. De La Peña notes that two credible witnesses or conflicting statements could establish such rumours, leading to proceedings (Eymerich 1993: 116). This reliance on unverified reports often resulted in convictions with little factual basis, reflecting a system designed to intimidate society by fostering fear. As Franco Cordero observed, this approach prioritises hypothesis over facts—a model that surprisingly persists today:

> the solitude in which inquisitors work, never exposed to contradiction, unbound by dialectical constraints, may perhaps assist police work, but it fosters paranoid mental frameworks. Let us call this the 'primacy of hypothesis over facts': the investigator pursues one of them, sometimes blindly; nothing guarantees it is better founded than the alternatives, nor does the role encourage, as a precaution, self-criticism; just as all the cards are in his hand and he alone lays them on the table, he steers the outcome towards "his" hypothesis. We know what persuasive means he possesses [...] using it, he directs the result wherever he wishes. (Cordero 1986: 51)

In the inquisitorial system, evidence management was entirely controlled by the magistrate, which is its defining feature (Coutinho 2001: 24). Canon law rules mainly served to confirm hypotheses already held by the judge (Carvalho 2003: 22), leading to outcomes that were predetermined (Carvalho 2003: 21–22). Cordero describes this process as a monologue with an appearance of flawless automation where nothing is left to chance (Cordero 2000: 319). As a result, so-called "truth" in these proceedings reflected the inquisitor's personal views, compelling the defendant to confirm the judge's assumptions. Coutinho explains that decisions were made in advance and evidence was interpreted only to support these preconceived choices, creating a "paranoid mental framework" (Coutinho 2002: 186). The judge used deductive logic to justify decisions with evidence found after the fact (Coutinho 2001: 25). Roxin points out that this conflation of roles compromised judicial impartiality due to psychological strain from gathering and evaluating evidence (Roxin 2003: 122).

The introspective inquisitorial procedure is flexible and undefined, lacking fixed forms or timelines, and does not involve structured opposition (Cordero 1986: 50). It did not focus on objective standards or cognition, leading to increased subjectivity and reducing the accused to objects. This shift distanced proceedings from fact-finding, despite claiming to seek the truth. Cordero (1986: 317) states that inquisitors typically sought convictions, structuring procedures to this end. As Lopes

Jr (2005: 161) points out, the truths produced relied on fundamentally flawed concepts and methods. According to Ferrajoli, the model is based

> on the pursuit of substantive truth, which is therefore configured as a *maximal truth*, pursued without any normative limits on the means of obtaining evidence, and at the same time not bound, but discretionary, at the very least because the indeterminacy of the charges and their evaluative character require, more than evidence, value judgements that cannot be challenged by the defence [...] the end (of attaining the truth, whatever it may be) justifies the means (whatever procedures are used) [...]. (Ferrajoli 2002: 434–435)

For Coutinho, "a system with such a structure, as seems elementary, tends to prevail over time, although subject to secondary changes [...] and will continue to prevail—if only because it upholds the *status quo* and, therefore, *serves those who hold power in any regime* [...]" (Coutinho 2001: 24). It is a system that compromises the possibilities for the accused to resist the punitive power that encroaches upon his liberty and, therefore, is perfectly suited to dictatorial, totalitarian, and antidemocratic regimes.

Eymerich viewed the right of defence as merely delaying proceedings and sentencing, highlighting how procedural speed favours authoritarian purposes. De La Peña supports Eymerich, claiming defence is useless and that a lawyer's main job is to make the accused confess, repent, and request punishment (Eymerich 1993: 138–139).

The system was designed to symbolically subjugate the accused, using tactics like controlling physical space—such as seating the accused lower than the inquisitor—to assert dominance. Eymerich notes that the inquisitor's goal is to extract information, often without even disclosing the charge, using broad questions like "what have you done?" to confuse and undermine resistance. Cordero (2000: 19) describes the process as forcing the investigated, whether guilty or not, to speak under pressure, with a focus on achieving results rather than justice.

Eymerich's manual describes interrogation methods focused on persistent questioning, setting traps, and leveraging suspicion to prompt confessions (Eymerich 1993: 113, 117). De La Peña suggests repeating promises of mercy to elicit clear admissions, while Cordero highlights the inquisitor's extensive authority and belief that guilt is inherent, justifying coercive tactics (Cordero 2000: 22–23; Cordero 1986: 46). The investigation was viewed as therapeutic, with penalties seen as remedies, and the accused often forced to cooperate.

> If the accused continues to deny, and the inquisitor believes he is concealing his errors—even in the absence of evidence—the interrogations will be intensified by varying the questions. In this way, either a confession will be obtained or, alternatively, contradictory answers. If contradictory answers are given, the inquisitor will ask the accused why he suddenly responds one way and then another: he is pressed to tell the truth, being told that if he does not yield, he will have to be tortured. If he confesses, all is well. If not, this alone, together with other indications, will suffice to subject him to torture and thus extract a confession. (Cordero 1986: 46)

The procedure was designed to secure a conviction; the experimentation and manipulation of the accused, objectified as a source of knowledge, would invariably lead to this outcome, as the inquiry was already directed towards a predetermined end. If the offence is a sin, its acknowledgement by the perpetrator is a goal of the inquisitorial procedure; nothing stands in the way of this objective, which justifies all the means employed by the judge to obtain the confession of the accused (Alonso 1986: 41). As Cordero reflects, the inquisitor works as he pleases with animals that must confess; once a hypothesis is conceived, he builds inductive manoeuvres upon it; the absence of debate allows for paranoid thinking; facts are eclipsed by hypotheses. Master of the board, he arranges the pieces as he wishes, for the Inquisition is a verbal world akin to a dream: times, places, things, people, and events float and move within manipulable frameworks. It is a dangerous game, for the inquisitor establishes facts with total freedom, selectively attentive or deaf to the data, according as they confirm or contradict his hypothesis; since words are a malleable material (the accused utter them in torrents), any conclusion becomes possible; a narcissistic sense of omnipotence develops, in which all caution and self-criticism vanish (Cordero 2000: 23).

Confession was indispensable to the inquisitorial system, and there were no limitations regarding the means used to extract it, as these were justified by the sacred mission of uncovering the truth (Coutinho 2001: 26–27). The inquisitorial apparatus developed a theorem: guilty or not, the accused holds the historical truth; every question will surely be resolved, provided the inquisitor can penetrate his mind. There was no formally regulated dialogue: the system was directed at an animal that confessed (Cordero 1986: 48). According to Lopes Jr.,

> the interrogation was regarded as an essential act, requiring a special technique. There were five progressive types of torture, and the suspect had the "right" to be subjected to only one type of torture per day. If after 15 days the accused did not confess, he was considered "sufficiently" tortured and was released. Nevertheless, the methods employed were effective, and perhaps only a few managed to withstand the full 15 days. Worse still, in some cases the punishment was less severe than the tortures endured. (Lopes Jr 2010: 65)

The procedure took place in what Cordero calls the inquisitorial environment: the person under investigation is an animal that confesses or at least must do so; since suicidal outpouring is generally repugnant, it must be stimulated. The investigators manipulate souls, causing the accused to soon become unrecognisable compared to who he was outside the inquisitorial environment, which requires a sophisticated technology: enclosed spaces and a cyclical time subject to indefinite schedules, typical of the inquisitorial art, which employs deep psychological work on the accused, alternating moments of harshness and gentleness. It is a true instructional confinement, designed to extract the truth (Cordero 2000: 393–394). The Inquisition's obstinacy in pursuing a supposed truth through torture represented a regression in evidentiary matters, as it often led to the conviction of the innocent, who could not withstand the torment, or to the acquittal of those who demonstrated greater resistance to suffering (Moura 1994: 12).

The ambition for truth emerged in the Inquisition and persists to this day in the Western criminal justice system. In the pursuit of this "real truth", pre-trial detention becomes the general rule: once in possession of the heretic's body, torture may be used to extract a confession (Lopes 2010: 64). As I have already observed, a mere rumour was sufficient to initiate an investigation, and detention was inescapable, for this allowed the inquisitor to have the accused at his disposal for torture and obtain a confession. The institution of preventive custody had no fixed regulation, being left to the discretion of the inquisitor, who acted according to the status of the individuals and the gravity of the offence (Manzini 1951: 58). As an art directed at obtaining confession, the inquisitorial procedure required time to manipulate the accused; as an evidentiary measure, this custody was an official instrument: in a normal environment, the accused would not confess (Cordero 2000: 392). The characteristics of the system entailed an objectification of bodies: for the inquisitor, it was necessary to have the heretic's body at his disposal. This body was scrutinised, analytically dissected and reassembled as the object of possible knowledge, in accordance with the dogmatic framework of a set of pre-established truths and procedures.

But as already indicated, the purpose of the system did not lie in the purification of individual souls. In discussing the apparent madness of an accused, Eymerich recommends that both the truly and the falsely insane must be tortured, with no reason to fear the death of the accused during torture; and he concludes by revealing the true meaning of the system, stating that.

> it must be remembered that the most important purpose of the trial and the death sentence is not to save the soul of the accused, but to pursue the common good and to intimidate the people (*ut alii terreantur*). Now, the common good must take precedence over any other considerations of charity aimed at the benefit of an individual. (Eymerich 1993: 122)

Eymerich's discourse is unequivocally foundational, establishing a rationale that informs the criminal justice system through a punitive framework evident across different historical periods. This approach is exemplified by Brazilian Minister of Justice Francisco Campos's arguments in the explanatory memorandum to the Brazilian Code of Criminal Procedure of 1941:

> Our current criminal procedure laws guarantee defendants, even those caught in the act or overwhelmed by the weight of evidence, such an extensive catalogue of safeguards and privileges that repression necessarily becomes defective and delayed, resulting in an indirect encouragement of criminality. It is urgent to abolish the unjustifiable primacy of the individual's interest over that of social protection. We cannot continue to compromise with pseudo-individual rights to the detriment of the common good. (Campos: 2010: 349)

It is unsurprising that these two conceptions can be compared, as each represents a rationale aimed at the removal of individuals designated as enemies by authorities vested with the power to determine such classifications. Both the Inquisition and Vargas's Estado Novo exemplify how authorities have historically employed punitive logic to suppress opposition. This longstanding approach—using collective fear through prompt and decisive punishment—continues to influence contemporary legal perspectives on trials, including those held by "rationalist" scholars such as Ferrer Beltrán. According to Beltrán (2007: 30), a trial serves as a deterrent to future murders only when it successfully identifies the perpetrators and enforces appropriate penalties. Beltrán's arguments reveal his authoritarian political leanings, visible in the belief that exemplary punishments can have a deterrent effect—a principle present in Eymerich's manual.

Rationalism and inquisitorialism are politically and epistemologically intertwined. For this reason, reimagining criminal justice requires closely examining the dominant truth-seeking epistemology, rooted in inquisitorial principles and reinforced by the "invented tradition" of evidentiary rationalism (Graham, 1987: 1209).

Eymerich advises inquisitors to avoid declaring the accused innocent in acquittals, recommending they simply state nothing was proven against them. This allows for future convictions if the person returns before the Tribunal (Eymerich 1993: 15–151).

The inquisitorial system prioritises its own version of truth, seeking conviction above all else. Within this framework, Eymerich's manual provides several direct references to truth, indicating that the prevailing discourse of the contemporary criminal justice system's "search for the truth" is characterised by an inquisitorial approach. According to the decision-making model proposed by Eymerich,

> we investigated everything you were accused of in order to know the truth [...] taking our seat in the Tribunal, in accordance with our function as judge, with our gaze fixed only on God and concerned only with the truth, with the Holy Gospels before us, so that our judgement may emanate from the face of God and that our eyes may see the truth. (Eymerich 1993: 150)

In another passage, the reference to truth appears again, indicating that the inquisitors "will continue the interrogation until they have obtained the whole truth from his lips" (Eymerich 1993: 155).

Eymerich believed that if two reliable witnesses testified, it was enough to establish guilt and justify a conviction (Eymerich 1993: 219). Inquisitors could even order witnesses to be tortured, aiming to force them to tell the truth and penalise them for lying under oath. Torture was intended to reveal the truth—or what inquisitors believed to be the truth—within a system designed to amplify punitive control (Eymerich 1993: 221).

Given how the term truth was understood, it is understandable that authorities would recommend torturing a suspect when only one witness testified against them, since a rumour combined with a statement was considered a semi-proof (Eymerich 1993: 208). As Ferrajoli explains, "in the medieval trial, if the evidence was insufficient but still left some suspicion or doubt regarding guilt, this was seen as a semi-proof. Such cases resulted in a verdict of semi-culpability and a reduced sentence" (Ferrajoli 2002: 441). In this view, simply being suspected meant you could not be presumed innocent—an idea that eventually found its way into secular legal systems, as will be discussed later.

The *Directorum Inquisitorum* is not the sole inquisitorial treatise deserving of scholarly consideration. The *Malleus Malleficarum* exemplifies punitive thinking, justifying inquisitorial authority by arguing for the existence of witches and stressing the gravity of their alleged crimes, attributed to the devil, the accused, and God's will (Zaffaroni et al. 2003: 513). Politically, the Inquisition presumed anyone with differing beliefs was a threat to Christian unity, using coercive tactics like torture to force confessions and assert their perceived inferiority. This objectification was widely directed at women as well as heretics and political opponents. According to Zaffaroni et al.:

> The *inquisitio* represented not just a shift in criminal law, but, by integrating all forms of knowledge, it initiated a significant cultural shift that started with the elite, motivated by the desire to include the entirety of society. During the late Middle Ages, pagan traditions persisted across Europe, and the elites themselves had not yet completely assimilated. Women serve as the bearers of culture; thus, to sever ties with the former culture and establish a new one, it was essential to impose control over women. (Zaffaroni et al. 2003: 512–513)

The relationship between the *Malleus* and the subjugation of the female body is manifest. One point that deserves closer scrutiny concerns the various temporalities assumed by the Inquisition and how these altered its object, the intensity of repression, and, to a greater or lesser extent, how the early stages of capitalism—which coincided with overseas expansion and the logic of colonialism—ushered in an unprecedented aesthetic of repression of the feminine.

Federici's hypothesis links emerging capitalism's needs with the witch-hunt, arguing it targeted women's resistance and agency in sexuality, reproduction, and healing. Her study combines a gender lens, statistical data, and sociological analysis, emphasising the witch-hunt as a tool to build a new patriarchal order and facilitate capitalist development. Older women who were branded as witches frequently found themselves excluded from society, struggling to adjust to life in an urban capitalist context. Federici identifies the witch-hunt's roles in establishing a new sexual division of labour, solidifying patriarchal structures that excluded women from waged work, and transforming women's bodies into instruments for reproducing the labour force (Federici 2017).

It is important to note that the pre-capitalist witch-hunt occurred at the same time as both the extermination of Indigenous peoples in the Americas and the English-led slave trade (Federici 2019: 40). The *Malleus Maleficarum* was published in 1486, just before Columbus's voyage to the Americas. Manuals on demonology played a crucial role in shaping and perpetuating efforts against this perceived crime (Ankarloo et al. 2002: 125).

Many leading scholars agree that colonisation played a key role in developing demonology. Parinetto suggests that witch-hunts in the American colonies deeply influenced European ideas about witchcraft. He describes the word "witch" as a flexible label used to target very different groups, even entire populations (Parinetto 1998: 101). The term "witch" doesn't have a fixed meaning; instead, it changes over time. Parinetto also notes that under accusations of witchcraft and sodomy, around 69 million Amerindians were killed (Parinetto 1998: 09). He argues that witch-hunts functioned as an effective disguise for colonial actions (Parinetto 1998: 10). Essentially, the large-scale witch-hunts in sixteenth-century Europe were shaped by earlier persecutions in the Americas. Parinetto's research relies on accounts of "cannibal savages" from the Americas, reports that demonologists later used, showing clear links between these two waves of persecution.

Unlike other countries or colonies, Brazil never had its own inquisitorial tribunal. Spain, for instance, established these courts in Lima and Cartagena in 1569 and 1610, respectively. While Portugal did not set up an Inquisition tribunal in Brazil, it did establish tribunals in Évora and Goa (in Portuguese India), both under the Portuguese Holy Office. Even though colonial Brazil lacked a formal Inquisition tribunal, the influence of the Holy Office was nevertheless strong and far-reaching within the colony. Therefore, any study aiming to go beyond criminal procedure texts and understand deeper social attitudes in Brazil must consider this subtle but significant legacy (Batista 2016: 26).

The Tribunal of the Holy Office was established in Portugal in 1536 and lasted until 1821, with jurisdiction extending over the entire Empire, including Brazil. Although attempts to set up an Inquisition tribunal in Brazil failed due to financial issues, economic dependencies, and the territory's size, Lisbon's Tribunal maintained authority. The Inquisition continued to act in Brazil and other colonies despite these challenges (Costa 2018: 43–44).

Although Brazil never had a permanent inquisitorial court, the Portuguese colony saw several visits from inquisitorial authorities. Notably, major visitations occurred in Bahia and Pernambuco at the end of the 1500s, Bahia in 1618, and Grão-Pará in the late eighteenth century. Additional visits are documented, such as a minor one to the southern captaincies in 1626. These records indicate that such visitations were likely more frequent than historical accounts typically suggest (Feitler 2019: 89).

The Inquisition strongly influenced Brazil's legal system, as shown by the Philippine Ordinances of 1603, which governed criminal law and procedural law until the reforms of 1830 and 1832. These codes reflected an inquisitorial tradition and did not incorporate accusatorial elements.

The Philippine Ordinances, marked by inquisitorial rationality, became colonial Brazil's first penal and criminal procedural code. Unlike earlier ordinances, they saw widespread application, reaffirmed by King João IV in 1643 and later monarchs. Their enforcement persisted in Brazil after independence, as confirmed in 1823, until replaced by the Penal Code (1830) and Code of Criminal Procedure (1832).

Contemporary criminal justice scholars generally distance themselves from the violence of past inquisitions. Many consider references to the Inquisition in current debates irrelevant, arguing that the ongoing search for truth in criminal proceedings does not reflect actual continuity. However, some critics note that focusing on a search for truth underpinned by a concept of relative or approximate truth can subtly sustain inquisitorial influences in accusatorial systems and risks perpetuating human rights violations.

Coutinho, Lopes Jr, and Martins demonstrate that inquisitorial approaches continue to shape truth-seeking in contemporary legal discourse. The inquisitorial system spread quickly across Continental Europe, was renewed by scientific rationality, and remains central to civil law traditions. The main issue is not whether inquisitorial influence exists, but how much. As Carvalho (2008: 78) notes, it is more coherent to assess varying degrees of inquisitorial logic throughout history and legal systems, rather than framing criminal procedure as simply accusatorial or inquisitorial.

The epistemological and political principles established by these frameworks continue to shape the Western legal tradition, largely because inquisitorial systems were incorporated into secular jurisdictions, as discussed further below.

The Spread of the Inquisitorial Procedure in Secular Jurisdiction

The rise of inquisitorial epistemology was closely linked to the monopolisation of punitive power by the State. Zaffaroni, Alagia, and Slokar point out that when the conflict ceased to be *an injury against the victim* and became *an offence against the sovereign*, that is, when its essence shifted from harm to a human being to an offence against the lord, it detached itself from the injury and became increasingly subjective, as *enmity* towards the sovereign. The investigation of harm to one's neighbour lost its meaning, as the aim was no longer reparation but the neutralisation of the sovereign's enemy. What was exceptional in Germanic law (the community acting against the traitor) became the rule: *every offender became a traitor, an enemy of the sovereign* (Zaffaroni et al. 2002: 235–236).

As secular legal systems developed, the ancient Roman idea of the "enemy" resurfaced, leading to new methods of persecution. With the sovereign now seen as the aggrieved party, disputes could no longer rely on adversarial proceedings, prompting the shift from accusatorial to inquisitorial procedures. Though *cognitio*'s frameworks faded after the Carolingian Empire, the Church preserved it as both a spiritual and administrative practice, later influencing secular courts—especially as centralised power grew in the thirteenth century (Foucault 2003: 68–71).

Inquisitorial interrogation was shaped by religious ideas from medieval Church practices. Foucault observes that legal violations became linked to religious faults, so harming the sovereign was seen as both a sin and a crime (Foucault 2003: 73–74; Carvalho 2003: 15). This connection led to viewing crimes as offences against both secular and sacred authority.

The inquisitorial system moved beyond church courts, spreading through Continental Europe as monarchies centralised judicial power (Prado 2006: 81). This transformation marked the rise of absolutist states in the late Middle Ages, with kings controlling justice via appointed judges (Foucault 2003: 67; Maier 2006: 288–289; Cordero 1986: 27). According to Zaffaroni (2007: 31), when victims were sidelined, public authorities gained broad control over conflicts, selectively intervening and maintaining surveillance over groups seen as threats to social order.

In the thirteenth century, professional royal courts replaced earlier judicial systems, centralising justice. By the fifteenth century, they absorbed all former court functions as nation states rose (Maier 2006). Judicial authority followed a strict hierarchy, allowing appeals and reserving final judgement for the king (Maier 2006). Zaffaroni notes that inquisitorial procedures, which used torture to force additional accusations, spread rapidly and were implemented more strictly in secular courts than ecclesiastical ones (Zaffaroni 2007).

The creation of compulsory conflict resolution marked a major shift, ending individuals' rights to manage their own disputes and requiring submission to external authority as both judiciary and political power (Foucault 2003: 65). Foucault explains that the accusatorial system faded out around the twelfth and thirteenth centuries. The second half of the Middle Ages brought new justice procedures, which were pivotal to European history and its global influence. This legal evolution mainly affected the forms and foundations of knowledge, introducing a specific type of legal understanding that significantly shaped the Western world (Foucault 2003: 62).

As Zaffaroni, Alagia, and Slokar point out, "the model of conflict or party-based resolution persisted as long as a central, vertical power had not emerged, but when such a power appeared and gained sufficient strength, it confiscated the victim through the punitive model" (Zaffaroni 2002: 233). The onset of this process brought about a significant innovation, with the invention—or reinvention—of the notion of offence: harm now extended also to the sovereign, who could demand retribution (Foucault 2003: 67). In this way, the state gradually and steadily appropriated the entire judicial process, the whole mechanism for the interindividual settlement of disputes characteristic of the High Middle Ages (Foucault 2003: 66).

Power became more centralised with the rise of the inquisitorial system, which dominated secular law in continental Europe from the thirteenth to eighteenth centuries (Maier 2006: 288). In the nineteenth century, this model transformed but still influences modern criminal procedures. England diverged by instituting checks on authority with acts like the Bill of Rights (1689), while other monarchies reinforced judicial control under the inquisitorial approach—a structure only partly reformed in the nineteenth century. The system expanded across Spain, Portugal, France, Germany, and their colonies, including Spanish America and Brazil (Prado 2006: 84–87). Zaffaroni observes that secular courts adopted the inquisitorial method, often targeting political dissenters through public executions. In Spain, the monarchy mainly opposed political adversaries—labelled as heretics—with the Inquisition lasting until the nineteenth century (Zaffaroni 2007: 34).

The incorporation of inquisitorial principles into secular law was not merely a matter of legal technicality but represented a profound shift in justice and governance. By adopting inquisitorial procedures, secular states reinforced their capacity to control dissent and enforce conformity, often under the guise of maintaining order or rooting out heresy. This blending of ecclesiastical and state mechanisms for investigation and punishment blurred the boundaries between religious and civil authority, embedding inquisitorial logic deep within the fabric of emerging nation states. Such developments laid the groundwork for modern legal systems, where the search for truth and the prosecution of perceived threats to authority became central to the administration of justice.

The inquisitorial system emerged not from rationalising punishment, but from evolving political structures and shifts in power intended to control opponents of new regimes. Foucault notes that state inquiries mainly served administrative and governmental functions, acting as tools for exercising power (Foucault 2003: 73). Therefore, the inquisitorial method aimed to efficiently manage the developing continental European power structure (Prado 2006: 81). According to Foucault,

> the inquiry is precisely a political form, a form of management, of the exercise of power which, through the judicial institution, became a way, in Western culture, of authenticating truth, of acquiring things that would

> be regarded as true and of transmitting them. The inquiry is a form of knowledge-power. (Foucault 2003: 78)

Consequently, employing inquiry as a method for assigning responsibility—rather than resolving disputes between parties—should not be misconstrued as a humanitarian advancement over the arbitrariness or randomness of ordeals. This transition signifies both a revolution in epistemological approaches and a prosecutorial requirement within systems of authority. It embodies an authoritative model of knowledge.

The inquiry's significance extends beyond its political role, as it introduced a systematic method for investigating past events and establishing truth. Designed to determine whether a crime occurred and who was responsible, inquiries replaced the need to catch offenders in the act by relying on witness testimony under oath. Over time, this process developed specialised knowledge and procedures for uncovering historical events. As Foucault notes, inquiries allowed past actions to be examined as if witnessed in real time, reshaping how history and truth were understood (Foucault 2003: 72). This innovation made aligning facts with investigative findings central to the concept of truth. As Foucault states, "Here we have a new way of extending the present, of transferring it from one era to another and offering it to the gaze, to knowledge, as if it were still present. This insertion of the inquiry, re-actualising, making present, tangible, immediate, true, what happened, as if we were witnessing it, constitutes a major discovery" (Foucault 2003: 72).

Over time, the search for truth became a tool of punitive mechanisms, expanding beyond material evidence to include perceived enemies as objects of inquiry. Torture was standardised as a method for uncovering truth, disregarding humanitarian considerations. This shift redefined the accused from procedural subjects to objects of investigation and proof (Maier 2006: 297).

Carvalho (2003) argues that the courts served as both legal tools and political apparatuses, legitimised by the Church, leading to a framework marked by intolerance and exclusion. Heresy was viewed as an offence against both religion and its supporting political system (Carvalho 2008). According to Lopes Jr. (2009), this system's benefits led legislators to apply it widely across all categories of offences.

Manzini argues that the inquisitorial procedure arose from social necessity, evolving out of the accusatorial system while keeping compatible elements. He notes it was more effective for crime suppression and better suited to the ethos and government structures after municipal liberties (Manzini 1951: 49). The model, run by officials within a hierarchy, became an efficient tool for centralising power, as seen in the French absolutist monarchy (Winter 2008: 16).

In the inquisitorial system, judges collect evidence independently to determine if a crime has been committed, treating victims and the accused mainly as sources of information. The accused is compelled to provide truthful testimony, and limits on uncovering facts are viewed as unnecessary. Gössel argues that this approach centralises punitive power within a single institution, reflecting sovereign authority and prioritising truth over individual rights (Gossel 2007: 19). This system facilitated absolutist regimes, where prosecution and judgement were unified, evolving into permanent institutions. Over time, judging became the domain of specialists rather than the public (Orbaneja and Quemada 1997: 125), leading to technocracy and replacing local courts with stronger centralised jurisdiction (Maier 2006: 295).

In 1532, Germany (then part of the Holy Roman Empire) enacted its first imperial criminal law, the *Constitutio Criminalis Carolina*, which drew mainly from Roman law but retained some Germanic traditions. The code introduced inquisitorial procedures, replaced traditional accusatorial systems, and led to public, official prosecutions and uniform regulations—including the use of torture—across Germany (Maier 2006; Prado 2006).

The inquisitorial procedure emerged in Spain in the thirteenth century and became dominant by the fourteenth (Prado 2006: 84). It replaced accusatorial methods with written, secret investigations aimed at factual accuracy, where torture was allowed given sufficient suspicion or a defendant's poor reputation (Deu 1995: 41).

By the late fourteenth century, Italy had adopted the inquisitorial procedure due to the need for criminal prosecution beyond private accusations. The system became entrenched and prevailed until the nineteenth century (Manzini 1951: 50–51). Unlike Spain, Germany, or France, Italy's Inquisition was less severe, partly because it preserved Roman-Germanic traditions. Italian scholars helped shape features like location-based jurisdiction, written and secret trials, authority-led prosecutions, legal proof, and the use of confession and torture (Maier 2006: 324).

Roman-canonical law was introduced to France by Louis IX in 1254, marking the rise of royal jurisdiction and new legal procedures. Despite some early resistance, the inquisitorial system became formalised through the Ordinances of 1498 and 1539, which reformed judicial organisation and accelerated proceedings. The 1670 Ordinance later strengthened this system with only minor structural changes (Maier 2006: 310).

A review of the Ordinance of 1670 shows that inquisitorial systems do not always lack party involvement; for example, the king's prosecutors had sole authority to initiate cases (Cordero 1986: 47). The main distinction in criminal procedure appears to lie in control over evidence: even though French law separated prosecution from judgement, judges retained control over evidence, maintaining the inquisitorial approach. Thus, despite changes in heresy prosecutions, the structure stayed inquisitorial, with judges overseeing evidence (Carvalho 2008: 68). Unlike in England, seventeenth-century France used secret inquisitorial proceedings, excluding both the public and the accused (Foucault 2008: 32).

Criminal prosecution became a state process, with the king's attorney or similar officials as principal prosecutors. The accused lost active participation and many legal rights due to secret proceedings, which limited defence and legal assistance. Detention became standard, and torture for confessions was common. State penal power peaked during this era (Maier 2006: 315), with defence counsel roles severely restricted or banned for serious offences (Zaffaroni 2007: 86), exemplified by their explicit abolition in Austria's 1788 Penal Code (Gossel 2007: 18).

The secular inquisitorial procedure relied on investigation, confidentiality, and documentation—focusing on an official search for truth rather than equal debate. Conducted in secret and recorded in writing, this system aimed to suppress offences and maintain public order, reflecting epistemological standards intended to strengthen the *Ancien Régime*'s authority (Maier 2006: 316).

The system relied on a classificatory hierarchy of legal proofs, which made legal truth a complex art, emphasising its aspect as a specialised knowledge—accessible only to experts—which reinforced the principle of secrecy and distinguished the judge's conviction from that which any reasonable person might have (Foucault 2008: 34).

Historically, legal proof was linked to authoritarian procedures aiming for absolute truth—even through extreme methods like torture (Ibañez 2005: 67). Cordero argues this is incompatible with contemporary criminal justice, as relying solely on statistical reasoning is unethical. The inquisitorial method presumed the accused knew all facts and sought confessions, often resulting in forced testimony and rigid verdicts. Judges had broad discretion, using algebraic terms for fractions of proof. Conviction depended on two consistent, uncontested witnesses whose testimony had to be clear and positive (Cordero 2000: 28–29).

Proceedings shifted from oral to written forms, making secrecy standard and leaving accused individuals passive and often unable to defend themselves (Maier 2006). Cordero calls this judicial concealment—an imbalanced system where the accused lacks information and fairness (Cordero 2000). Goldschmidt observes that while public hearings once promoted transparency in Roman and Germanic courts, this openness disappeared with the rise of inquisitorial procedures (Goldschmidt 2010).

Documenting judicial events is central to the inquisitorial system, where only information recorded in official records is considered valid, making notaries essential. By the thirteenth century, this documentation process had become sophisticated (Cordero 2000: 283). The inquisitorial method involves detailed verbal exchanges, requires the accused to speak, and treats proceedings as psychological investigations, with every detail formally recorded. As Foucault notes, secret written records governed by strict rules serve as mechanisms for producing truth, even without the accused present (Foucault 2008: 34).

While authority can establish truth without the accused present, their involvement is crucial for the proper operation of inquisitorial procedures. Foucault notes this point:

> although in strict law this is not necessary, this procedure will necessarily tend towards confession. For two reasons: firstly, because it constitutes such strong proof that there is no need to add others, nor to enter the difficult and doubtful combination of clues; confession, provided it is made in the correct form, almost relieves the accuser of the need to provide other proof (at least, the most difficult ones). Secondly, the only way for this procedure to lose all its unequivocal authority, and to become truly a victory achieved over the accused, the only way for the truth to exercise its full power, is for the criminal to take upon himself the crime itself and to sign what was wisely and obscurely constructed by the information. (Foucault 2008: 34)

Legal requirements for conviction often led to torturing defendants for confessions, as it was difficult to convict without sufficient witnesses or evidence, making confessions central to evidentiary activity (Maier 2006: 299). Moura notes that the focus on confession prioritised formalities over genuine legal evaluation of evidence and allowed convictions based mainly on confessions (Moura 1994: 13).

Because legal proof was required, courts did not assess evidence independently and instead focused on obtaining and recording written confessions (Winter 2008: 23). Confession played a central yet complex role: it was both one type of evidence and also surpassed others by having the accused acknowledge and accept the charges. Foucault notes that confession involves the accused participating in producing penal truth by affirming the information's validity (Foucault 2008: 34–35).

Within this procedural framework, the judge's role extends beyond independently determining the facts; instead, the judge engages directly with the accused to obtain acknowledgements that corroborate the findings of the investigation. The process of securing such admissions from the accused was historically characterised by formalised procedures. Confession has played—and continues to play—a central role in the inquisitorial system. During interrogation, the aim was to obtain what was regarded as the most compelling form of evidence: a confession from the accused. Foucault's (2008: 32) analysis highlights the rarely addressed consequences of judges combining prosecutorial and adjudicative functions: interrogation becomes a procedure in which the inquisitor seeks to dominate the accused, who is viewed more as an object than as a participant. The confirmation of the truth is thus extracted from the accused through a combination of coercion and persuasive techniques.

Thus, by torturing until confession was obtained and drawing conclusions deemed truthful from such torment, the procedure was typically marked by an acute experimental curiosity (Cordero 1986: 317). As Gossel points out, confession was assigned an absolute and objectively certain probative value, and had to be obtained, even using torture. The author considers that the equation of confession with truth leads to the mistaken belief that man can always know objective truth (Gossel 2007: 17). The interrogation of the accused could be preceded or followed by torture, which was even used against reluctant or suspect witnesses (Manzini 1951: 65). Torture was divided into three stages (Manzini 1951: 70–71):

(a) During the initial phase, the accused faces threats of torture and may also be subjected to stripping and binding, instilling significant fear.

(b) In the subsequent phase, the torment commences alongside the interrogation process.

(c) In the final phase, the accused endures severe torture, leading to extreme fatigue.

Should there be adequate evidence, this process may be reiterated multiple times, extending over several days.

Modern and contemporary legal systems, unlike their inquisitorial predecessors, do not force individuals to testify and allow them to remain silent (Cordero 2000: 93). However, some still believe that an accused person's silence can be seen as incriminating.

In inquisitorial epistemology, judgements often lacked reasoning, fact descriptions, and explanations for differing outcomes, obscuring the court's rationale (Manzini 1951: 76–77). Though reasoned judgements briefly emerged in the thirteenth century, courts soon resumed hiding their reasoning and case details. Explicit reference to facts in judicial decisions only became mandatory just before the French Revolution (Cordero 2000: 284).

The system did not declare innocence after acquittals, only noting insufficient proof for conviction, following Eymerich's recommendation later used by secular courts. Judgements could be revised repeatedly to continue prosecution, and public punishments served as displays of authority to the community.

In the inquisitorial system under absolutist regimes, judges act on authority delegated by the king. Appeals to the sovereign both reinforce central power and monitor judges, confirming the king as the ultimate punitive authority. This structure legitimises sovereign power and requires its demonstration in judicial proceedings (Prado 2006: 81).

Significant reforms to the inquisitorial system occurred in the late eighteenth and early nineteenth centuries, but its fundamental aspects persisted within a mixed framework and a new political order. Understanding this process explains why radical change was neither achieved nor possible; the inquisitorial method remained, disguised under a hybrid system and renewed by the philosophy of consciousness.

This persistence of inquisitorial elements, even amid reforms, underscores the difficulty of uprooting deeply entrenched legal traditions. Despite new philosophical influences and political changes, the framework remained largely intact and camouflaged within hybrid systems. As a result, the evolution of criminal procedure in Europe reflected a complex interplay between old and new, with incremental adaptation rather than wholesale transformation.

Before examining these topics in the next chapter, a summary is needed of the English common law system, which maintained an accusatorial structure free from inquisitorial influence. Punitive practices evolved differently in Europe: England expanded accusatorial procedures and limited punitive power, whereas the continent adopted widespread inquisitorial proceedings with few restrictions.

Digression: The English Adversarial Legal System

While most European nations adopted the inquisitorial system, England implemented an adversarial framework rooted in the evolution of common law principles. Common law, characterised by reliance on precedent and established customs, also contributed to procedural reforms in France; however, its impact diminished following the establishment of a mixed legal system in 1808 (Garapon and Papapoulos 2008: 23).

England's criminal procedure developed from several influences. After 1066, royal courts gained authority over local ones and earned public trust (Garapon and Papapoulos 2008: 27). According to Coutinho, disputes between the monarchy and feudal lords led to legal reforms that moved away from Germanic and feudal traditions for reasons distinct from those motivating the inquisitorial system (Coutinho 2001: 32–33).

England began consolidating centralised state power earlier than Continental Europe, with monarchs reducing local jurisdictions in the twelfth and thirteenth centuries. Crown-appointed judges oversaw courts and criminal cases, establishing procedures that formed the basis of common law (Prado 2006; Zilli 2003). Under Henry II, common law's structure emerged, including trial by jury influenced by Frankish traditions (Coutinho 2001; Zilli 2003). This led to a divide between English law and continental Romano-canonical systems (Taruffo 2010), as England favoured an accusatorial model with community involvement. In 1215, while European churches banned ordeals, King John accepted the Magna Carta, which limited royal authority and promoted early citizenship through linking taxation and political participation (Coutinho 2001: 36). The Magna Carta established legality, habeas corpus, jurisdictional limits, and presumption of innocence—principles absent from Germanic and early medieval law dominated by custom (Ferrajoli 2002: 308). These changes distinguished common law from civil law, a difference still present today (Taruffo 2010: 35).

Initially, jurors acted as both judges and witnesses due to their knowledge of the facts (Zilli 2003: 99). Later, they focused on assessing evidence and testimony (Taruffo 2010: 36). Since the twelfth century, Grand Juries have indicted serious crimes, while Petty Juries reviewed evidence unless defendants pled guilty (Prado 2006: 89).

In England, the accusatorial system developed separately from inquisitorial reforms, with the Petty Jury serving as the trial body by the fifteenth and sixteenth centuries. Prado (2006) notes that this approach remains fundamentally accusatorial, emphasising impartial judges and public prosecution, unlike the Continental model. Garapon and Papapoulos (2008) emphasise the distinct roles of judges, who oversee procedure, and juries, who decide facts and verdicts; convictions rely only on facts presented by prosecutors. Dias (2004) adds that this structure prioritises defendants' rights over seeking material truth.

England's distinct procedural systems resulted from its sustained political openness, especially after the Glorious Revolution of 1688, which led to liberal reforms and diminished aristocratic influence. Unlike France, England unified its law without codification, allowing the accusatorial adversarial system to develop independently of inquisitorial practices (Garapon and Papapoulos 2008: 125).

Although most continental law scholars see a link between medieval English accusatorial procedures and the current adversarial system, recent work by Richard Vogler challenges this notion. Vogler asserts that the Anglo-American criminal procedure is not accusatorial but adversarial—a system that arose in eighteenth-century England with new legal protections like due process, presumption of innocence, and rights to remain silent and cross-examine witnesses (Vogler 2008: 181). He contends the adversarial model stems mainly from the European Enlightenment and shares little with medieval accusatorial methods (Vogler 2008: 182).

In any case, regardless of Vogler's thesis, the fact remains that England did not undergo the so-called inquisitorial revolution and, as a result, its system was not tainted by the inquisitorial features that still permeate continental and Latin American systems (including those considered accusatorial, it should be said). As Coutinho summarises,

> the English criminal procedure, thus, within the common law tradition, emerges as an authentic party-driven procedure, distinct from that which previously existed. In essence, adversarial proceedings are fully realised; and the *state judge* occupies a passive role, *always distant from the gathering of*

> *evidence*. The proceedings, therefore, arise as a *contest between the parties* who, in a public setting (including town squares), argued before the jury, which, as a representation of society, pronounced the truth, *vere dictum*. A procedure based on such foundations would foster a *procedural culture* more resistant to manipulation, especially because the defendant, before being an accused, is a citizen and, therefore, the holder of inalienable and respected rights. (Coutinho 2001: 36–37)

Figueiredo Dias characterises the pure accusatorial system as the classic English criminal procedure, with the prosecutor and defence operating independently and the judge remaining impartial (Dias 2004: 247). This model distinctly separates prosecution from adjudication. Ferrajoli points out that, while interrupted by the Inquisition in continental Europe, the accusatorial tradition persisted in England (Ferrajoli 2002: 111–112). The enduring legacy of the common law tradition in England is thus manifest in a system that, while adapting over centuries, has consistently resisted inquisitorial influences and maintained a commitment to open contestation between the parties.

Had England not preserved the accusatorial system, the adversarial model likely would not have developed there, nor would France have limited judicial power in its post-1789 procedural reforms. These reforms ultimately failed, leading to the revival of the inquisitorial system within a mixed framework that spread across Continental Europe and Latin America under civil law traditions, as discussed in the next chapter.

CHAPTER 3

The Inquisitorial Nature of Mixed Procedural Systems

The Rise of Modern Criminal Law and the Development of the Mixed Procedural System

The work of Beccaria, Verri, and other classicist thinkers significantly influenced the development of contemporary judicial and administrative structures for prosecuting criminal cases. Their contributions laid the foundation for a criminal justice system designed to address a wide range of cases while implementing procedures that adapt to changing societal norms and requirements for social control (Khaled Jr and Morrison 2024). Although certain inquisitorial elements endured, judicial authority became more limited, thereby offering enhanced safeguards against procedural injustices for defendants. Nevertheless, judicial discretion persisted and continues to serve functions of social control, stemming from the judge's cognitive privilege—a concept associated with the solipsistic tendencies of zero-point epistemology and a steadfast search for truth, both core characteristics of the inquisitorial tradition (Khaled Jr and Gloeckner 2026).

Classicism established mechanisms intended to ensure consistency and reduce discretionary punishment that had been prevalent in secular and ecclesiastical courts since the thirteenth century. Nevertheless, commentators have observed that these theories may fail to address the potential

S. H. Khaled Jr., *Reimagining Criminal Justice, Search for Truth and Human Rights*, https://doi.org/10.1007/978-3-032-27227-0_3

arbitrariness inherent in criminal laws themselves, note that equal treatment can yield unjust outcomes when circumstances vary, and highlight that the selective nature of penal practices stands in contrast to their idealised representation. Furthermore, there is a lack of empirical evidence supporting the fulfilment of official penal functions, and inquisitorial features remain evident within civil law systems (Khaled Jr and Morrison 2024).

One of the most significant features of Beccaria's work is the incorporation of broader social and political ideas that were in vogue among progressive European intellectuals during the eighteenth century and can be found, for example, in Hobbes, Locke, Rousseau, and Montesquieu. His methodology consists in integrating narratives already accepted as images of the human condition and relating them to create the social space proper to a "rational penology" (Khaled Jr and Morrison 2024).

"On Crimes and Punishments" (1764) addresses various aspects of criminal law beyond technical legal considerations, offering an extensive re-evaluation of law and punishment through philosophical, moral, and economic perspectives on society. The book is not radical but recommends substantial reforms such as critiquing aristocratic property rights, advocating for the separation of powers, limiting Church authority, endorsing religious pluralism and tolerance, promoting legal equality, and eliminating both judicial torture and capital punishment. Beccaria's arguments are rooted in utilitarianism, social contract theory, and the principle of inalienable natural rights (Yar 2010: 4–5). Based on contractualism, informed by utilitarian and social contract principles, Beccaria's approach emphasises coexistence and societal harmony—a concept evident in the philosophies of Hobbes, Locke, and Rousseau (Batista 2011: 39). While Hobbes and Montesquieu are directly cited, Beccaria's adoption of the social contract concept aligns more closely with Locke's interpretation, which allows for resistance to government authority.

Beccaria's work is frequently characterised as a response to a period marked by punitive practices that were both arbitrary and severe. Consequently, many regard Beccaria as a proponent of humanitarian reform. This perspective highlights a historical context defined by secret indictments, public executions, torture, inconsistent sentencing, and disparities in punishment based on social class (Khaled Jr and Morrison 2024).

While calling Beccaria a humanitarian oversimplifies his role, equating classicism with contemporary "administrative or legalist criminology" also misrepresents its scope. Recognising the cultural and political effects of classical criminology is important, as it draws attention to criminal justice's boundaries—an issue not previously central (Khaled Jr and Morrison 2024). According to Vera Andrade, classicism carries liberal and humanitarian values, focusing on the justification and limits of punitive power versus individual freedom (Andrade 2003: 47).

Modern criminal law developed with a focus on minimal state intervention (*ultima ratio*) and the protection of individual freedoms from state overreach (Carvalho 2003: 43). This framework aimed to limit punitive power, emphasise individual liberty, and rationalise the penal system to safeguard against authoritarianism. Carvalho summarises these features as follows:

> The project of rationalising criminal justice thus stems from the articulation of the principle of legality (*nullum crimen, nulla poena, sine lege praevia, stricta et scripta*), the establishment of criteria of reasonableness and proportionality in sentencing, and, above all, the envisioning of a procedural apparatus based on an accusatorial structure in which the roles of judge and prosecutor are separated, the defendant is guaranteed full rights of defence, and mechanisms for the control and evaluation of evidence and judicial reasoning are activated to safeguard the accused. (Carvalho 2006: 28)

In 1789, the Declaration of the Rights of Man and of the Citizen established the presumption of innocence and legal jurisdiction.

A prevalent view associates the introduction of this declaration with the evolution of human rights, often assuming it marks a specific phase within theories that promote successive generations of rights. However, as outlined in the opening chapter, my perspective asserts that human rights are inherent to all individuals and do not depend on state recognition. Furthermore, the declaration's provisions were officially recognised but selectively implemented within society. Historically, citizenship was restricted solely to adult white male property owners, who alone benefitted from these rights.

Nevertheless, it is evident that notable progress was made in the field of criminal justice, even if these advancements were not fully established across all contexts—selectivity continued to characterise the operations of the modern criminal justice system.

While Beccaria's system included humanitarian elements, it primarily rationalised criminal justice as a mechanism of social control, not just as a humanitarian model. As Andrade notes, Eurocentric modernity balanced conflicting goals of regulation and emancipation (Andrade 2012: 43). The heirs of modern criminal law from classicism may look back to Beccaria—and to questions relating to "rights"—and thus blind themselves to what he actually proposed: an instrument designed for control, legitimised by mediating the explicit power of the sovereign and the latent power of the subject; above all, a criminal justice system aimed at social control (Khaled Jr and Morrison 2024).

A thorough analysis of Beccaria, even when approached at a superficial level, clearly demonstrates that criminal law serves as an instrument of social control. Provisions related to individual rights contribute to maintaining the legitimacy and authority of the criminal justice system. Although constraints on punitive power are not established solely for social control, they are also informed by the moral and political values prevalent in modern society. The implementation of boundaries within criminal justice is consistent with its regulatory function and forms an integral component of it. These boundaries ensure that the discourse surrounding justice remains within the formal parameters of the criminal justice framework. As Vera Malaguti Batista points out, classicism's critical attitude aimed to re-legitimise punitive power (Batista 2011: 40).

In summary, at least two points should be made regarding the consequences of the widespread implementation of the model outlined by classicism.

Firstly, crime prevails over "non-crime". As modernity spreads, all aspects of social interaction involving "harm" come to be interrogated as follows: "can this be framed within the rational scheme of criminal law?" (primary criminalisation). This form of questioning has led to the scope of punishable conduct expanding indefinitely, so that its limits have become unknown in the contemporary Western world (Khaled Jr and Morrison 2024).

Secondly, crime becomes the technique par excellence of "formal social control", surpassing and hindering other forms of conflict resolution. The result is a concentration of functional power in the hands of criminal justice professionals and their agencies in general, particularly the police, who are responsible for the initial selection (secondary criminalisation). This power is legitimised by specific conceptions of performance, which raises endless questions about the limits in the exercise of these powers and the modes of entry/selection into such careers, which vary according to spatial/historical context. Modern criminal justice organisations are, therefore, not only a technique for ensuring formal social control, but also products of the type of social control sought in modernity (Khaled Jr and Morrison 2024).

According to Carvalho (2003), as states and laws became secular, crime was redefined as a deliberate breach of state law, not a religious or moral failing. Foucault (2003) notes that offences became seen as violations of civil law set by legislative authorities.

With the advent of modernity and the emergence of legality and codification, it was also believed that the inquisitorial system would finally be superseded by an accusatorial model. Carvalho notes that "the overcoming of theological belief and the attempt to impose reason in order to bring rationality to the actions of procedural actors indicate an undeniable trend towards secularisation in the sphere of criminal procedural law" (Carvalho 2008: 71).

Within the rational-legal model, truth became regulated by formal procedures to counter authoritarianism. As Misse (2007) observes, crime is defined both by law and its official legal interpretation within procedural safeguards. Enlightenment-era reforms in the eighteenth century restricted secret denunciations, coerced confessions, and torture (Alonso 1986), aiming to limit power more than ever before.

Nevertheless, the intended character of the system was compromised during practical implementation; inquisitorial elements were rapidly adopted, even though torture had been definitively abolished, as will be discussed below.

After the French Revolution, there was initially a reaction against the inquisitorial system and an attempt to introduce an accusatorial system inspired by English law. Marat's *Plan for Criminal Legislation*, published in 1790—at the height of the revolutionary period—was clearly inspired by the English accusatorial system:

> It is not for judges to establish evidence of the offence, but rather to impartially examine that which is presented and to determine whether it is sufficient to declare the accused guilty. It is not, therefore, based on private knowledge that they should do so, much less on suppositions that they should decide against the accused. Everything they do not learn from the accuser, they must ignore, and anything not legally established must remain null in their eyes. They must never seek to entrap an accused, confuse him with tricky questions, force him into contradiction, or obtain from him, by false promises, a confession of his crime—precautions alien

> to their functions and unworthy of their character. Created to prevent the scales of justice from wavering, they must aim for the triumph of truth and seek to maintain its balance only by honest means. (Marat 2008: 172)

Marat's text does not fully abandon the concept of truth, but it removes the judge's authority to seek it, breaking from inquisitorial tradition. He notes that procedures should be regulated, requiring judges to act methodically and preventing impulsive decisions. Marat also insists justice be public, warning that secrecy allows unjust methods for gathering evidence. His aim is to limit the discretion typical of inquisitorial systems (Marat 2008: 180). For him,

> It is essential that the conduct of proceedings be subject to fixed, precise, and regular forms, so that the gravest matter in the world is not handled arbitrarily. Therefore, this part of criminal legislation requires great attention. Not only is it indispensable to regulate all its acts and the form of each act, but also to ensure compliance with these rules, rendering null anything contrary to them. (Marat 2008: 181)

Marat's plan, anonymously drafted in 1778 and later attributed to him in 1790, influenced French law by encouraging reforms. As Prado notes, the shift from monarchy to republic led to the end of torture and the adoption of criminal procedures modelled after Republican Rome and England (Prado 2006: 58).

In 1790, the monarchy's courts were formally abolished, which paved the way for significant reforms in 1791 that repealed the Criminal Ordinance of 1670 and implemented a more complex accusatorial system (Cordero 2000: 35). The Constitutional Assembly subsequently enacted the Revolution's inaugural criminal procedural law, thereby establishing a new legal framework for criminal proceedings. The September 1791 legislation demonstrates an ongoing tension between the inquisitorial principles of the 1670 Ordinance and the English law-inspired measures advanced by the new regime; although there was an intent to replace them, some inquisitorial elements persisted. Reforms were notably influenced by English law, particularly through the adoption of grand and petit juries, which introduced lay participation into judicial processes, as well as public and oral hearings and comprehensive access to defence (adversarial principle) (Maier 2006: 342). The formal method of legal proof was entirely abrogated (Moura 1994: 21). Legislation enacted in 1790 mandated that judgements explicitly state the factual findings agreed upon by the parties or established by evidence and required the citation of legal premises when no statutory provision was applicable (Gomes Filho 2001: 63). By 1794, the notion of a "reasoned judgment" had been established (Cordero 2000: 288).

Despite early influence from English accusatorial procedures, public criminal prosecution—a legacy of the Inquisition—remained dominant and reinforced inquisitorial practices (Maier 2006: 345–351). Ferrajoli observes that the accusatorial approach soon faded in Europe post-revolution (Ferrajoli 2002: 454), and Carvalho notes that nineteenth-century reforms, though secularising, did not remove inquisitorial logic from penal culture (Carvalho 2008: 71).

The overhaul of the old system ultimately failed. In 1795, the Thermidorian Reaction brought the *Code des délits et de peines*, which established a public prosecution monopoly and introduced a jury president—an early form of investigating judge. Investigations became written and confidential under the prosecution jury director's authority. Only witness statements and defendant questioning were done orally, strictly during formal debate, and written investigation details could be read aloud if testimony differed from the record (Maier 2006: 347; Cordero 2000: 35).

The inquisitorial shift arose from concerns that revolutionary criminal law overly emphasised citizen safety at the expense of effective public prosecution. In response, the Public Prosecutor's Office was established in 1801, implementing secret preliminary investigations led by judges and new pre-trial measures. While juries remained, their role faced criticism, especially in courts of exception that resembled the 1670 Ordinance system, though some safeguards persisted (Maier 2006).

> before the '*terror*' there was room for an attempt to recognise *procedural democracy*, unimaginable under Napoleon, a dictator like any other who, among other things, directly influenced the move back towards the structure of the *ancien régime* (the inquisitorial spirit attracts people of such stature, in any place and time), but he only managed to abolish the *prosecution jury*, which apparently would not have a major effect (*although it actually did*). (Coutinho 2008: 38)

The 1808 *Code d'instruction criminelle* shaped later European criminal procedure by reviving elements of the 1670 French Criminal Ordinance, such as investigations led by a judge. This system divided investigation and trial phases but made defence rights largely ineffective during investigations due to secrecy, written procedures, and prosecution dominance, echoing earlier inquisitorial practices (Maier 2002; Winter 2008; Ferrajoli 2002).

The decision to proceed with prosecutions was entrusted to an investigating judge rather than council chambers (Maier 2006: 355–356). In this initial inquisitorial phase, judges compile case files that guide proceedings (Cordero 2000: 36). Documents from this stage may be used as trial evidence but are not intended to be decisive (Maier 2006: 357–358).

The outcome was predictable: evidence secretly gathered by the investigating judge during the inquisitorial phase compromised the accusatorial phase. Instead of merely diminishing their influence, such evidence should be excluded entirely. Judges' access to preliminary investigation materials risks bias and premature conclusions (Winter 2008: 40).

The secretive investigative process, led by a judge and concealed from the accused and their defence (Maier 2006: 353), was separate from the public trial phase. However, this separation was mostly superficial because investigation records often determined trial outcomes, especially when testimonies differed or witnesses were absent (Cordero 2000: 58). According to Ferrajoli, the trial's debates became largely repetitive of the investigation (Ferrajoli 2002: 454).

In the second stage—oral and public debate—the accused and prosecution were treated equally through public hearings and legal representation (Maier 2006: 353–354). Despite this, judges could still seek evidence and question witnesses, reflecting inquisitorial traditions seen in Napoleonic-influenced systems like Spain's 1882 law. This contrasts with Marat's more passive legislative model.

As Cordero points out, this two-stage model became the archetype for continental European systems in the following centuries (Cordero 2000: 36). The Napoleonic Codes and the mixed continental procedure reintroduced bureaucratic and inquisitorial forms of jurisdiction (Ferrajoli 2002: 461). Furthermore, there was also a return to the Inquisition model regarding the accused's liberty during proceedings, which was not guaranteed (Maier 2006: 354).

Maier contends that the code resulted from a compromise between the 1670 Ordinance and the 1791 procedural law, blending inquisitorial principles with republican ideals of freedom and dignity (Maier 2006: 351–352). He argues that although this reconciliation seems favourable, it is ultimately unachievable, as key inquisitorial methods—like disrupting party control over evidence—remained. Cordero adds that the 1670 French Criminal Ordinance established rigid formalism in justifications, which endured even after the old regime through systems influenced by inquisitorial practices (Cordero 2000: 59). Despite appearing accusatorial, the system essentially restored inquisitorial principles, incorporating only superficial accusatorial features (Maier 2006; Zilli 2003).

The creation of the mixed system aimed to balance inquisitorial investigations with the introduction of debates, but its reliance on the "intimate conviction" standard allowed judges to rule based on personal belief without justification or transparency (Badaró 2008). This lack of reasoning led to judicial arbitrariness and preserved the influence of evidence gathered inquisitorially (Filho 2001; Mora 2006). Critics argue that intimate conviction undermines truth-seeking in legal proceedings and is fundamentally incompatible with epistemic standards (Taruffo 2010).

Secrecy primarily restricts information to experts, and instructional secrecy remains key (Cordero 2000: 298). Pre-trial investigations determine facts, with judges confirming them and sometimes seeking further validation. Ferrajoli argues that judges should not assume investigatory roles, though mixed systems grant them control over evidence and investigations alongside prosecutors (Ferrajoli 2002: 488). As Carvalho notes,

> Modern procedural technology, in adapting the mechanisms of the medieval inquisitorial procedure, renames the system as *mixed*, proposing the adaptation of the procedure into two stages (first inquisitorial, second accusatorial). However, this *two-headed monster* (Cordero), universalised by the Napoleonic Code, not only maintains the inquisitorial logic but also reconditions the work of the procedural actors, especially the judge, in the relentless pursuit of truth in criminal proceedings. (Carvalho 2008: 177)

Without checks on power, knowledge became authoritarian and inquisitorial investigations shaped historical truth by presuming guilt. This undermined safeguards, making later phases mere formalities to confirm earlier findings. Disputed evidence could trigger more inquiries, further blurring prosecution and judgement roles. Ferrajoli argues the Napoleonic Code of 1808 worsened this by mixing inquisitorial and accusatorial systems (Ferrajoli 2002: 566).

Criminal procedure became arbitrary, prioritising truth-finding over human rights protections typical of accusatorial systems. Ritualistic processes served to suppress state opponents, with the inquisitorial model enabling the inquisitor to control proceedings and employ any method to establish facts about the accused (Cordero 2000: 186).

In this system, truth served mainly as a tool of power, established by authorities and seldom questioned—similar to the Inquisition. Contemporary civil law criminal procedures still reflect these inquisitorial and authoritarian traits. Unlike European models, preliminary investigations in Brazil are carried out by the police, a system that presents several significant challenges. As Lopes Jr. observes,

> the fraud lies in the fact that evidence is gathered during the inquisitorial inquiry and then fully incorporated into the proceedings, so that, in the end, a persuasive speech by the judge suffices to legitimise the decision. This discourse is masked by various formulas, such as: the evidence from the inquiry is corroborated by the evidence produced in court; comparing police evidence with judicial evidence; and thus a whole exercise in immunisation (or rather, a labelling fraud) is performed to justify a conviction that is, in reality, based on elements collected in the secrecy of the inquisition. The trial ends up becoming a mere staging or repetition of the first phase. (Lopes Jr 2010: 68)

Rosa adds that "pseudo-evidence" from the police inquiry should only be used to assess procedural admissibility, as it has not undergone adversarial testing (Rosa 2006: 319). Despite this, authoritarian elements of the mixed system persist, enabling preliminary material to affect judicial decisions.

The continued need to address this issue highlights the considerable distance yet to be covered before a fully accusatorial system is realised in judicial practice.

Kant de Lima observed "the ambiguity of our procedural system, which calls itself mixed, while police practices 'are handed over', 'negotiated', constituting a genuine inquisitorial tradition" (Lima 1989: 75). According to Misse, the police phase of the incrimination process gains autonomy and greater significance in proportion to the degree of exclusion and social segregation of the accused. Depending on how the relationship between criminal subjection and social distance is established, the social reach of criminal subjection may extend to the streets, *favelas*, neighbourhoods, or entire parts of the city, as well as to distinctive social characteristics such as class, gender, age, and race. Not to mention the collection of Lombrosian images accumulated by the police over the years and the opening of avenues to reduce social distance and enable "negotiation" (Misse 2007: 23–24).

Both Kant de Lima and Misse highlight that there is little room for "negotiation" within criminal proceedings; instead, negotiation shifts to the police, where it takes very different forms depending on the social standing of the individual under investigation. Often, this negotiation turns violent, particularly for those who are socially vulnerable. Kant de Lima examined these challenges by comparing negotiation issues between common law and civil law systems. Likewise, Misse observes that Anglo-Saxon legal traditions have built-in mechanisms allowing criminal prosecutors to negotiate charges—a practice absent from the Brazilian system, where prosecution can't legally be lessened through negotiation—an option available only for minor offences. This gap leads to an illegal, hidden market for negotiations involving the police. As a result, there's a "moral" microsocial aspect to negotiation, legalism, and broader social norms (Misse 2017: 18–19). According to Lima, "Police justify their unauthorized actions by claiming they have firsthand knowledge—they were present. They also assert that, at times, it is necessary to 'take justice into their own hands'" (Lima 1989: 76). The general approach police often take—exceptions acknowledged—towards suspects suggests the weak nature of evidence obtained early in investigations, indicating such evidence should typically be excluded at trial unless repetition is impossible.

These findings support progressive legal views that only procedural truth—established within a dialectical, adversarial trial structure—should be admissible (Lopes Jr 2005: 257). However, many judges still rely on evidence from police inquiries, overlooking the original role of the trial phase and allowing investigative elements to influence decisions. This blurs the distinction between accusatorial and inquisitorial systems—perpetuating power imbalances, especially against vulnerable groups. Such practices are incompatible with democratic ideals.

In recent years, an initiative was established to strengthen the protection of rights during preliminary investigations by introducing the safeguards judge. This judge was intended to oversee the legality of the investigative process and conclude their involvement upon receipt of the complaint from the Public Prosecutor's Office. The purpose was to maintain impartiality in subsequent procedural phases and prevent potential bias arising from prior assessments of the accusation's merit. However, the implementation of the safeguards judge took considerable time, and, ultimately, the responsibility for receiving complaints was eliminated from the role.

Most concerning, the myriad problems regarding the investigative phase are not the most significant challenge facing contemporary proceedings. While these issues are pronounced, the inquisitorial characteristics underlying procedural truth-finding processes are even more profound. As Lopes Jr. observes, the inquisitorial nature of criminal investigations and penal enforcement has long been acknowledged, thereby obscuring the issue of inquisition during the trial phase (Lopes Jr 2010: 75). According to Prado,

> here, too, the same type of psychological bias will be observed as that which underlies concerns about the judge's own power to initiate proceedings, insofar as the judge will generally base their reasoning on the evidentiary elements that they themselves have incorporated into the case, considering them important for resolving the matter. This will ultimately distance the judge from the desirable position of secure detachment from the parties and their opposing interests, a position that would allow for the best weighing and conclusion. (Prado 2006: 137)

The links between the search for truth, inquisitorialism and the mixed system of criminal procedure are deep and persistent. A significant feature of the inquisitorial tradition in contemporary legal systems is the judge's involvement in the collection of evidence. This approach blurs the distinction between prosecution and adjudication and challenges the party-driven evidence management central to accusatorial systems. The rationale for this shift often centres on the pursuit of truth—a consistently emphasised principle, even as its expressions vary. Although this prerogative has an authoritarian theoretical foundation and leads to arbitrary judicial outcomes, it remains strongly supported and is considered compatible with hybrid procedural frameworks, including the Brazilian procedural system.

The relationship among the pursuit of truth, inquisitorialism, and the mixed model of criminal procedure is both longstanding and significant, yet scholarly debate on this subject remains active. Some experts contend that the mixed system does not qualify as an independent third model, whereas others assert that its second phase is purely accusatorial and that the commitment to truth-seeking does not undermine this nature.

A detailed review of Brazil's procedural system provides insight into debates about mixed systems and whether they have unique principles compared to accusatorial or inquisitorial models, as outlined in the next section.

The Fundamentally Inquisitorial Nature of the Brazilian Procedural System

Debate over whether procedural systems are accusatorial, inquisitorial, or mixed is highly contested in socio-legal studies, mainly due to differing views on defining characteristics. This overview sets out the key points of the debate and presents a position, focusing on its relevance to truth production in criminal proceedings.

One of the foremost critics of the so-called mixed system is Jacinto Nelson de Miranda Coutinho, whose views align with those expressed in this study. Coutinho clarifies the legal-procedural meaning of "system" describing it as "a set of legal concepts which, when unified by an overarching principle, become an organic whole with a defined goal" (Coutinho 2001: 16). He argues that the dispositive principle forms the foundation of the accusatorial system, while the inquisitorial principle serves as the basis for the inquisitorial system:

> except for the less informed, everyone maintains that today we do not have *pure systems*, in the classical form in which they were structured. If that is the case, then *mixed systems* always prevail, of which, not infrequently, there is a mistaken (or distorted) view, precisely because, in their *entirety*, they end up being received as a third system, which is not true. The so-called *mixed system*, *reformed* or *Napoleonic* is the combination of the other two, *but it does not have its own unifying principle*, so it is either *essentially inquisitorial* (as ours is), with some (secondary characteristics) derived from the accusatorial system, or it is *essentially accusatorial*, with some characteristic elements (again secondary) borrowed from the inquisitorial system. For this reason, *we can only formally consider it as a third system*, always keeping in mind the notion of its *unifying principle*, since this is perhaps the starting point of the alienation observed in legal practitioners, especially proceduralists, relieving them of the responsibility for

> conduct required by the system or, worse, failing to immunise them against the vices it generates. (Coutinho 2001: 16)

Coutinho contends that Brazil's criminal procedural system is fundamentally inquisitorial because judges primarily control evidence, making this the defining feature rather than the formal separation of prosecutorial and judicial roles (Coutinho 2001: 29; 2002: 185). Lopes Jr. agrees, noting that simply separating these functions at the outset does not characterise the accusatorial system if judges can still actively seek evidence and perform prosecutorial acts (Lopes Jr 2010: 67, 70).

The French Criminal Ordinance of 1670 established a distinct separation between prosecutorial and judicial responsibilities, while preserving an inquisitorial framework in which judges oversee evidence and actively pursue factual accuracy. Eymerich's Manual recognised third-party accusations as exceptions to the conventional dual role typically held by judges. The Napoleonic legal system formally differentiates between prosecutorial and judicial functions yet adheres to inquisitorial methods; judges are responsible for managing evidence and determining the truth, notwithstanding prevailing misconceptions regarding its classification as a third system.

The debate centres on the risk of reviving inquisitorial practices if judges are empowered to produce evidence. Coutinho (2001) argues this allows judges to support their own hypotheses, replacing truth with belief—regardless of the obsession with the search for truth. Lopes Jr. (2005) cautions that such investigative powers compromise judicial impartiality, as judges may unknowingly favour their own theories, predetermining outcomes. Prado (2006) concurs, stating that when judges generate evidence, they confirm their own assumptions. He underscores that the accusatorial and inquisitorial systems assign fundamentally opposing roles to judicial authorities.

Rui Cunha Martins examined the discourse regarding the unifying principle of the system, noting that the inquisitorial framework's focus on factual truth resulted in assigning evidence management to a magistrate less receptive to nuanced tensions (Martins 2010: 93). As stated by Cunha Martins,

> strictly speaking, the procedural system inspired by democratic-constitutional principles can only conceive of one and only one "unifying principle": democratic legitimacy; just as it can only conceive of one and

> only one systemic model: the *democratic model*. To say "democratic" is to say the opposite of "inquisitorial", the opposite of "mixed", and it is to say more than "accusatorial". The system cannot legally be inquisitorial; nor can it be mixed (for if it is mixed, there will be at least one part that violates legality); it can be accusatorial, as this is a model encompassed within the arc of legitimacy. But it can only be so on one condition: that this accusatorial model proves capable of embodying such adequacy. More than accusatorial, the model must be democratic. The choice of an accusatorial model is merely the means chosen to ensure something more fundamental than itself: its banner is that of democracy, and it is the instrumental means of guaranteeing it. There is little virtue in preserving a model, even if labelled accusatorial and thus presumed to be legal, if it contains elements capable of undermining the general bond of the system (the so-called "unifying principle": democratic legitimacy), even if these elements may not be sufficient, in technical terms, to deny the accusatorial character of the model. It is not the accusatorial model as such that the democratic procedural system must preserve, but the democratic legitimacy that governs it. (Martins 2010: 93–94)

Although democratic legitimacy may not serve as the most appropriate primary standard for criminal procedural systems, there are substantial arguments for supporting a significant relationship between the accusatorial model and democratic principles. Nonetheless, the management of evidence offers a more robust and historically substantiated criterion, given its reliance on established practices and studies—unlike "democratic legitimacy" which often leads to protracted debates due to ongoing ambiguities in defining democracy today. Consequently, it appears prudent to regard "democratic legitimacy" as a valuable supplementary rather than principal criterion.

In this context, Cunha Martins asserts that any mechanism, element, or practice within the procedural system should be evaluated by asking: *Is this mechanism, element, or practice, regardless of its type, compatible with the democratic-constitutional framework underlying the system in which it operates?* According to Martins, this inquiry holds primary importance and ought to be posed consistently (Martins 2010: 94).

Cunha Martins considers that democratic legitimacy—as produced by the political-constitutional framework—should be conceived as a governing model that must serve as a *limit* to authoritarian procedural tendencies, imposing a procedural system that can itself be regarded as a limiting apparatus on punitive power (Martins 2010: 95). According to Lopes Jr.,

> Initially, our Constitution does not—expressly—guarantee a criminal procedure guided by the accusatorial system. However, we have no doubt as to its enshrinement, which arises from a systematic interpretation of the Constitution. To this end, it suffices to consider that the democratic constitutional project requires the valorisation of the individual and the value of human dignity, which are basic premises of the accusatorial system. It should be recalled that the transition from the inquisitorial to the accusatorial system is, above all, a transition from an authoritarian political system to the democratic model. Thus, democracy and the accusatorial system share the same epistemological foundation. (Lopes Jr 2010: 182)

The Brazilian Constitution establishes an accusatorial model with provisions such as the Public Prosecutor's exclusive authority to initiate criminal proceedings (art. 129, I), adversarial process and defence rights (art. 5, LV), due process (art. 5, LIV), presumption of innocence (art. 5, LVII), and transparency in judicial decisions (art. 93, IX). Carvalho suggests that constitutional protections in criminal law help check excessive state power and safeguard fundamental rights (Carvalho 2008:101). Prado notes that the Constitution and Criminal Procedure share key concerns—protecting fundamental rights and supporting separation of powers—and highlights their connection to democracy (Prado 2006:41). A democratic state's criminal policy will lack coherence if it ignores legal standards and fails to recognise human dignity as the core principle of democracy (Prado 2006: 28).

Democracy relies on a criminal justice system that values human dignity. Unlike inquisitorial methods focused on social control, democratic frameworks demand respect for everyone's rights and differences. Prado argues that law and democracy are linked through genuine participatory and inclusive models, which have significant impact on criminal procedure and help build a culture of democratic social coexistence (Prado 2006: 40).

Recent political and constitutional changes have prompted a rethinking of criminal jurisdiction, emphasising the importance of protecting human rights and limiting punitive authority. Lopes Jr. (2010) argues that accusatorial procedures require reconsidering how judicial knowledge is constructed, which helps set limits on power. He also suggests moving away from inquisitorial traditions centred on convictions, noting judges may feel their role is incomplete without guilty verdicts.

Given these circumstances, it is important to clarify that criminal jurisdiction is often seen as a form of power, typically through inquisitorial lens. Tucci describes it as the authority to administer state justice (Tucci 2002: 46), while Lopes Jr. considers it a function that reviews prosecutorial claims to determine if state punishment should be applied (Lopes Jr 2008: 401). Lopes Jr. suggests moving beyond viewing jurisdiction solely as power, emphasising oversight to prevent authoritarianism. The key challenge is making criminal jurisdiction a fundamental right, ensuring fair trials before impartial judges within reasonable timeframes, thereby strengthening protections against abuse and advancing human rights. Both Lopes Jr. and Coutinho argue that jurisdiction should be understood not only as state power but also as a constitutional safeguard for citizens (Coutinho 2000; Lopes Jr 2008).

Traditionally, safeguarding citizens from arbitrary actions has been a complex task, as jurisdiction was predominantly regarded as the authority to impose penalties. This restrictive perspective confines criminal jurisdiction solely to the aspect of punishment. Consequently, it is essential to establish a framework of minimum safeguards that effectively restricts punitive powers.

Ferrajoli highlights that criminal jurisdiction reflects a knowledge-power interplay, where effective trials depend on balanced cognition and authority (Ferrajoli 2002: 39). When power dominates, it undermines procedural safeguards and jeopardises protection for weaker parties. An accusatorial system, supported by constitutional norms, enables jurisdiction to check state overreach. Thus, seeing jurisdiction as solely an unchallengeable expression of state interests is outdated. As Lopes Jr. argues, a contemporary understanding of jurisdiction should align with democratic principles and the rule of law (Lopes Jr 2008: 402).

Lopes Jr. contends that jurisdiction should act as a safeguard against excessive punitive power in a democratic legal system, requiring clear procedures and solid proof before punishment. The system relies on formal decision rules and strong evidence standards to prevent abuse. Essential safeguards include proper evidence collection, the right to defence, and adherence to due process (Lopes Jr 2005: 73). The idea of a democratic criminal procedure leads to the view that its structure should follow a dialectical model: the judge adjudicates but does not initiate prosecution, manages evidence or searches for the truth, reflecting the core principles of the accusatorial system (Prado 2006: 33).

It is important to note that, although this model offers significant advantages, it has not been fully adopted in practice, largely due to prevailing power dynamics that outweigh considerations of potential harm to human rights.

Although Brazil has made constitutional progress, its criminal procedure remains influenced by Francisco Campos's 1941 perspective. Campos argued that the Code avoids traditional legal leniency towards criminals, reduces excessive formalism, and eliminates criteria driven by individualism or sentimentalism, prioritising efficient criminal justice (Campos 2010). As Prado notes, the democratic structuring of criminal procedure is not simply imposed from above, even if rooted in the Constitution; it must contend with strong cultural opposition from those who favour an inquisitorial model aimed at pursuing absolute truth (Prado 2006: 37).

The key issue is identifying the essential elements of a procedural framework that treats jurisdiction as a fundamental right in a reformed criminal justice system. This matters for both academic reasons and because it influences human rights protections and cognitive functions within the system. To understand what defines an accusatorial system based on party-driven evidence and democratic values, its core features must be examined.

According to Goldschmidt, the accusatorial system requires judges to base their decisions on evidence presented by the parties involved, resulting in adversarial proceedings that uphold impartiality and protect the rights of the accused. Conversely, when judges are permitted to conduct independent fact-finding, the procedure is characterised as inquisitorial (Goldschmidt 2010: 780). Giacomolli (2006: 129) highlights the accusatorial principle as a key safeguard in criminal procedures, where prosecutor and defendant act as adversaries before an impartial judge. In such systems, parties are responsible for presenting evidence, and judges serve strictly as impartial arbitrators, without proposing evidence (Giacomolli 2006: 227).

Bachmaier-Winter argues that assigning one person to investigate, collect evidence, and deliver a verdict violates impartiality (Winter 2008: 22). Prado notes that in inquisitorial systems, judges act as prosecutors, while accusatorial models maintain independent prosecutors to uphold judicial impartiality (Prado 2006: 106). Prado further warns that an adjudicator seeking conviction risks bias (Prado 2006: 137). Ferrajoli adds that the accusatorial system requires judges to remain impartial observers, contrasting with the inquisitorial model, where judges play an active prosecutorial role (Ferrajoli 2002: 461). Lopes Jr. emphasises that.

> It is elementary that granting investigative powers to the judge fatally violates the guarantee of impartiality upon which criminal procedure and the accusatorial system are based, and furthermore, there is no possibility of a "proper use" of such powers, as they will only ever be invoked by inquisitors, whose benevolence must always be doubted. (Lopes Jr 2010: 508)

For this reason, Lopes Jr. maintains that "to conceive of the accusatorial system disconnected from the principles of impartiality and adversarial proceedings is to fall into grave reductionism" (Lopes Jr 2010: 70). Impartiality is not a personal quality of the judge, but a quality of the accusatorial system itself (Lopes Jr 2010: 183). Impartiality is ensured by the accusatorial model but compromised in the inquisitorial system; it exists only when prosecution and adjudication are separate and judges are uninvolved in investigations and management of evidence (Lopes Jr 2010: 70).

The points above align with Cunha Martins' standard for democratic legitimacy and endorse a criminal jurisdiction model that avoids power prioritisation. Undermining parties' control over evidence violates judicial impartiality and results in inquisitorial, antidemocratic conduct by the magistrate.

This approach stands in contrast to the democratic principles of due process and regulated punitive authority, which are foundational to the rule of law and the protection of human rights. Despite this divergence, there is ongoing debate regarding the matter; within Brazil and the broader civil law tradition, numerous scholars advocate for the compatibility of the accusatorial system with truth-seeking and evidence management by the judge. The following section will critically evaluate opposing perspectives to determine their merit and whether such compatibility exists or may contribute to human rights violations.

Judicial Authority and the Gathering of Evidence: Reassessing the Inquisitorial Nature of Criminal Justice Procedure

To present a comprehensive range of perspectives on this subject, I will first address the views of Badaró, whose position contrasts with those held by Aury Lopes Jr., Alexandre Morais da Rosa, Jacinto Nelson de Miranda Coutinho, and Geraldo Prado. For him, there is no incompatibility between the accusatorial criminal procedure and an active judge, endowed with powers to take evidence, which allow him to order the production of evidence necessary for the discovery of the truth. Badaró argues that the essence of the accusatorial procedure lies in the separation of the functions of prosecution, adjudication, and defence. The absence of powers to take evidence on the part of the judge is merely a historical characteristic of the accusatorial system, but not an essential feature (Badaró 2003: 154).

Badaró, Zilli, and Grinover maintain that a judge collecting evidence does not undermine impartiality (Zilli 2003: 144; Grinover 1999). Drawing on Cunha Martins, I question whether such judicial conduct fits with democratic legitimacy or checks on punitive power required for the defence of human rights. My initial view is negative, but further evaluation of contrary opinions is needed before reaching a final judgement.

Gomes Filho argues that while judges may introduce elements into proceedings on their own, these must be subject to adversarial scrutiny and party arguments (Filho 2001: 101). Taruffo similarly asserts that a judge's evidentiary powers are essential for impartiality but clarifies that judges should not dominate the fact-finding process. Instead, judges should ensure parties provide all necessary information for truth-seeking, intervening only as needed. While Taruffo notes that judges are responsible for safeguarding the truth—since parties may lack such interest—he maintains that evidentiary powers must be balanced by allowing parties to challenge and counter evidence introduced by judges. He advocates for the effective functioning of the adversarial principle rather than limiting judicial evidentiary powers (Taruffo 2010: 1999).

Taruffo's argument might seem convincing at first, but he confuses the proper roles of judge and party. Expecting parties to debate with the deciding judge, especially over evidence introduced by that judge, is illogical. Taruffo downplays concerns about judicial investigation, arguing truth-seeking ensures impartiality; I disagree, as history shows this can harm defendants' rights and democratic legitimacy. Judicial activism of this kind risks harmful outcomes. As Lopes Jr. notes, presenting evidence is the prosecution's job, not the judge's (Lopes Jr 2010: 183).

The issue remains debated, with many prominent scholars revising their views. Cordero sees judges' evidentiary authority as a necessary residual aspect, noting that judicial systems differ mainly by the extent of adversarial debate and consideration of each party's input (Cordero 2000: 49, 201). Similarly, Armenta Deu accepts that judges may introduce evidence in limited cases, treating such actions as supplementary to the evidentiary process (Deu 1995: 27–28).

Many scholars argue this practice should be residual and limited, yet it is challenging to find instances where it does not infringe on the accused's rights and conflict with democratic standards. Disregarding the *in dubio pro reo* principle, further evidence gathering during uncertainty can prioritise convictions over impartiality. In a democratic accusatorial system, doubt should lead to acquittal, aligning with the very meaning of *in dubio pro reo*.

If the principle of *in dubio pro reo* is not employed as a constraint on punitive authority, any prospects for criminal justice effectively addressing criminal selectivity are significantly diminished. In fact, the opposite effect occurs: the pursuit of truth may reinforce police selectivity by not only accepting evidence obtained during the preliminary investigation but also seeking additional evidence intended to substantiate the initial findings.

Montero Aroca argues that only the accusatorial procedure truly exists, yet he defends the judge's power to order evidence independently—a trait typical of inquisitorial systems—as part of it. He contends that judicial evidence gathering supports the aims of criminal trials without violating their principles (Aroca 2006: 540, 557). However, this stance is debatable, since in rights-based criminal justice, the prosecution carries the burden of proof; judges should ensure due process, not build cases. Thus, I maintain that judicial initiative in evidence collection is inherently inquisitorial and challenges democratic legitimacy, even if some see it as fitting within an accusatorial model.

Gomes Orbaneja and Herce Quemada describe an "accusatorial" system where judges independently investigate, regardless of party actions (Orbaneja and Quemada 1997: 111–112). Kai Ambos considers systems mixed if judges can investigate autonomously and are not restricted by charges (Ambos 2008: 69). In Germany, the Public Prosecutor acts in the accusatorial role while judges' investigative authority reflects the inquisitorial aspect, making the criminal procedure both accusatorial and inquisitorial (Ambos 2008: 70).

Figueiredo Dias explains the principle of accusation: courts can only examine cases within substantiated charges made by another authority (Dias 2004: 136–137). He notes that following this principle does not guarantee a fully accusatorial process, as it may also exist in systems with inquisitorial aspects (Dias 2004: 137). Dias also refers the principle of investigation, where courts independently clarify facts beyond what parties present—known as the principle of material truth (Dias 2004: 148). He distinguishes between purely accusatorial procedures and those combining accusatorial structure with investigative powers, emphasising that the latter is not strictly inquisitorial (Dias 2004: 149).

While I do not intend to simply dismiss the views of respected author Figueiredo Dias, I ultimately agree with Coutinho and Cunha Martins. Their arguments lead me to believe that, regardless of claims about its compatibility with an accusatorial system, the principle of material truth embraces an inquisitorial approach. More importantly, it conflicts with democratic legitimacy and the constitutional requirement for due process.

Roxin, like Figueiredo Dias, contends that the principle of investigation (or material truth) is central to criminal proceedings (Roxin 2003: 99). He observes that German criminal procedure merges inquisitorial and accusatorial features, characterising it as an accusatorial procedure with investigative elements (Roxin 2003: 122–123).

However, the investigation principle often conflicts with both the accusatorial model and the democratic legitimacy necessary in a rule-of-law state. The acceptability of a procedural system depends on limiting judicial prerogatives within an accusatorial, democratically legitimate structure that contains punitive power. Proactive judicial involvement in pursuit of truth can undermine the impartiality expected in a framework where evidence should be managed by the parties. Positions tolerating judicial activism risk shifting towards an inquisitorial, and thus antidemocratic, model—potentially leading to infringements on the human rights of the accused under the guise of justice.

According to Coutinho's framework, the absence of a unifying principle precludes the existence of a truly "new" mixed system. From this standpoint, systems labelled as inquisitorial-accusatorial, accusatorial-inquisitorial, mitigated inquisitorial, or accusatorial systems with judicial investigative powers are essentially variations of the inquisitorial model, all rooted in the inquisitorial principle—namely, the pursuit of material, relative, or approximate truth. Cunha Martins further characterises these systems as antidemocratic. As previously discussed, the inquisitorial system is defined by the judge's *ex officio* investigation and their active role in seeking material truth (Lopes Jr 2010: 73).

This system relies on the controversial concept of "real truth", which contradicts the principles of the accusatorial system and democracy in contemporary criminal justice. Following Lopes Jr., who, like Coutinho, opposes superficial reforms, I agree that the Brazilian system—and others with similar traits—is (neo)inquisitorial and fundamentally undemocratic (Lopes Jr 2010: 67). If legal culture is viewed as a system of truth production and evidence management defines criminal procedure, then Brazilian legal culture is shaped by the dominance of the inquisitorial tradition and its emphasis on the search for the truth. As noted by Sentis Melendo (1959), the handling of evidence reveals whether a system is authoritarian or not. In accusatorial and democratic systems, parties are responsible for presenting evidence, while judges remain impartial adjudicators to protect the rights of the accused and uphold due process. Goldschmidt explains that adopting an accusatorial procedure ensures judicial impartiality by restricting judicial initiative in prosecution and requiring accusations to come from external parties (Goldschmidt 2010). Legal rules and safeguards are important because they set clear boundaries, reducing judges' subjectivity in legal proceedings. Aragoneses Alonso argues that true impartiality requires criminal proceedings to follow the accusatorial principle, ensuring the decision-maker is a third party (Alonso 1960: 131).

The accusatorial model focuses strictly on procedure distancing itself from inquisitorial ideologies by emphasising rules over outcomes. In this model, formality increases as the judge's role decreases. In a re-envisioned criminal justice paradigm, it logically follows that structured regulation should be prioritised over the influence of individual judicial perspectives. Such an arrangement serves to limit subjective interpretation and procedural decisionism, thereby fostering a system intended to minimise potential harms.

Cordero argues that in accusatorial procedures, justice is maintained by strictly following rules, whereas inquisitorial systems focus on utility, valuing evidence only for its usefulness. This technocratic approach dismisses formal safeguards and can lead to abuses since the judge's subjective conviction holds sway. In inquisitorial proceedings, any fact or act providing insight into events is considered evidence, prioritising historical truth over legal boundaries and often bypassing established rules, resulting in inherent illegality. This idea reappears in the post-inquisitorial era, under principles that allow countless abuses stemming from the judge's free conviction (Cordero 2000: 40). As will be discussed in the penultimate chapter, significant risks arise from the narrative formation of the judge's unfettered conviction. Therefore, it is essential to limit the means available to the judge when constructing their account, preventing it from devolving into a manifestation of monologically driven authority.

At this stage, the critique concerning the continuity of the Inquisition is especially relevant: the method of pursuing the truth—even when understood in approximate or relative terms—facilitates evidentiary experimentation and validation of previously established hypotheses. These practices raise the risk of wrongful convictions, an aspect that Cordero may not have fully recognised when he amended his perspective to acknowledge ongoing residual judicial management of evidence.

The accusatorial structure offers an alternative that matches shifting expectations for criminal jurisdiction in democratic societies. Prado (2006: 104) notes its main aim is to protect the accused's rights from arbitrary punishment. While truth matters in this system, it does not dominate, allowing the accusatorial procedure to serve as a check on punitive power without the issues seen in the inquisitorial model.

In contrast, the inquisitorial system pursues truth regardless of procedural form, aiming for conviction rather than truth and resulting in authoritarian outcomes. Ferrajoli describes this as "procedural decisionism" where decisions rely on authority (Ferrajoli 2002: 36). Carvalho emphasises the need for stronger safeguards for fundamental rights, given the historical preference for inquisitorial practices in penal systems (Carvalho 2008: 78).

Alcalá-Zamora y Castillo highlights the ongoing issue of the judge-prosecutor, first seen in inquisitorial criminal procedures where judges acted as prosecutors (Castillo 1992: 249–250). The main concern is not just secrecy or torture, but the concentration of judicial functions in one person, which persists today in various forms (Castillo 1992: 266–267). Modern procedural codes, including Spanish and Brazilian law, still allow judges to take actions typically reserved for the parties, justified by the pursuit of factual truth. According to Lopes Jr., such provisions, as is the case with Article 156, items I and II, of the Brazilian Code of Criminal Procedure, express the adoption of the inquisitorial principle, which underpins an inquisitorial system, as they represent a breach of equality, of adversarial proceedings, and of the very dialectical structure of the proceedings. As a result, they undermine the main guarantee of jurisdiction, which is the impartiality of the judge. An inquisitorial procedure is thus outlined (Lopes Jr 2010: 73).

It is not unexpected that a legal code influenced by the oppressive reasoning of Italian fascism and created during a repressive era in Brazilian history—specifically during the Estado Novo in 1941—would inherently oppose democratic principles and do so overtly, as evidenced by the remarks of Francisco Campos in the justification statement:

> The judge will cease to be an inert spectator in the production of evidence. His intervention in procedural activity is permitted, not only to direct the course of the criminal proceedings and deliver the final judgment, but also to order, *ex officio*, any evidence deemed useful for clarifying the truth. In the pursuit of this, the judge is not subject to *preclusions*. As long as the facts underlying the accusation or the defence have not been fully established, and there remains an unexplored source of evidence, the judge should not invoke *in dubio pro reo* or *non liquet*. (Campos 2010: 352–352)

The inquisitorial epistemology's emphasis on prosecution is evident in the authority given to judges. For example, in public prosecution cases, judges can still convict someone even if the Public Prosecutor has suggested acquittal, and they may also identify aggravating circumstances that were not previously mentioned (Campos 2010: 355).

Asserting that truth should not be sought at any cost—as rationalist scholars advocate—nonetheless implies that the pursuit of truth remains essential and is viewed as a fundamental objective of criminal proceedings. The same reasoning applies to arguments regarding the need for a "necessary balance" between this pursuit and the rights of the accused. Therefore, there is a persistent interconnection between discussions of truth and the judge's initiative in evidence gathering—an approach which, as previously noted, tends to enhance rather than limit punitive authority. Simply relativising the ambition for truth or the judge's capacity to initiate evidence gathering does not suffice to establish the ritualised procedural safeguards required to contain punitive power and safeguard human rights.

The incompatibility of this way of thinking with the constitutional rules meant to limit punitive authority is so obvious that it barely needs elaboration. As Lopes Jr. points out, "all inquisitorial aspects of the Code of Criminal Procedure are fundamentally unconstitutional and should be dismissed" (Lopes Jr 2010: 184). From a legal standpoint, it's clear that the inquisitorial basis of Brazilian criminal procedure does not resist constitutional examination—a view strongly supported by scholars such as Aury Lopes Jr., Jacinto Nelson de Miranda Coutinho, Alexandre Morais da Rosa, and Geraldo Prado.

In the absence of clear constitutional guidance regarding the responsibility for managing evidence in criminal proceedings, recent legislation has addressed this issue. Law 13.964/2019 (Article 3-A) clarifies that judges cannot take over the prosecution's evidentiary role or manage evidence, reinforcing constitutional limits on judicial power in criminal cases. The law ensures judges do not act as prosecutors or investigators and may only seek clarification when needed. Article 3-A thus strengthens protections against judicial overreach and clearly assigns the burden of proof to the prosecution.

Although the debate over the search for truth in criminal proceedings should be settled, inquisitorial attitudes persist, driven by the belief that judges can uncover factual truth. Scholars such as Lopes Jr. (2010: 74) and Gimeno Sendra (Sendra 1996: 372) discuss the link between procedural systems and truth-finding, noting that courts in some systems are required to seek historical truth, even by independently gathering evidence. Bettiol (1973: 249) similarly argues that judges may compensate for inactive parties when substantive truth is at stake in punitive matters. However, this approach risks continuing a tradition of persecutory justice, subordinating defendants' rights and viewing them primarily as objects of condemnation.

In the end, one must decide between two approaches: an accusatorial and democratic procedure that values human dignity and upholds human rights—based on the presumption of innocence—or a system rooted in inquisitorial principles focused on objectification. Within the first approach, judges are inclined to acquit, acting in a receptive role while the burden falls on the prosecution to overturn the presumption of innocence. Conversely, under the inquisitorial model, judges become active participants driven by a relentless pursuit of truth, displaying a tendency towards condemnation reminiscent of Eymerich's inquisitorial philosophy.

The inquisitorial approach to criminal proceedings, rooted in maintaining *the status quo*, originated in Rome and primarily served institutional punitive power. After the fall of Rome, its truth-seeking focus survived mainly in Church administration, later reemerging with the Inquisition, which solidified the notion of uncovering absolute truth through inquisitorial methods. Modern reforms did little to change this; punitive authority continued to dominate how truth was defined. The so-called "mixed" procedure gained legitimacy from emerging scientific arguments, further entrenching this model—a theme explored in the next chapters. As Lopes Jr. observes,

> The key point is to deny "truth" as a function of the proceedings (if only to avoid the trap of the inquisitorial system, founded on the search for truth). It is a naivety that reflects a belief in the omnipotence of modern legal knowledge. The equation, up to now, is (was): modern reason + judge + judicial ritual = the myth of truth. And the founding myth of the judgement and even of the (inquisitorial) process is truth. That is why unveiling is necessary, so that, freed from the mission of revealing the truth, we may move towards an accusatorial and democratic criminal procedure. (Lopes Jr 2010: 540–541)

In this context, it can be asserted that the discourse of corresponding truth, as well as truth-seeking in general, functions as an arguably flawed argumentative device, arising from contested origins that its proponents often do not acknowledge. In practice, this paradigm may introduce significant challenges to due process of law, including the potential for human rights violations. The search for truth is frequently used to justify and legitimise judicial authority—powers that diverge from the democratic principles of the accusatorial system and enable elements of inquisitorial epistemology within perceived accusatorial frameworks, thereby reinforcing the objectification of the accused.

This perspective relies on the belief in the judge's capacity, as the subject of knowledge, to uncover the essence of matters through a defined methodology and thus discover the truth, which is then articulated in the judicial sentence—the textual expression of the rational observer's understanding of reality. The following chapters will address and critically examine this belief, aiming to advance a more equitable and democratic approach to criminal justice. Before proceeding, however, I will analyse a case that exemplifies the persistent influence of inquisitorial practices in

Brazil, specifically the most prominent criminal proceeding in the nation's history.

Operation Lava Jato and the Conviction of Luiz Inácio Lula da Silva

This section presents a short case study that examines certain aspects of Operation Lava Jato, focusing on its authoritarian tendencies and the inquisitorial approach taken in the proceedings against Luiz Inácio Lula da Silva.

Operation Lava Jato represents the most extensive investigation into corruption and money laundering in Brazilian history, commencing in March 2014 and concluding officially in February 2021. The operation uncovered an elaborate scheme involving the misappropriation of resources at Petrobras, commonly referred to as "Petrolão". This arrangement consisted of major construction firms, including Odebrecht, providing bribes to executives of the state-owned enterprise and politicians in return for inflated contracts. Led by the Federal Police and the Federal Public Ministry—initially overseen by Judge Sergio Moro in the city of Curitiba—the inquiry resulted in the detention and examination of several prominent individuals, among them former President Lula (whose conviction was later rescinded). The operation faced diminished momentum following debates regarding judicial and prosecutorial impartiality, particularly after the disclosure of communications known as "Vaza Jato". Ultimately, these developments contributed to the Federal Supreme Court (STF) annulling numerous convictions on grounds of procedural errors and lack of jurisdiction—Moro's role as judge who acted in his own interests is now widely documented and difficult to dispute.

Over the past decade, particularly following the initiation of Operation Lava Jato in 2014, the Brazilian criminal justice system increasingly operated under exceptionalist frameworks that elevated inquisitorial approaches to new heights. The invocation of truth-seeking and anticorruption efforts served to justify authoritarian measures and shift attention away from the primacy of fundamental rights. This pattern extended beyond criminal proceedings, influencing broader society through punitive narratives that promoted intolerance, selective moralism, and the criminalisation of difference—especially within the political arena.

Operation Lava Jato represented a significant departure from traditional punitive approaches in Brazil, as it marked one of the first occasions where the criminal justice system took decisive action against privileged sectors of society, including leading corporations. This shift away from historical selectivity in enforcement was initially received favourably, with many analysts regarding it as a meaningful step forward in addressing corruption.

Nonetheless, scholars who support the restriction of punitive authority have observed a notable outcome: the permissible scope in criminal proceedings expanded considerably in subsequent years, while the selective nature of criminal justice persisted, albeit at a different level. Operation Lava Jato has since become a primary example of lawfare, as prosecutorial efforts focused predominantly on politicians associated with the political left.

One historically significant example is that of Sérgio Moro, a first-instance judge who convicted former president Luiz Inácio Lula da Silva in a case widely regarded as lacking sufficient proof for guilt. From the beginning of Operation Lava Jato, Moro's approach was characterised by procedural decisions that have been criticised for undermining the principles of the accusatorial system and due process.

Moro conducted the proceedings by adhering to a rationale that prioritised outcomes over procedural integrity, forgoing the impartial stance expected of a judge in an accusatorial system, particularly considering his frequent confrontations with defendants: concerns regarding the right to silence emerged when interrogations served not as a platform for the accused to present their perspective but rather as a coercive method for eliciting confessions, suggesting potential procedural impropriety (Lopes Jr 2014: 655).

Given the potential for bias arising from Moro's involvement and his alignment with predetermined hypotheses, it would have been prudent to address at the outset who would judge subsequent Lava Jato proceedings. These circumstances raised legitimate concerns about whether the proceedings risked becoming performative, merely affirming previously adopted conclusions—something that the Supreme Court later recognised, annulling numerous convictions, including Lula's.

The employment of psychological coercion by Moro during interrogations is reminiscent of methods detailed by Nicolau Eymerich in the *Manual of Inquisitors*. Ideally, such approaches would remain solely within the realm of history, with the Inquisition and its associated rhetoric relegated to scholarly study. However, as Moro's interrogation strategies illustrate, these methods persist, indicating an ongoing connection between inquisitorial epistemology and present-day breaches of procedural legality.

Operation Lava Jato's impact extended well beyond its officially stated aim of combating corruption. The measures enacted during the operation had notable effects on individuals from socially disadvantaged backgrounds. Emphasising outcomes over procedural integrity led to a significant reduction in due process protections. Judge Moro's approach served as a model for many judges, who adopted his methods and sought similar public recognition. Consequently, vulnerable populations experienced increased exposure to inquisitorial practices within the criminal justice system, which contributed to higher incarceration rates.

The inquisitorial approach was not simply adopted by the Lava Jato initiative – it was reinterpreted and heightened, resulting in a criminal justice system increasingly characterised by precautionary interventions. This period also saw a rise in pre-trial detentions based on perceived intentions or expected actions of political activists, alongside renewed use of detentions for investigative purposes or statements.

Amid rapidly declining institutional standards, authoritarian measures advanced through repeated concessions to unchecked punitive power, all justified by so-called "noble" causes. There appeared to be no limits to the authoritarian redesign of criminal justice: Moro's public hate speech towards the left became deeply entwined with criminal procedure, ultimately leading to the unprecedented criminalisation of the legal profession within a democracy. This resulted in many lawyers being openly defamed by the media, as if they were actual criminals.

The prioritisation of judicial outcomes over procedural integrity in Brazil reflects the broad implementation of criminal proceedings that often contravene human rights standards. This situation highlights both the enduring influence of authoritarian practices rooted in an inquisitorial tradition and the challenges faced by Brazil's democratic culture in resisting the appeal of prosecutorial efficiency. During Operation Lava Jato, Brazil's criminal procedure became a forum for legal experimentation, resulting in the dilution of procedural safeguards and the reinforcement of inquisitorial tendencies. Judicial activism notably elevated the judge to a central role within the proceedings. Furthermore, media coverage, attracted by crime-fighting narratives, extended the influence of these judicial decisions and transformed trials into widely publicised events, frequently subordinating the presumption of innocence to public demands for swift punishment.

The legal environment, contaminated by social expectations for a swift and effective response to corruption, often enthusiastically and uncritically assimilated investigative and prosecutorial strategies that relegated fundamental principles such as accusatorial proceedings and the right to a full defence to the background. The rhetoric of fighting crime—especially corruption—justified, in the eyes of much of society, the relaxation of constitutional safeguards, paving the way for exceptional measures that, once normalised, eroded the very structure of democracy.

Operation Lava Jato had significant repercussions across Brazil's legal and political spheres, impacted the nation's economy, influenced cultural discourse, and altered the social fabric of society. While the initiative was widely recognised for its anti-corruption efforts, its overall effect is subject to debate, particularly given observations that enforcement was largely selective, focusing primarily on one segment of the political spectrum.

The distortion of legal principles is unacceptable, particularly when influenced by personal interests, as exemplified by Lula's conviction under Judge Moro, who subsequently transitioned from the judiciary to a political role as Minister of Justice within the Bolsonaro administration.

Thus, when we look at the trajectory of the last decade of criminal procedure in Brazil, it becomes inescapable to recognise that the roots of authoritarianism, fuelled by successive institutional crises and the rhetoric of intolerance, found fertile ground to flourish and expand through criminal prosecution. The risk of normalising judicial arbitrariness, wrapped in moralising justifications, was—and remains—that of perpetuating exclusionary and selective structures, which turn criminal procedure into an instrument for maintaining historical inequalities.

Due process of law is a substantive principle—legal proceedings must adhere strictly to established rules, ensuring that judicial discretion is not exercised arbitrarily or based on an inquisitorial approach that seeks to confirm pre-existing hypotheses. When such practices are allowed, legal proceedings risk becoming procedural formalities culminating in predetermined convictions. Replacing procedural standards (focusing on methods) with an overriding emphasis on outcomes—such as prioritising the fight against corruption—may appear justifiable to some; however, this fundamentally undermines the protective safeguards inherent in criminal law and favours manipulation. Criminal law and criminal procedure should serve as vital checks within a system established to protect fundamental rights and uphold constitutional safeguards. It is inconsistent with these principles for a judge to advance personal agendas under the guise of judicial duty. In criminal proceedings, it is essential that the judge exercises judicious restraint over punitive authority, ensuring the proper functioning of mechanisms designed to prevent excesses of power (Zaffaroni et al. 2003).

The Lava Jato case introduced a new judicial paradigm in which the judge openly adopted prosecutorial functions and appeared to take a central role in proceedings. Within this framework, actions previously considered inappropriate were justified as part of an initiative that permitted blatant deviations from standard due process.

The term "spectacle criminal procedure" refers to a form of criminal prosecution that disregards legal standards in favour of garnering media attention (Casara 2015). In this context, the judge frequently occupies a central role, and judicial reasoning may be influenced by prevailing political or criminal agendas. Such procedures tend to reinforce punitive expectations rather than uphold impartial justice (Martins 2013).

The pursuit of truth continues to play a role in current legal proceedings, often within the framework of rationalist theories based on established postulates. These theories support the view that judges serve an epistemic function in seeking truth during trials, thereby preserving inquisitorial procedural characteristics. While inquisitors asserted that they confronted evil, the accusatorial procedure remains a technical procedure where what prevails is strict adherence to established protocols, aligning with democratic principles.

For these reasons and more, the choice between accusatorial and inquisitorial models is not simply an academic or theoretical exercise. These two models represent fundamentally different procedural approaches: (a) the inquisitorial model, which is characterised by an authoritarian structure focused on uncovering truth; or (b) the accusatorial model, which emphasises democratic principles centred on human dignity and the presumption of innocence.

The first procedural parameter facilitates the expansion of the police state and leads to a corresponding erosion of democratic principles. By contrast, the second procedural parameter strengthens the democratic rule of law and serves to regulate any residual elements of the police state within its framework (Zaffaroni 2003). As Rui Cunha Martins observes, "Perhaps one of its greatest virtues lies here: when demanded to shed blood, it instead offers the right to adversarial proceedings. When urged to convict, it resists adopting the mindset of the executioner". Martins underscores this point: if upholding justice requires enduring unpopularity amid public outcry, such a stance should be maintained (Martins 2013: 98–99).

When the democratic rule of law is detached from rigorous adherence to democratic procedures, it becomes susceptible to inquisitorial practices that may undermine its institutions, under the mistaken assumption that arbitrarily applied punitive authority promotes the common good.

Does this imply that procedural frameworks and their classifications take precedence over combating corruption? The issue is more nuanced. As noted by Rui Cunha Martins, the Rule of Law is maintained only when individuals with power or those engaged in corruption are held accountable through due legal process; any deviation from this standard constitutes mere populism (Martins 2013: 105).

Operation Lava Jato exemplified populist tendencies in Brazilian criminal procedure, shifting focus from legal formality to outcomes driven by urgency and public demand. Media-fuelled spectacle led to relaxed constitutional safeguards and elevated judicial figures, causing due process principles to erode. As a result, judicial performance became based on satisfying popular expectations rather than technical standards, reinforcing inquisitorial practices and undermining the democratic foundation of Brazil's criminal justice system.

In this context, Lula's coercive detention in 2016 marked a turning point for Operation Lava Jato—in many ways, it was a rehearsal for Lula's inevitable conviction. The Supreme Federal Court only formally recognised that coercive detention for interrogation was illegal about two years later.

For the purposes of this brief case study, the key issue is to examine the reasoning behind the measure, the ways it was justified, and how misinformation about it spread through the media. The underlying motive for the action seems clear: Judge Moro's order to detain former president Lula was not simply to obtain his testimony—especially since he wasn't even asked to appear voluntarily—but instead served as an unlawful restriction of his freedom of movement for several hours.

The sequence of events leading to Lula's detention demonstrates a methodical and coordinated approach marked by significant complexity and the involvement of various agents and institutions. This process established a moral economy (Thompson 1998), which provided justification for numerous unlawful actions. Participants shared an understanding regarding both their objectives and the limits of acceptable conduct required to achieve them. This ideological alignment resulted in certain authoritarian actions being perceived as legitimate and appropriate within the group. Advancements towards the collective goal fostered increased solidarity and further unified those working towards a common aim.

Over time, the social conventions guiding the operational dynamics of Operation Lava Jato fostered an increasingly collaborative environment among principal participants fulfilling their respective roles. This cooperation resulted in blurred boundaries between responsibilities and functions, sometimes leading to practices that diverged from established legal protocols and engaged public opinion on matters involving rights infringements. Consequently, the relationship between those involved in Operation Lava Jato and the media organisations disseminating information became notably stronger. Major media outlets operated as strategic partners, serving as primary channels for public communication and facilitating the garnering of public support—an element pivotal to the prosecution's progress and overall success.

The phenomena I conceptualise here as "moral economy of illegalities" played a significant role in a sequence of events that included selective information disclosures, infringements on fundamental rights framed as legal strategies, selective media coverage, and highly publicised criminal proceedings. The widespread use of both persuasive and coercive tactics was so extensive that creating a complete record of actions undertaken by the authorities is nearly impossible. Retrospective analysis suggests that this mechanism was deliberately established with the objective of securing Lula's conviction, thereby allowing for a range of measures irrespective of their compliance with constitutional standards.

The coercive detention of former President Lula may be interpreted in at least three complementary ways:

(a) It served as a preliminary measure designed to gauge potential public response to a possible future arrest.

(b) It functioned as an explicit demonstration of authority, intended to undermine the resolve of the primary individual targeted by the operation.

(c) The direct intervention involving the former president was undertaken to enable a targeted method of interrogation, characterised by the examiner's pursuit of information from the subject. This approach departs notably from the conventional practice of permitting the suspect to present their account and reflects elements of inquisitorial investigative techniques.

I will briefly explore these three points.

The initial point is sufficiently articulated. For a procedural framework that effectively incorporates public opinion into the exercise of jurisdiction, it is necessary to assess the opposing party's capacity for response—namely, to evaluate their resilience within the public sphere, which is considered a pivotal arena in achieving anti-corruption objectives (albeit such efforts may be selective, leading to the targeted criminalisation of certain political actors while immunising others). This approach can be presented as something morally justified, thus legitimising both concrete and symbolic measures. Alternatively, this matter may be examined through the lens of "techniques of neutralisation" as proposed by David Matza and Gresham Sykes. In this context, an analysis of the subjective justifications employed by advocates of Operation Lava Jato to maintain a positive self-perception while engaging in unlawful conduct would be pertinent. Denial of the victim and denial of harm are particularly prominent in this regard (Sykes and Matza 1957).

This leads to my next point: the intended impact of Lava Jato's showcase of power. The operation's strategies mirror contemporary military guidelines, notably the Shock and Awe doctrine, which aims to swiftly dominate opponents through overwhelming force and dramatic displays designed to undermine resistance and willpower. According to Ullman and Wade, the creators of this tactic, its goal is to influence the adversary's perception and understanding by applying enough pressure—both physical and psychological—to eliminate any possibility of resistance. Success relies on disrupting the opponent's will and capacity to respond.

The Shock and Awe doctrine has attracted considerable attention, with its advocates contending that rapid dominance allows for the more effective and efficient achievement of military or political objectives by incapacitating the opponent's ability to respond. As previously discussed, Lula's coercive detention had implications extending beyond legal matters; it was employed with a specific political intent to assess the opposition's resilience and secure public support—something openly sought by Operation Lava Jato. Judge Sérgio Moro publicly remarked that "cases involving serious corruption offenses and influential public figures can only progress with the backing of public opinion and organised civil society. That is your responsibility".

The similarities between Operation Lava Jato's methods and the Shock and Awe doctrine become more obvious when considering their media strategies. According to Shock and Awe, dominance is achieved by creating overwhelming conditions that force opponents to accept desired strategic or military aims. To accomplish this, large amounts of misleading information—such as lies, confusion, selective withholding of details, and disinformation—are often widely distributed.

The Lava Jato operation utilised similar strategies; however, a significant distinction lies in the focus of its efforts. The dissemination of "false information, confusion, selective denial of information, and disinformation" was aimed at shaping public opinion through the media presence associated with Lava Jato, which initiated an extensive intelligence campaign that, arguably, targeted the Brazilian populace. This suggests Lava Jato may have treated the general population as enemies, subjecting them to narratives that could potentially undermine fundamental rights.

Finally, it is essential to examine interrogation within the context of the previously discussed moral economy. Interrogation is driven by an ambition for truth and serves as a structured mechanism through which the judge systematically acquires information. This process is motivated by a commitment to validate what the judge believes to be the truth, thereby creating an environment in which the accused is required to demonstrate their innocence.

In subsequent months, legal proceedings in Brazil were depicted as a contest between Judge Moro and former President Lula, with hearings and testimonies frequently accessible via YouTube. Judge Moro ultimately convicted Lula in a case that has faced criticism for lack of substantial proof, leading to a judgement noted for its extensive digressions and reliance on judicial discretion.

Judge Moro's conviction of former President Lula in 2017 serves as a notable example within the Brazilian judicial system. The judgement raised concerns regarding whether "motivated" free judicial decisions can effectively prevent judges from forming conclusions prior to the comprehensive evaluation of evidence. Spanning 238 pages, the decision relies significantly on inference, abstraction, and conjecture, which has prompted critical analysis.

The case highlights ongoing inquisitorial elements within Brazilian jurisprudence and underscores the complexities that arise when considerations of morality, media influence, and judicial reasoning intersect. Observers have noted that Judge Moro faced considerable pressure to convict, as both his professional reputation and the integrity of the Lava Jato operation were perceived to be at stake. As a result, the outcome of the proceedings was widely anticipated. Moro had to convict Lula—no other outcome was acceptable or even possible.

Although fully aware of the level of scrutiny his ruling would face, Moro was ultimately unable to meet the standards required for such a significant task. The outcome highlighted that the concept of motivated free judicial conviction alone does not sufficiently curb the influence of a judge's personal moral judgements, particularly when shaped by pre-existing conviction hypotheses. This underscores the need to reconsider the structure of criminal justice, moving away from an epistemology centred on the judge's pursuit of truth, lest inquisitorial practices persist in subtle forms.

Moro consistently cited the notion of motivated free judicial conviction and referenced terms such as "standard of proof" and "beyond any reasonable doubt". However, the evidentiary standard applied proved inadequate, conflicting with principles of due process grounded in epistemic rigour. His approach effectively reversed the burden of proof, obligating the accused to establish innocence beyond doubt. The presumption underlying his judgement appeared to favour guilt, becoming firmly established early in the proceedings: the case against Lula thus unfolded as a steady progression towards conviction.

The underlying motivations of key figures associated with what is now referred to as Lavajatismo have become increasingly apparent. Sérgio Moro's resignation from his judicial post, following his statement that his mission was complete, further highlighted these motives. The Intercept's investigative reporting, known as Vaza-Jato, provided substantial evidence supporting longstanding suspicions: there existed significant role ambiguity and functional overlap among individuals representing different institutions, including the Federal Police, the Federal Public Prosecutor's Office, and most notably Judge Sérgio Moro within the Federal Judiciary. These findings called his impartiality into question. Rather than acting as an impartial guarantor of legal norms and fundamental rights, Moro engaged in frequent communication with public prosecutor Deltan Dallagnol, suggesting a coordinated effort towards shared objectives. For those closely following these developments, such dynamics were already apparent; what stands out is the extent of the collaboration and the regular exchange of information, particularly via WhatsApp.

In this context, it becomes clear that the gap between the utopian project of a democratic state governed by the rule of law and the effective realisation of its promises remains vast. With each new historical cycle, Brazil faces the challenge of building robust institutions and practices capable of breaking the vicious cycle of authoritarianism, whose legacy silently permeates the rituals of daily legal proceedings and the habits of legal practitioners themselves. The inquisitorial past is not merely a distant shadow, but an active and persistent element that resurfaces with surprising force during moments of political and social tension, reviving the drive for inquisitorial objectification in the pursuit of truth.

It is within this contradictory scenario, marked by constitutional advances and practical setbacks, that Brazilian criminal justice continues to provide fertile ground for disputes over the scope of citizenship and the exercise of state power. The tension between the letter of the Constitution and the reality of criminal procedure lays bare the urgent need for profound reform—not only normative, but above all cultural and epistemological—capable of dismantling the foundations of decisionism and the inquisitorial logic that still prevail.

As will be discussed in the following chapter, this challenging situation largely continues because of the prevailing political and epistemological emphasis on the pursuit of truth, which is rooted in the correspondence theory of truth and the judiciary's perceived ability to discern such truth during legal proceedings.

CHAPTER 4

Correspondence Theory of Truth, Scientificity and Legal Positivism

The Search for Absolute Truth and Its Political Implications

This section will examine the relationship between knowledge and power in criminal proceedings, analysing how the epistemological dimension of corresponding truth and the political dimension involved in the pursuit of truth interact within contemporary legal scholarship. Furthermore, it will demonstrate the necessity for new frameworks to ensure the effective protection of human rights.

Contemporary evidentiary law still retains features influenced by nineteenth-century scientific methods, emphasising correspondence truth, neutrality, and a precise alignment between factual occurrences and judicial determinations. This positivist framework prioritises the pursuit of truth as the central objective within criminal proceedings.

Throughout much of the twentieth century, this political and epistemological perspective prevailed, highlighting an epistemology centred on the pursuit of "absolute truth", "material truth", or "real truth". In recent years, evidentiary rationalism—articulated by scholars such as Michelle Taruffo and Jordi Ferrer Beltrán—has introduced a more relative approach while maintaining the quest for absolute truth as the principal goal in legal proceedings. For the purposes of this analysis, the discussion will initially address the earlier framework before advancing to an examination of the latter.

S. H. Khaled Jr., *Reimagining Criminal Justice, Search for Truth and Human Rights*, https://doi.org/10.1007/978-3-032-27227-0_4

Many contemporary scholars describe criminal procedure as adhering to a logic wherein truth aligns with reality, a concept derived from what are termed "facts" as illustrated in Bettiol's assertion:

> the aim of every trial is the pursuit of truth. In criminal proceedings, this becomes even more dramatic due to their nature. Given the intensity with which the search for truth is pursued in criminal cases, we can say that a fundamental principle of criminal procedure is the investigation of the material or substantive truth of the facts under discussion, so that they may be proven in their historical existence, without obstacles or distortions. This compels the legislator to eliminate all restrictions on evidence from the code and requires that the judge be left free to form his own conviction. (Bettiol 1973: 205)

Bettiol's position reflects a modern epistemological approach to the subject's ability to determine truth, a stance historically linked to anti-formalist theories that advocate expanded judicial discretion in evaluating evidence to better facilitate the pursuit of truth.

Bettiol's proposal is problematic for two reasons: chiefly, truth cannot be the sole focus in criminal proceedings due to necessary evidentiary limits, like the exclusion of illegal evidence. As Aragoneses Alonso notes, although freedom of evidence generally applies, certain evidence can be required or prohibited. Therefore, the pursuit of truth must not override the due process and human rights protections that criminal procedure demands. Calamandrei's view, encapsulated as "person, not thing", underscores this necessity by prioritising respect for the accused over objectification—a risk inherent in procedural systems focused solely on truth that harken back to the Inquisition. As Lopes Jr points out,

> the myth of real truth is intimately connected with the structure of the inquisitorial system [...] with authoritarian systems; with the pursuit of a 'truth' at any cost (even to the point of legitimising torture at certain moments in history); and with the figure of the judge as actor (inquisitor). (Lopes Jr 2005: 262)

Historically, the pursuit of truth has been closely linked to an authoritative approach in criminal proceedings. According to Manzini, the principal objective of criminal trials is to secure punishment for those adjudged guilty, thereby enabling the State to implement its punitive measures once culpability has been established (Manzini 1951: 250). Manzini argued that criminal proceedings should be seen as tools for protecting society by repressing crime and for safeguarding individual and collective freedoms (Manzini 1951: 251). However, he believed that suppressing crime was more important than liberty, with the criminal procedure meant to uphold the State's right to prosecute (Manzini 1951: 253). To him, it was incorrect to claim procedural rules aim to protect innocence, since innocence should only be presumed until conviction; the presumption of innocence does not mean the prosecution carries the burden of proof, as judges can gather evidence independently and accusations are already supported by initial indications. In essence, during proceedings, there is neither guilt nor innocence—only suspicion (Manzini 1951: 255).

Manzini describes a persecutory logic that reveals how dubious ideas connect with the principle of material truth. According to him, procedural certainty in the State's punitive claim is declared based on this principle (Manzini 1951: 259). He argues that, during criminal proceedings, material truth takes precedence, giving the judge both the right and responsibility to form an independent conviction—meaning they must seek facts that most accurately reflect reality. The judge is not bound by the evidence presented only by the prosecution or defence; instead, they have the power to initiate and conduct any investigations they believe will help uncover the truth (Manzini 1951: 262). Clearly, Manzini's approach—which many Brazilian legal scholars also adopt—continues an inquisitorial and antidemocratic tradition and therefore should be rejected.

Like Manzini, authors such as Leone equate free judicial conviction with material truth in criminal proceedings. Leone argues that criminal cases rely on the judge's discretion in choosing evidence, emphasising freedom not in judgement but in establishing proof (Leone 1963: 155–157). This concept is controversial, as it enables judges to direct outcomes, potentially undermining the safeguards of the accusatorial system and threatening the rights of the accused. Neves Baptista notes that the principle of material truth is often regarded as central to criminal procedure and frequently highlighted as a defining feature in legal scholarship (Baptista 2001: 6).

The pursuit of truth described by Bettiol, Manzini, and Leone warrants rejection on epistemological grounds as well. There is no methodology capable of overcoming the myriad barriers to achieving a truth that precisely corresponds to reality—one allowing for the establishment of historically verifiable facts free from distortion. This perspective reflects an antiquated notion of scientific rigour, as it disregards complexity and places undue confidence in technical means to discern the essence of reality.

Calamandrei provides a comparable critique, observing that "the most serious error of procedural science in the last fifty years has been, in my opinion, this: the separation of procedure from its social purpose; the study of procedure as an isolated field. As a self-contained world, it was believed possible to create around it a form of proud isolation, increasingly distancing it from substantive law, substantive matters, and ultimately from justice" (Calamandrei 1999: 178–179).

The concept of truth as mere correspondence to reality proves insufficient for addressing the complexities inherent in acquiring knowledge about the past and does not adequately reflect the dynamic characteristics of such epistemological processes. This simplified perspective can hinder the development of more nuanced frameworks that align with the multifaceted nature of criminal proceeding phenomena.

This authoritarian and epistemologically simplifying perspective is sustained based on the tenacious defence of a permanent isolation of law from other fields of knowledge. For instance, Bettiol attributes a predominantly sociological, rather than legal, character to Goldschmidt's theory of process as a legal situation (Bettiol 1973: 245)—refuting what should recognised as the best theory to illustrate the complex phenomenology of the criminal proceedings.

Bettiol's analysis suggests a reversal of the principles that ought to guide scientific inquiry: the aspect of Goldschmidt's theory—namely, his effort to capture the practical realities of criminal proceedings—which should be regarded as a strength, is instead presented as an epistemological weakness.

Elements that highlight criminal procedure's intrinsic dynamics, uncertainty, and complexity are often met with scepticism by proponents of the search for truth, who uphold principles such as certainty, security, control, and correspondence truth—concepts deeply rooted in modernity yet clearly epistemologically outdated and inadequate. As Prigogine notes, "the idea of certainty dominated science for centuries" (Prigogine 1996: 236).

The epistemological foundations underlying this "science of criminal procedure" are increasingly considered outdated and untenable within other disciplines that examine past events, such as history or philosophy. The pursuit of absolute truth lacks coherent epistemological foundations, yet it persists primarily for its implicit political function: supporting an authoritarian perspective within criminal procedure. As Salo de Carvalho remarks,

> The persistence of the inquisitorial style, grounded in the investigation of truth, softened by the ideological inversion of the liberal humanitarian discourse and by modern scientific rationality, fuels the narcissistic dream of the procedural subjects to extract, through evidentiary mechanisms, data that reconstructs the past event in precise correspondence with that distant reality. The aspiration to find a symmetrical adequacy of the past reality (the criminal act), based on the evidentiary elements presented by the parties, underpins the purpose that will come to govern the science of criminal procedure: *real truth*. (Carvalho 2008: 177)

Carvalho argues that prioritising the search for truth in criminal procedure has justified inquisitorial practices (Carvalho 2008). Relying on a concept of truth as factual correspondence can lead to procedural authoritarianism. Instead, Oliveira suggests that truth in trials is always a version reconstructed by participants (Oliveira 2005). Calamandrei notes that judges are limited by human perception, so judgements assess plausibility rather than absolute truth (Calamandrei 1999). Carnelutti contends that judgement seeks values but cannot access true understanding, equating it to seeking forbidden knowledge (Carnelutti 2001). Gauer observes that even seemingly clear facts remain partially obscure (Gauer 2006), and Pozzebon adds that scientific certainties are absent from case files (Pozzebon 2006). Carvalho concludes that criminal procedure is an artificial, fallible system, where adopting a position involves selecting among competing narratives rather than establishing indisputable truth (Carvalho 2003).

These arguments are compelling and present considerable challenges to counter; in essence, the concept of truth as correspondence with reality can only effectively function discursively within a monological framework. Proponents of this viewpoint seldom scrutinise the premise, often regarding it as incontrovertible. Studies that favour the search for truth over the defence of human rights tend to adopt an epistemological model aligned with methodologies from the natural sciences—even though even these disciplines have moved beyond such a reductionist approach to their subject matter. Notably, mathematics and physics have evolved away from the pursuit of absolute exactness, embracing chaos and uncertainty as underlying principles of reality. This raises important questions as to why applied social sciences have yet to experience a similar paradigm shift and why continued adherence to the concept of "real truth" or "material truth" persists.

To better understand this concept, which is notably inquisitorial in nature, it is useful to reference Mirabete. He articulates that conviction arises when the judge "is convinced that certain facts are true, reaching the truth when the idea formed in their mind aligns precisely with the reality of the facts" (Mirabete 2002: 256).

This perspective underscores a strong reliance on the judge's capacity to interpret reality through their cognitive abilities, assuming they can fully apprehend and analyse the facts to reveal the underlying truth. Such a position reflects an epistemological and ontological presumption regarding the possibility of uncovering absolute truth about past events—a notion that contrasts sharply with the perspectives held by more progressive procedural theorists.

Many scholars argue that truth in criminal proceedings is simply agreement with reality, assuming reality is fully knowable and observable. However, defining truth as mere correspondence with reality is limiting and can justify authoritarian approaches in criminal justice, such as the principle of material truth, which supports inquisitorial systems (Lopes Jr 2005: 262).

The Association of Federal Judges of Brazil (AJUFE) opposes restricting judges' pursuit of truth, citing traditional legal values (Martins 2010: 37). Oliveira observes that a police-centric Criminal Procedure Code has left generations of jurists clinging to outdated ideas (Oliveira 2005: 6). As Thums notes, "criminal procedure is built upon the myth of truth" leading only to extended trials under the pretence of legal certainty (Thums 2006: 187, 190). Based on this myth, cases that should be resolved quickly based on the absence of proof of guilt become exercises in evidentiary prospection conducted by magistrates who actively seek convictions.

However, it is important to recognise that the views of authors such as Bettiol, Manzini, Leone, and Mirabete represent just one aspect of the broader inquisitorial search for truth ideology and its underlying correspondence theory of truth.

In addition to scholars who advocate for an unremitting pursuit of truth, there are those who adopt a more nuanced perspective, viewing knowledge of the truth as approximate or relative and characterising it as a continuous yet inherently limited search for absolute truth. These authors endorse judicial initiative in the collection of evidence but acknowledge that legal constraints define and limit the judge's so-called "epistemic function" in the pursuit of truth.

For instance, Ferrer Beltrán observes that while the pursuit of truth is undeniably the primary objective of evidentiary procedures in judicial contexts, it does not stand alone; multiple aims may coexist (Beltrán 2007: 32). He takes a position that relativises the knowledge of the truth yet preserves the search for absolute truth as the primary aim of the proceedings. Beltrán establishes the pursuit of truth as the most important driving force of contemporary legal procedure. According to him, procedural provisions designed to provide safeguards may entail epistemological trade-offs that could hinder the core purpose of establishing factual truth (Beltrán 2007: 77–78).

Although Beltrán may not explicitly state this, his position suggests that procedural knowledge should emphasise the exercise of power rather than its limitation. From his perspective, human rights safeguards are regarded as obstacles to the search for truth. This perspective closely resembles Manzini's political understanding of criminal procedure.

The inquisitorial tradition finds renewed expression in a rationalist commitment to a solipsistic monologue and an "epistemic function of seeking the truth", presenting rational and abstract approaches to issues of evidence and truth. This perspective integrates both objectivism and subjectivism, resulting in an incongruous synthesis of philosophical paradigms. Although the notion of "truth" in evidentiary rationalism was shifted towards relative truth or "knowledge of the truth", defined by the elements available within legal proceedings rather than direct reference to historical events, the pursuit of "knowledge of the truth" continues to aim for an approximation of "absolute" or "objective" truth. As a result, it is incumbent upon the judge to seek this truth, reinforcing the objectifying aspect embedded in rationalist philosophy, which revitalises the inquisitorial ambition for truth.

This framework upholds confidence in the judge's capacity, as an epistemic authority, to examine case matters through a systematic and abstract methodology, thereby aiming to approximate the truth. The judgement is regarded as the narrative outcome of this evidentiary process conducted by the judge, reflecting their rational analysis based on the evidence presented throughout the proceedings.

According to its main proponents, who label conceptions of evidence situated outside the rationalist tradition as "irrational", the search for truth is the primary means to achieve justice (Twinning 2006: 78). Evidentiary rationalism establishes a teleological relationship between evidence and truth (Beltrán, 2006: 3). In this sense, the criminal justice system operates as an "epistemic engine" whose purpose is the discovery of truth (Laudan, 2013, p. 23). This teleological relationship is explained as being the most appropriate mechanism for the institutional objective of the procedure—the pursuit of truth—to be achieved (Beltrán 2021: 17). For rationalists, the pursuit of truth is an essential element of democracy, and fundamental rights themselves are grounded in this objective conception of truth (Taruffo 2012).

While these arguments may initially appear compelling, it is crucial to examine the political ramifications of evidentiary rationalism. Specifically, it is important to consider how prioritising the search for truth influences human rights, legal safeguards, and exclusionary evidentiary rules.

A thorough grasp of evidentiary rationalism necessitates an examination beginning with Jeremy Bentham, who is widely acknowledged as a central figure within this tradition. While Bentham is frequently categorised within classicism, his writings did not incorporate the humanitarian considerations emphasised by Beccaria (Khaled Jr. & Morrison, 2024).

Bentham's perspective on criminal procedure is fundamentally anchored in the belief that, although multiple values merit consideration during fact-finding, the accuracy of judicial decisions must take precedence. Such a stance results in procedural formalities being relegated to matters of secondary importance. This approach also exhibits a clear alignment with inquisitorial epistemology, characterised by its anti-formalist tendencies. Consequently, the commitment to "seeking the truth" often stands in direct opposition to rules governing the exclusion of evidence. Not coincidentally, the Benthamite framework—frequently referenced as an aspirational standard in evidentiary rationalism—closely parallels prevailing authoritarian concepts of the State. Importantly, this alignment extends beyond mere subordination of exclusionary rules to utilitarian principles.

Benthamian consequentialism encompasses utilitarianism and serves as a foundation for contemporary interpretations, including those associated with libertarianism and the economic analysis of law. Bentham supported the use of torture (Twinning & Twinning 1973), and more recently, Posner (2006) and Wigmore (Chiesa 2010: 44) have presented arguments in favour of torture under specific circumstances, deliberately setting aside human rights considerations within these theoretical frameworks. This line of reasoning reveals an association with objectification aims historically connected to inquisitorial practices.

Jeremy Bentham's evaluations of the Declaration of the Rights of Man and of the Citizen remain influential in contemporary discourse. In his work, *Anarchical Fallacies* (Bentham, 1843), Bentham systematically critiques the document, challenging the concept of imprescriptible human rights and emphasising the primacy of state authority over individual rights. While he did not explicitly identify as a positivist and articulated his arguments prior to the emergence of legal positivism, Bentham's analyses are notably aligned with its principles (Zaffaroni, 1998, p. 109). He argued that notions of inalienable rights or contractual restrictions on governmental power lack substantive value under the principle of utility, referring to them as ambiguous or ineffectual constructs (Khaled Jr. and Morrison 2024: 380). This philosophical approach underpins what is referred to as the "rationalist tradition", which prioritises accurate resolution of criminal cases through substantive law over ethical constraints such as rules of evidentiary exclusion. Consequently, Bentham's procedural model integrates police investigative functions with minimal limitations, reflecting a marked affinity for authoritarian political frameworks.

Graham Jr. (1987: 1214) observes that the ethos of Bentham's philosophy was to reinforce and expand control within a statist and hierarchical framework. According to the author, Bentham's ideas could be characterised as "proto-Stalinist" in nature. Bentham's preference for authoritarian political structures is reflected in his approach to procedural (criminal) law, particularly through his proposal to abolish existing evidentiary rules and the perceived right of parties to present evidence as they see fit. This perspective reduces criminal proceedings to a mechanism primarily concerned with the production of evidence, where normative considerations are treated largely as obstacles and viewed, at best, as necessary concessions.

Ultimately, Bentham can be seen as fundamentally opposed to proceduralism. The reduction of criminal procedure to the management of evidence is expressly discussed by Bentham in his Treatise. To leave no doubt, I repeat here verbatim his words: "the art of the process is in reality nothing but the art of managing evidence" (Bentham 1825: 2).

More recently, Larry Laudan has emerged as a contemporary proponent of similar epistemological frameworks. Laudan states that all rules of evidence exclusion that exclude relevant evidence should be regarded as "suspect" (Laudan 2013: 46). The starting point is the argument that the better informed the decision-makers are, the better the decision will be (Laudan 2013: 46). Regarding exclusionary rules, he questions several of them, listing a series of rules that he believes could be perfectly abandoned: a) rules that exclude confessions in which the accused was not informed of his right to remain silent; b) rules that prohibit the use of illegally obtained evidence; c) the fruit of the poisonous tree doctrine; d) testimonial immunities; e) instruction (in the *Griffin* case) to the jury that it cannot draw a negative inference from the accused's silence; f) exclusion of evidence that would show the defendant's character and use of prior bad acts; g) rules requiring the prosecution to prove that the confession was likely given voluntarily; h) rules regarding the rejection of evidence that could cause the jury to make an unfair prejudgement; i) rules on excluding confessions taken more than eight hours after detention of the accused, without the suspect having appeared before a judge; j) rules prohibiting informing the jury of the reasons for the defence's refusal to allow a witness with immunity to testify; k) rules dealing with the exclusion of a confession corroborated by other evidence when the arrest was made without probable cause; l) rules that limit the information given to jurors about witnesses who refused to testify based on the Fifth Amendment; m) rules regarding the inadmissibility of hearsay; n) rules prohibiting informing the jury of a codefendant's plea deal in cases of mutual accusation/plea; o) rules prohibiting informing the jury of the defendant's refusal to testify (the *Doyle* rule) at the preliminary investigation stage (Laudan 2013: 199).

Laudan also presents the "principle of indifference between acquittals and convictions": this principle establishes that if it is possible to set a standard of proof that incorporates what society believes to be the appropriate value for false convictions, it would be a mistake to propose that other aspects of the proceedings, including evidentiary rules, should grant the accused additional benefits beyond the benefit of the doubt already offered by setting the standard of proof (Laudan 2013: 119). This is because "in such a regime, there would be very few guilty convictions and practically no crime prevention" (Laudan 2013: 207). He continues: "from the moment a criminal procedure begins, the average guilty defendant can be confident that, even if guilty, it is unlikely he will be convicted" (Laudan 2013: 207). Finally, "the ultimate response to those defence attorneys who insist on a 'fair fight' is to remind them that if they truly want fair play between the prosecution and the defense, then the 'beyond a reasonable doubt' standard should be replaced by another standard of proof that awards victory to the side with the more plausible argument" (Laudan, 2013: 218). Laudan is not alone in this fight: he has the intellectual (and political) support of Ferrer Beltrán for the proposition that the standard of proof must be able to reflect and produce the *ratio* of error distribution that is deemed socially acceptable (Beltrán 2021: 125).

In contrast to the aforementioned interpretation, my perspective views a reimagined criminal justice system as a safeguard against excessive punitive power, deriving its legitimacy from rigorous evidentiary standards and strict adherence to procedural protocols rather than an emphasis on uncovering the absolute truth. This approach is characterised not as a compromise but as an intentional decision to uphold the defence of human rights, establishing the presumption of innocence as the foundational principle guiding criminal proceedings instead of prioritising the judge's role in the pursuit of truth.

In line with Beltrán, Taruffo observes that certain exclusionary rules lack an epistemic function, as they are not designed to facilitate truth discovery. Instead, these rules pursue objectives distinct from accurate fact-finding, as they may restrict or exclude relevant evidence, thereby negatively affecting the epistemic purpose of legal proceedings (Taruffo 2010: 167).

An important perspective to consider is presented by Ferrajoli. In contrast to Laudan, Taruffo, and Beltrán, Ferrajoli does not prioritise the pursuit of truth over procedural safeguards. However, within his epistemology of criminal procedure, he also upholds the correspondence theory of truth. Ferrajoli maintains the foundational framework of the correspondence model in criminal proceedings, opting to relativise the prevailing discourse rather than completely depart from it.

Ferrajoli critiques the ideal of absolute correspondence in evidentiary standards geared towards establishing absolute or material truth. However, he suggests that the Enlightenment ideal of perfect correspondence can be reinterpreted as an approximation, which he terms procedural truth. As Ferrajoli states, procedural truth "can be understood as an approximate truth relative to the Enlightenment ideal of perfect correspondence" (Ferrajoli 2002: 42).

Although he does not support evidentiary management by the judge, he sometimes describes the criminal procedure as a pursuit of truth. For Ferrajoli, "the only meaning of the term 'true'—like 'reliable', 'probable', or 'plausible'—is the more or less reasoned and approximate correspondence between propositions and objective reality, constituted in proceedings by the facts adjudicated and the norms applied" (Ferrajoli 2002: 50–54).

Proponents of judicial initiative in evidence fail to properly acknowledge the incompatibility between truth-seeking and the due process required for regulated punitive power. They overlook how redefining truth as nuanced or approximate correspondence perpetuates inquisitorial practices and undermines democratic proceedings that protect fundamental rights. Advocates of the correspondence theory of truth—except Ferrajoli—still view truth-seeking as central to criminal proceedings, thus consciously or not reinforcing the inquisitorial paradigm and maintaining judicial interference in evidence management. In extreme cases, evidentiary rationalism defends that exclusionary rules dedicated to the protection of human and fundamental rights must be abolished to facilitate the search for truth.

Given these considerations, it's crucial to remember that, historically, limitless authority has often resulted in a version of "truth" that simply echoes the beliefs of those in power or serves authoritarian aims. In such situations, truth is dictated arbitrarily, similar to what occurred under the Napoleonic biphasic system or inquisitorial structures—whether secular or religious—which have shaped procedural practices that continue to affect us today. These systems have inflicted serious harm on the rights of accused individuals. The irony is clear: an overzealous pursuit of truth can move legal proceedings further away from genuine understanding and respect for human rights. As Ferrajoli observes, an increase in authority tends to diminish knowledge (Ferrajoli 2002: 39). Moreover, simply relativising this ambition for truth amounts to only a minor improvement compared to the fundamental changes needed to safeguard the rights of the accused. Ultimately, empowering judges with investigative authority to "seek the truth" often leads to wrongful convictions that a democratic, accusatorial legal system should strive to prevent or minimise.

Establishing clear boundaries for judicial evidentiary involvement is essential to uphold fairness in legal proceedings. Allowing judges unrestricted discretion over the extent of their participation in evidence management can pose significant risks to the rights of the accused. The most prudent solution is to prohibit all forms of judicial evidentiary initiative, thereby ensuring the judge fulfils the impartial role expected under the dispositive principle of the accusatorial system.

As previously discussed, when judicial evidentiary activities are permitted, the accusatorial system is not fully implemented and inquisitorial practices tend to dominate. By contrast, increasing oversight over evidence management—particularly through adversarial proceedings—promotes improved understanding and facilitates greater regulation of judicial authority. This underscores the importance of establishing well-defined and uncompromising procedural rules, which should not be relaxed for prosecutorial objectives.

When a judge takes on the role of a party rather than maintaining impartiality, judicial objectivity is undermined. Practices such as selective evidence evaluation and subjective decision-making can compromise procedural safeguards that are designed to restrain punitive authority and ensure due process in criminal law. Such a departure elevates individual authority above legal principles, contradicting the foundations of democratic governance and the protection of human rights. This perspective is rooted in the simplistic epistemological notion that corresponding truth can be established when a judge acts as a central figure in the proceedings.

The belief in the notion of corresponding truth—even if considered relative or approximate—undermines the accusatorial system by straying from its democratic ideals. How cases are handled can differ greatly depending on a judge's role in the proceedings. For instance, when there is doubt about reaching a verdict, pursuing absolute truth allows a judge to take an inquisitorial approach, seeking evidence specifically to resolve uncertainties in forming their conviction. Many believe this empowers judges to implement measures to clarify questions, conduct fresh interrogations, or revisit witnesses, acting on the premise that pursuing truth is both possible and necessary. Eventually, gaps may be filled by a judge's own assumptions, confirming pre-existing hypotheses and gathering information until the case fits the cognitive framework they have previously constructed. Sometimes, missing parts of the judge's belief are supplied from police investigations—sources of information meant solely for prosecutors rather than judges. When these materials are included in court proceedings, they can negatively impact the accused's interests.

Conversely, when a judge adopts a comprehensive perspective and acknowledges the impartiality required by the accusatorial system, they must dismiss the accusation if there is insufficient evidence supporting the prosecutorial hypothesis. Acquittal does not require aspirations for uncovering absolute truth; under the *in dubio pro reo* principle, reasonable doubt alone should be sufficient.

However, Francisco Campos observes in his explanatory memorandum to the Code of Criminal Procedure that application of this principle should be restricted—the procedural framework established in the 1941 Brazilian Criminal Procedure Code is fundamentally inquisitorial. Following this approach, Campos allows the judge to initiate supplementary or additional evidence during the criminal investigation or before issuing a verdict. Additionally, Campos makes clear the relationship between inquisitorial logic and the pursuit of truth: "If it is true that the judge is bound by the evidence in the case file, it is equally true that the judge is not limited by any *a priori* criteria in determining, through such evidence, the material truth" (Campos 2010: 352).

Granting judges investigative powers to "seek the truth" primarily serves the enhancement of punitive authority, as any reasonable doubt supposedly warranting judicial intervention should instead result in acquittal—not in an endless search of evidence to convict the accused. As Neves Baptista notes,

> For the accused, this truth is, quite evidently, irrelevant. If guilty and unrepentant, their interest lies in preventing its discovery; if guilty and remorseful, they are better served by a swift resolution of the case, allowing them to satisfy their own conscience by bearing the consequences of their acknowledged wrongful act; if innocent, a protracted investigation into their innocence is of no use, as the State's recognition of it suffices. Ultimately, the interest in any investigation is that of the latter—the State—as justification for the exercise of its punitive power. (Baptista 2001: 199)

Nassif asserts that a constitutional state of innocence is a pre-established truth in legal proceedings, not just a presumption (Nassif 2005: 122–123). He believes judges need not be convinced of innocence—it is assumed. The relentless quest for truth often empowers authority at the expense of procedural safeguards. This raises questions about criminal jurisdiction: should it enforce punitive power or regulate it? Ultimately, emphasising truth risks undermining safeguards, creating an unacceptable imbalance and potentially reinforcing the selectivity of secondary criminalisation.

This raises several key issues: how can the idea of truth as correspondence be surpassed, how can power's influence on knowledge in criminal proceedings be limited, and how can criminal procedure foster respect for human rights instead of serving punitive aims? Addressing these concerns calls for fundamentally rethinking the role of truth and viewing the criminal procedure as more than a technical instrument. According to Calamandrei,

> we proceduralists cannot resign ourselves to being merely patient and meticulous clockmakers, whose work is exhausted in arranging the gears, without asking whether the mechanism that emerges from our hands will mark the hour of happiness or the hour of death. We refuse to be likened to magnificent mechanics manufacturing electric chairs; we want to know where our work leads, to what human ends it must serve. (Calamandrei 1999: 183)

Calamandrei's perspective underscores the importance of not interpreting criminal procedure as a mechanism for pursuing truth, as such an approach risks diminishing its function in constraining punitive authority. Traditionally, criminal law scholarship has concentrated on theories of crime and punishment, often overlooking procedural aspects, which has led to adverse consequences. Criminal law and procedure are intrinsically linked, with procedure serving as a critical conduit between legal theory and practical application (Lopes Jr 2008).

Historically, an unwavering commitment to the pursuit of absolute truth has often resulted in significant infringements on the dignity of the accused—and simply adopting a more relativistic stance towards the knowledge of the truth can perpetuate similar errors if driven by an excessive focus on fact-finding. This underscores the need to reconsider current paradigms and advocate for the reformation of criminal justice systems. To this end, two interconnected objectives are identified: first, establishing the scope of attainable truth within legal proceedings; and second, pursuing the humanitarian imperative to restrict arbitrary punishment, as required by democratic principles. These goals are inherently linked and have frequently been neglected—a condition that Carnelutti characterises as the core dilemma within criminal justice, which unfortunately continues to exhibit inquisitorial elements:

> punishment, unfortunately, does not begin with the conviction, but much earlier, with the trial, the investigation, the preliminary acts, even with the first suspicion cast upon the accused; so much so that criminal proceedings are from the outset a punishment, and often the accused is subjected to it *in vinculis*, as if already convicted; the drama is that he is punished in order to determine whether he should be punished. (Carnelutti 2004: 36)

Carnelutti argues that criminal proceedings are expected to achieve more than they realistically can. However, while these proceedings are necessary, it is important to recognise their limitations (Carnelutti 1965: 87).

According to Taruffo, "the issue is not, in reality, to suppose that mythical absolute truths can be reached, but rather to determine which relative and reasonable truths are actually ascertainable" (Taruffo 2005: 46). Badaró, a prominent proponent of evidentiary rationalism in Brazil, asserts that "from an epistemological perspective, the central question is whether truth can be attained" (Badaró 2003: 19).

Nevertheless, evidentiary rationalism's response to this issue presents fundamental flaws: it upholds the correspondence theory of truth in a relativised manner, and continues to defend the pursuit of absolute truth, thereby requiring the judge to manage evidence accordingly.

A new framework for criminal justice ought to consider both political and epistemological factors. This includes reaffirming limits on punitive power and scrutinising suitable standards of truth within criminal proceedings. Criminal procedure studies must recognise the inherent challenges in reconstructing historical events and the associated limitations, necessitating a departure from a correspondence theory of truth.

Ferrajoli argues that an adequate concept truth is essential not only for developing a theory of legal procedure but also because of its role in judicial practice (Ferrajoli 2002: 40). He maintains that while a criminal justice system based entirely on truth is an unattainable ideal, one completely devoid of truth would lead to arbitrariness (Ferrajoli 2002: 38).

Ferrajoli's argument is sound: the concept of truth (epistemological dimension) and the pursuit of truth (political dimension) are closely interconnected and mutually reinforcing. An insufficient understanding of truth informs the continued search for truth in criminal proceedings, indicating that this notion warrants comprehensive examination.

Rui Cunha Martins contends that truth should be regarded as one significant component—yet neither absolute nor preeminent—in legal proceedings. Elevating truth to a central position risks facilitating an authoritarian perspective (Martins 2010).

He argues that establishing truth as the primary aim of the criminal procedure raises important political issues, contending that such an approach could undermine the protection of human rights. Accordingly, Martins (2010) suggests that both the concept and the emphasis on truth should be reconsidered.

Rather than focusing solely on the attainability of absolute truth, it is crucial to establish an appropriate definition of truth within criminal procedure—one that addresses both the complexity inherent in the context of criminal proceedings and the historical nature of past events, without positioning the pursuit of truth as the primary objective.

To accurately define the function of truth within this updated model of criminal justice, it is necessary to move beyond the correspondence theory of truth that forms the foundation of both Ferrajoli's approach and the evidentiary rationalism articulated by Taruffo and Ferrer-Beltrán.

The Correspondence Theory of Truth as Formulated by Alfred Tarski

Within the current landscape of procedural studies, Alfred Tarski's correspondence theory of truth has been embraced by several prominent scholars, notably Michelle Taruffo, Jordi Ferrer-Beltrán, and Luigi Ferrajoli.

Although these authors may differ in certain respects, they share a foundational postulate: the notion of corresponding truth as articulated by Alfred Tarski, the renowned Polish scholar recognised for his contributions to logic and mathematics. Tarski's theory distinctly embodies what is often termed rationalist abstraction. His conception of truth is fundamentally a logical and mathematical enterprise that seeks to engage with epistemological concerns; however, Tarski himself identified it as a subject within the philosophy of the exact sciences (Mancosu 2008).

At least two of Tarski's works merit attention due to their examination of the concept of truth. In his article *The Concept of Truth in Formalized Languages*, Tarski provides only a concise overview of truth within common or natural languages, using this as a prelude to his principal focus: the analysis of truth in formalised languages. Formalised languages, such as programming, mathematical, and chemical languages, are intentionally designed for specific applications and stand in contrast to common or natural languages, which have evolved through historical and cultural processes.

In this text, he posits that "x *is a true statement if and only if* p" can be demonstrated; for example, *"it is snowing" is a true statement if and only if it is snowing* (Tarski 2007: 156). This formulation appears to reference Aristotle's classical concept of truth as correspondence. However, Tarski does not confine his analysis to this perspective and proceeds to examine additional considerations, including aspects unrelated to the "correspondence" between statements and reality. Instead, he addresses the internal coherence of statements, suggesting that the inherently open nature of common language presents challenges when compared with formalised languages.

In a later text, *The Semantic Conception of Truth and the Foundations of Semantics* Tarski returns to the topic in more detail. On this occasion, he openly proposes to reinterpret the Aristotelian correspondence, that is, to refine the formulation "*To say of what is that it is not, or of what is not that it is, is false, while to say of what is that it is, or of what is not that it is not, is true*". His (re)formulation is very different from the original and extraordinarily well-known: *the statement "snow is white" is true if and only if snow is white.*

The use of quotation marks on the left side of the equivalence signifies that the "name" of the statement appears there, whereas the statement itself is presented on the opposite side. This method is referred to as the T-scheme (derived from "*truth*"). According to Tarski, this approach offers a more concise and sophisticated definition, which can be adopted independently of any particular epistemological perspective. The semantic conception of truth, therefore, remains "neutral" regarding naive realism, critical realism, idealism, empiricism, or metaphysical positions (Tarski 2007: 190). While seemingly straightforward, the proposal is ambitious. It seeks not only to enhance the Aristotelian correspondence definition but also aspires to universality.

The classification of Tarski's work as a "correspondence" theory warrants careful consideration. While Tarski appeared to intend a correspondence conception of truth, the definition he formulated does not align with criteria where the truth of a statement depends on its relation to external reality. Tarski's T-scheme does not clarify the connection between statements and objective, observable facts. Specifically, the formulation "the statement 'the snow is white' is true if and only if the snow is white" remains abstract and self-referential, lacking explicit criteria for direct comparison with the world to determine its truth or falsity—a key requirement of the correspondence notion. Thus, Tarski's framework seems not to constitute a genuine correspondence theory; rather, it delineates conditions under which a statement may be considered true based solely on internal logical coherence. If this interpretation holds—as supported by substantial scholarly literature—Tarski's semantics do not address the narrative representation of reality in textual, oral, or visual forms. The sole requirement is internal consistency within the statement itself. Such an abstract concept, detached from empirical verification, may suffice for formal logic but does not account for evidentiary phenomenology, such as in criminal or civil procedures. Accordingly, it appears inadequate for these applications and potentially many others, as will be demonstrated subsequently.

Tarski's proposal generated significant debate within academic circles. Some logical positivists attending the First International Congress on the Unity of Science in Paris in 1935 perceived his ideas as a reemergence of the correspondence theory of truth, linking language with reality. However, contrasting perspectives were also present—Otto Neurath, for example, expressed concern that logical formalism might entice individuals towards metaphysical positions, essentially constructing abstract formal frameworks appealing to those with a logical orientation. Neurath maintained that the semantic conception of truth was incompatible with a strictly empiricist and anti-metaphysical stance, particularly one opposed to untestable scientific claims (Mancosu 2008: 196–197). In his correspondence with Tarski, Neurath contended that the constraints Tarski sought to enforce on his notion of truth would not be upheld and that these formulations could facilitate various forms of metaphysical speculation. Neurath cautioned against an inappropriate extension of Tarski's theory—from formal languages to common or natural ones—and specifically challenged Tarski's use of the concept of "truth" (Mancosu 2008: 198).

Another prominent critique of Tarski's theory merits consideration. Hilary Putnam strongly challenged Tarski's claim that his framework constitutes a correspondence theory. To support his argument, Putnam references an example from Lewis Carroll: *"The Snark was a Boojum" is true if and only if the Snark was a Boojum.* He elaborates further: "But what does this statement actually convey? If it conveys anything—though some might argue it conveys nothing—it merely suggests that the expressions on either side of 'if and only if' are in some sense equivalent; for instance, anyone who accepts one is logically committed to accepting the other. While this may be significant information regarding the use of 'true', it does not align with the type of insight sought by proponents of the correspondence theory (Putnam 1979: 71)". In Putnam's view, as a philosophical account of truth, Tarski's theory fails as thoroughly as a theory possibly can (Putnam 1985: 64).

The critiques offered by Neurath and Putnam are neither postmodern, psychoanalytic, decolonial, rooted in philosophical hermeneutics, nor shaped by the linguistic turn—approaches that would arguably present even stronger challenges. Rather, their criticisms arise from the perspective of a contemporary counterpart to Tarski or stem from ambitions articulated but not realised within the theory itself. Consequently, if one were to adopt a "correspondence theory" in criminal proceedings (which appears, at best, questionable), the selection of Tarski as a foundational model warrants careful scrutiny. According to Putnam, it would have been preferable for Tarski to confine his efforts to formulating "definitions of truth" within formalised languages, refraining from making broader philosophical claims—a stance closely aligned with that of Neurath (Putnam 1979: 72).

Is Tarski's "theory" best characterised as a theory of truth as correspondence? Does it restore the notion that truth entails a relationship between language and reality? Furthermore, is Tarski's semantic definition of truth genuinely a reinterpretation of Aristotle's classical correspondence theory of truth? According to Tarski, the answer is affirmative; he asserts that his work represents a formalisation of the concept of truth as correspondence. Certain scholars, such as Ferrajoli, Ferrer-Beltrán, and Taruffo, have embraced this position without substantive critical examination or epistemological scrutiny.

The persistent reliance on Tarski's correspondence theory, and its unquestioned adoption within legal discourse, underscores the tendency of the legal field to privilege scientific models as the ultimate arbiters of truth. Yet, this uncritical approach neglects the profound epistemological distinctions between scientific inquiry and legal reasoning, particularly in contexts where complexities and ambiguities predominate. Such reliance often results in oversimplification, with legal processes attempting to emulate scientific precision in settings where certainty is elusive and competing narratives must be weighed. As a result, the pursuit of scientific truth within legal proceedings can inadvertently reinforce existing power structures, privileging the perspectives of those who wield authority in the name of rationality.

This persistence highlights the tendency of legal scholars to appropriate the epistemological tools of science, often without adequate consideration of their suitability or limitations when applied to the intricacies of legal reasoning. Among these three, only Ferrajoli (2002) advances the discussion by directly engaging with the concept of truth in criminal proceedings, though his treatment remains somewhat limited and must be reviewed and expanded. In *Law and Reason* (2002) he employs Tarski's framework to construct a notion of relative corresponding truth, which nevertheless retains an abstract character and is potentially vulnerable to appropriation by punitive tendencies.

In his book *Simply the Truth*, Taruffo contends that defining truth is an inherently unsolvable problem. Nevertheless, he notes that, in line with widely accepted philosophical and epistemological perspectives, Tarski's criterion is generally regarded as valid: the assertion "snow is white" is true if and only if snow is white (Taruffo 2010: 98). To illustrate the necessity of adopting the correspondence theory of truth within legal processes, Taruffo (2010: 95) directs readers to Jordi Ferrer-Beltrán's work, *Proof and Truth in Law* (2007).

In the referenced work, characterised as a "philosophy of law" Ferrer-Beltrán clarifies that he will not address the concept of truth. The author explicitly indicates his reliance on a correspondence theory of truth, drawing from Tarski, and dedicates the book to examining the relationship between this notion of truth and proof. Ferrer-Beltrán argues in a footnote that the diverse issues and theories associated with truth warrant more comprehensive study and would demand an extensive bibliography; therefore, he references a single publication on the subject (2005: 18).

After criticisms regarding the supposed "irrationality" of other theories, Tarski's formulation is employed with the following implication: *"snow is white" is true if, and only if, snow is white*. According to Ferrer-Beltrán, this suggests that truth requires a correspondence between a statement and the facts of the world (2005: 73). Nonetheless, as previously noted, it remains highly debatable whether Tarski's theory genuinely encompasses correspondence within its scope. The discussion on this subject is limited to less than a paragraph. The epistemological framework of evidentiary rationalism is fundamentally based on Tarski's theory of truth; should this foundation prove unsound, the entire structure would consequently be undermined. The unwavering endorsement of Tarski's correspondence theory of truth by Taruffo and Ferrer-Beltrán may be interpreted more as a matter of belief than based on rigorous justification—an observation that is particularly noteworthy given the emphasis on "epistemology" within evidentiary rationalism. Across the works of proponents of evidentiary rationalism, there appears to be no clear explanation of how a framework originally designed for formal languages—Tarski's primary aim—can be effectively applied to legal contexts. This principle tends to be accepted without question, despite its apparent misalignment with Tarski's own theoretical foundations.

To be fair to Ferrer-Beltrán, it must be acknowledged that throughout his trilogy, he aims to establish criteria by which correspondence could occur and be verified intersubjectively. In his view, "it is proven that *p*" implies *"there are sufficient elements of judgment supporting* p" and thus the internal coherence of a statement alone does not suffice for its truth; the statement must also be tested against an external reality. However, for a theory purporting to represent the state-of-the-art of epistemology, such treatment is arguably inadequate.

One clear observation emerges from the work of the three referenced authors: Tarski's concept of truth is adopted without substantial epistemological analysis or adaptation to legal contexts. Although Tarski aimed to refine the notion of correspondence, his resulting concept does not fully align with this intention. Ferrajoli, Taruffo, and Ferrer-Beltrán integrated Tarski's concept into their theoretical frameworks, considering it an appropriate model of correspondence for legal phenomena. The outcomes of these incorporations merit careful consideration.

Ferrajoli's methodology demonstrates certain limitations but does not advocate for the search for truth. He references Tarski's definition to partially revise the correspondence theory of truth (Ferrajoli 2004: 41); however, this approach remains constrained by a conceptual framework of correspondence that is inadequate for criminal procedure, despite its frequent perception as the sole or most rational standard.

In contrast, Taruffo and Ferrer-Beltrán introduce a scenario that merits further scrutiny: Tarski's concept plays a significant role within the context of legal procedure and proof, emphasising the pursuit, demonstration, and verification of truth, although its substantive validity remains debatable. Additionally, Taruffo and Beltrán's evidentiary rationalism is positioned by them as the exclusive legitimate approach to epistemological frameworks for legal proceedings, with alternative viewpoints characterised as irrationalism.

Taruffo, for instance, provides an extensive discussion in his work *Simply the truth* (2010) where he critiques what he describes as postmodern influence, suggesting that it has led to the rejection of concepts such as truth, reason, history, and knowledge as trustworthy instruments. Nevertheless, several inaccuracies are evident in his analysis, beginning with his categorisation of certain authors as postmodern—including Heidegger, who does not fit within the context Taruffo criticises. Moreover, Taruffo's critiques of Lyotard, Vattimo, and Derrida rely on secondary sources rather than direct engagement with their original texts, resulting in a misinterpretation of their arguments (notably, Derrida, Heidegger, and Vattimo do not appear in his bibliography). Although Taruffo acknowledges that what he terms postmodernity was not detrimental to philosophical thought and that it triggered a lasting crisis in some outdated ideas, he ultimately evades addressing the issue of truth by deeming its definition insoluble. He concludes by endorsing the "classical criterion" proposed by Tarski, wherein the statement "snow is white" is true if and only if snow is white (Taruffo 2010: 89–98).

Taruffo and Beltrán critique modern epistemological models of positivism, including syllogistic reasoning and the simple determination of facts. However, their framework offers limited contribution to current discussions regarding the concept of truth in legal proceedings and demonstrates consistent support for modernity's epistemological and political assumptions. This tendency is particularly evident in Taruffo's work on the topic. All perspectives that criticise modernity are crudely portrayed as "irrational" in a generic manner by Taruffo, including feminism (2010). He concludes his narrative with Tarski, asserting that we have reached the "post-post-modernity", which would represent the "return of truth". Considering Taruffo's critiques, my perspective aligns with Timm de Souza, who asserts that.

> *The accusation of irrationality is one of the preferred rhetorical strategies of hegemonic models of rationality to attempt to disqualify other rationalities, or even other possibilities of rationality.* Nothing new under the sun: the history of philosophy has, over the centuries, been the tension between the promulgation of systems and theories as truths and the ever-present

> suspicion that truth lies beyond the scope of systems and theories. (Souza 2004: 165)

It follows that a more nuanced engagement with the philosophy of science is required—one that acknowledges the limitations of strict correspondence and the necessity for pluralistic, context-sensitive approaches to truth. By critically evaluating the epistemic ambitions underpinning contemporary legal practice, one can better appreciate the ways in which truth claims are constructed and maintained, thus fostering a more reflective and equitable system of justice.

An essential preliminary step is to critically examine and deconstruct the prevailing modern scientific paradigm underpinning the concept of corresponding truth. Transcending the pursuit of absolute truth in criminal proceedings necessitates a departure from entrenched traditions in knowledge construction. The subsequent section will address this subject in greater detail.

Modern Thought and the Ambition for Scientific Truth: Knowledge as Power

The contemporary understanding of the correspondence theory of truth embodies a particular epistemological viewpoint grounded in modern scientific principles and methodologies, that provide the foundational and legitimising basis for procedural practices that contrast with the structure of the accusatorial system, empowering the judge—as a holder of knowledge—to supposedly discern underlying realities. This notion of scientificity has facilitated the evolution of inquisitorial reasoning, albeit under distinct premises, as will be further elaborated below.

Modern scientific thought has profoundly influenced the legal sphere, shaping the expectations placed upon judges and procedural frameworks. The authority vested in judicial actors, grounded in the perceived reliability of scientific knowledge, has contributed to the persistence of inquisitorial tendencies within contemporary criminal justice. This dynamic warrants careful scrutiny, as it raises questions about the balance between epistemic ambition and humanitarian safeguards in criminal justice.

The modern paradigm conceptualises knowledge in ways that can be considered insufficient for addressing the nuanced complexities of reality. Employing this approach as a benchmark for truth within procedural settings may adversely affect the accused, as it enables inquisitorial epistemological methods to continue operating within proceedings that are nominally accusatorial.

While numerous scholars disregard the debate concerning the exhaustion of the modern scientific paradigm—often attributing it to what they broadly term the "irrationality of postmodernity"—the recognition of this paradigm's limitations is not a recent development and harkens back to the second half of the nineteenth century.

In this sense, an additional critique of Taruffo concerns his deliberate decision to omit in-depth analysis of complex topics, despite acknowledging their importance. This is particularly relevant to issues such as time and causality, which he references but refrains from examining extensively, observing that these areas involve philosophical and scientific debates with which he chooses not to engage. This methodological choice recurs throughout several subjects addressed in *Simply the Truth* (Taruffo 2010: 68).

The resulting epistemological framework offers a simplified perspective on issues within criminal justice, neglecting the pastness of the past, the importance of exclusionary rules, the need to uphold human rights and the nuanced experiences of individuals involved in criminal proceedings, which are inherently characterised by uncertainty.

Such omissions raise significant concerns regarding the adequacy of prevailing rationalist models for capturing the multifaceted nature of legal reality. The adoption of scientific standards, while offering a veneer of rationality, can inadvertently reinforce the authority of judges as truth-seekers, and perpetuate inquisitorial elements. This calls for a more reflective stance—one that embraces the plurality and contextual sensitivity required for justice, rather than defaulting to rigid epistemic ambitions inherited from modernity.

It is important to advance beyond reductive forms of scientism. As Gauer observes, "from the late nineteenth century to the present day, the debate concerning the theoretical limitations of science became central, particularly within the humanities" (Gauer 2006: 13). Consequently, this study maintains that it is no longer justifiable for an outdated model—one now reconsidered by the exact sciences, which have moved from strict precision towards embracing complexity—to continue as the dominant framework within the legal field. The continued reliance on such models is problematic due to the limited insights they produce and their diminished effectiveness in constraining punitive authority.

The current focus on the search for truth within contemporary criminal procedure, along with the confidence in judges' capacity to realise this objective, should be understood against the broader backdrop of modern scientific thought. Albeit based on fundamentally different assumptions, the intellectual developments characteristic of this period altered and redefined the approach to truth that was a central feature of the Inquisition.

According to Baumer's definition, "modern" does not pertain to recent advancements but rather to a distinct set of concepts and perspectives that emerged during the seventeenth century, thereby establishing a new worldview that has profoundly shaped European civilisation (Baumer 1977: 44–45).

The legal field maintains a strong commitment to the modern scientific paradigm—a framework that, despite no longer being adopted in its originating scientific disciplines, remains prevalent in legal scholarship not only due to epistemological considerations but also because it aligns closely with the aims of punitive authority.

Modernity is often praised as a victory for reason and enlightenment, marking the shift from religious knowledge to scientific thinking and establishing progress as a central value in shaping a new world. This view of progress connects to the concept of becoming, which suggests movement and change. Becoming challenges any fixed truths or eternal ideals by implying that everything is always developing into something different. According to Baumer, this focus on change and evolution is at the core of the modern mindset, setting it apart from the stability and permanence associated with the medieval perspective (Baumer 1977: 37–38).

Beginning in the seventeenth century, the transition from being to becoming was spurred by groundbreaking ideas that slowly gained traction, dramatically reshaping society. Baumer notes that, during this period, more educated individuals started to consider themselves as "Moderns", distinguished from the "Ancients". Even if they didn't use the specific term, they saw themselves as initiating something historically unprecedented, such as ushering in a new era of thought (Baumer 1977: 43).

This transition resulted in a significant shift in temporal orientation: the past was no longer revered but began to be regarded as something to surpass. The Moderns exhibited a pronounced disregard for tradition and placed strong confidence in the potential of future endeavours guided by science and rationality. Nevertheless, as Gauer observes,

> the scientists of that era, in seeking to understand cosmic phenomena independently of religious belief, did not prevent the sacralisation of a new belief, namely, belief in scientific "truth". Scientific truth consists of the set of laws developed by the moderns, with the primary function of regulating societies. In this rationalisation lies the intention to eliminate faith, myth, and beliefs in all events that could not be explained by scientific rationality. (Gauer 2009: 12)

In the seventeenth century, new ideas began to surface that would eventually drive sweeping changes to Europe's landscape and, because they were spread worldwide, influence the entire globe. These shifts stemmed from the development of a modern worldview, which challenged the traditional ways of understanding politics and society. This shift also led to major reforms in punishment practices across the Western world. This transformation holds particular significance for modern law, given that modern legal systems emerged directly from this process—acquiring their respective advantages and intrinsic constraints.

Baumer explains that the rise of a new world system, as described by Galileo, gradually replaced Greco-Christian theory. This shift, accelerated by events like the Crusades, Columbus's discovery, and especially the realisation that Earth is not the universe's centre, significantly challenged the medieval worldview. Philosophical shifts led to a new European worldview, replacing the medieval vision of nature as controlled by a Creator with one of self-sustaining processes. Thinkers like Copernicus, Galileo, Descartes, Bacon, and Spinoza contributed to viewing the universe as a machine or clock that functions independently after its creation, contrasting with earlier beliefs that required continual divine intervention (Baumer 1977). The modern worldview marks a clear break from the ancient perspective: nature used to be seen as guided by purpose, but modernity treats it as a machine governed by fixed laws. This shift led to a mathematical interpretation of the world, as Galileo described the universe as a book written in mathematical language (Baumer 1977: 68).

The drive for uniformity through scientific laws arose during Europe's major religious conflicts, to restore order and stability. Newton's system succeeded by offering movement governed by permanent natural laws, reflecting modern thought's aim for universal truths and diminishing plurality. Science gradually displaced theology, leading to secularisation in the eighteenth and nineteenth centuries and promising, at least theoretically, the replacement of inquisitorial punishment with more limited power structures.

Modern innovations set boundaries and enabled the secularisation of punitive practices, marking progress. However, inquisitorial methods remained, though secularised. Punitive power persisted through these changes and adapted to new foundations despite efforts to restrict it. Ultimately, science did not create a utopia, as it soon became intertwined with political power.

The most significant development in seventeenth-century intellectual history was the emergence of a new conception of knowledge—one that quickly gained acceptance as true—which fundamentally shifted the focus from contemplation to utility. As Baumer observes, "this utilitarian perspective was at odds with the traditional conceptions of knowledge, Aristotelian and Augustinian, which emphasised knowledge or wisdom in itself" (Baumer 1977: 48). As knowledge became associated with practical use, it started to take on an instrumental role, reflecting a drive for control and eventually transforming the idea of knowledge as liberation into a source of new oppression. Baumer points out that "among scientists and natural philosophers, the focus was more on power—the feeling of authority their novel ideas and methods provided" (Baumer 1977: 77).

In addition to the authority exercised by those controlling scientific and philosophical discourse, modern science was employed in the service of destruction, facilitating the development of more efficient and expedited methods for eliminating diversity—whether among populations rendered vulnerable by emerging capitalism, colonial and neocolonial dominance, or ongoing ecological harm. Accordingly, Gauer (2004) observes that "a knowledge that was intended to be utilitarian and functional ended up being recognised less for its capacity to deeply understand the 'real' than for its ability to transform and dominate it".

The capacity to arbitrarily establish truths was integral to this framework. This reconceptualisation of knowledge not only corresponded with, but also enhanced, confidence in the investigative and inquisitorial authority vested in judges. As a result, such investigatory powers continued to exist even after the dissolution of the Inquisition. The emergence of discursive and argumentative methods in the seventeenth century, founded on scientific principles, offered additional rationales for the exercise of punitive authority within legal proceedings. Ultimately, the production of hierarchical truths remained indispensable to the maintenance of power, as it facilitated the regulation and formation of individuals according to prescribed standards, thereby ensuring the preservation of the existing social order. For Foucault,

> we must admit that power produces knowledge (and not simply by encouraging it because it serves power or by applying it because it is useful); that power and knowledge are directly implicated; that there is no power relation without the correlative constitution of a field of knowledge, nor knowledge that does not presuppose and simultaneously constitute "power-knowledge" relations. (Foucault 2008: 27)

This dynamic of interaction is integral to certain conceptions of knowledge; power is present within domains of knowledge and truth beyond inquisitorial forms alone. As Foucault observes, "even in science we find models of truth whose formation reveals political structures that are not imposed externally upon the subject of knowledge but are themselves constitutive of the subject of knowledge" (Foucault 2003: 27). Foucault further references Nietzsche, noting that "behind all knowledge, all cognition, what is at stake is a struggle for power. Political power is not absent from knowledge; it is interwoven with knowledge" (Foucault 2003: 51). Thus, Foucault contends that the possible forms and fields of knowledge are determined by the processes and contests that traverse and constitute power-knowledge (Foucault 2008: 27).

The relationship between power and knowledge is deeply interconnected. Knowledge and power do not exist separately; rather, as modern criminal law emerged, it was shaped by powerful strategies that directed its creation, language, and legal development—it was not simply used by those in authority to maintain control. This close connection meant that legal-criminal mechanisms were formed alongside power, often pushing safeguards and procedural protections into the background. In essence, the pursuit of truth stayed largely unchanged, and the system retained many inquisitorial traits, some of which are still present today.

In this regard, modern thought has imparted a legacy to contemporary criminal procedure that is doubly problematic: firstly, by legitimising authoritarian practices through the attribution of scientific authority; secondly, by employing methods that significantly oversimplify reality, thereby disregarding its inherent complexity in favour of an imposed—or intended—homogeneity. Vattimo (1980: 13) observes that the modern era fostered a mode of thinking characterised by unifying, sovereign, and generalising categories. The author argues that the comprehensive system of cause-and-effect, anticipated within metaphysical worldviews and actualised through technological means, represents an underlying will to dominate (Vattimo 1980: 96).

The authoritarian tendencies of power perpetuated the violent nature of inquisitorial truth, characterised by an intent to eliminate divergence. Conversely, modern thought introduced the concept of legality, which marked a notable, though limited, advancement in restricting punitive authority. Accordingly, the history of punitive practices should not be viewed solely as a linear progression towards humanisation; the modern process of reform is inherently ambiguous, despite prevailing narratives of continuous social development.

As the pace of change continued to quicken, progress emerged as a central idea in modern thinking. This concept offered Europeans the chance to comprehend and exert influence over their surroundings, with the promise of building what was described as an earthly paradise. As Gauer notes,

> modern science linked the investigation of the forces of nature to their usefulness in benefiting humanity. The scientific field came to be conceived as a possibility for progress and, through it (progress), the definitive and total emancipation of humanity—still submerged in the Platonic world of shadows—was envisaged. The civilisation of the Enlightenment spread across all continents; from Europe came progress, and the sciences advanced in England, Germany, and other countries. (Gauer 2009: 46)

Baumer states that Bacon envisioned a scientific era empowering humanity to control the world, shifting focus from human flaws to capability (Baumer 1977: 108). Modern thought redefined humans as rational beings; Galileo supported the limitless potential of human intellect and anticipated advances in understanding nature (Baumer 1977: 114). Gauer further notes,

> movements such as the Reformation and Protestantism freed individual conscience from religious institutions and the church, placing the individual directly under the eyes of God. Humanism placed man at the centre of the universe, and the scientific revolutions made the individual a decipherer of the mysteries of nature. The Enlightenment, in turn, endowed man with a rationalism detached from subjectivism; this rational individual,

> freed from dogma and intolerance, had before him the entirety of human history to be mastered. (Gauer 2009: 39–40)

The seventeenth century is often regarded as the first modern century; during this period, individuals increasingly distinguished themselves from their predecessors, and approaches to understanding and interpreting the world underwent significant transformation. As Baumer observes, “Descartes was a modern who disregarded the philosophical systems of the past, Aristotelian or Scholastic, a defender of the science of Galileo” (Baumer 1977: 56). Nevertheless, Descartes pursued order and clarity, culminating in the establishment of “rules” and “principles”—the central themes of his major works—to structure both thought and the universe (Baumer 1977: 56). Thus, the conviction in a stable universe remained prevalent, albeit occasionally manifesting in new forms, such as Cartesianism or Newtonianism (Baumer 1977: 58). According to Gauer,

> the creation of the paradigm of modernity, whose foundation lies in the work of Descartes, enabled the emergence of dualism: body-mind, persons and things, lawful and unlawful, objectivity and subjectivity, reason and emotion. In this way, the entire structure of modern thought was established, which fostered the belief in the possibility of pursuing perfection. This pursuit, however, was ultimately hindered by the very conception of the apprehension of reason. (Gauer 2009: 40)

When considered in this manner, the binary framework underlying modern thought becomes apparent: it is a structure that tends towards the simplification of reality and overlooks its intrinsic complexity. Modern thought operates through a binary lens and—despite assertions regarding the boundless capacity of reason—such an approach remains fundamentally simplistic, irrespective of any apparent sophistication. As Lovejoy observes,

> thus, for two centuries, the efforts made to improve and correct beliefs, institutions, and art were, in general, governed by the assumption that, at every stage of his activity, man should conform as closely as possible to a standard conceived as universal, uncomplicated, immutable, and uniform for every rational being. The Enlightenment was, in short, an era dedicated, at least in its dominant tendency, to the simplification and standardisation of thought and life—its standardisation through simplification. (Lovejoy 2005: 290)

The removal of religious categories from thought processes that came to be regarded as neutral, objective, and impartial did not address their fundamental problems; rather, it may have exacerbated them. By concentrating on the development of closed, self-referential systems, there was a propensity to disregard reality, replacing it with the internal consistency of these conceptual frameworks. While the modern understanding is frequently labelled as "universal" it ultimately serves as merely a representation of humanity, rather than its authentic nature—and a highly selective one, as the only individual considered rational is the white European male. Other cultures were not regarded as legitimate: they were thought to generate merely curiosities and exoticism, rather than knowledge (Khaled Jr and Morrison 2024).

As ideas about humanity evolved, religion gradually lost influence in the seventeenth century. A divide emerged between those who believed God created the world but no longer intervened, and those who thought divine providence guided history—a view that was becoming less credible. These different beliefs shaped very distinct perspectives on the penal system. Viewing the universe as a machine or clock opened the door to moving past the inquisitorial model, questioning the religious dogma at its core. In this way, modern thinking offered subversive potential and marked a moment of openness, even if it was only partly achieved during the shift towards the Rule of Law.

Baumer argues that the scientific revolution introduced the belief in consistent natural laws and encouraged critical views towards past intellectual achievements (Baumer 1977: 152). New scientific approaches, such as those of Bacon and Descartes, led people to see the present as more knowledgeable than the past, fuelling the Moderns' sense of superiority over the Ancients (Baumer 1977: 153). This shift implied a new confidence in discovering truth, once reserved for theology, with reason now seen as the primary tool for solving human problems. Foucault observes that Western philosophy began to place the subject at the centre of all knowledge, linking freedom and truth to individual reasoning (Foucault 2003: 10).

Descartes' *Discourse on the Method* presents his approach to reasoning and scientific truth, combining elements of logic, geometry, and algebra to form a method that arguably retains their strengths without their flaws. He recommends only accepting ideas that are completely clear and distinct, breaking knowledge into manageable parts, and advancing from simple to complex concepts to ensure nothing is missed. Descartes highlights that mathematicians alone have achieved true demonstrations, appreciating that his method applies reason universally (Descartes 2008: 24–27).

Nevertheless, notwithstanding Descartes' philosophical convictions, his purported division between subject and object ultimately led to the ascendancy of the subject, thereby rendering the external world voiceless in this monologue, as noted by Octavio Paz (Paz 1977: 97). Foucault notes that "Descartes established a somewhat sacred priority of the subject in Western thought" (Foucault 2003: 10), and Gauer agrees, suggesting that since Descartes, dialogue has become overly focused on the subject (Gauer 2004: 6). Lenio Streck further argues that the term subject itself shifted, with the subject now "subjecting" things—this is what he calls the subject-object scheme, where reason is used to explain and justify the world (Streck 2010: 13). The procedural model based on the syncretism of contradictory paradigms (Streck 2023), which underpins the assumption of the judge's omnipotence, still endures because it continues to sustain the search for truth in contemporary criminal justice. It has persisted for so long precisely due to its simplicity—that is, because it employs the very model of thought (par excellence) of Western civilisation (Coutinho 2018: 117).

There was no real separation between subject and object; the subject imposed meaning externally. Scientific certainty became much like an inquisitorial judge's preference for hypotheses over facts, and these approaches combined into a procedural system promising truth. This model ignored the hidden complexity beneath apparent clarity, assuming rational observers could illuminate all ambiguities.

Although reliance on reason in modern thought represented progress compared to the religious dogmatism underlying inquisitorial practices, it introduced new complexities. Over time, excessive confidence in rationality developed into another form of dogma—specifically, nineteenth-century scientism—which, alongside the so-called mixed system, diminished legal protections in favour of preserving a new *status quo*. Consequently, it is inaccurate to interpret history as a linear progression from ignorance to enlightenment. The rational methodology aimed at discovering the truth has proven to be harmful to human rights, regardless of its theoretical and epistemological distinctions from inquisitorial structures, maintaining the propensity for the objectification of the accused.

As previously discussed, although modern criminal law demonstrated significant strengths in limiting punitive authority, evolving demands for social control over emerging threats to the *status quo* ultimately influenced the formation of a hybrid procedural system—the so-called mixed system. This development was legitimised through a new form of dogmatism—scientific dogmatism—which had been evolving since the seventeenth century. Consequently, the epistemology of truth-seeking became increasingly aligned with scientific paradigms derived from the natural sciences. As Gauer (2004: 1) observes, in modernity, the connection between knowledge and the Galilean-Newtonian model, and the privileging of science as the principal means for revealing truth, established a vital framework within Western intellectual tradition. Under this scientific paradigm, the concept of truth was redefined according to the adequacy between object and rational judgement, as outlined by Descartes, thereby fostering an ambition for "the verification of a new truth, precisely that dictated by science" (Gauer 2004: 1). In summary, religious dogmatism was supplanted by a new form rooted in scientific knowledge, wherein science began to assume an authoritative role reminiscent of religious doctrine, ultimately taking on responsibilities traditionally reserved for theological discourse—being chief among them, the revelation of truth.

In nineteenth-century science, truth was not just a goal but an unquestionable belief. Gauer notes that scientists' pursuit of understanding turned scientism into a quasi-religion, treating scientific methodology as the route to truth (Gauer 2004: 1). Ricoeur describes scientism as science's methodological aim elevated to a claim—that science assumes a role akin to religious salvation (Ricoeur 1968: 199).

A pronounced emphasis on truth is a defining trait of Western civilisation, rooted in the foundational developments of the nineteenth-century scientific paradigm. The transition from religiosity to scientific thought shifted explanatory authority from religious institutions to the emerging value system of scientific rationality. This evolution marked a departure from the historic alignment between Church and Absolutist State—represented by clergy and nobility—to a new association between the scientific community and the secular Liberal State, which advanced the interests of the burgeoning bourgeoisie amid capitalist expansion. Scientific rationality functioned as an effective instrument for legitimising authority, becoming an integrated component of social and political organisation and, in turn, influencing the progression of scientific knowledge.

The modern scientific paradigm, modelled after the natural sciences, promised that a rigorous method applied to clearly defined subjects would yield verifiable truths and ultimately create an ideal society through reason

(Gauer 2006: 75–76). This view fostered the idea of progress and a future better than the present. Gauer describes this paradigm's main trait as a "will to truth"—linking reality, truth, visibility, universality, and immutability (Gauer 2004: 8–9). Modern science established methods based on notions of absolute truth, viewing knowledge as universal and eternal. Its foundation—experimentation, objectivity, neutrality, and generalisation—shapes both scientific and legal thinking. Experimentation emphasised technique, while objectivity reinforced claims of neutrality in science and law (Gauer 2006: 9).

Scientism reinforced a dominant paradigm of truth that served as a tool for power and the emerging bourgeois order. After gaining control, the new elite focused on creating mechanisms to justify and legitimise their authority, including establishing and regulating truths. Foucault argues that truth is inseparable from power and shaped by systems of dominance, with science gaining authority through these dynamics and truth defined by the rules set within such power structures (Foucault 2002: 12–13).

The rise of scientism and the transformation of truth into a tool for legitimising authority marked a profound shift in the intellectual landscape of modernity. Scientific discourse, once seen as merely a method for understanding nature, became deeply entwined with the mechanisms of power and governance. This entanglement meant that the pursuit of truth in criminal procedure was shaped by, and served, the interests of the emerging bourgeois class and the secular state. The scientific paradigm provided a framework that justified social control and regulatory practices, while simultaneously reinforcing the values and ambitions of those in positions of authority.

The modern secular view of history suggests that progress aims to build an ideal city shaped by rationality rather than divine purpose (Gauer 2004: 3). This vision serves the interests of those in power. As Gauer notes, after the eighteenth century, the philosophy of history increasingly centred on scientific progress as a replacement for Christian teleology (Gauer 2004: 2–3). Science was regarded not simply as an abstract theoretical discussion, but as a practical means of directly engaging with reality to achieve objectives valued by emerging ruling groups. This shift from contemplation to active intervention is fundamental to the modern conception of the world.

However, to prevent any misinterpretation, it is essential to clarify that this does not constitute an anachronistic critique of modernity; nineteenth-century science, much like any other text, is inherently tied to its time. Its development was shaped by specific economic, political, social, and cultural conditions. As Chartier notes, "What is real, in fact, is not only the reality targeted by the text, but the very manner in which it targets it, in the historicity of its production and in the strategy of its culture" (Chartier 2002: 56).

The guiding principles of that era aligned with the prevailing scientific understanding of the 19th century and addressed the interests of those in authority, leading to their incorporation into the developing criminal justice system.

Nevertheless, ongoing reliance on an epistemological framework rooted in former realities remains problematic, as it disregards significant advancements in science and philosophy. More importantly, this persistence overlooks the imperative for political and epistemological reform towards a model centred on human rights protection.

The search for truth is closely linked with forms of political authoritarianism that have historically contributed to social injustice and with early stage scientific approaches intended to legitimise emerging political and social structures. In this context, the search for truth functioned primarily as an instrument for legitimising, securing, and promoting authority in service of early capitalism elites—whether intentionally or unintentionally. Consequently, reformist ideologies that initially sought openness were often redirected to serve the consolidating powers, becoming mechanisms for reinforcing established power dynamics through direct intervention in societal realities. This transformation is evident in classical thought, particularly within Bentham's philosophy, which departed from formalism and legal safeguards in favour of evidentiary anti-formalism and search for truth—a position largely at odds with the humanitarian principles advanced by Beccaria (Khaled Jr and Morrison 2024).

Legal Positivism, Syllogism, and Mere Finding of Facts

By the late eighteenth century, the longstanding conflict between Ancients and Moderns was fading, leading to major shifts in political structure and power dynamics, with scientific discourse playing a key role. Modernity promised a rational, progressive society and secularisation offered a move away from punitive traditions towards regulated, less harmful systems. However, this ideal was not realised; inquisitorial epistemology soon re-emerged, reinforced and renewed by the Cartesian subject-object framework.

By the early nineteenth century, revolutionary enthusiasm had faded, and Napoleon took power to restore order and support the new ruling class. Law became a central means of regulating society, leading to more legislation, most notably the introduction of the *Code d'instruction criminelle* in 1808. This period marked a turn towards repression under the guise of security, ending post-Revolution accusatorial procedures and reducing legal protections.

> Modernity created this compulsion, this irresistible desire, for order and security. The perfect world, the utopia of the Enlightenment thinkers, would be entirely clean and self-identical, transparent and free from contamination. The rationality expressed through conventions and laws aimed to immunise society against violence, corruption, the seduction of beliefs, and other impurities. The moderns forgot, however, that there would be no immunity against selfishness, nihilism, and the exploitation of a vast number of human beings. (Gauer 2009: 85–86)

This topic explores how scientificity, positivism, and a renewed pursuit of truth became linked in nineteenth-century criminal procedure. While legal positivism did not originate from inquisitorial motives, its alignment with the search for truth has, and still can, elevate it—sometimes misleadingly—under claims of neutrality.

Support for an inquisitorial approach was strengthened by the philosophy of consciousness and early positivist reasoning. This alignment legitimised potentially harmful legal practices, linking prosecutorial strategies with what Ferrajoli named paleopositivism—an influence that persists today and warrants re-examination. Lenio Streck also highlights the connection between the inquisitorial system and the philosophy of consciousness (Streck 2010: 32).

It's important to remember that, while the inquisitorial pursuit of truth suited the dominant regime, simply reverting to the mindset of the seventeenth-century Criminal Ordinances was not an option. Instead, punitive practices needed to be presented as scientific, suggesting they balanced prosecution interests with citizens' rights—a goal that fit well within the early nineteenth-century legal-scientific discourse. As a result, legal positivism—and its focus on scientific principles—ultimately supported the ongoing use of inquisitorial punishment, updating it rhetorically for the new era while preserving its central aim of uncovering the truth.

During the nineteenth century, scientific standards began to influence every discipline, introducing clear methods and objectives for acquiring knowledge. The field of law aimed to embrace these standards as well, seeking to gain the credibility and authority associated with science. Morin observes that separability was one of the central concepts underpinning modern science; as Descartes noted, addressing complex problems requires breaking them down into smaller, manageable components (Morin 1996: 240).

This principle led to the emergence of scientific disciplines through a systematic fragmentation of reality, resulting in independent spheres of inquiry and a gradual divergence between science and philosophy—a trend that continued well into the twentieth century as a justified development (Morin 1996: 240). The evolution of modern law was notably influenced by this process, which sought to eliminate elements that could impede its perceived scientific rigour.

Modern law's connection with scientific principles stems largely from positivism, which distinguishes positive law from natural law—a concept traced back to Greek philosophy. The emergence of positive law enabled civil law's integration into nineteenth-century models, leading to codification efforts aimed at enhancing legal predictability and certainty, as noted by Bobbio (1999: 21) and Carvalho (2008: 35).

Positive law aimed to create a clear, objective legal framework that minimised interpretation and reduced unpredictability. By insisting on strict adherence to the letter of the law, predictability and legal certainty were prioritised. Influenced by thinkers like Montesquieu and Beccaria, this approach distrusted judge-made law due to past abuses, resulting in limits on judicial discretion and the eventual codification of law.

Although humanitarian considerations played a role in this intellectual development, legal positivism advanced a state-centred interpretation of law, prioritising legislative authority and de-emphasising alternative sources such as customary or natural law. This led to France's exegesis school, later criticised for its rigid reliance on statutes and assumption that the *Code de Napoléon* addressed all cases, treating law as a complete, gapless system.

The concept that a legal system can be complete is closely tied to the idea of law as a science: precise, unchanging, and exact—a reflection of the mathematical ideal at the heart of this way of thinking. According to Carvalho, codification is seen as the Enlightenment's dream, aiming for a perfectly structured system without gaps, inconsistencies, or contradictions, which represents the ultimate *ratio iuris* (Carvalho 2008: 36). Yet, this paradigm has significant shortcomings—positivism's belief in a completely flawless legal order is one of its biggest misconceptions. As Carvalho comments, "few things demonstrate the narcissism of jurists more than insisting that the legal system is a *complete and coherent* entity, where gaps and conflicts are only apparent and easily resolved" (Carvalho 2006: 40).

Given the emphasis on achieving intrasystemic coherence within the emerging field of knowledge to ensure its scientific integrity, the systematic elimination of unpredictability was unsurprising. Consequently, complexities inherent in the process of judicial decision-making were discursively excluded from the framework, with legal application addressed through a simplified epistemology that overlooks the nuances of reality and consciousness in favour of maintaining internal consistency within legal discourse. As Bobbio observes, from the positivist perspective,

> the legal procedure would consist solely of a finding of fact (that is, ensuring that the facts provided for by law are verified), since the law would become so clear that the *questio juris* (namely, the determination of the legal norm to be applied in the case at hand) would present no difficulty, as all the legal questions traditionally involved in judgement (and which required the intervention of legal experts) were exclusively the result of the multiplicity and irrational complication of laws. (Bobbio 1999: 67)

In the nineteenth century, the modern regulatory approach to law reached its zenith, shaped by an *esprit géométrique* that prioritised normativity over empirical reality. In this context, doubts arising in legal cases were often addressed by appealing to the legislator's intent, conceived as a *deus ex-machina* capable of resolving any perceived gaps within the system. This framework reinforced the notion of the judge as a "mere mouthpiece of the law" refraining from subjective interpretation and reducing factual issues to neutral determination by a rational evaluator, thereby promoting certainty and predictability in judicial decisions. The reliance on mere fact-finding reflects a conception of truth as correspondence—aligned with Cartesian rationalism—which emphasises the straightforward and accurate assessment of reality, coupled with the application of legal norms by the rational subject. According to Ferrajoli, truth as correspondence underlies Enlightenment conceptions of jurisdiction as fact-finding and the image of the judge as the law's mouthpiece (Ferrajoli 2002: 41).

Classical legal positivism treats law as a closed system focused on norms and their application, often overlooking real-world context. In this view, legal decisions are seen as syllogistic conclusions: judges simply apply laws to facts without introducing new reasoning, aiming for consistency and predictability. Beccaria encapsulated this by arguing that judges should strictly follow the law's premises—general and specific—without personal interpretation, to avoid uncertainty (Beccaria 2003: 22).

Coutinho mocks the thinking structured around syllogistic premises, stating that "in the end, everything is reduced to *syllogisms*, often without any *meaning*; or, what is much worse, they categorically provide 'the' meaning" (Coutinho 2002: 180). It was not only reality that was forgotten, but also everything that makes the judge a being-in-the-world. For Coutinho, it is pretended that subjectivity does not exist, or rather, its existence, when admitted, is considered to be under total control through motivated free conviction. The judge is generally presented as a robot, a transparent being through whom the "will" of the law flows; and some, in all seriousness, truly believe that he possesses it. The human being is almost entirely ignored, in an extraordinary effort to instil in him—and in all of us—the awareness that his function is to mirror a will that is not his own (Coutinho 1998: 139).

Consequently, Western legal thought, founded on the philosophy of consciousness, reason, and methodologies derived from the natural sciences, has largely overlooked the role of historical context and subjectivity in human existence. This oversight has contributed to enduring challenges that continue to significantly influence legal practice today. According to Coutinho,

> We are confronted with a significant distortion of reality; ultimately, this kind of unsettling positivism—often favoured by authoritarian governments and their supporters, even among us—works to legitimize the current state of affairs, sometimes at the cost of disregarding the individual. The individual often feels lost and finds no answers to their questions, not because of malice, but usually due to unconsciousness, ignorance, or a form of knowledge that leads elsewhere: if the law's will prevails, the judge's intentions become irrelevant. There is little discussion about this, or its impact,

> which can be severe and deeply troubling, especially for those who recognise that our world is made up of human beings—something greater than just physical objects—and is not simply mechanical in nature. (Coutinho 1998: 139)

The failure to acknowledge subjectivity in decision-making is tied to the idea of scientific objectivity. The positivist approach overlooks factors like consciousness, language, and the judge's perspective, treating law application as simply matching a norm to objective facts—a process described as mere finding of fact—and neglecting the complexities of reconstructing historical events. According to Lopes Jr., it is

> clear that it is not a mere matter of fitting the fact to the norm. This activity is permeated by a series of variables of an axiological nature, inherent to the specific subjectivity of the decision-making act, not least because every reconstruction of a historical fact is tainted by contamination arising from the very selective activity involved. (Lopes Jr 2005: 266)

The logic of the syllogism, when based solely on mere factual findings, reflects the scientific model typical of the *ésprit géométrique*, which is generally seen as objective, impartial, and devoid of values. This approach defines positivist law: a system where norms are applied hierarchically and their validity stems simply from their origin in the State—a concept Ferrajoli refers to as mere legality.

While this perspective on decision-making has become widespread, it offers little insight into how decisions unfold. According to Morais da Rosa, Beccaria's view was that truth mirrors reality (Rosa 2006: 142). For Ferrajoli, however, Beccaria's portrayal of the judge as an unbiased seeker of truth is quite naive (Ferrajoli 2002: 46). Ferrajoli argues that to truly grasp how procedural truth is accepted, one must examine judicial reasoning, which is about applying the law and does not even formally fit the logical structure of the "perfect syllogism" that Beccaria and formalist Scholasticism envisioned (Ferrajoli 2002: 52). Taruffo points out that every legal rule, even those that seem least ambiguous, must be interpreted; therefore, identifying the legal prerequisite always involves interpretative work (Taruffo 2010: 225). Ferrajoli believes that the basic epistemological realism supporting the Enlightenment image of judges as mere "mouthpieces of the law" is clearly outdated and untrustworthy today (Ferrajoli 2002: 39). He notes that the Enlightenment idea of a perfect "correspondence" between legal rules and real events, and of verdicts as mechanically applying the law, is philosophically naive and influenced by metaphysical realism (Ferrajoli 2002: 39). Still, Ferrajoli suggests we can preserve its theoretical and political significance if—and only if—we redefine it as a limiting model: something never fully achievable but rather an ideal that can be approached, especially if we clarify the circumstances under which it may be more or less satisfied (Ferrajoli 2002: 39).

Nevertheless, the assertion that the correspondence theory of truth can operate as a limiting factor does not withstand historical analysis. Historically and presently, the correspondence concept of truth has functioned as a foundational principle legitimising the judicial pursuit of truth.

In the particular historical context in which it was first implemented, this procedural structure was primarily designed to reinforce mechanisms of social control. As a result, the criteria adopted often led to the marginalisation of lived realities within criminal law, with significant adverse effects. The integration of inquisitorial principles with positivist methodologies and scientistic reasoning has produced, and continues to produce, detrimental outcomes for punitive practices. This environment allows analytical experimentation to generate a distorted form of truth that subtly perpetuates inquisitorial logic. Consequently, reducing "facts" to what can be readily processed by methodological frameworks creates conditions in which inquisitorial epistemologies of truth-seeking are revived and accusatorial principles are undermined. It is not coincidental that procedural stages have become performances aimed at affirming initial investigative outcomes. This synthesis causes the epistemological perspective to oscillate between factual objectivism and subjective consciousness—supporting the doctrine of judicial free conviction (Streck 2023)—and ultimately sustains the continued pursuit of inquisitorial truth that reaffirms the selectivity of secondary criminalisation.

The proceedings are structured to facilitate the pursuit of truth, with factual determinations made by the judge rather than being subject to the parties' control over evidence characteristic of accusatorial systems. While codified law may impose certain constraints on judicial discretion, inquisitorial practices persist, granting judges significant authority in matters of fact and enabling considerable decision-making latitude. As a result, principles such as predictability and legal certainty frequently led to an emphasis on securing convictions. The framework is designed to address individuals identified as threats to society through punitive measures, under the guiding objective of uncovering truth. This methodology is justified through the rhetoric of scientific objectivity in the assessment of facts—portraying legal application as a formal syllogism that ostensibly guarantees neutrality. Accordingly, the judge, often described as the "mouthpiece of the law", essentially serves as the administrator of a system characterised by authoritative social regulation.

Although this paradigm has faced well-founded criticism, it effectively served its prosecutorial purpose. Remarkably, it still influences legal practice and the judiciary in much of Latin America (Carvalho 2008: 36). Its structure maintains the inquisitorial pursuit of truth and supports a discursive-normative framework that enables arbitrary punitive power.

Modern reforms, grounded in scientific rationale, have reinvigorated inquisitorial principles and imparted an air of legitimacy to procedures fundamentally inquisitorial in character. This epistemological framework has maintained its veiled emphasis on confirmation of hypotheses rather than empirical facts and has seldom regarded accusatorial principles as the prevailing standard.

As Morais da Rosa observes, "the 'paranoid' structure in criminal procedure appears subtly, as it is concealed by ordered rhetorical devices, both in the adoption of an inquisitorial stance in the management of evidence and in the interpretation of conduct" (Rosa 2006: 316). As further noted by Lopes Jr.,

> the truth in criminal proceedings is inaccessible, but, aware of this, (they) construct a framework that must legitimise submission to power by asserting that the judgment and the judge are bearers of the revelation of the sacred (truth). This is the device we can no longer tolerate, for it is also designed to deny subjectivity and all the various psychological factors that affect the act of judging, persisting in the dream world of a judge who is otherworldly, neutral, the mouthpiece of the law, etc. (Lopes Jr 2010: 541)

The criminal procedural system built by Napoleon was designed to increase social control. Though reform movements and the French Revolution suggested a shift to an accusatorial model inspired by English law, the Napoleonic regime's need for control reversed this change. As scientific discourse merged with political objectives, legal standards began prioritising rationality and the systematic pursuit of absolute truth. Judicial practices soon followed Cartesian principles, leading to the return of inquisitorial methods in criminal proceedings, now legitimised by secular norms.

The epistemological framework underpinning criminal proceedings did not adequately account for the ramifications associated with the construction of "truth". While positivist methodologies systematically relied on factual determinations, truth frequently emerged as an assumption established during preliminary phases and later confirmed, rather than as an objective outcome derived from empirical reality and relevant norms. Within the positivist tradition, truth was seldom considered a prominent concern, reflecting a fundamental reliance on the judge's capacity to analytically evaluate factual accuracy and scientifically apply appropriate legal standards. The procedures employed to establish facts subject to codified law were rarely contested, nor were ontological inquiries introduced regarding the portrayal of historical events. Additionally, prevailing scientific dogmatism discouraged philosophical or interpretative exploration, as such perspectives were regarded as lacking scientific validity and believed to hinder access to substantive truths.

The positivist model is recognised as a framework derived from the natural sciences, characterised by its mechanistic methodology that tends to oversimplify intricate phenomena, thereby omitting complexity within cognitive processes. The integration of the positivist paradigm, philosophy of consciousness, and inquisitorial epistemology established a system primarily utilised for social regulation and coercion, which contrasts with the humanitarian principles envisaged by eighteenth-century reformers regarding the regulated application of punitive authority. Significantly, criminal sciences persist in upholding the epistemological logic of positivism and remain committed to the pursuit of truth. As observed by Carvalho,

> the procedural criminal dogmatics of the twentieth century followed the general programme of the modern sciences, adapting itself to the Cartesian ideal. After the break with the confessional system and the secular staging to maintain the fundamental principles of inquisitorialism, under renewed inspiration it projected as the purpose of the nascent science (criminal procedural dogmatics) the creation of mechanisms for the pursuit of truth. Criminal proceedings thus became the laboratory in which historical reality, through the instruments of evidentiary procedure, would be adapted to the judge's decision. (Carvalho 2008: 77)

With few exceptions—most notably Goldschmidt—early twentieth-century criminal procedural dogmatics has typically concentrated on defending prosecutorial methods shaped by legislation influenced by the 1808 *Code d'instruction criminelle*. As previously mentioned, this code reinstated the inquisitorial search for truth. In Brazil, much of the scholarship on legal procedure is based on the explanatory memorandum of the 1941 Code of Criminal Procedure, often repeating its technical flaws (Lopes Jr 2010: 328). More troubling than these mistakes is the field's tendency to focus on infra-constitutional legislation and prosecutorial priorities rather than its proper role: limiting the state's punitive power and safeguarding human rights, as mandated by both the Constitution and international treaties.

Achieving progress in criminal justice requires a reassessment of concepts that have historically justified punitive practices and a reimagining of justice aligned with democratic-constitutional principles. Over the past decade, significant scholarly contributions, including those by Jacinto Nelson de Miranda Coutinho, Geraldo Prado, Aury Lopes Jr., and Alexandre Morais da Rosa, have advanced this endeavour. The adoption of a procedural dogmatics that avoids perpetuating the violence inherent in prevailing discourses is essential to fostering the possibility of moving beyond the inquisitorial paradigm that continues to influence judicial practice. As Salo de Carvalho notes, "aside from the narcissism of penal dogmatics in establishing the conditions for attaining truth, it is crucial to consider the consequences arising from the very definition of this goal" (Carvalho 2008: 74).

The persistence of inquisitorial logic within criminal procedure underscores the enduring complexity of legal epistemology. Despite the emergence of reformist ideologies and the gradual incorporation of scientific rationality, the foundations of punitive practice remain deeply rooted in inquisitorial traditions that privilege the judge's interpretative authority and the systematic confirmation of hypotheses. This has resulted in a legal landscape where the search for truth is less an objective endeavour and more an exercise shaped by established power structures and discursive strategies.

Therefore, any genuine advancement in criminal justice must involve not merely technical modifications to procedure, but a fundamental re-examination of the conceptual frameworks that underpin the administration of criminal justice. By interrogating the nature and consequences of truth-seeking within criminal proceedings, it becomes possible to challenge the legacy of authoritarianism and move towards a system that prioritises the limitation of punitive power and the protection of human rights. Such an approach demands openness to interdisciplinary perspectives, inviting dialogue between legal theory and other fields of knowledge to foster a more nuanced and humane conception of justice. Accordingly, I intend to outline and elaborate upon this approach in the subsequent section.

Challenging the Established Principles and Accepted Truths of Modern Science

Ideally, the transition from an explicitly inquisitorial system—where the inquisitor establishes the truth—would have led to the implementation of an accusatorial model defined by adversarial proceedings and limited state authority, reflecting political and epistemological shifts towards greater respect for human rights. However, this evolution did not materialise; despite changes in foundational principles, the dynamic between knowledge and power remained essentially unchanged. The revised framework for criminal procedure was primarily oriented towards preserving social order rather than safeguarding the rights of the accused.

While the foundational pursuit of truth in criminal proceedings initially seemed at odds with the shifting social, political, and scientific landscapes of the era, it was subsequently reinterpreted to reinforce the judge's enduring cognitive authority. The commitment to truth-seeking persisted as an essential mechanism for social regulation, now justified by an emerging scientific doctrine that lent further legitimacy to institutional power. Furthermore, it is notable that Enlightenment thought, which originally enabled the rise of the bourgeois elite, gradually lost much of its humanistic emphasis as its significance to the new dominant class diminished.

Thus, it's not sufficient to focus solely on the internal logic of a discourse; one must also account for its practical effects. When theory was translated into practice, the model became noticeably distorted—not by chance, but according to what benefited the emerging power structure. In this light, modernity is inherently ambiguous. The modern era is filled with contradictions: it claims to restrict power yet also justifies persecuting enemies and enhances inquisitorial ways of thinking with new tools. Put simply, regarding criminal procedures and punitive measures, the shift was less substantial than expected. What was meant to be an objective, neutral, fair, and non-interpretive system supported dogmatic notions of truth intertwined with aspirations for greater social control.

It is reasonable to state that the ideology of progress and the discourse regarding the enemy—central elements of modern thought—were instrumental in legitimising numerous acts of violence. Most modern intellectuals either explicitly supported colonialism or downplayed its violent aspects, as illustrated by Hobbes, Locke, Montesquieu, Beccaria, and others (Khaled Jr and Morrison 2024). The punitive practices associated with Nazi fascism were, to a significant extent, enabled by the ideology of progress—criminal law was closely connected to the events of the Holocaust (Conde 2005). Timm de Souza contends that the Holocaust does not represent.

> in any sense, some kind of perverse accident along the way, or a sudden and unexpected contamination of reason by unreason, or a deranged deviation of foundations or trajectory; rather, it is the *effective realisation* of an extreme and congenital possibility of Western culture itself, of the *logos* abandoned to itself, of Being with meaning in itself, of the definitive resolution of the great equation of reality and the summit of dialectics and the will to power. (Souza 2010: 30–31)

The Holocaust should not be considered merely an aberration in the development of modern rationality; instead, it can be interpreted as a culmination of its logic, with criminal law playing a notable role (Conde 2005). While contemporary systems of widespread incarceration are not directly comparable to the Nazi regime's industrial-scale methods of extermination, mechanisms for systematically managing and imprisoning individuals while violating their human rights persist. These mechanisms are often legitimised through discursive strategies that present such practices as rational and civilised approaches aimed at protecting society.

Thorough evaluation of the rational thinking that drives criminal proceedings is crucial, since pursuing the truth lies at the heart of these processes. Breaking away from an authoritarian tradition is essential, so that criminal justice can be reconsidered in a way that restricts, rather than arbitrarily applies, punitive power. Previously discussed issues show that this inquisitorial method partially persists because the importance of the subject matter is often undervalued—oversimplified and accepted as fact due to presumed reliability. Overcoming this perspective demands a fundamental rethinking of knowledge and a restructuring of the concept of truth, using principles different from those found in modern natural science. As mentioned before, simply redefining corresponding truth as relative or approximate does not suffice to disrupt the inquisitorial tradition.

Contrary to popular belief, questioning the foundations of modern thought is not a recent development; such scrutiny dates back to the late nineteenth century. Foucault, interpreting Nietzsche, argues that knowledge does not naturally connect to its objects but involves power, domination, and even violence (Foucault 2003: 18). He suggests knowledge is shaped by an underlying will to distance itself from, rather than resemble, its object—a "radical malice" (Foucault 2003: 21). Nietzsche sees knowledge as historically contingent and marked by conflict and perspective, lacking an inherent essence (Foucault 2003: 22, 24–25). As Nietzsche observes, people remain mired in illusions, perceiving only surfaces without accessing truth (Nietzsche 1983: 46).

> what, then, is truth? A mobile army of metaphors [...] a sum of human relations which have been poetically and rhetorically intensified, transferred, adorned, and which, after long use, seem to a people to be solid, canonical, and binding. Truths are illusions of which one has forgotten that they are illusions, metaphors that have become worn out and powerless to affect the senses [...] the whole material with which, and upon which, the so-called *man of truth*, the researcher, the philosopher, works and builds, comes, if not from Cloud-Cuckoo-Land, at any rate not from the essence of things. (Nietzsche 1983: 48–49)

For Nietzsche, there is not a single point that is "true in itself", effective, and universally valid, without reference to man: truth is not a true proposition, but a general order of the world, a historical structure, a form of life, or an epoch of being. In other words, what was understood as truth was nothing more than what acquired this character through an arbitrary attribution by science. Nietzsche exposed the will to eradicate difference, a defining feature of knowledge that aims at universalisation:

> Every concept arises from the equalisation of the non-equal. Just as it is certain that no leaf is ever completely identical to another, it is certain that the concept of leaf is formed by arbitrarily disregarding these individual differences, by forgetting what is distinctive, and thus evokes the idea that,

in nature, beyond the individual leaves, there is something called a "leaf", a sort of primordial leaf. (Nietzsche 1983: 48)

Nietzsche asserts that the researcher "forgets, therefore, the original intuitive metaphors as metaphors, and takes them for the things themselves" (Nietzsche 1983: 50). From this standpoint, absolute universalisation via conceptual frameworks should be understood as a human construct. Nietzsche explains, "within this dice game of concepts, however, truth is called using each die as it is designated, counting its points exactly, forming correct categories, and never transgressing the order of castes and the sequence of hierarchical classes" (Nietzsche 1983: 49). He further contends that individuals build with the fragile substance of concepts, which are self-fashioned (Nietzsche 1983: 49). As interpreted by Foucault, for Nietzsche,

> Knowledge is at once the most generalising and the most particular of things. Knowledge schematises, ignores differences, assimilates things to one another, and does so without any foundation in truth. For this reason, knowledge is always also a form of ignorance. On the other hand, it is always something that targets, maliciously, insidiously, and aggressively, individuals, things, situations. (Foucault 2003: 26)

According to Vattimo, Nietzsche believes our standards for truth and falsehood stem from a specific form of life shaped by power relations, not from absolute requirements for living. Even evidence as a measure of truth is just part of this particular social framework (Vattimo 1980).

Nietzsche provides an incisive observation: "when someone hides something behind a bush, then looks for it there and finds it, there is not much to boast about in this seeking and finding; it is just the same with the seeking and finding of 'truth' within the domain of reason" (Nietzsche 1983: 50). According to Nietzsche, "the investigator of these truths is, in the end, only seeking the metamorphosis of the world into man, striving for an understanding of the world as something in the likeness of man, and at best achieves the feeling of an assimilation" (Nietzsche 1983: 50).

Consequently, knowledge itself becomes an exercise of power: when hypotheses are predetermined, one pursues confirmation rather than genuine discovery. Ultimately, Nietzsche's critique closely aligns with

Franco Cordero's assertion regarding the predominance of hypotheses over facts.

Not only philosophy challenged modern science's concept of truth; Einstein's theory of relativity also undermined it from within the natural sciences (Einstein 2002). If time is perceived differently by each observer and absolute truth depends on aggregating all perspectives, how can we claim a single corresponding truth? What does this mean for the pursuit of truth?

The idea of corresponding truth suggests that perfect observation can reveal absolute reality, but Einstein's theory of relativity disproved this, showing knowledge is both changeable and influenced by perspective. Scientific understanding is provisional, as Gauer explains, since uncertainty about time means universal laws are no longer reliable (Gauer 2004: 6). Ferrajoli notes scientific theories are always replaced by new ones, making truth temporary and based on current evidence (Ferrajoli 2002: 42). Merleau-Ponty argues science creates models rather than fully engaging with reality (Merleau-Ponty 1969: 25), while Soares adds that in the modern viewpoint:

> [...] it is up to the agent of knowledge to discover, beneath the mutable, the constant. Therefore, life, as the generator of contingencies and producer of differences irreducible to an integrating unity, will escape scientific treatment. From life, only regularity is taken for the scientific treasury. (Soares 2004: 47)

Through the identification of consistent patterns, what remains is often incomplete knowledge. The notion that any subject can wholly encompass truth has become untenable. Gauer observes that "the ongoing fissures, fragmentations, discontinuities, and displacements have erased the vision of certainties, meaning that humanity's actions are no longer assured by the Cartesian logic which once supported the unified whole of modern reason" (Gauer 2006: 139). Unity has been supplanted by fragmentation; certainty by uncertainty; and order by complexity. This evolution in the understanding of meaning is necessary for the progression of science and knowledge beyond the limitations of modernity.

The world exhibits an inherent complexity, characterised by discontinuity, disorder, and unpredictability. While broad explanatory frameworks aim to simplify this complexity, they may inadvertently prioritise internal coherence over faithful representation of the subject, thus potentially undermining the objective of attaining genuine understanding. As Merleau-Ponty notes,

> to say that the world *is*, by nominal definition, the object X of our operations is to absolutize the scholar's epistemic situation, as if everything that was or is had only ever existed to enter the laboratory. "Operative" thought becomes an absolute artificialism. (Merleau-Ponty 1969: 27)

Objectivist scientism has tended to distance itself from human experience by positioning science as the exclusive means of discerning truth about reality, which can result in a dogmatic perspective. When scientific methodologies are the sole focus, valuable insights from literature and art that contribute to understanding real-life experiences may be disregarded. For instance, Kafka's *The Trial* provides a nuanced depiction of punitive practices that contrasts with more abstract procedural accounts. Gauer (2004: 4) observes that scientism improperly discounts subjectivity as merely illusory, despite its integral role in reality. Rethinking criminal justice therefore necessitates expanding beyond restrictive scientific definitions of truth and avoiding conflation between mental constructs and their referents (Souza 2004: 107). As Ricoeur reflects,

> if science enjoys a unique status in the provisional edifice of truth, it is because, in our eyes, it is the touchstone and model of all truth. All truth, we think, should be, if not *of* science, at least *like* science. Science could serve as an exemplary model of truth for as long as the very ideal of *Episteme*, born of Greek geometry, appeared to us free of opacity, as a satisfactory answer, fully saturating the question that gave rise to it. The Galilean era, now drawing to a close, rests on a total faith in the exemplary nature of mathematical knowledge inherited from the Alexandrians; and upon this foundation of clarity, the mechanistic exploration of the entire realm of the visible was inaugurated and advanced, with the success we know. (Ricoeur 1968: 172–173)

Gauer explores the relationship between modernity and the concepts of truth, time, narrative, and myth. She proposes that science may be regarded as a narrative framework through which meaning is ascribed to the universe, drawing parallels with myth due to its pursuit of absolute truth. Referencing Levi-Strauss, Gauer contends that scientific truth functions as a narrative elucidating universal logic, thereby underscoring its similarity to myth. This analogy is significant, as Gauer asserts that the modern ideal of cumulative truth integrates truth within historical time, consequently requiring a narrative methodology (Gauer 2004: 10–11).

The rationale underlying the so-called "grand narratives" was to provide coherence and structure to reality by presenting uncertain, unpredictable, and fragmented aspects as certain, grounded in humanity's collective rational pursuit of truth through science. Gauer (2004: 11) notes that "the notion of an absolute truth from modern science, which aimed to impose order on a world not previously shaped by its standards, was crafted in narrative form, and could only exist as such". She further asserts that these legitimising metanarratives once conferred meaning upon both present circumstances and future developments but have since lost credibility. According to Gauer (2004: 11–12), "we are in a position where the truths conveyed by these metanarratives—once used to justify various eras and perspectives, maintaining continuity over fragmentation—are no longer relevant". In this context, "the crisis prompted scientists to realise that there isn't just one science, nor a single, absolute, universal, and eternal truth" (Gauer 1998: 25). Nonetheless, this insight remains only partially embraced, as it challenges deeply rooted convictions, as Gauer observes:

> if we accept as a solid vocation of this paradigm the association between "reality" and truth, or between the pursuit of the visible and the will to truth, it is understandable that any deviation of the problem towards a repositioning of obscurity and opacity among the priorities of knowledge should, in itself, be a source of disturbance to the canonical understanding of that will to truth. (Gauer 2004: 8)

Despite the potential for these new understandings to enhance knowledge, significant resistance remains. As Baptista asserts, "the provisional nature, however, of scientific proof—an inescapable consequence of the transitory character of the convenience or utility of theoretical models and the ever-accelerating pace of their succession—ultimately reduces this truth to mere verisimilitude, generalising uncertainty and relativism" (Baptista 2001: 30). Science provides only provisional knowledge concerning its subject matter and does not, nor can it, represent absolute truth. Nonetheless, "this abandonment of the will to truth as a quest for the absolute brings about a certain disorder in the tradition of scientific knowledge" (Gauer 2004: 8).

The challenge of confronting fragmentation and relinquishing universal claims is significant. Still, Gauer and Timm de Souza emphasise that "the multiplicity of perspectives does not mean disorder or disorganisation, but rather the integration, real or potential, of senses of discovery, over time, of the meanings that time may, today, assume" (Gauer and Souza 2004: xi). This represents an emergence of new interpretative possibilities—an openness to plurality. As Ricoeur observes, "at the level of the concrete life of a civilisation, the spirit of truth lies in respecting the complexity of the orders of truth; it is the recognition of plurality" (Ricoeur 1968: 194).

It is essential to evaluate how the criminal justice system could be restructured based on an evolved understanding of truth, thereby mitigating inquisitorial and authoritarian tendencies. A decisive shift away from correspondence theories of truth, as well as residual inquisitorial methods and nineteenth-century scientism, is required. Coutinho (2002: 176) asserts that a genuine epistemological break necessitates the determination to move beyond entrenched dogmatism. Similarly, Gauer (2006: 10) notes that the "end of certainties" has influenced fields such as physics, mathematics, and neuroscience, but its effect on the applied social sciences remains limited. Carvalho (2003: 76) further underscores the importance of reinvigorating secularisation processes, observing that authoritarian elements—expressed through constructs of risk and persecution—persist in legislation, legal scholarship, law enforcement, sentencing frameworks, and penitentiary law. Despite widespread acknowledgement of the need for such transformative change, the discursive fallacy intrinsic to the prevailing search for truth ideology persists, continuing to function as a foundational legal doctrine which underpins the cognitive privilege of the judge.

Adherents of modern frameworks may perceive the current crisis in knowledge as addressable only by establishing a new paradigm, one that provides reassurance similar to that offered by earlier modernist solutions. Evidentiary rationalism seems like an effort that hopes to fulfill this aspiration. However, this view highlights a conceptual limitation: it neglects the core issue, which is not solely the insufficiency of modernity's answers, but rather the problematic assumption that overarching narratives or pre-existing solutions can fully encompass the complexities of time or deliver objective truths. The intricacies of reality exceed what traditional modernist responses—or any single narrative aspiring towards predictability and definitive truth—are capable of capturing.

It is preferable to embrace complexity rather than adhere to the potentially misleading certainty associated with nineteenth-century dogmatism. This scenario does not inherently constitute a crisis; rather, it involves recognising and addressing sophisticated challenges. Nevertheless, even if one interprets it as a crisis, such moments need not be viewed solely in a negative light, as Heidegger observed:

> The "movement" proper to the sciences unfolds through the more or less radical and invisible revision, for the sciences themselves, of their fundamental concepts. The level of a science is determined by its *capacity* to undergo a crisis in its fundamental concepts. In these immanent crises of science, the relationship of positive investigations with the things themselves wavers and is shaken. Nowadays, there are tendencies in almost all disciplines to place research on new foundations. (Heidegger 2005: 35)

As Carvalho observes, "the belief in the unity of discourse and in the power of scientific methods forged in modernity blinds the researcher, preventing them from perceiving the scale of contemporary revolutions and challenges (risks)" (Carvalho 2006: 25). It is in this sense that Timm de Souza's critique is directed, denouncing:

> The "logical apparatus" which, with its power of abstraction, enabled the emergence and advance of modern science and technology, has become a fetish. From being a critical instance of reality, it has turned into an instrument legitimising a reflection of reality whose main constitutive feature is the claim to replace, to its own advantage, reality itself. (Souza 2004: 109)

As Timm de Souza notes, objects resist objectification far more than a certain idealising rationalist logic has led us to believe (Souza 2004: 124). For this reason, it is necessary to move beyond a model of rationality that does not recognise its own limitations (Souza 2004: 125). This is particularly evident when considering criminal procedure and the problematic fixation on security and truth. As Lopes Jr. observes, "the world of criminal proceedings is a world of instability, so it is not appropriate to speak of judgments of security, certainty, and stability when dealing with the world of reality, which is inherently risky" (Lopes Jr 2004: 158).

Our epistemological linkage to modernity must either be dissolved or pushed to its furthest boundaries—a process that inevitably presents challenges, particularly for those who strongly adhere to prevailing dominant theories.

Unexplored ideas often evoke discomfort because familiarity with established concepts fosters a sense of ease (Lyotard 1997: 28). Bachelard's imagery provides insight into the resistance to novel experiences that challenge deeply held convictions. He observes, "the house *is our corner* of the world. It is, as is often said, our first universe. It is a true cosmos. A cosmos in every sense of the word" (Bachelard 1960: 22). Consequently, it is logical that "the house is regarded as a space of comfort and intimacy, as a space that must condense and protect intimacy" (Bachelard 1960: 50). The familiar environment thus serves as a fortress for personal sensitivities (Bachelard 1960: 23*)*, with additional fortresses existing within, such as cupboards. Bachelard notes, "the interior space of the old cupboard is deep. The interior space of the cupboard is a space of intimacy, a space that is not opened lightly" (Bachelard 1960: 70). He further states, "in the cupboard lives a centre of order that protects the whole house from boundless disorder" (Bachelard 1960: 70), indicating the cupboard's role in providing stability, security, and apparent certainty.

However, this certainty can be precarious, as illustrated in the statement, "the nest— we shall immediately understand—is precarious and yet it triggers in us the reverie of security" (Bachelard 1960: 86). Bachelard argues, "there are ideas that dream. Certain theories, believed to be scientific, are great reveries, boundless reveries" (Bachelard 1960: 92). These reveries find refuge and shelter, supported by the enduring structures of the house. He posits, "every corner of a house, every angle of a room, every small space where we like to hide, to confide in ourselves, is, for the imagination, a solitude, that is, the germ of a room, the germ of a house" (Bachelard 1960: 108). Bachelard asserts that "in many respects, the 'lived' corner refuses life, restricts life, hides life. The corner is, then, a negation of the Universe" (Bachelard 1960: 108), which may also represent a negation of complexity, chaos, and uncertainty.

Given these considerations, a transition is warranted—one that moves beyond the limitations imposed by certain aspects of modern scientific methodology. Merleau-Ponty refers to a fundamental historicity, wherein the dynamic reasoning of science must reorient itself towards both its objects of inquiry and its own foundational principles, ultimately reconnecting with philosophy (Merleau-Ponty 1969: 29). The trend within modern science to distance itself from philosophical interpretation and pluralism—a tendency once regarded as an objective—should be critically reassessed to facilitate the emergence of new questions and innovative approaches to persistent issues. As Gauer notes,

> the production of knowledge, deprived of universal truth, can only be supported by an attitude of provisional knowledge. The idealised objectivity of scientific knowledge is superseded by a pluralism of truths; to the necessity of methodological rules is added the necessity of legal-political mediation. (Gauer 2004: 6)

According to Timm de Souza, "philosophical wisdom would thus consist in accompanying the unfolding of temporality in which the real is constituted, without forcing it into schemes which, though very useful for its paralysed intelligibility, say little about the way things actually occur" (Souza 2006: 5).

Criminal procedure must move away from the conceptual schematism characteristic of modernity, which tends to oversimplify complex realities under the guise of uncovering truth. In the context of criminal proceedings, such an approach may prompt judges to assume excessively active roles. Accordingly, I recommend reconsidering both the inquisitorial tradition and the scientific methods that have implicitly supported it.

A shift in perspective is necessary—legal scholars should let go of claims to absolute truths, which are illusionary and rooted in arrogance. Morin suggests that "the universe is a mixture of order and disorder, and this blend changes greatly depending on circumstances, conditions, places, and moments…" (Morin 1996: 242). He also asserts that "the major discovery of this century is that science does not offer certainty" (Morin 1996: 239). Morin points out that the question "what is real?" has re-emerged as a challenge, since reality can be both continuous and discontinuous at once (Morin 1996: 224–245). Timm de Souza describes this as a "multiplicity where meaning arises from the mutual irreducibility among perspectives, which remain essentially and permanently dispersed and constitute reality" (Souza 2006: 6). The world can only be interpreted; precise knowledge is beyond our grasp. Lyotard argues that "matter neither asks anything of us nor expects any answer. It is indifferent to us" (Lyotard 1997: 20). Heidegger believes that "reality is resistance or, more specifically, the sum of resistances" (Heidegger 2005: 276). As Maffesoli observes, life goes beyond any theory trying to explain it (Maffesoli 2003).

This prompts consideration of assertions regarding access to truths that accurately represent reality, particularly when existing scientific, technological, or theoretical methods are insufficient to comprehensively resolve such intricate matters. Timm de Souza points to the current challenge: the continued existence of the real as something that stimulates thought following the crisis of Totality (Souza 2006: 7). He states, "A single perspective on the world, such as one solely based on scientific models, cannot adequately understand the true human world" (Souza 2004: 126).

The modern Cartesian idea of separating disciplines is now being re-examined, which is encouraging different fields of knowledge that were once divided to reconnect (Morin 1996: 242). Philosophy, in particular, plays a crucial role in this process, as reviving a philosophical perspective—previously set aside in favour of scientific ideals—is seen as essential. The main goal is to bring together what has been split apart and assemble the pieces again to create better tools for understanding. As Morin puts it, "relevant knowledge is the kind that can provide context—that is, it brings things together and makes connections" (Morin 1996: 253).

As Gauer notes, "any and every form of illicit act can be regarded as a complex phenomenon and, therefore, cannot be adequately explained through the lens of a single discipline predicated on absolutized 'truth' and judicial impartiality" (Gauer 2006: 13). Additionally, the *Charter of Transdisciplinarity* highlights the presence of multiple levels of reality, each subject to its own logic, and advises against reducing reality to one level governed by a singular logic.

As physics shifts from notions of absolute precision towards embracing uncertainty and indeterminacy, it becomes increasingly important for the human and applied social sciences to consider adopting comparable methodologies. The quantum revolution fundamentally challenges established paradigms and rigid legal frameworks, prompting a reconsideration of our conceptualisation of reality. Henri Atlan, a noted biophysicist, contends that reality necessitates interpretation, introducing the concept of "interpretands" (Pessis-Pasternak 1992: 67).

Ilya Prigogine notes that uncertainty and an appreciation of complexity present challenges. He observes that "we are still quite unaccustomed, at the end of the twentieth century, to this very different view of things, which takes into account the complexity of the universe" (Prigogine 1996: 233). Prigogine further states, "we are beginning to understand that the universe is very different from that timeless geometry which corresponded to the ideal of classical science. The world we are beginning to decipher is more like a novel, like the *One Thousand and One Nights*" (Prigogine 1996: 232). This perspective reflects a philosophical approach characterised by curiosity and respect for the intricacies of reality. The title of his article, "*The Re-enchantment of the World*" underscores an intellectual stance appropriate for frameworks that acknowledge the diversity and complexity inherent in human life.

A re-enchanted world offers countless possibilities and subtle layers of meaning. Merleau-Ponty argues that instead of simply describing space and light, we should allow them to reveal themselves, prompting us to revisit questions once thought resolved (Merleau-Ponty 1969: 76). Rather than seeing this as a crisis, it is an opportunity to realise that what seemed certain before depends on myriad factors.

Nassif argues that nobody holds absolute truth. Instead, we have only "truths", which are just hypotheses open to constant scrutiny and can be changed if proven wrong (Nassif 2005: 128). Lopes Jr. adds that, considering uncertainty, chaos is generally the norm while order is the rare exception (Lopes Jr 2005: 57).

In contrast to modern proposals advocating the elimination of uncertainty in favour of predictability and regularity, it must be accepted that chaos and uncertainty are not inherently negative; rather, they play a constructive role. As Prigogine (1996) notes, disorder does not impede but actively stimulates organisational processes and the continual renewal of the universe. Therefore, the objective should be to analyse and engage with chaotic phenomena, instead of abolishing them under an arbitrary explanatory framework that oversimplifies reality in pursuit of truth. Gauer (2004: 9) suggests that while it may perhaps be premature to speak of an "epistemology of uncertainty"—where scientific laws possess a markedly reversible nature—there is, at minimum, a perspective that favours interpretations and narratives over universal and immutable truths.

It remains uncertain whether this emerging scientific perspective—characterised by its openness to philosophical inquiry and acknowledgement of ambiguity—will effectively navigate the complexities ignored by modernity or ultimately yield to the persistent quest for absolute truths. But one thing can be said: unlike the predetermined and assured frameworks inherent in modernity's grand narratives, this developing epistemology demands ongoing critical assessment rather than offering fixed certainties. This perspective encourages the recognition that truth is not a static or singular entity, but rather a dynamic process influenced by context, interpretation, and the interplay of multiple viewpoints. In the realm of law, this means adopting more flexible and reflexive approaches, allowing for the coexistence of diverse narratives.

As Morin highlights, "the great discovery of this century is that science is not the realm of certainty" (Gauer 1996: 239). Similarly, Carvalho notes that criminal procedure often conflates truth with reality and substance, even advocating for the pursuit of a "real truth" (Carvalho 2006: 40). Today, it is imperative to acknowledge and embrace uncertainty. The paradigm must shift from pursuing certainty, consistency, and clear definition towards accepting unpredictability, discontinuity, and complexity. Gauer suggests reconsidering our methodologies to address intricacy rather than oversimplifying in favour of absolute truths. Ultimately, the issue of what constitutes truth remains unresolved (Gauer 2004: 14). Echoing Bachelard's viewpoint, "all values must tremble. A value that does not tremble is a dead value" (Bachelard 1960: 57).

Such an epistemological transformation requires the cultivation of intellectual humility and openness, fostering a culture in which questions are valued as much as answers. Instead of striving for unattainable certainty or absolute truth, legal practitioners and scholars must engage with the provisional and contingent nature of knowledge, acknowledging that their interpretations are subject to revision in light of new evidence or perspectives. This approach ultimately promises a more nuanced and humane legal system, better equipped to respond to the intricacies of lived experience and the multifaceted character of truth, as will be explored on the next chapters.

CHAPTER 5

Past Events Framed as Legal Facts

Events, Construction of Facts, and the Search for Truth

The interpretative approach outlined here seeks to transcend the prevailing inquisitorial, positivist and rationalist emphasis on absolute truths. It advocates for an epistemological transition from an objectifying criminal procedure towards one that acknowledges the complexity of past events while upholding the rights of the accused. This approach entails distancing from nineteenth-century notions of scientific neutrality as well as contemporary evidentiary rationalist models focused on judicial truth-seeking.

Distinguishing between facts and events serves as a foundational element in the epistemological analysis presented herein. In legal discourse, the term "fact" commonly implies a connection to truth: facts are usually understood as established or verifiable truths concerning past occurrences, encompassing both what transpired and its generally accepted significance. Nevertheless, the presumed objectivity associated with facts highlights the fundamental limitations of evidentiary reasoning inherited from modern frameworks. Accordingly, this discussion distinguishes between facts—conceived as outcomes of legal evaluation applied to historical events—and events themselves, which serve as their historical referents rooted in lived experience and, thus, are open to varied interpretations regarding their meaning. Within the legal context, a "fact"

S. H. Khaled Jr., *Reimagining Criminal Justice, Search for Truth and Human Rights*, https://doi.org/10.1007/978-3-032-27227-0_5

emerges from the intersection of an actual life event and its interpretation within legal language.

Ferrajoli investigated the interplay between legal norms and historical events and concluded that it challenges the Enlightenment model of perfect correspondence, notwithstanding his decision to retain a relative form of this ideal. Ibañez also examined this issue, noting that one prevalent misunderstanding regarding truth originates from the legacy of the exegetical school and the syllogistic approach. These perspectives persist, and it is therefore unsurprising that judges are still sometimes regarded as passive recipients of purportedly established facts—as inert material subject only to intuitive judgement and mere classification into predetermined legal categories (Ibañez 2005: 116).

This viewpoint is appropriately open to critical examination, as facts are inherently influenced by interpretation and construction rather than existing in isolation as objective realities.

In criminal law, "facts" are largely shaped by legal language and procedures, meaning they do not simply reflect reality but are discursively constructed and given specific meanings, distancing them from the original event they aim to represent.

Rather than reflecting a transparent window onto past events, the judicial finding of fact is a product of interpretative engagement, in which factual statements are scrutinised, contested, and ultimately situated within the framework of legal meaning. This dynamic not only challenges the notion of an unmediated correspondence between fact and past events but also demands a critical awareness of the limitations and possibilities inherent in legal fact-finding.

Taruffo (2010) argues that only facts relevant to the case—those defined by applicable legal rules—serve as the main objects of proof. Sendra et al. (1996) note that criminal proceedings consider only typical facts, as determined by normative criteria, and that historical judgements are shaped by both factual activity and the affected legal interests. According to Aragoneses Alonso (1997), facts are understood through their legal importance rather than as mere events, and legal application involves integrating analysis of conduct with interpretation of norms. Thus, the fact emerges from a blend of real-world events and their legal meanings, challenging the ideal of direct correspondence and highlighting the intertwined nature of historical and legal truths within proceedings.

Recognising this dynamic contrasts sharply with the nineteenth-century positivist model, which assumed truth was easily obtainable from facts. Many scholars still rely on this outdated view, believing judges can simply find the truth—sometimes out of a misguided "scientific" conviction. This stems from law's tendency to mirror the modern ideal of natural sciences, seeking universal laws through logical reasoning. However, this nomothetic approach, rooted in mathematical ideals, is ill-suited for understanding complex past events. As Gil observes, in mathematics, objectivity and truth are essentially the same, but such certainty cannot be transferred to the unpredictable nature of human society (Martins and Gil 2002: 17). Einstein also showed that mathematical certainty only exists in abstraction, not when applied to reality, meaning the precision of exact sciences cannot extend to social phenomena (Einstein 2002: 66–68).

The past comprises unique events; accordingly, knowledge of historical occurrences is inherently idiographic. The idiographic method addresses unique circumstances and nonrecurring, contingent events. As Ferrer Beltrán notes, there is a clear distinction between idiographic sciences and nomothetic sciences, with the latter aiming to establish general laws applicable to phenomena that can be repeated indefinitely (Beltrán 2007: 34).

In the context of criminal proceedings, however, both universal principles and particular circumstances coexist. Ferrajoli identifies two types of propositions: factual (*de facto*) and legal (*de jure*). He explains that "the truth of the first is a factual truth, as it is demonstrable through evidence of the event's occurrence and its attribution to the accused; the truth of the second constitutes a legal truth, in that it can be established by interpreting the meaning of normative statements that classify the act as an offense" (Ferrajoli 2002: 40). Gadamer further reminds us that Aristotle recognised the inherent tension between the universality of legislation—whether codified or unwritten—and the uniqueness of each specific case (Gadamer 1992: 301).

The interplay between referencing past events—viewed as singular occurrences—and anticipating their normative implications through general laws raises important questions about truth production in legal proceedings. As noted by Gimeno Sendra, determining criminal responsibility and appropriate punishment requires judges to make two key assessments: firstly, a historical evaluation focused on verifying whether certain events occurred; and secondly, a legal assessment aimed at classifying these verified facts as criminal offences and considering the imposition of penalties (Sendra 1996: 602–603). Cordero argues that convictions depend on positive historical judgements: confirming the existence of the alleged act, establishing the defendant's involvement, clarifying the mental state (intent or negligence), and affirming the conditions necessary for punishment. Consequently, the judge evaluates these facts within the framework of criminal law (Cordero 2000: 276–277). Aragoneses Alonso observes that the application of law entails the jurist identifying relevant facts and applicable legal norms, thus integrating abstract rules with individualised conduct (Alonso 1996: 552).

Alonso's analysis underscores a point not often acknowledged within legal scholarship: The "facts" considered in criminal proceedings emerge from the assessment of a life event as relevant through the application of legal norms. This process is far more complex than a simple determination of fact; legal facts are dynamic constructs rather than static, objectively observable phenomena.

This tension requires careful analysis, as misconstruing its essence may result in overly simplistic syllogisms based solely on perceived factual determinations. Such reasoning assumes that past "truth" can be objectively established by an observer who neutrally identifies facts and applies rules within a normative framework expected to consistently produce unambiguous solutions—a notion reflective of nineteenth-century scientistic ideals and the *esprit géométrique*.

The concept of document offers illustrative examples that merit thorough consideration and demonstrate the limitations of positivist epistemology with respect to facts and interpretation. As noted by Aragoneses Alonso, documentary evidence encompasses any object that may be introduced as evidence in court proceedings. A document is fundamentally a movable object admissible as evidence during litigation. This category includes a range of materials assembled throughout the legal proceedings, such as written texts, fabrics, papers, and books, all of which may be incorporated into the case file (Alonso 1986: 310). Chiovenda offers a broader definition, characterising a document as any tangible item intended to capture or reproduce a particular expression of thought (Chiovenda 1998: 151).

Scientific methodologies enable the verification of documents, statistics, and sources, thereby facilitating the clear communication and reproducibility of results. This methodological rigour serves to prevent unsupported assertions. Nevertheless, concerns regarding objectivity in historical research arise when facts are construed within broader systems of value judgements (Koselleck 2006: 185). Even in apparently unambiguous cases, verification methods have inherent limitations, as belief formation and judgement involve complex processes. While a document may be authentic and not forged, this does not ensure the accuracy of its content; documents inherently represent their own perspectives, unless interpreted through indirect analysis. As Ginzburg observes, “there are no neutral texts; even an official inventory employs a code that must be decoded: any indirect statement, as Jakobson noted, is reshaped by the individual quoting it”. [...] Nonetheless, this does not imply that a text solely reflects itself or its concepts. [...] Even rigorously regulated documents, such as those produced during inquisitional proceedings, can reveal underlying cultural contradictions (Ginzburg 1989: 209).

In positivist epistemology, documents are often seen as direct representations of factual reality. Yet this view overlooks an important reversal: facts aren’t simply produced by documents or testimonies—instead, these materials are chosen based on what is considered significant about the “fact” itself. As Ricoeur observes, “The document was not a document before the historian considered examining it, and thus the historian, so to speak, institutes the document as a document after his intervention and observation; at the same time, he institutes historical facts” (Ricoeur 1968: 26).

In other words, a document only becomes evidence when it’s paired with a guiding hypothesis. Facts do not arise directly from documents; rather, documents are selected according to specific practices. Every “fact” emerges from questioning—such as “who did it”, “how”, “why”, and similar inquiries. This process constantly involves selecting and reconstructing aspects of reality. According to Ricoeur,

> A vigilant epistemology warns against the illusion of believing that what is called a fact coincides with what actually happened, even with the living memory of eyewitnesses, as if facts lay dormant in documents until historians extracted them. (Ricoeur 2003: 235)

Positivist epistemology tends to overlook the historical context, contingency, and uniqueness that characterise each event, treating facts as objective entities that merely reflect past reality. In legal proceedings, the fact under consideration serves only as a simplified representation of the genuine complexity inherent in real-life events.

Although this positivist ideal continues to prevail, it often obscures the nuanced relationship between factual information and its interpretation. While the authenticity of a document might be verified by the appropriate methods, individual judges may assign varying degrees of significance to such evidence during deliberation. This divergence arises because reaching a decision entails more than simply aligning facts with objective reality, as will be discussed in subsequent chapters. As Calamandrei observes,

> Place two painters before the same landscape, side by side, each with their easel, and return an hour later to see what each has painted on their canvas. You will see two entirely different landscapes, to the point where it seems impossible that the model was the same. In such a case, would one say that one of them betrayed the truth? (Calamandrei 1996: 125)

The complexities surrounding the concept of "fact" have been long acknowledged by historians, as Febvre notes:

> And what do you call facts? What do you place behind that little word 'fact'? Do you think they are given to history as substantial realities, which time hides more or less deeply and which must simply be unearthed, cleaned, and presented in the light of day to our contemporaries? [...] all sciences manufacture their object. (Febvre 1978: 105)

Febvre describes facts as "hooks on which theories are hung" emphasising that these hooks must first be forged before they can be put to use, rather than simply taken from "the past" or assumed to be synonymous with "history" (Febvre 1978: 105).

The assumption that facts may be observed and classified independently of the observer's perspective and contextual background overlooks the inherent subjectivity present in recognising and evaluating historical occurrences. The establishment of facts is influenced by cognitive, cultural, and normative biases of the individuals involved, thereby challenging assertions of complete objectivity. A quotation from Koselleck may help clarify how factual and legal truths are intertwined:

> the factual content established *ex post* in relation to the events under investigation is never identical to the totality of past circumstances, supposedly taken as real at that time. Every event investigated and represented historically is nourished by the fiction of the factual, but the actual reality can no longer be apprehended. This is not to say that the historical event is established carelessly or arbitrarily, since the control of sources ensures the exclusion of what should not be said. But this same control does not guarantee what can be said. (Koselleck 2006: 141)

This passage underscores the nuanced relationship between events and facts, as articulated by Koselleck's concept of the "fiction of the factual". While past events exist independently of subsequent interpretations, they acquire historical significance only when historians elect to research them or when they satisfy specific criteria that introduce legal considerations and prompt criminal justice involvement. The assignment of meaning to any event is ultimately an external imposition, illustrating the inherent challenges and limitations associated with attributing meaning in historical interpretation. Furthermore, such "facts" demand evaluative judgement. As Ricoeur notes, "there is no action that does not elicit, to some degree, approval or disapproval, according to a hierarchy of values of which goodness and badness are the poles" (Ricoeur 1994: 94).

According to Gimeno Sendra, the punishable act may be examined from two distinct viewpoints: either as a historical event devoid of legal interpretation, or as an act defined within the parameters of the Penal Code. The author contends that determining the subject of criminal proceedings requires an appropriate integration of both perspectives (Sendra 1996: 210). Nonetheless, the process of legal adequacy remains problematic; the inherently uncertain and unpredictable nature of life events resists comprehensive resolution by the universal application of legal norms. Each occurrence is intrinsically novel, singular, and contingent—real-world phenomena often surpass the scope of legal regulations, which may intentionally simplify complexity in pursuit of an idealised notion of truth. Koselleck observes that

> the before and after of an event retain their own temporal characteristics, which can never be fully reduced to long-term conditions. Each event produces more and, at the same time, less than is contained in its previous circumstances: hence its surprising novelty. (Koselleck 2006: 139)

A challenging question for legal-criminal theory must be pondered here: while legal typification structures reduce complexity and serve as a safeguard due to modern concepts of legality, they also select only certain characteristics from what is considered a crime, ignoring other aspects. This means that when analysing a case, only certain features are focused on, and from a theoretical standpoint, the prosecution must not only prove the act occurred but also that it qualifies as typical, unlawful, and culpable. This presents a real issue, since, as Aragoneses Alonso highlights, reality is livelier and less structured than any formal approach and forcing it into rigid frameworks strips it of its true nature (Alonso 1997: 551–552). Leone further argues that life's complexity, full of unknowns and unique circumstances, cannot be fully represented by ready-made models of reality (Leone 1963: 157)—surprisingly, Leone recognises this complexity but endorses the concept of "real truth".

Modern legal thinking often ignores the intricacies of real life, becoming preoccupied with normative structures and their execution in prosecution. This tendency to overlook complexity has lent the blending of facts and law a harsh, sometimes damaging quality for defendants. As Carnelutti notes,

> precisely because the concepts, or rather the dogmatics that bring them together, serve as instruments, we must not confuse them with the knowledge of Law. If only the concepts they represent, better or worse, were enough to know reality! The danger of dogmatics is precisely this: that the world of concepts, instead of the world of things, becomes the object of knowledge. There is no more insidious danger for us, law professors; precisely because rules, or if we prefer, legal norms, are nothing more than concepts, when we establish the latter as what we must know, we end up confusing the world of concepts with the real world. (Carnelutti 2004: 49)

This matter relates to the methodology employed in legal research, which Carnelutti (2004: 63) characterises as inherently dogmatic—a conceptual framework developed to a high degree of sophistication for the precise interpretation of phenomena through a legal perspective and the proper application of law.

The ongoing debate concerning the limited training of judges in the humanities is, therefore, not unexpected. Normative knowledge alone provides only marginal benefits when it comes to understanding and addressing complex real-world issues.

In contrast, Taruffo presents a divergent perspective, asserting that while judicial education is primarily grounded in legal doctrines rather than factual matters, it nonetheless derives significant value from regular exposure to practical casework. Such engagement enables judges to cultivate the skills required to perform their epistemic responsibilities, which Taruffo identifies as the pursuit of truth. As a result, Taruffo contends that civil law judges are appropriately equipped to undertake this search for truth (Taruffo 2010: 206–207).

Carnelutti is not nearly as optimistic. He recognises the inherent limitations of the dogmatic method:

> The drawbacks of the dogmatic method are twofold: on the one hand, the world of phenomena may be lost from view and, on the other, it may be considered that this world exhausts reality; when this defect is not corrected, *dogmatics* turns into *dogmatism* or *positivity* turns into *positivism*, which leads to a serious degeneration of science. (Carnelutti 2004: 63–64)

Ferrajoli approached this line of reasoning when he identified another element of subjective distortion of truth, linked to the professional training of judges, which "is constituted by the legal filters interposed between the judge and the reality of the world of norms, within which the facts to be proven must be subsumed" (Ferrajoli 2002: 48). In this sense, the author points out that the set of norms constitutes

> a language that transcendently conditions the operative language of the judge and, in turn, his or her approach to the facts to be judged. It thus amounts to a system of interpretative schemes of a selective type, which isolates only those elements of the fact deemed criminally 'relevant' and ignores all others. This disposition to read reality *sub specie juris* generates a form of misunderstanding, sometimes even blindness, regarding the events judged, whose complexity is thereby simplified and distorted. (Ferrajoli 2002: 48)

This interplay between legal structures and factual reality reveals the inherent limitations of legal adjudication. The law, in its effort to enforce consistency and predictability, necessarily abstracts and categorises events, which can lead to a distortion of the richness and complexity of lived experience. Judges, constrained by legal definitions and procedural requirements, may inadvertently overlook crucial aspects of a case that fall outside these established frameworks. This selective attention is not merely a technical issue but touches on fundamental questions of justice and fairness, as it shapes which narratives are heard and which are silenced in the courtroom.

Recognising these constraints invites a more reflective legal practice—one that is open to the ambiguities and uncertainties inherent in human affairs. Rather than striving for an unattainable objectivity, legal actors might benefit from acknowledging the interpretive nature of their work and the provisional character of their findings. Such an approach does not undermine the rule of law; rather, it enhances its legitimacy by fostering humility, critical engagement, and a deeper sensitivity to the particularities of each case.

A robust framework for analysing life's phenomena should incorporate the particularities of individual cases, including personal circumstances that may affect the evaluation of censure directed at the agent, while also recognising the victim—whose perspective has frequently been marginalised by mainstream criminal justice systems, an issue that restorative justice initiatives aim to remediate. Furthermore, it is essential to maintain a stringent standard of proof, safeguarded through adversarial proceedings, as reliance on general patterns and uniformly applied rules is better suited to large-scale phenomena. Analytical reductionism, which concentrates solely on regularities and disregards unpredictability, can undermine the integrity of criminal adjudication. For instance, inferring culpability in a current case based solely on prior offences exemplifies the limitations inherent in this methodology.

An additional element frequently overlooked by the criminal justice system is the dynamic between singular incidents and broader societal frameworks. Extensive oppressive systems, such as global capitalism, structural racism, and patriarchy, are often disregarded—individual events tend to be isolated from their wider context and examined solely through a legal perspective.

Structural analysis examines the relationship between individual events and broader systemic frameworks, underscoring the intricacy of human activities. Koselleck asserts that specific structural conditions facilitate certain occurrences, yet these structures only become apparent through the events they enable (Koselleck 2006: 138). He observes that this dynamic presents a substantive methodological challenge: there exists a disconnect between events and structures, as their temporalities diverge, preventing seamless integration in practical or scientific contexts (Koselleck 2006: 139).

Criminal law frequently resolves this complexity by disregarding structural considerations altogether. In contrast, Zaffaroni's (2003) concept of co-culpability seeks to integrate structural factors into assessments of legal responsibility. Co-culpability in criminal law is a principle that divides responsibility for committing a crime between the perpetrator and the State, when the latter fails to provide social and economic opportunities. Defended to reduce the sentence, it recognises the vulnerability of the agent, whose self-determination was affected by state omission. This perspective enriches legal theory by advocating for measured approaches to sentencing, although it remains rarely discussed or implemented in practice.

The tendency to overlook underlying structures is among several factors that highlight the complexity intentionally obscured by modern theoretical frameworks. The primary issue stems from the geometric orientation of modern thought, which aimed to exclude interpretive considerations that were necessary for properly evaluating the specific details of individual cases. This perspective has contributed to the misconception that cognition possesses an unlimited capacity to distil the essence of phenomena solely through factual judgement, thereby enabling a facade of neutral—and ostensibly scientific—application of pertinent norms.

This methodological challenge underscores a critical tension in legal-criminal theory: the reduction of complex realities to typified concepts, while necessary for procedural clarity and safeguarding legality, inevitably results in the selective omission of important contextual elements. The process by which facts are subsumed under legal norms, as Ferrajoli observes, is inherently shaped by interpretative frameworks that filter and simplify the multifaceted nature of events. Consequently, this oversimplification risks distorting the lived reality of the individuals involved. To counter this tendency, it becomes essential for legal analysis to integrate a more nuanced appreciation of individual and structural factors, recognising the limits of dogmatic and positivist approaches and advocating for a methodology that acknowledges, rather than suppresses, the richness and unpredictability of life.

The interplay between fact and law, as discussed above, necessitates a nuanced approach to criminal justice. It is not enough to rely solely on the conceptual frameworks provided by legal dogmatics; rather, the legal system must remain sensitive to the unpredictable and multifaceted nature of real events. This sensitivity is crucial to prevent the reduction of complex human circumstances to simplistic legal categories, which risks eroding the fairness and integrity of judicial proceedings.

As previously discussed, positivist epistemology gained prominence within the legal profession because of law's commitment to rationality and its aspiration to be regarded as an exact science. This motivation fostered an emphasis on universal principles and the belief that reality can be understood through scientific objectivity and neutrality. In the nineteenth century, historiography adopted similar aims.

However, contemporary historians have largely rejected these earlier foundational assumptions. Furet observes that "history, even scholarly history, is not and never will be an exact discipline, in the way we refer to the exact sciences" (Furet 1979: 31). In a comparable vein, Gay asserts that "unlike a natural scientist, the historian is fundamentally similar to those they study. This makes history the most delicate of sciences, easily influenced by new theories and open to charges of bias and ideology" (Gay 1990: 194). Similarly, Gadamer observes that while philologists work with a fixed text before interpretation, historians must continually reconstruct their foundational text: historical reality (Gadamer 1992: 27). Lopes Jr. stresses that history involves not constructing but reconstructing the past within the present (Lopes Jr 2005: 262). Ibañez also points out that facts are not pre-existing realities; instead, they are elements to be reconstructed (Ibañez 2005: 61).

What is expected is an opening of dogmatics to life, abandoning the autopoietic dream of modern positivism. For Carnelutti, "the law, in order to fulfil its task, must compress the fact [...] the fact, in order to be represented, is compressed until it becomes a thing". Thus, "the law seeks to detain the fact and the fact to escape the law" (Carnelutti 2001: 39). As the author highlights,

> a fact may constitute a contract even independently of the civil judge's decision and, thus, by the mere concordant judgement of the parties, produce the effects of a contract; but *on the other hand, a fact cannot be a crime without the judgement of the criminal judge*; for it to be a crime means, in effect, that a penalty is applied to it, but this can only be done by virtue of the criminal judge's decision. [...] *the crime does not exist, that is, a fact does not exist as a crime unless the judge has declared it so, that is, has considered it as such.* A fact, even when it appears similar to one abstractly provided for, is not a crime before the judicial declaration of certainty; without it, there may exist a crime in an ethical sense, but not according to the Law. The declaration of *positive* certainty of the crime is a *necessary* condition for the existence of the crime, just as the declaration of *negative* certainty is a *sufficient* condition for its non-existence. (Carnelutti 2001: 39)

While certainty is a concept that merits cautious consideration—a point to be further analysed—Carnelutti demonstrates that criminal law serves not only affirmative purposes but also a crucial negative function in restricting punitive authority. This is exemplified in cases where typicity is absent or when conduct is rendered neither unlawful nor culpable due to justificatory or exculpatory circumstances. The legal barrier functions not solely as a controlled gateway, but fundamentally to limit the exercise of punitive powers.

To accurately apprehend reality rather than distort it through self-referential frameworks, it is essential to address practical issues directly and adjust the application of criminal law as necessary to accommodate this complexity. Prioritising lived experience over theoretical classifications necessitates micro-historical analysis in criminal cases, highlighting uncertainty, conflict, and negotiation while integrating broader structural considerations. As Carvalho observes, it is essential to open up dogmatics, beginning with an engagement with the reality of life, since the particularities of circumstances in cases involving drugs, gender-based violence, the environment, the financial system, property crimes, for example, demand a sophistication of the structures of criminal law and procedure, without this entailing a rupture with the system of safeguards (Carvalho 2008: 32–33).

Advancing historical understanding in criminal proceedings necessitates moving beyond the constraints of the subject-object paradigm and engaging in inquiry with humility, acknowledging the inherent depth and complexity in examining the past. This approach requires setting aside modern assumptions that suggest objective truths can be discerned solely through the rational subject's methodological capabilities. Timm de Souza, drawing on Rosenzweig, critiques "the prejudice that philosophical intellect harbours towards the objects of its investigation, regarding them *a priori* as realities to be completely laid bare by the analytical power of the philosophical mind" (Souza 2004: 67). In a similar vein, Gadamer asserts that "the naive belief in the objectivity of the historical method was an illusion" (Gadamer 1992: 46).

The key question is how to move beyond this way of thinking. For Taruffo, the activity that establishes the correspondence between fact and norm in the effects of the decision and identifies the legally relevant element escapes the syllogistic scheme, which is not well-founded but continues to inspire the common sense of jurists (Taruffo 2005: 99).

Taruffo's research centres on the concept of facts. Although his methodology is notably more advanced than that of legal positivism, his theoretical structure is still fundamentally based on the same epistemological principles, namely a correspondence theory of truth and the subject-object schema.

For Badaró, it's less crucial to determine whether legal proceedings should or even can seek the true discovery of facts; what's important is to clarify what "truth of the facts" means within a legal context (Badaró 2003: 27).

While I do not share Badaró's perspective regarding the pursuit of truth, I acknowledge that he rightly emphasises the importance of clearly defining the term "fact".

The argument advanced herein is based on a refined conception of fact, which supports moving beyond a simplistic view of factual findings. Within this framework, I agree with various criticisms offered by rationalist scholars who adopt the theory of relative or approximate correspondence truth, though I find that their conclusions lack the desired level of innovation, as will be discussed further. As Gomes Filho has observed,

> Above all, the relative indifference of legal doctrine and practitioners towards the assessment of facts should be emphasised, even though this activity is not only as important as the choice of the norm, but above all because it is precisely here that judicial discretion is most broadly manifested, which should, as a consequence, require greater attention to its control. (Filho 2001: 145)

To commence, it is essential to specify the reference point intended when addressing the concept of proving matters within the domain of facts. Legal scholars frequently overlook the complex interrelations inherent in this context, resolving the issue by simply invoking the term fact. The expression *mere finding of fact* suggests an assumed dominance of the observer over the observed, indicating a dynamic that disregards underlying intricacies. Given that the notion of fact is often ideologically charged and fails to reflect past events accurately, a more thorough analysis and critical assessment are necessary. As Taruffo observes, the task of defining what constitutes a fact involves numerous philosophical considerations (Taruffo 2010: 53). He maintains that "there is no simple or universally accepted definition of 'fact' that can serve as an unquestioned starting point" (Taruffo 2005: 92). According to Carnelutti,

> the aim of criminal proceedings is to determine whether the accused is innocent or guilty, which means, above all, whether a particular fact did or did not occur. But it would be necessary, first, to know what a fact is; a word that is used intuitively, but which deserves greater reflection. (Carnelutti 1965: 71)

Gimeno Sendra maintains that establishing the scope of criminal proceedings based on an objective fact prior to trial—such as identifying a particular act allegedly committed by the defendant—serves to protect defence rights, uphold *res judicata*, and reinforce legal certainty (Sendra 1996: 210).

Sendra correctly points that the categorisation of a specific life event as a legally significant fact serves a safeguard function, associated with the predetermined outline of punishable actions in line with the principle of legality.

Criminal procedure does not engage with reality itself but selects aspects of it, as explained by Coutinho: judgements address structured interpretations, not just events, focusing on how acts are legally classified through typicity, unlawfulness, and culpability, which can have serious outcomes for the accused. Maier notes that substantive legal rules narrow down social conflicts to only relevant elements, excluding the rest (Maier 2006: 855), illustrating the simplification inherent in criminal cases. Neves Baptista adds that the fact to be proven is a legally defined one, already shaped by law before evidence is considered (Batista 2001: 66, 115).

Evidentiary activities should not be perceived through traditional interpretations of "facts" which could simplify intricate situations into basic frameworks and bolster the judicial quest for truth. Carnelutti observes that the legal definition of "fact" intrinsically encompasses aspects of ambiguity.

> is there a word more frequently used than fact? I believe that only *thing* could compete for first place. Both are like certain coins which, through constant circulation, have become so worn that neither head nor tail can be distinguished. Everyone uses them, believing they know their meaning, and so, when someone asks what they mean, the answer does not come as easily as expected. (Carnelutti 2001: 36)

Carnelutti notes that jurists utilise the term *fact* in various contexts without thoroughly examining its conceptual boundaries, thereby necessitating a clear semantic understanding to achieve consensus on its significance.

Taruffo emphasises that we must recognise a fact is never simply straightforward or uniform, nor can it be fully captured by a basic statement like “x exists”. Every fact is made up of various circumstances—such as time, place, temperature, colour, sound, actions, and connections to other events—that together constitute what we call a fact (Taruffo 2010: 223). As Taruffo explains,

> Anyone who attempts, in general terms, to define what constitutes a “fact” will be faced with a very complex problem. When we try to identify, in a generic and approximate way, the situation or portion of experience at issue, the problem arises when we attempt to analytically define this situation and the fact or facts that compose it. Indeed, no descriptive proposition is *a priori* capable of capturing and exhausting the fact, and it cannot even be maintained that it can be *completely* described by a series, however extensive, of propositions. (Taruffo 2005: 93)

Guasp suggests that to truly understand what constitutes a fact, we should view it as an event with three specific dimensions in time and space. According to Guasp (1996: 294), this spatio-temporal aspect is fundamental to the very concept of a fact—his notion of fact acknowledges the pastness of the past, an important point that will be explored in the next chapter.

A thorough assessment of the significance of factual evidence in criminal proceedings is essential. This evaluation is predicated on the understanding that factual references in legal settings reflect the intricacies of empirical reality, necessitating critical scrutiny as part of human experience. While both criminal law and historiography focus on the investigation of human actions rather than natural phenomena, criminal law does so within the structured parameters established by the analytical concept of crime in legal doctrine—a very peculiar lens through which events experienced in life are interpreted according to their legal consequences.

The dogmatic approach distils from an interconnected life narrative a structured framework, analysing actions and omissions based on their consequences, which may align or diverge from the agents' original intentions, to which they may either assent or simply acquiesce. These acts occur within defined spatial and temporal contexts and are motivated by reasons that clarify why individuals chose specific courses of action or inaction. Agents, as those responsible for acting, omitting, allowing, or contributing to outcomes, can therefore be held accountable and subject to censure. Context and circumstances, not always created by the agents themselves but nonetheless influential, may facilitate, impede, or occasionally justify their conduct. Typically, these actions are directed towards others—either against, in favour of, or in cooperation with individuals—or may pertain to material and immaterial goods. They can involve various means or instruments, ranging from complex to simple. Such actions generally result in harm—they usually produce effects and potentially legally significant side consequences, whether intended, unintended, or merely accepted by the agents. All these elements are deeply intertwined, interconnected, and mutually significant, in addition to being permeated by all the layers of complexity inherent to human society.

This intricate interplay between action, context, and consequence illustrates the profound difficulty in isolating and defining the factual substratum of legal proceedings. The narrative constructed in the courtroom is not a mere recitation of neutral events but an interpretative act, shaped by the perspectives of those recounting and those evaluating these legally established facts. Each participant—be it the accused, the witnesses, or the legal practitioners—contributes to a layered understanding, where the meaning of what occurred is continually negotiated and reinterpreted. Thus, the factual question in criminal law is not simply a technical matter of evidence gathering but also an exercise in understanding the multifaceted nature of human behaviour within its real-life context through legal lens while being conscious that such lens does not equate reality. As Carnelutti observes,

> we cannot do without these puppets; but we must not forget that they are mere copies of the original, which is the human being. In short, I mean that anything may happen in my classes; but that my students should confuse the man who steals with the puppet of theft, or the man who kills with the marionette of homicide, that, God willing, will not happen. (Carnelutti 2004: 50)

Although Carnelutti's cautionary perspective warrants consideration, it is essential to emphasise that the prevailing legal framework mandates these entities, as their safeguards are fundamental unless one envisages completely forgoing modern criminal law—a course neither recommended nor feasible in contemporary circumstances. As Carvalho observes, "criminal law and criminal procedure remain necessary as alternatives to politics, presenting themselves as technologies for minimising violence and the arbitrariness of punitive power" (Carvalho 2008: 212).

It has been determined that the concept of a "fact" involves considerable simplification. Nevertheless, considering an event as a solitary fact within the framework of legal interests does not preclude the existence of numerous subtleties. While criminal proceedings might superficially appear to follow a binary framework—resulting in verdicts of either guilt or innocence—the process of reaching such decisions pertains to past occurrences and necessitates addressing a multifaceted set of inquiries. These questions exceed the scope of modern scientific inquiry both in their significance and context, posing substantial challenges even to those directly witnessing the events, let alone those attempting to fully resolve their complexity by merely surmounting historical obstacles.

This complexity becomes apparent when one acknowledges that the interpretation of a "fact" must address several aspects: what occurred, why, who was involved, how, when, with or against whom or what, in what manner, at what location, and for what purpose. As Koselleck, citing Gentz, observes, whether Louis XVI was assassinated, executed, or punished—a matter debated by historians—matters more than the mere fact that he was killed by guillotine (Koselleck 2006: 185). Similarly, in criminal law, focusing solely on the outcome is inadequate; the deprivation of life is only part of a broader inquiry that includes demonstrating causality, considering exonerating circumstances, confirming intent and volition towards the result or acceptance of risk, and identifying any failure to exercise required objective care, among other considerations.

Life as Lived Experience and Statements About Facts

As Taruffo observes, the events relevant to justice are *tranches de vie*, that is, events or sets of events related to people's lives (Taruffo 2010: 55). From my interpretative perspective, the focus here is on *life*, in the sense given by Dilthey and later refined by the hermeneutic tradition: the realm of contingency and unpredictability.

This perspective posits that life should be understood through categories inherent to its nature, necessitating the inclusion of sensibilities in analysis as opposed to relying solely on methodological rigour and the supposed impartiality of rational inquiry. Souza (2004: 24) asserts that the essence of life extends beyond its conceptual boundaries. For Dilthey, life is not a metaphysical construct but rather consists of lived experiences—a foundational notion (Palmer 1997: 109). Similarly, Soares maintains that when interpreting life, it is essential to regard it holistically, ensuring that both parts and the whole reciprocally inform and assign meaning to one another (Soares 2004: 43). Such an approach is grounded in premises distinct from those underlying modern determinism. According to Soares,

> It is typical of life to give rise to difference, the singular, the radically new, the particular in an irreducible sense. Life is, therefore, contingency, accident, chance. It is the ungovernable or unforeseeable generation of events. Facticity gives way to lived experience, internally unravelled by arbitrariness, by chance. (Soares 2004: 40)

Soares considers that "like life, history produces more than regularities that can be grasped by explanations aimed at establishing laws and causal links: it is the realm of contingency and requires a hermeneutic treatment *a posteriori*, so that phenomena acquire meaning" (Soares 2004: 43). In this sense, life and history—at the margins of their regularities—create singular phenomena, are sources of irreducible particularities, and carry, even if only virtually, the rupture of the laws that analytical monitoring of their unfolding would allow to be formulated (Soares 2004: 45).

Therefore, any attempt to understand an event must necessarily acknowledge this complexity, so that the web constituting the event represents a narrative that is fundamentally opaque to those who seek to know it—a task not facilitated by the adoption of a linguistic-formal structure for addressing such events. In this regard, according to Ibañez, the judicial treatment given to facts assumes that they are natural facts, previously and definitively constituted as such from the moment of their occurrence, requiring only objective identification (Ibañez 2005: 49). Given this definition of fact, it would be possible for the judge, spontaneously and without mediation, to establish a relationship of total exteriority with them, with minimal subjective implications. However, as the author points out, the pure fact of philosophical positivism does not exist and, therefore, factual judgements understood as mere findings of brute data are not possible (Ibañez 2005: 49). According to Taruffo,

> The common-sense idea that for every fact there exists *an* objective and appropriate description seems, therefore, clearly unacceptable, not based on subjectivist approaches, but because the levels of analysis of the same situation can be very different (in theory: unlimited). (Taruffo 2005: 94)

Taruffo points out that legal philosophers have essentially concerned themselves with the interpretation and application of norms, without delving particularly into the analysis of facts, except in terms of their reduction (or subsumption) to normative premises (Taruffo 2010: 226). For Gomes Filho, the indifference of legal doctrine and practitioners towards facts

> has as its most visible causes, the false consciousness that factual judgments are mere findings of realities that have no independent existence and, therefore, do not need to be justified; in other words, facts are *evident* and, as such, do not require justification, even if such *evidence* has been obtained indirectly. (Filho 2001: 145)

A focus on normative structures over past reality can lead to harmful outcomes. Ibañez (2005) notes that facts never explain themselves; factual judgement is always necessary. Döhring (1986) argues that jurists must determine the relevant facts before applying legal norms, as legal science is not solely about rules. He points out that it's rare for facts to be clear from the start—uncertainty often lies in reconstructing events, particularly in criminal cases. When both facts and law are unclear, clarifying the facts becomes the main challenge. The purpose of evidence, according to Döhring, is to establish those facts upon which legal consequences depend or from which other legally significant facts may be inferred.

However, the main challenge is that these are not simply objective facts; rather, they constitute assertions or narrative representations of past events. As observed by Taruffo,

> When we speak of the construction, definition or identification of the fact, or of the individualisation of the level of reality or the degree of precision at which it is determined, or also of the way in which norms individualise legally relevant facts, it seems evident that reference is not being made to

> the fact as an occurrence in empirical reality, but to statements, of various kinds, referring to occurrences that are supposed to take place in the world of empirical reality. (Taruffo 2005: 113)

Consequently, these are not objectively established facts, but rather statements shaped by narrative intent that serve to construct an argument about their significance. While Taruffo stops short of pursuing this argument to its logical endpoint—a limitation I regard as one of the key conceptual gaps in the author's approach to truth—I believe that acknowledging this dynamic creates a significant challenge for asserting a corresponding truth, even one that is relative or approximate, as a regime of truth within proceedings. Badaró states that

> The facts debated in the proceedings are statements about facts in the real world, that is, what is said about a fact: it is the statement of a fact and not the fact itself. Consequently, the object of proof is not the fact itself. What is proven are the allegations of facts made by the parties as the basis for the prosecution and the defence. What can be true or false, veracious or untrue, or "proven", are the allegations about the fact. (Badaró 2003: 159-160)

While this approach does not distinguish between fact and event as proposed here, the contemporary rationalist viewpoint recognises that legal proceedings do not access an unmediated reality. Instead, language serves as a tool for interpreting past occurrences within a legal framework to ascertain guilt or acquittal.

According to Taruffo, "the truth of the fact is merely an elliptical formula to refer to the truth of the statement whose object is a fact" (Taruffo 2005: 117). The author observes that the facts in proceedings are not empirically determined entities: they are narratives relating to facts, and it is necessary to determine which of these narratives best corresponds to the best possible interpretative application of the relevant norm (Taruffo 2010: 226).

This is a critical consideration, as the evaluation of the meaning of truth with respect to narrative representations derived from arguments presented during proceedings challenges the underlying model of corresponding truth more fundamentally than Taruffo acknowledges. Put differently, evidentiary processes are informed by assumptions that extend beyond not only the perception of an objectively discernible reality through straightforward factual judgement but also surpass the more nuanced concept of relative corresponding truth.

Ibañez provides a more comprehensive analysis of the issue than Taruffo. According to Ibañez, judges do not engage directly with facts but rather with propositions regarding facts—cognitive representations that refer to events in the real world. The acquisition of knowledge about facts is inherently mediated by language, which introduces elements of relativism, uncertainty, and ambiguity into this cognitive process (Ibañez 2005: 50). The author asserts that, for judges, discursive mediation is not merely a straightforward description of phenomena existing independently of judicial activity; instead, it constitutes a process of reconstructing the fact, wherein the judge plays an active role from within, thus incorporating subjectivity inherent to any reconstructive endeavour (Ibañez 2005: 51–52).

Although not thoroughly analysed, the linguistic aspect should be regarded as an important limitation on the cognitive privilege of the judge—a factor not addressed by evidentiary rationalism.

Rationalists assert that truth is absolute while recognising that knowledge of the truth is inherently relative. For them, although absolute truth may be unattainable, the pursuit of it remains essential so that relative understanding can approximate this ideal as closely as possible. Within this framework, the judge serves as the central epistemic agent, responsible for diligently seeking the truth by consistently expanding the scope of evidence considered. This Bentham-inspired process aims to enhance the likelihood that judicial decisions reflect the closest possible approximation to absolute truth.

The rationalist argument presents a strong case for a criminal justice system founded on the pursuit of truth, ideally resulting in convictions when the individual is accountable and acquittals when they are not. However, although this perspective may seem persuasive in theory, practical experience demonstrates otherwise. This theoretical framework reinstates the pursuit of inquisitorial truth by emphasising a commitment to uncovering factual accuracy at the expense of procedural safeguards and human rights protections. It endorses an approach to uncertainty that favours ongoing investigation over exoneration, with the goal of attaining absolute truth. Extensive historical evidence indicates that a criminal justice system predominantly centred on uncovering the truth is susceptible to bias, selective or widespread incarceration, and an elevated likelihood of judicial errors and wrongful convictions.

Evidentiary rationalism correctly identifies the limitations of modern legal epistemology when it comes to "mere finding of facts", "syllogism", and "real or absolute truth". But the solution that evidentiary rationalism presents to the epistemological limits it encounters is problematic: acknowledging the inherent limitations of knowledge regarding historical realities—specifically, the impossibility of reaching absolute corresponding truth—the approach taken in lieu of the alternative of outright falsehood is to revitalise the framework of corresponding truth through the concept of relative truth (the pursuit of knowledge about the truth), while continuing to maintain the aspiration for material or absolute truth. Within this revised perspective, corresponding truth refers not to the past event itself (the "unattainable material or absolute truth"), but rather to the alignment between judicial decisions and the evidentiary statements submitted during proceedings (relative truth or knowledge of the truth). Nevertheless, striving for "absolute, material, or objective truth" remains significant and desirable, necessitating that judges undertake an epistemic role in the quest for truth, including an expansive consideration of evidentiary material that disregards the importance of procedural safeguards. This establishes an intrasystemic model of justification, wherein a judicial decision is deemed true when the judge's assessment aligns with what is substantiated in the proceedings; conversely, it is considered false when such correspondence is absent (Beltrán 2005: 43–44).

Within this framework, judicial decisions are deemed valid when supported by factual proof originating from the judge's direct efforts, thereby reflecting a substantiated knowledge of the truth. Citing such proof and articulating the rationale underlying the decision adequately establish its legitimacy. Where an epistemic and foundational distinction exists between absolute truth (which may be unattainable) and knowledge of the truth (as derived from evidence), the evidentiary record functions both to ratify the decision and to justify the epistemic role undertaken by the judge in pursuing absolute truth.

In other words, the ruling's legitimacy is established based on the evidence submitted by the judge throughout the proceedings. This perspective, which adheres closely to self-reinforcing principles, may be susceptible to various types of confirmation bias.

Departing to some extent from positivist reasoning, rationalist scholars acknowledge that it is unrealistic to expect judges to reach identical outcomes when assessing the narrative accounts provided by parties during legal proceedings—variations in the interpretation of facts and the application of rules are unavoidable and uncertainty abounds.

It must be recognised that they make concerted efforts to develop objective criteria and standards to mitigate these challenges. But the proposed framework proves to be inconsistent. The pursuit of truth as a political and epistemological goal is consistent only with a system that genuinely regards absolute truth as attainable. A system that treats the knowledge of the truth as relative and acknowledges numerous epistemological limitations in its pursuit should favour human rights. It should be conscious that wrongful convictions are very likely and uphold a harm reduction programme. Yet rationalist scholars continue to adhere to correspondence theory and uphold the cognitive authority of the judge—which is at odds with their own reasoning. Their arguments provide enough relativism to prompt a re-evaluation of established beliefs about evidentiary practices. Rather than simply reaffirming the search for truth, it should be critically reconsidered—the corresponding theory of truth does not account for the lived experience of criminal proceedings.

The rationalist epistemology does not seem to account for the principle that uncertainty regarding historical facts should operate in favour of the accused. Rather, it prioritises the pursuit of truth, which is considered both the principal objective and the institutional cornerstone of criminal proceedings. Such an approach facilitates human rights violations and wrongful convictions. In judicial proceedings, a judge's personal intuition—consciously or not—can sometimes take precedence over objective evidence, prompting a search for additional evidence that aligns with their expectations. Under such circumstances, there is a tangible risk that assumptions may influence the determination of factual findings. Therefore, it is essential to extend arguments that challenge the epistemological foundations of positivism to their logical endpoints, which would necessitate the abandonment of the search for truth in criminal justice.

Taruffo contends that designating judges as truth-seekers addresses a primary issue: the perceived lack of commitment to truthfulness by the parties, thus necessitating judicial responsibility in upholding truth. However, his approach is consistent with judicial activism, which has faced significant scrutiny in recent years and is frequently regarded as incompatible with human rights safeguards, as it can favour authoritarian measures under the justification of societal protection. While it is important to acknowledge the inherent limitations in the knowledge of truth, this recognition should not, as some rationalists suggest, justify expanding judicial evidentiary frameworks indefinitely under the rationale of "better informing" decisions. Such an approach can inadvertently increase the risk of wrongful convictions while ostensibly striving for absolute truth. Historical evidence indicates that judge-centred truth-seeking practices often foster authoritarian tendencies and unchecked judicial authority. Therefore, understanding epistemological boundaries necessitates a critical strengthening of constraints on punitive power.

In contrast, my stance diverges significantly from Taruffo's; I contend that adversarial proceedings—rooted in dialogue—constitute the most reliable evidentiary framework for examining allegations. Criminal trials are inevitably influenced by the dynamic between factual narratives and the interpretative paradigms established by legal norms. This relationship implies that evidentiary activity should be intrinsically linked to the argumentative strategies deployed by the parties and the wider discursive environment in which evidence is introduced and assessed under the watchful eye of a judge strongly focused on the rules of due process.

This does not require judges to assume a truth-seeking function, nor does it oblige them to act as passive recipients of information akin to bureaucratic officials. Rather, judges play an active part in upholding due process and constructing meaning, mediating between divergent narratives and endeavouring to justify their rulings within the parameters of procedural fairness and impartiality to mitigate wrongful convictions. As Gomes Filho remarks,

> this complex operation of legal qualification of facts does not dispense with a certain degree, more or less intense depending on the characteristics of the case under examination, of judicial creativity, which is manifested through evaluative judgments, both in the application of the norm to the fact and in the very ascertainment of the fact itself. (Filho 2001: 171)

The term *judicial creativity* merits recognition for its significance. Although its ramifications will be addressed in the concluding chapter, it is notable that the phrase itself does not immediately illuminate the substantial risks associated with this imaginative aspect.

Consequently, such impulses—regardless of whether they are conscious or not—should be regulated by a framework intended to constrain punitive authority and limit the discretion intrinsic to judicial creativity. Achieving this necessitates the removal of truth-seeking logic.

In light of these considerations, it becomes clear that the pursuit of truth in legal proceedings cannot be approached as a purely objective or scientific endeavour as evidentiary rationalism advocates. The interplay between evidence, interpretative frameworks, and evaluative judgements means that the adjudicative process is inherently shaped by the perspectives and preconceptions of those involved—as will be explored later, the judge is a being-in-the-world. This subjectivity does not undermine the importance of striving for fairness; rather, it highlights the necessity of procedural safeguards and critical reflection to mitigate the risks of arbitrariness.

Evaluation in criminal law relies on objective criteria set by processes of primary criminalisation (criminal law), binding judges to act-based legal structures rather than inquisitorial subjectivity. The analytical concept of crime underpins and frames the meaning of legal cases. However, judges still must interpret and construct narratives when deciding cases, which introduces elements of creativity. The persistence of an inquisitorial epistemology in evaluating facts can undermine legality by allowing subjective truth-making. Ultimately, if such an approach prevails, legal restrictions become ineffective, as evidentiary boundaries are shaped by the dominant epistemology (Cordero 2000: 10).

Although rationalist methods attempt to temper the pursuit of absolute truth, they remain influenced by its inherent appeal. Consequently, it is necessary to reconsider this methodology, as redefining the search for truth does not resolve underlying challenges; rather, it perpetuates the notion that a judge's primary responsibility is the epistemic pursuit of truth.

Taruffo's critique is both relevant and significant, with the author offering a framework for legal reasoning that extends beyond a purely positivist perspective. Nevertheless, it appears necessary to take his analysis further, as Taruffo still relies on the rational individual's cognitive abilities to pursue and broaden the evidentiary scope, without fully accounting for the complex and context-dependent nature of legal processes in their entirety.

Evidentiary rationalism tends to overlook that the judge constructs, rather than merely discovers, the truth. Some scholars, like Taruffo, acknowledge reconstructive activity but overlook the risks when one individual controls the evidentiary proceedings. This approach, while claiming that truth should not be sought "at any cost" fails to set boundaries and perpetuates inquisitorial practices by allowing judges to pursue a subjective version of truth. Ultimately, this maintains undemocratic orientations in criminal justice and threatens the rights of the accused.

Taruffo's rejection of syllogistic logic and the mere finding of fact is well-documented; however, the alternative framework he offers does not sufficiently address the challenges posed by persistent inquisitorial frameworks—in many ways, it reinvigorates them. According to Taruffo, judges are not presented with facts as concrete historical events readily perceivable in their particularities. Instead, judges must construct or reconstruct the facts from available elements: (a) the parties' submissions regarding primary and secondary facts; (b) information arising from procedural activity, particularly the management of evidence by the judge—an epistemic function of search for truth; and (c) insights derived from experience and common sense (Taruffo 2010: 230). With respect to the "maxims of experience" cited by Taruffo, these principles present a potential risk of judicial subjectivity, as they may allow for considerable interpretive discretion.

Crucially, the fundamental concern with Taruffo's position is that he envisions an active judicial role guided by a notion of corresponding truth, thus placing considerable confidence in the judge's capacity to directly operationalise such reconstruction and exercise what he describes as an epistemic function aimed at discovering the truth. While his criticisms of the mere finding of fact may be valid, his proposed solution is ultimately inadequate.

In contrast, my perspective diverges from "evidentiary rationalism", advocating for a sophisticated understanding of factual determination that includes clear procedural safeguards to mitigate the risks of decisionism. Excessive reliance on the judge's discretion in pursuit of truth can result in violations of the accused's human rights, reducing them to mere objects of inquiry. Therefore, criminal justice should be reconceptualised as a ritual designed to minimise such risks. The essential distinction lies in the imperative to limit reliance on the judge's presumed goodwill, opting instead for systemic impartiality upheld by the accusatorial model. This deliberate trust in procedural safeguards serves to constrain punitive authority, thereby protecting against judicial arbitrariness and ensuring that the outcome does not depend solely on the personal inclinations or subjective reasoning of the judge.

The limitations inherent in judicial fact-finding underscore the necessity for a more nuanced and restrained approach to adjudication. Rather than relying solely on the judge's interpretative authority, criminal proceedings must be structured to ensure transparency and accountability, with the accused's rights firmly protected throughout. This involves recognising the interpretative nature of evidence and the constructed character of factual narratives, thereby fostering a climate in which procedural fairness and impartiality are prioritised above subjective truth-seeking.

In legal proceedings, the notion of truth should be considered as contingent upon the specific circumstances and context of each individual case. While the prosecution seeks to persuade the judge, securing a conviction is neither assured nor presumed, in accordance with the presumption of innocence. The fact-finding process does not rest on an independent pursuit of absolute truth by the judge; instead, it relies upon the arguments and evidence introduced by the parties during trial. If the judge is satisfied beyond reasonable doubt of the accused's guilt, the facts may be determined based on the prosecution's case. Conversely, where uncertainty remains, acquittal is required, indicating that reasonable doubt takes precedence over the attainment of absolute truth.

As previously noted, advancing beyond the constraints of modern scientific methods requires a thoughtful approach characterised by collaboration and respect for both the subject of investigation and the rights of the accused. This approach differs significantly from viewing the judge's role as performing an "epistemic function" focused on the pursuit of truth in criminal proceedings. This calls for thoughtful analysis and the establishment of explicit guidelines, instead of promoting discretionary approaches by judges when faced with uncertainty. The challenge, then, is to design institutional mechanisms that balance the necessity for judicial interpretation with robust procedural safeguards. Such mechanisms should constrain the scope for unchecked subjectivity, ensuring criminal proceedings remains firmly anchored within the boundaries of legality and due process. Safeguarding the rights of the accused requires not only procedural formality but also an ongoing critical awareness of how narratives are constructed and facts are understood within the courtroom context.

Adjudication, therefore, focuses less on reconstructing an absolute historical reality and more on identifying which narrative best withstands critical evaluation based on the presented evidence and applicable legal standards. This approach highlights the necessity for transparency, robust argumentation, and procedural safeguards to ensure that judicial outcomes are both legally sound and epistemically justified, while upholding human rights. As will be discussed in the next chapter, the pastness of the past serves as a crucial element when examining truth in criminal proceedings—an aspect that Taruffo and Ferrer-Beltrán completely overlook.

Ferrajoli's approach, by contrast, foregrounds the inherent limitations of reconstructing past events within the context of legal proceedings. He emphasises that the so-called procedural truth achieved in court is not an objective or absolute reflection of historical reality, but rather a contingent, context-bound outcome shaped by the adversarial process and the available evidence. This perspective recognises the impossibility of fully accessing the past and cautions against any judicial aspiration to omniscience or unfettered authority in fact-finding.

Accordingly, Ferrajoli's stance aligns with a more restrained and principled conception of adjudication—one that accepts the provisional nature of factual determinations and insists on procedural safeguards against arbitrariness. By rejecting the notion of the judge as an active seeker of truth, Ferrajoli underscores the primacy of the presumption of innocence and the necessity for rigorous standards of proof. This approach not only mitigates the risk of judicial overreach but also serves to protect the accused from the dangers of retrospective certainty, thus reinforcing the fundamental values underpinning the rule of law.

Regarding the pursuit of truth and the pastness of the past, Ferrajoli's perspective differs markedly from that of Taruffo and Ferrer-Beltrán. Ferrajoli posits that "factual procedural truth is, in reality, a specific kind of historical truth, concerning statements about past events that cannot be directly experienced" (Ferrajoli 2002: 43). Although he does not examine the implications in detail, Ferrajoli's focus on historical truth led him to reject the notion that judges should actively seek the truth.

Accordingly, the focus of the analysis now shifts to the theory of history. The following section introduces the examination of the concept of pastness by revisiting a longstanding debate within socio-legal studies: the comparative analysis of the roles of the judge and the historian.

The Roles of the Judge and the Historian—A Reappraisal of a Traditional Analogy

Within the framework for reimagining criminal justice presented here, the comparison between the roles of judge and historian is of central importance, given their shared engagement with the interpretation of past events.

Scholarly literature has extensively discussed the parallels between these professions; it is a longstanding analogy that frequently illuminates the potential risks inherent in narratively reconstructing history. The persistence of this comparison stems from clear reasons: both judges and historians attribute significant importance to evidence when establishing the occurrence of historical events. Numerous scholars examine the concept of evidence by drawing analogies between these roles. Cordero, for instance, introduces the notion of *historical typicality*, asserting that judicial deliberations address historical cases (Cordero 2000: 381). Calamandrei and Aragoneses Alonso employ the term *historical judgement*, explicitly likening judges to historians (Alonso 1996: 558; Calamandrei 1999: 243). Carnelutti discusses a retrospective orientation in both civil and criminal proceedings—the former concerning contractual execution and the latter focusing on punishment of offences. For Carnelutti, this orientation signifies engagement with the past, equating it with history, thereby designating such judicial processes as historical judgements (Carnelutti 2001: 56). He contends that evidence enables this retrospection, serving as the mechanism for reconstructing history. In his view, determining whether an event occurred is inherently a backward-looking endeavour—precisely the work of history.

When considering history, one is confronted with the complexities of reconstructing past events—challenges that parallel those faced within judicial proceedings (Carnelutti 1965: 72). Similarly, Gomes Filho highlights the convergence between the functions of judges and historians, noting that both are engaged in reviving past events in the present through the analysis of evidence (Filho 1997: 44). Ferrajoli asserts that "the trial is, so to speak, the only case of historiographical experimentation" (Ferrajoli 2002: 48). Maier argues that judicial procedure largely constitutes a legally regulated form of historical inquiry, as it seeks to verify the truth of a historical hypothesis—whether affirmative or negative—that forms the core of the proceedings (Maier 2006: 844). He further maintains that criminal law's focus on the retribution of individual unlawful acts necessarily entails an evidentiary process oriented towards investigating and understanding the past (Maier 2006: 149). According to Maier, the aim of the proceedings is to establish the veracity of a historical hypothesis via a legally structured process of historical investigation (Maier 2006: 847). Coutinho observes that after a crime has occurred, sanctions are imposed only following a judicial decision, which must be based on the procedural reconstruction of the criminal act to the extent that a procedurally valid truth demonstrating culpability is established (Coutinho 1998: 137).

Accordingly, much of the literature on criminal procedure suggests that criminal evidence inherently involves a form of historical reconstruction, irrespective of differing perspectives on truth. The comparison between judicial and historiographical methods is thus well-established and continues to provoke thoughtful consideration of the judge's function in criminal proceedings. Historians have also drawn such parallels, exploring the issue from the standpoint of historical theory. Ginzburg, for instance, states that "judges and historians are united by their concern with the definition of facts, in the broadest sense of the term, including everything that is, in some way, inscribed in reality" (Ginzburg 2002: 62). Within philosophy, Ricoeur notably examined the enduring comparison between historians and judges, describing it as a *locus classicus* for multiple reasons (Ricoeur 2003: 421).

The prevalence of this analogy is not accidental; the historical development of both professions reveals substantial overlap. Bann notes that both jurists and historians originated from identical institutions and often operated within the same social circles. He explains, "University historians of the last century initially found themselves, willingly or otherwise, in close association with academic lawyers. At Cambridge, the moral sciences examination instituted in 1848 encompassed economics, politics, moral philosophy, jurisprudence, law, English, and history. In 1867, jurisprudence and history were removed and combined into a law and history examination, which was short-lived, before history became an independent discipline in 1873" (Bann 1994: 41).

It is important to recognise legal influences that shape historians' methods, even if these origins are sometimes disputed. Bann notes that law shares controversial methodology and judgement with history, prompting historians to separate their work from legal institutions (Bann

1994: 9). The judge-historian analogy persists, yet jurists often misunderstand historical analysis, wrongly assuming it still follows Leopold von Ranke's nineteenth-century concept of reporting facts exactly as they happened. Koselleck explains Ranke's approach aimed for neutral and objective representation by critically studying authentic sources, pursuing a singular comprehensive truth (Koselleck 2006: 165).

Some legal scholars claim historians can pinpoint what happened in the past and when, treating them as ultimate authorities on historical truth. This assumption leads some to compare judges to historians, suggesting criminal trials reveal objective reality. However, this reflects outdated nineteenth-century historiographical ideas, which assume facts lead directly to hypotheses and explanations are simply cause-and-effect. As Hobsbawm notes, such models presume history's exact truth is fully reconstructable (Hobsbawm 2001: 156).

The matter is considerably more intricate than a traditional notion of corresponding truth may suggest. Chartier notes that historical knowledge can no longer be viewed as merely a straightforward reproduction or equivalence between an object and discourse, nor simply between the past and its portrayal through historical narration (Chartier 2001: 136). He further comments that "the certainties of critical objectivity and the epistemology of coincidence between reality and its knowledge no longer protect history from an unease regarding its regime of truth" (Chartier 2001: 139). This sense of unease serves a constructive purpose and should always be acknowledged and addressed.

Contemporary historiography challenges the positivist view of historical truth, arguing that facts are shaped by questions, sources, and interpretation rather than existing independently. This perspective suggests that equating judicial findings with historical truth overlooks inherent subjectivity and idiosyncrasies in both fields. Legal scholarship, like history, must recognise the constructed nature of its fact-finding, and yet has to fully utilise the analytical tools of historical theory—particularly regarding the "pastness of the past", which remains underexplored even in advanced studies such as the one undertaken by Ferrajoli (2002).

Misinterpretations of modern historiography, coupled with insufficient interdisciplinary training among jurists, frequently lead legal analyses to prioritise the legal perspective while relegating history to a subsidiary role. Consequently, this approach produces partial and biased viewpoints that neglect the distinct methodologies and contributions of other disciplines—an issue this study aims to systematically address. As Ricoeur

(2003: 419) articulates, the functions of both judge and historian necessitate assuming an independent, third-party perspective regarding the public sphere, thereby upholding a standard of impartiality—one that maintains distance from subjective pursuits of truth and recognises impartiality as an essential and foundational criterion. According to Carnelutti,

> indeed, the judge, like the historian, makes history, or more precisely, historiography. The only difference is that, in most cases, while the historian deals with great deeds, the judge concerns himself with small ones. But this is not an absolute rule: there are historical works dedicated to seeking out small things from the past; and there are judges upon whom fate has placed the burden of punishing a people (Carnelutti 2001: 57) [...] the judge—we have said—is also a historian, with only a difference between great and small history. Since the history the judge makes, or rather reconstructs, is small history, it may seem that his task would be easier than constructing great history. However, I wonder whether it is easier to handle the microscope than the telescope: is not the difference between people and individual the difference between microcosm and macrocosm? To attach too much importance to the distinction between small and great things is an aspect of our blindness; the experience of the atom should already have revealed this. (Carnelutti 1965: 81)

Irrespective of discussions regarding the scale of events of interest—which may have been rendered less significant by developments such as microhistory—the central premise is that historians investigate topics they select and critically analyse themselves. Historically, inquisitorial judges initiated *ex officio* proceedings based on mere rumours; in contrast, contemporary cases are brought before judges according to established jurisdictional rules that determine which cases are subject to adjudication. The principal function of judges is to reach decisions regarding conflicts and harm, a duty that notably differs from that of historians. This distinction highlights the power exercised by the judiciary, particularly its authority to impose sanctions. Judges must operate within procedural constraints prescribed by the accusatorial system, whereas historians enjoy greater latitude in constructing their narratives. The most notable divergence lies in these limitations: judges must develop their accounts within fixed legal frameworks, while historians are afforded substantial freedom and are not bound by requirements of impartial judgement.

Within accusatorial epistemology, judges face constraints on their decision-making that historians do not. Judges are bound by legal procedures and can only evaluate facts deemed relevant by the parties, operating within strict boundaries set by law (Calamandrei 1973: 112; Coutinho 2002: 177). This contrasts with historians, who may freely use any method to uncover historical truth. Legal truth must fit within formal evidentiary rules, so even if a judge personally believes something outside these methods, it cannot be accepted in court (Calamandrei 1973: 112–113). While impartiality is safeguarded through such restrictions, historians would use all available information regardless of method (Taruffo 2010: 161). Ultimately, the rules governing judges fundamentally separate their epistemological approach from that of historians.

However, although such limits exist, they are often ignored in practice. Judges, citing their pursuit of truth and subtly veiled inquisitorial methods, may exert broad authority that risks more than simple errors in historical analysis. Therefore, judicial boundaries must be defined more clearly and strictly than those for historians, especially due to the magistrate's punitive powers.

Examining the impact of doubt clarifies the difference between judges and historians. When evidence is lacking or conflicting, historians must refrain from drawing conclusions and label their findings inconclusive until credible documentation emerges (Calamandrei 1973: 113). Judges, however, are required to reach decisions even in uncertainty; under the *in dubio pro reo* principle, they must acquit if doubts remain rather than pursue endless investigation. Unlike historians, judges are not tasked with finding historical truth but with protecting the rights of the accused and ensuring due process. The search for absolute truth becomes relevant only for conviction, reflecting a punitive approach contemporary criminal justice should avoid. Ginzburg highlights this key divergence between judge and historian.

> for the former, the margin of uncertainty has a purely negative meaning, and may lead to a *non liquet* —in contemporary terms, to an acquittal for lack of proof. For the latter, it compels a deepening of the investigation, linking the specific case to the context, understood here as a field of historically determined possibilities. (Ginzburg 1989: 183)

Judges are not required to justify acquittals or explain verdicts of innocence, unlike historians who must cite sources. Only convictions need to be supported by proof. In accusatorial systems, parties manage evidence and the judge remains impartial; if doubt exists, the defendant is acquitted. In contrast, inquisitorial systems involve judges in truth-seeking, which can disadvantage defendants and weaken procedural protections, highlighting the importance of keeping evidence management separate from judicial roles.

The pressure to decide is especially significant for judges confronting historical events. Unlike historians, who can delay their conclusions, judges must make timely decisions to resolve disputes and reduce defendants' hardship (Calamandrei 1999: 270). As Carnelutti notes,

> unfortunately, human justice is so constituted that it causes men to suffer not only because they are guilty, but also to determine whether they are guilty or innocent. This, unfortunately, is a necessity from which the procedure cannot escape, even if it were humanly perfect. (Carnelutti 1965: 75)

Leading an investigation affects outcomes: historians seek evidence supporting their own hypotheses, focusing on information relevant to their research interests. Judges, especially in accusatorial systems, may develop opinions but are not meant to direct proceedings, avoiding pitfalls of subjective inquiry. Calamandrei noted that historians resemble lawyers more than judges:

> the lawyer acts upon reality like the historian, who gathers facts according to a pre-established selection criterion, and disregards those which, considering that criterion, seem irrelevant. The lawyer, like the historian, would betray their profession if they altered the truth by inventing facts; but does not do so when they merely select and organise from raw reality only those aspects advantageous to their case. (Calamandrei 1996: 128)

Lawyers may take sides, but judges must remain impartial, especially in accusatorial systems. However, unconscious biases can lead judges to reinforce their own views or seek evidence for their assumptions. Unlike historians and lawyers, this lack of impartiality is problematic for judges, whose neutrality is essential in democratic proceedings. As Calamandrei notes,

> it is true that, as intended by the law, the means of evidence are instruments for discovering the truth; and it is also correct that the judge can be compared, as an impartial investigator of the truth, to the historian, but

> in reality the history written by the judge is not simply the history of the truth, but rather the history (the "sports chronicle", we might say) of the contest through which one of the parties has succeeded in making their truth prevail in the proceedings, *secundum allegata et probata* (according to what has been alleged and proven). (Calamandrei 1999: 243)

When judges seek truth by presenting evidence, they take on roles usually held by the parties, similar to historians or inquisitorial judges. However, criminal proceedings are designed to protect the accused's rights and limit punitive power—unlike historians, judges must face strict boundaries. These limitations need clear definition due to legal complexity and the importance of due process. While historians interpret past actions, judges make decisions affecting living people, often imposing severe consequences that extend beyond punishment and impact society, reaffirming prevailing hierarchies of class, race, gender, sexuality, and spirituality (Khaled Jr and Gloeckner 2026).

This distinction between the judge and the historian, therefore, does not rest solely on the scale or significance of the events under scrutiny, but rather on the fundamental differences in their respective roles, methods, and constraints. While both are invested in reconstructing the past, the judge is bound by procedural rules and the necessity of reaching a decision within a defined framework, whereas the historian enjoys greater latitude in both the scope of inquiry and the methods employed. The historian may pause, revise, or even abandon a line of investigation in the face of uncertainty, but the judge is compelled by the demands of justice to deliver a verdict, even when confronted with ambiguity or insufficient proof. This procedural imperative underscores the unique responsibilities and pressures inherent in judicial decision-making, distinguishing it from the often open-ended and reflective process characteristic of historical scholarship.

Furthermore, the consequences of judicial decisions carry immediate and tangible effects on individuals' lives and liberties, whereas the historian's conclusions, while influential, do not bear the same direct impact. This reality highlights why the legal system should focus on rigorous procedural safeguards and the principle of impartiality, recognising that the cost of error in a courtroom far exceeds that of scholarly debate. Ultimately, acknowledging these distinctions not only clarifies the limits of the traditional analogy but also reinforces the need for a nuanced and critical approach when considering the intersections between law and history.

The implications of this divergence are far-reaching; while historians may revisit and reinterpret evidence as new sources emerge, judges must operate within the parameters established by due process, ensuring that their judgements are not only historically informed but also procedurally sound. This distinction underscores the broader philosophical debate regarding the nature of truth and objectivity in both fields, highlighting the importance of recognising the constructed and contingent aspects of fact-finding in criminal justice.

While it is important to recognise the authority to impose sanctions and refrain from ascribing undue judicial activism in fact-finding, the relationship between sentencing procedures and the act of documenting history is more substantial than often acknowledged, particularly concerning narrative issues, as will be discussed in the concluding chapter. Accordingly, following Ginzburg's analysis, although many differences exist,

> this does not prevent a partial overlap between the two perspectives, which is strikingly brought to our attention when historians and judges find themselves working physically in contact, within the same society and around the same phenomena. [This is] a classic problem, which might have seemed definitively overcome—the relationship between historical inquiry and judicial inquiry—but which reveals unexpected theoretical and political implications. (Ginzburg 1989: 181–182)

Examining these implications highlights a key contrast: while *res judicata* judgements are final, historical accounts remain open to reinterpretation. Historiography is not definitive or unchangeable; it gains meaning through comparison with other narratives, audience engagement, and scholarly debate. Thus, as Bann notes, there is an essential difference between judicial decisions and historical interpretation.

> the controversial historical text cannot have the same immediate and practical purpose as discourse in a courtroom [...] even if the mode of demonstration is similar, in the sense that authorities are specifically cited. The aim is not acquittal or conviction, but rather an authorised historical text. Thus, the "final judgement" is indefinitely suspended [...] the approval granted by the academic public is, ultimately, the only criterion of legitimation. (Bann 1994: 37)

Historians acknowledge that historical narratives are subject to continuous reassessment; widely accepted works are frequently reevaluated and updated in light of new interpretations. Seminal texts by authors such as Herodotus and Michelet are now primarily regarded as literary references rather than definitive histories, due to the progression of contemporary scholarship. As observed by Ricoeur (2003: 426), the discipline of history is characterised by an ongoing process of revision. Conversely, the legal system does not inherently undergo such self-correction (Ferrajoli 2002: 47), underscoring a fundamental distinction in how the concept of "truth" is approached within the disciplines of history and law.

> relevant is the distinction between the "truth" constructed in the proceedings and fixed by the judge in the sentence, and scientific or historical truth. The former has the judge as the sole investigator, whereas the others do not. The competence to investigate this historical fact and to judge is established by law, as an exclusive prerogative of the judge. Thus, once this decision is reached and becomes *res judicata*, it will, as a rule, be immutable. (Lopes Jr 2005: 266)

Criminal cases, unlike historical research, are limited by judicial scope and cannot be investigated indefinitely. Adversarial processes, overseen by impartial judges, partly address this limitation by managing evidence between parties rather than allowing continuous inquiry. This accusatorial approach supports democratic values and favours a harm reduction programme. Ferrajoli (2002: 48) observes that judicial errors, unlike academic ones, can irreversibly harm the accused. While post-conviction reviews exist (criminal review), they are hindered by the principle of *in dubio pro societate*—of fascist origin—which upholds convictions when in doubt for presumed societal interests.

Criminal review may occur when a conviction contradicts clear law, relies on false proof, or new evidence demonstrates innocence or justifies a reduced sentence, even posthumously for family compensation. While nullity, *mandamus*, or *habeas corpus* can challenge final judgements, the principle of *in dubio pro societate* generally limits these remedies.

This principle reflects an inquisitorial mindset and, as Lopes Jr. observes, lacks constitutional support and consistency: doubt can lead to acquittal at trial but not in criminal review. This inconsistency raises issues with rejecting new evidence that would have led to acquittal during trial but is considered insufficient in criminal review (Lopes Jr 2010: 252–253).

According to Ricoeur, the capacity for ongoing revision distinguishes a judicial sentence from the work of the historian. This distinction is emphasised by the author, who notes that

> it is a characteristic of judicial judgment to interrupt the interplay of arguments and counterarguments, bringing them to a close, even if this closure is only provisional, at least for as long as avenues of appeal remain open; but there will ultimately, somewhere or at some point, be a final judgment that enforces public authority. (Ricoeur 1995: 164)

Taruffo observes that law centres on decision-making, with legal procedures designed to produce outcomes (Taruffo 2010: 219). This contrasts with historical analysis, since judicial narratives enable the State's punitive power, meaning errors can have severe consequences compared to mistakes in historiography.

Although historical research is subject to ongoing revision as new evidence emerges, judicial decisions attain finality once all avenues of appeal have been exhausted. While criminal review remains theoretically possible, it is generally constrained by the principle of *in dubio pro societate*—an interpretative standard that stands in fundamental opposition to my proposal of reimagining criminal justice with a focus on human rights and a comprehensive reassessment of truth in criminal trials.

If the achievement of absolute corresponding truth is unattainable—as suggested herein—this inherent limitation cannot be resolved through legal procedures that enable convictions under the pretext of safeguarding society. Criminal law primarily addresses conduct rather than character, with its structure designed to constrain the exercise of punitive authority; consequently, any adjudicated matter should remain open to review when new evidence arises that may undermine the conviction's legitimacy. As Nassif notes, a judge's determination of "the truth" in convictions is invariably provisional (Nassif 2005: 126).

Clearly, this standard does not extend to the reassessment of acquittals, since accusatorial proceedings are fundamentally constructed to prevent undue harm. The enduring risk to individuals typified the evidentiary standards of the height of the inquisitorial system, an era when acquittals were nonexistent—only judgements based on insufficient proof were rendered, allowing cases against the accused to be reopened at any point.

Given that uncertainty is an intrinsic aspect of interpreting historical events, criminal convictions should not be regarded as absolutely conclusive. The knowledge informing such decisions remains inherently limited, given that absolute truth is unattainable. This uncertainty persists even after final adjudication. As Lopes Jr. observes, "a conviction is only maintained in the absence of evidence that raises well-founded doubt. Hence, *in dubio pro reo* serves as a pragmatic standard for addressing procedural uncertainty, regardless of the stage at which it is identified". He further explains that "certainty (security) cannot be claimed, even after a final judgment, because *res judicata* is a legal construct that does not always align with reality [...] Uncertainty is intrinsic to the criminal procedure, as its domain is reality itself" (Lopes Jr 2005: 63–64).

As in the field of historiography, conviction narratives should not be regarded as definitive but must remain open to revision when they fulfil the criteria for criminal review, following harm reduction principles. Consequently, legal outcomes are inherently provisional, permitting continued revaluation in response to new information that may serve the interests of citizens regarding punitive authority. Accordingly, judicial decisions must balance their finality with a willingness to reconsider, acknowledging the provisional character of knowledge concerning past events. Treating truth as an absolute can reinforce power structures in ways that jeopardise justice and the safeguarding of fundamental rights. Therefore, criminal law should recognise the analogical relationship between the roles of judge and historian, considering the complexities and limitations inherent in both as they seek to interpret and reconstruct past realities.

In light of these considerations, it becomes apparent that the criminal justice system must embrace an approach that acknowledges the inherent limitations of human cognition when dealing with past events. Rather than persisting with rigid frameworks that seek unattainable certainties, the law should foster mechanisms that allow for the ongoing scrutiny and, where necessary, correction of judicial determinations. Such an orientation not only aligns with fundamental human rights but also ensures that the administration of justice remains vigilant against the dangers of irrevocable error.

The analogy between judicial and historical inquiry thus serves as a powerful reminder: both disciplines are ultimately engaged in the interpretative reconstruction of realities that can never be fully recaptured. This shared predicament calls for humility and adaptability in legal reasoning, reinforcing the imperative to keep the possibility of revision alive in the face of new evidence or interpretative advances. Only by doing so can criminal law uphold its commitment to fairness and the protection of individual dignity.

The forthcoming chapter will further integrate the theory of history into procedural frameworks by introducing the concept of traces of the past.

CHAPTER 6

Beyond the Ambition for Truth: The Duality of the Traces of the Past and the Hallucinatory Character of Evidence

Traces of the Past

After conducting an initial assessment of the limitations associated with the correspondence theory of truth in previous chapters, I aim to establish an epistemological framework that does not overlook the pastness of past events. This approach seeks to address the intricacies of historical occurrences while preserving respect for human rights concerning accused individuals. The proposed framework intentionally departs from a fundamental characteristic of inquisitorial, positivist and rationalist epistemologies—their conceptual violence—which overlooks the temporal complexity of past events in pursuit of an absolute conception of truth. According to Timm de Souza, the analytical rigour demonstrated by many philosophical traditions, which adopts an experimental scientific model to dissect reality in search of foundational elements, constitutes a form of violence against the real (Souza 2004: 27).

This proposal is grounded in an epistemological approach that fundamentally prioritises what should be central to procedural knowledge—namely, the inherent pastness of the evidentiary context established by the criminal case. When properly appreciated, this aspect gives rise to a complex array of questions. As Ibañez notes, because these events are historical, procedural truth is primarily subject to the same constraints as historical truth (Ibañez 2005: 122). In this regard, one must consider,

S. H. Khaled Jr., *Reimagining Criminal Justice, Search for Truth and Human Rights*, https://doi.org/10.1007/978-3-032-27227-0_6

drawing on Bachelard's terminology, the "aesthetics of the hidden" (Bachelard 1960: 19).

The relationship between criminal proceedings and significant life events is characterised by substantial complexity. The inherent resistance of past occurrences challenges the methodologies—be they inquisitorial, positivist, or rationalist—utilised by individuals engaged in the pursuit of absolute truth.

This chapter provides an in-depth examination of the concept of pastness, emphasising that the cognitive framework foundational to criminal proceedings must thoroughly address this complex issue—a matter neglected by inquisitorial epistemology, modern positivist approaches and evidentiary rationalism.

While methodological debates tend to focus on core epistemological concerns—specifically, the formation and treatment of evidence (to be discussed later)—the ontological challenge relates to engaging with the "pastness" of past events, a fundamental aspect for reconceptualising criminal justice. From this perspective, the key issue becomes how judges should approach the temporally remote nature of legally significant events upon which their judgements are based—an element neglected by evidentiary rationalism frameworks. For example, Ferrer Beltrán, when comparing the roles of judge and historian, contends that this comparison holds limited relevance, asserting that evidentiary reasoning concerns the proof of singular, unrepeatable events regardless of their position in time (Beltrán 2007: 35). For Taruffo the comparison between the judge and the historian is valid in certain respects—though clearly not from all perspectives—yet even where it holds, its utility appears limited. It does not provide specific analytical frameworks or cognitive insights into how judges determine facts that are distinctively informed by the work of historians. Notably, this analogy offers no significant contribution concerning the concept of evidence or the rational application of means of proof within judicial proceedings (Taruffo 2005: 341). Taruffo acknowledges the depth of epistemological discussions in historiography but dismisses their relevance to legal evidence, which I view as a significant oversight (Taruffo 2005: 338–339).

Whether intentionally or not, both Taruffo and Beltrán avoid comparing law and historiography, thereby perpetuating law's isolation from the broader philosophical reflections on the past—an isolation that must be addressed to reform criminal justice and advance human rights. Contrary to their stance, I argue that reference to the past is fundamental to legal truth and should guide theories of procedural truth. Similar to Montero Aroca, whose dismissal of the notion of inquisitorial procedure was noted earlier, Taruffo and Ferrer Beltrán offer a novel perspective in procedural doctrine—one that does not take the pastness of past events into account.

In contrast, I assert that examining the differences among accusatorial, inquisitorial, and mixed frameworks, as well as comparing the roles of judges and historians, is essential for substantive and constructive dialogue in the field of criminal justice.

Ferrajoli argues that, at a semantic level, the truth behind judicial arguments is fundamentally similar to the truth found in scientific theories (Ferrajoli 2002: 42). According to Ferrajoli, challenges related to verification in legal propositions closely resemble those faced in verifying historical claims, meaning legal analysis can benefit from philosophical debates about these issues (Ferrajoli 2002: 43). While Ferrajoli's analysis was limited by his maintenance of Tarski's correspondence theory of truth, he acknowledges the importance of debates about historical claims in other fields, such as history and philosophy.

From this standpoint, it is important to emphasise the pastness of past events rather than overlook it, as it represents a critical foundation for a framework in which procedural integrity—anchored in the rules of due the process—is paramount. In this context, truth should be considered contingent and inherently elusive, which amplifies the risk of error, given that convictions cannot be regarded as definitive reflections of historical reality. While I recognise that this position may appear provocative and might seem to imply a total disconnect between judicial narratives and concepts of truth, that is not my intent.

My argument aims to move beyond a reductive distinction between absolute truth (commonly termed real, material, or substantive truth) and radical relativism. At the same time, it does not endorse an intermediate stance of approximate or relative truth, which maintains the ideal of correspondence and, as a result, upholds and reinvigorates inquisitorial authority and the pursuit of truth.

I have repeatedly contended that it is imperative to move beyond the correspondence model of truth in criminal proceedings, but this should not be interpreted as an endorsement of sceptical relativism. My stance aligns closely with that of Rui Cunha Martins, who suggests that the most productive approach is one that transcends the traditional paradigm of adequacy while resisting the tendency to exclude truth altogether—a notion he describes as the "paradigm of exiled truth" (Martins 2010: 87). Accordingly, this chapter will develop its analysis along these lines, framing the concept of the "pastness of the past" as a foundational postulate for redefining truth—not by rejecting it, but by reconfiguring its role within criminal proceedings.

Recognising pastness as an essential component of the procedural cognitive framework opens a space for fruitful dialogue with other fields, such as the theory of history and the philosophy of history. Historians analyse events that occurred in the past, focusing on actions taken by individuals over time. Similarly, judges issue rulings based on their assessment of prior actions, evaluated within the formal framework of legal proceedings. The use of verb tenses further emphasises reference to events situated in the past; the subject matter pertains to an empirical reality that has already transpired. If the event did not occur, there exists no factual basis for enquiry, as the absence of materiality precludes knowledge.

Given that cognitive reference relates to a past event—albeit processed through the distinct framework of legal-criminal discourse—the capacity to reconfigure temporality, as articulated by Ricoeur, raises important questions regarding the truth in criminal proceedings. The act of reconfiguration seeks, in essence, to render justice to elapsed time by partially reconstructing and reinterpreting it. Consequently, the process of narratively reconstructing historical events is inherently interpretive, entailing a retrospective effort to recover life narratives obscured by the passage of time. This task is highly complex, and its intricacy is heightened within the context of legal proceedings—a subject that will be explored further in subsequent discussion.

From this standpoint, it may be asserted that, for a conviction, the judge must construct a narrative based on evidence presented throughout the proceedings, wherein truth emerges as an essential standard: namely, the requirement to accurately represent the past. My position aligns with the view that legal processes produce a narrative reconstruction—necessarily incomplete and imperfect relative to the events they seek to depict—rather than an exact or approximate reproduction of historical reality. Achieving absolute truth is unattainable, as procedural uncertainty remains inherent; the past cannot be fully accessed through the cognitive tools available to humans. Criminal proceedings are intended as reliable mechanisms for reconstructing past events; however, the acceptance of certain evidence as proof may occasionally be incorrect, potentially resulting in judicial error.

In this sense, Carnelutti compares the reconstruction of the past in legal proceedings to that of the historian, "with this difference for the worse: the crime is a stretch of road, along which the person who travelled it tries to destroy the traces" (Carnelutti 1965: 72). Thus, Carnelutti asks, "how does one who, having walked across the fields, wish to retrace the same path in the opposite direction? He follows the traces of his steps" (Carnelutti 1965: 73). Taking into account Carnelutti's observations—which align to some extent with my own perspective—I am now able to present my concept of trace. This notion is fundamental for establishing a procedural epistemology that adequately addresses the issue of pastness and facilitates transcending the sign of corresponding truth as well as inquisitorial, positivist and rationalist frameworks.

It can be asserted that the epistemological inquiry—concerning the methods and validity of evidence, as well as norms—has historically masked, and continues to mask, the ontological question. The latter pertains to the potential for reconstituting past time through traces. Salo de Carvalho notes that

> The Cartesian method inspires the dogmatics of criminal procedure in the sense of considering the possibility of, through the fragmentation and microscopic study of the criminal case, recreating the past event that can no longer be experienced and reaching truths. Thus, after breaking down and meticulously studying the evidentiary elements incorporated into the case file, the truth would be attained through the free evaluation of the evidence. (Carvalho 2008: 74)

It must be acknowledged that an event under judicial consideration has already transpired—it is a time that has irreversibly passed and cannot be relived or directly replicated. As such, direct observation of the event is no longer possible. Bloch asserts: "The historian, by definition, is unable to witness the facts he studies himself [...] in contrast to knowledge of the present, that of the past will necessarily be indirect'" (Bloch 2001: 69).

Acknowledging that our understanding of the past is inherently indirect significantly limits the feasibility of pursuing a corresponding truth from a knowledge standpoint. The passage of time places historical events beyond the grasp of modern scientific methods, which define truth as correspondence between reality and observation. For instance, it is not possible to recreate a historical event under controlled conditions comparable to an experiment determining the boiling point of water. Consequently, the notion that legal proceedings could approximate the classical ideal of scientific experimentation is fundamentally flawed. Ferrajoli highlights this distinction, stating: "factual procedural truth, like historical truth, instead of being predicable in direct reference to the judged fact, is an inference from the 'proven' facts of the past and the 'evidentiary' facts of the present" (Ferrajoli 2002: 44). According to his perspective,

> What the judge examines are not the criminal facts under judgement, but their evidence. In no different manner from the historian, he cannot, therefore, examine the fact he is tasked to judge, which in any case escapes direct observation, but only its evidence, which are experiences of present facts, even if interpretable as signs of past events. (Ferrajoli 2002: 44)

According to Ferrajoli, this realisation "deeply fractures the ideal model of factual procedural truth as objective correspondence" (Ferrajoli 2002: 44). For him, "the 'certain', 'objective' or 'absolute' truth always represents the 'expression of an unattainable ideal' [...] the contrary idea that one can achieve and assert an objective or absolutely certain truth is, in reality, an epistemological naivety" (Ferrajoli 2002: 42). The conclusion the author draws from this line of reasoning led him to assert that truth must be conceived as a corresponding, but relative or approximate, truth, which led him to reject absolute truth and the judge's capacity to seek the truth. In this sense, Ferrajoli explicitly warns that the term *truth* should not be used with metaphysical implications in the sense of absolute correspondence (Ferrajoli 2002: 41).

Ferrajoli advances beyond positivist frameworks while still maintaining the plausibility of a relative or approximate correspondence theory of truth, drawing on Tarski's approach (Ferrajoli 2002: 42, 54, 56, 435). Although I concur with the rejection of absolute truth, I argue that endorsing a regime of truth grounded in relative correspondence remains vulnerable to discursive displacement. Evidentiary rationalism sustains the relativity of the knowledge of the truth but maintains the search for absolute truth—a framework driven by the ambition for truth. This position continues to uphold, whether implicitly or explicitly, the centrality of the pursuit of truth. Although Ferrajoli does not explicitly consider this potential outcome, his reasoning remains based on a rational framework that, historically, has not succeeded in fully departing from the dominant search for truth ideology within criminal justice.

Accordingly, it is necessary to critically evaluate ongoing reliance on correspondence theory, as it may inadvertently reinforce aspects of the inquisitorial tradition and positivist methods. Tarski's notion of truth remains closely associated with evidentiary rationalism and its pursuit of absolute truth, despite Ferrajoli's critique concerning the judicial search for truth. The adoption of a correspondence theory inevitably places truth at the centre of criminal proceedings and consequently leads to the persistent temptation to seek it—ambition for truth. As noted by Cunha Martins,

> As long as the debate remains within the same rules of the game that once led to the consecration of the "true" as the central axis of the procedural system, as long as the argument used to propose functional displacement stems from the same province of meaning as the argument used to reassert centrality, the possibility of producing an effective reconsideration of the problem will always be limited. (Martins 2010: 81)

Ferrajoli's reasoning concerning the impossibility of experimentation is not erroneous; however, it should be pursued to its logical conclusion, resulting in a definitive departure from the ideal of correspondence truth. Addressing this matter and progressing beyond the correspondence paradigm requires acknowledging that, without direct observation, alternative methods must be employed. The knowledge derived from these substitutes retains significance, but it exists at a distinct cognitive level, separate from the traditional framework of corresponding truth.

The requirement of proof for a conviction necessitates the presentation of evidence that is sufficiently persuasive to convince the judge of the accused's guilt. As Lopes Jr. observes, "Essentially through evidence, the trial aims to establish conditions enabling the judge to engage in recognitive activity, thereby producing the conviction reflected in the judgment" (Lopes Jr 2010: 500). Coutinho further notes, "Evidence serves as the vehicle by which truth enters the trial, providing the basis upon which the judge's conviction in the specific case is formed, even though it is acknowledged that this is not the sole foundation for judgment" (Coutinho 2002: 177).

Temporarily setting aside the subjectivity highlighted by Coutinho, it is clear that referencing evidence imposes upon both judicial proceedings and the judge's reasoning an obligation to adhere strictly to substantiated facts: judgements must be supported by robust proof. However, if direct experience of the "fact" is unattainable, how does the judge's conviction actually emerge from evidentiary processes? As Ariès (1989: 225) notes, "In history, we cannot repeat the experiment. In fact, we cannot even conduct an experiment". This underscores a significant ontological divide between past and present—between what exists and what once existed. The concept that mitigates this separation, or at least enables partial communication across it, is the notion of trace—a pivotal idea to which I now turn my attention for further analysis.

Both judges and historians are compelled by the necessity of evidence to engage with traces indicative of past occurrences. As Bloch asserts, "the knowledge of all human facts in the past, and of most of them in the present, must be [...] knowledge through traces" (Bloch 2001: 73). Traces serve as the fundamental basis of proof; legal proceedings are not abstract debates disconnected from historical reality, nor should they function merely as adversarial contests or as arbitrary games determined by the discretion of a judge. Rather, traces provide a conduit through which events from the past can be discerned.

But what exactly does a trace mean, and why does the notion proposed here truly acknowledges the pastness of the past, which cannot be said of knowledge structured on the premises of corresponding truth?

The Pastness of the Past and the Duality Inherent to It

The notion of trace refers to an element that originates from the past yet continues to persist in the present. This observation is not entirely unprecedented; Heidegger recognised the duality inherent in the notion of the past. He asserts, "the past belongs, indisputably, to an earlier time, to the events of then. But it can, nevertheless, still simply be given 'today', as, for example, the ruins of a Greek temple. With it, a 'piece of the past' is still 'present'" (Heidegger 2005: 183). Such a perspective challenges the prevailing ontological interpretation of the historical past as merely something that "has been". According to Heidegger, the "world" from which these artefacts originated no longer exists; yet, their intramundane character persists as objects now embedded in the present, maintaining significance despite their temporal distance. In essence, traces occupy a unique position, simultaneously belonging and not belonging to the past under investigation. Addressing Heidegger's stance and aiming to extend his analysis, Ricoeur posits that

> In particular, the scientist does not recognise what should be, for him, an enigma: that the past, which is no more, has effects, exerts an influence, an action (*Wirkung*) upon the present. This subsequent action (*Nachwirkende*)—one might say belated or post factum—should be surprising. More precisely, it is on the notion of traces of the past that perplexity should focus. Do we not say of the remains of a Greek temple that a "fragment of the past" is still "present"? The paradox of the historical past is entirely there: on the one hand, it is no more; on the other, the traces of the past keep it still within reach (*vorhanden*). (Ricoeur 1997: 129)

The notion of trace, as articulated by Ricoeur (1997: 10), simultaneously encompasses both a remnant and an indication of what once existed but no longer remains. The trace suggests absence—specifically, the event situated in a now-past temporal context—while also constituting a form of presence. According to Ricoeur (1997: 179), the trace signifies without directly manifesting its referent. It does not represent the past itself, but serves as a surviving mark that endures, pointing towards a past already rendered inactive by the passage of time. Through traces, individuals attempt to access what has ceased to exist (Ricoeur 1997: 11). This reveals a paradox: a past that has vanished yet undeniably once existed, possessing "reality" (Ricoeur 1997: 175). Ricoeur further interrogates the significance of leaving a trace.

> Littré provides the first meaning of the word *trace*: "a vestige left by a man or an animal in the place where it passed". Then, he records the more general usage: "any mark left by a thing". By generalisation, the vestige has become a mark: at the same time, the origin of the trace has extended from a man or animal to any thing; in compensation, the idea that something passed by has disappeared; what remains is only the record that the trace has *left*. This is the crux of the paradox. On the one hand, the trace is visible here and now, as a vestige, as a mark. On the other hand, there is a trace because *before* a man, an animal passed by; a thing acted. In the very use of language, the vestige, the mark *indicate* the pastness of the passage, the anteriority of the scratch, of the notch, without *showing*, without making appear, *that which* passed by. Note the fortunate

> homonymy, in French, between "*être pass*" (to have passed), in the sense of having passed through a place, and "*être passé*", in the sense of belonging to the past. (Ricoeur 1997: 200)

Consequently, the notion of trace exhibits a notable duality, signifying both the dynamic process of passage and the static quality of the residual mark that becomes fixed. Persistently examining this paradox, Ricoeur further analyses the dynamics inherent in the notion of passage:

> someone has passed by; the trace invites one to follow it, to return, through it, if possible, to the person or animal that passed by; the trace can be lost; it can itself become lost, leading nowhere; it can also be erased: for the trace is fragile and requires preservation in its intact state, otherwise, the passage truly occurred, but simply remains in the past; we may know from other evidence that people and animals existed somewhere: they will remain forever unknown if no trace leads to them. (Ricoeur 1997: 201)

In essence, the trace constitutes proof of a past event that enables its persistence into the present, thereby allowing—albeit within certain limits—the acquisition of knowledge about what has transpired. Consequently, ongoing reliance on the preservation of traces is unavoidable, as they serve as the tangible remnants of prior existence. The absence of such traces precludes the reconstruction of historical trajectories. According to Ricoeur,

> the trace indicates here, therefore in space, and now, therefore in the present, the past passage of living beings: it guides the hunt, the search, the investigation, the research. All of this is history. To say that it is knowledge by traces is, ultimately, to appeal to the significance of a finished past that, nevertheless, remains preserved in its vestiges. (Ricoeur 1997: 201)

Ricoeur characterises traces as conduits to the past, positing that they provide historians with access to realities that have been lost with the passage of time (Ricoeur 1997: 174). Through these traces, historical accounts are formulated; the reconstruction of the past is achieved via narrative representations of particular moments, events, or periods. Traces function as records of prior eras. They underpin both historical research and judicial verdicts, serving as foundational elements from which historical knowledge arises and constituting essential foundations for judicial decisions.

While traces may represent remnants of what has transpired, they are simultaneously tangible objects or marks:

> It suggests, first of all, the idea of a more solid, more enduring support than the transient activity of men [...] their works outlasted their labour; men pass; their works remain. But they remain as *things* among things. Now, this thing-like character is important for our investigation: it introduces a cause-and-effect relationship between the marking thing and the marked thing. (Ricoeur 1997: 202)

Accordingly, the trace encompasses both a dimension of significance, as a vestige indicating prior presence, and a causal relationship inherent in the materiality of the mark. The object itself, above all, invites further inquiry. Thus, as the author asserts, the trace functions as a sign-effect. This leads to the question: what does it entail to follow a trace? According to Ricoeur,

> to follow a trace is to reason by causality along the chain of operations constitutive of the act of passing by; on the other hand, to return from the mark to the marking thing is to isolate, among all possible causal chains, those which, moreover, convey the specific significance of the relationship between the vestige and the passage. (Ricoeur 1997: 202)

This intellectual process is inherently complex and resists reduction to the basic framework of correspondence truth theories; a nuanced and sophisticated perspective is required. Marrou asserts that "the historian can only resort to the notion of cause at the cost of an arbitrary schematisation, a crude simplification of reality" (Marrou 1978: 145).

Remnants of the past are indirect references. The distinction between indirect reference and direct experience is particularly significant, as it highlights that understanding the past does not strictly align with the framework of corresponding truth—contrasting the discourse with an external reality is not feasible.

Legal positivism posited that the evidentiary foundation presented in legal proceedings corresponds directly to past events, thereby assuming the possibility of establishing "real" or "absolute" truth. Evidentiary rationalism, by contrast, acknowledges the absence of absolute truth within legal processes, while continuing to assert the absoluteness of truth itself and recognising that our knowledge of it remains relative. Rather than interpreting this as an epistemological constraint necessitating greater emphasis on human rights and procedural safeguards, proponents suggest that judges should strive to align their findings with absolute truth, contending that such efforts would facilitate closer approximation to this ideal.

As previously discussed, the epistemic function of truth-seeking is susceptible to confirmation biases that reinforce the prioritisation of hypotheses over factual evidence. This approach is grounded in Tarski's correspondence theory of truth, which has notable limitations when applied to legal proceedings.

Knowledge derived from traces occupies a distinct cognitive domain separate from that of correspondence: the "third time" associated with historical reconstruction arises out of traces of events that persist into the present; this time is, in a way, intuited rather than directly experienced. Historiography addresses temporal aporias by formulating a third temporality which mediates between lived and cosmic time through connective procedures such as calendars, archives, documents, and traces (Ricoeur 1997: 174). Accordingly, the temporality inferred from traces should not be equated with elapsed time but rather seen as a time that is narratively represented without being fully restored.

One must ask whether this construction achieves perfect or even relative correspondence; clearly, it does not.

The question is imprecisely formulated. The reality of past events is not something the judge discovers absolutely or relatively; instead, the "truth" is narratively produced by the judge. It is a form of temporal narrative shaped from a particular perspective; one inextricably linked to historicity, tradition, and preconceptions. For this reason, truth in this context should be considered as produced rather than simply discovered, an issue that will be further explored in the penultimate chapter.

At present, attention must be directed towards the challenge of understanding the "pastness" of the past: historians and judges do not engage with the events themselves but with what endures in the perceptions of direct witnesses—an issue that introduces complexities surpassing even the concept of the trace, as will be addressed in chapter eight—or through material relics, expert examinations, occasional items or documents representing only fragments of a much larger whole that remains fundamentally inaccessible. Furthermore, there are additional considerations regarding the admissibility of evidence potentially recognised as proof—as traces of the past—during proceedings, the underlying discursive strategies, and the process by which a judge forms their convictions; these matters will be discussed in greater detail later.

Judges and historians encounter significant challenges when interpreting past events, as these occurrences are inherently separated from current experience. Therefore, it is not feasible to apply the standard of corresponding truth in the way one might in a controlled environment; criminal proceedings cannot serve as laboratories where historical reality is tailored to judicial decisions through evidentiary processes. Instead, interpretation relies on the available evidence which may or may not be recognised as traces of the past that persist into the present, enabling the narrative reconstruction of previous events, acknowledging that access to the past remains complex, indirect, and accompanied by considerable difficulty.

The subsequent section will expand upon these factors with the aim of establishing an appropriate framework for truth within criminal proceedings.

The Same, The Other, and the Analogous

The signs representing the Same, the Other, and the Analogous offer valuable frameworks for analysing the complex pursuit of "absolute truth" within criminal proceedings. Ricoeur's conceptualisation of the *Same* articulates both the ambition and the belief in attaining absolute truth concerning historical events. As Ricoeur states,

> The first way of thinking about the pastness of the past is to remove its sting, that is, temporal distance. The historical operation then appears as a de-distancing, an identification with what once was. This conception is not without support in the practice of historians. Is the trace, as such, not itself present? Is retracing the trace not making the past events to which it leads contemporaneous with the trace itself? As readers of history, are we not ourselves transformed into contemporaries of past events through a living reconstruction of their sequence? In short, is the past intelligible except as persisting in the present? (Ricoeur 1997: 244)

Nevertheless, the past cannot be considered identical to the present; rather, it approaches an "*Other*" that does not return nor can be replicated. The understanding of past events under the isolated sign of the

Same supports an ontology underpinned by presenteism, that supersedes both the past and its remnants, namely traces. Fundamentally, this perspective entails the negation of temporal distance, which is ultimately unattainable. The pastness inherent to the past remains insurmountable: no method can restore or re-enact what has already occurred—it simply lies beyond human reach. To consider a narrative supported by traces of the past as something equivalent to a past event—absolute truth—is indisputably a rudimentary epistemic excess. Criminal proceedings require engagement with a complex legal linguistic framework—one that further distances the observer from the intricacies of the past event in question.

No direct equivalence exists between the narrative articulated in a sentencing judgement and the historical event it references. The narrative constructed by the legal process is inherently distinct from the actual occurrence, as it is shaped by juridical interpretation and what can be intuited based on the remaining traces of the past. Again, the past cannot be considered identical to the present; rather, it approaches an "*Other*" that does not return nor can be replicated entirely. Thus, the present alone cannot serve as the sole foundation for truth. Instead, the present should remain receptive to the possibilities suggested by traces.

The epistemic landscape navigated by judges and historians is fraught with ambiguity and interpretative challenges, primarily due to the indirect nature of traces that survive from past events. As such, the process of reconstructing history or adjudicating facts in criminal proceedings involves a nuanced interplay between what is accessible in the present and what remains irrevocably lost to time. This interplay underscores the impossibility of attaining an unmediated or absolute truth about past occurrences, compelling both disciplines to operate within frameworks that acknowledge the persistent gap between narrative and reality. The resultant knowledge is best understood as a provisional construct, shaped by the limits of available traces and the interpretative strategies brought to bear upon them.

When it is asserted that corresponding truth is achieved within proceedings, the distinction between present and past is effectively eliminated due to the assumed primacy of the present. Consequently, this form of truth becomes coercive: rather than acknowledging difference, it nullifies and erases the unique characteristics of the past. Such an approach to truth assumes the possibility of eliminating both the inherent opacity of the past and the opacity of consciousness itself, thereby rendering consciousness fully transparent to preclude any form of contamination—a danger evidentiary rationalism underestimates. It presumes that the opacity of the past and the potential for contaminated consciousness are negligible, thus permitting the application of a standard of approximate or relative correspondence that justifies the persistent search for absolute truth in criminal proceedings.

The central flaw in this perspective lies in the fact that the trace cannot fully correspond to the past itself; rather, it merely indicates the past, embodying both presence and absence, as Heidegger noted. In essence, the trace, as a vestige of what has transpired, serves as a substitute for the past, performing a role of representation. This dynamic renders knowledge constructed upon traces inevitably subject to uncertainty. Such ambiguity persists even when the provisionality of the supporting element is resolved and the trace's authenticity as proof of the past is established: the trace always remains a fragment of a larger past event—a precarious substitute for a reality forever out of reach.

Nevertheless, it would not be appropriate to adopt a concept of truth in criminal proceedings that is solely based on the idea of temporal otherness, as there is also the presence of a tangible reality represented by the trace and its interpreter. This point highlights the enduring complexity and fundamental paradox involved in comprehending the past, which resists straightforward classification and ultimately emerges as a substantial aporia.

While the past cannot simply be regarded as the *Same*, it also cannot be considered an entirely separate *Other*, given its preservation through traces. Evaluating the past solely from the perspective of distance results in an ontology that denies its existence, since, despite having occurred, it endures as traces and therefore, in some sense, continues to exist. Knowledge grounded in traces is not a complete *Other* relative to elapsed time, nor is it devoid of meaningful connection to historical events. To clarify: knowledge of the past does not attain corresponding truth (in terms of the *Same*), but neither is it wholly an *Other*—which would imply absolute falsity, sever all ties to truth and undermine the ideal of justice. Instead, epistemic engagement with history maintains meaningful relations to both truth and justice.

A complete disregard for truth regarding the past is not a viable approach, as focusing solely on distance oversimplifies the matter by neglecting the distinction between the contemporary other and the other of the past—specifically, the significance of pastness and the distinct ontological status associated with the persistence of traces. The survival of the past within the present poses a particular challenge that must be acknowledged, as it is this very phenomenon that differentiates knowledge of the other from knowledge of the past. The otherness of the past cannot entirely supersede the enduring presence of the past through traces. Indeed, it is the recognition of an element's trace-like nature that forms the foundation of probatory value in procedural contexts—an aspect that cannot be dismissed. Traces carry intrinsic weight and cannot simply be disregarded at the discretion of either the parties or the judge.

While traces may not disclose every detail about the past to which they pertain, they nonetheless possess prohibitive authority: they establish boundaries by making it untenable to argue for or validate certain conclusions without acknowledging them, or by directly contradicting them. The judge is obliged to ensure that the requirement of truth is met in the core reasoning of their judgement, drawing upon tangible elements recognised as proof through the evidentiary process—traces which enable, at least in part, an informed narrative reconstruction of the past. It is insufficient for a judge merely to have reached a conviction; they must articulate, in narrative form, the probatory basis for their decision when they believe the accused to be guilty. Nonetheless, this responsibility appears to further accentuate the complexity surrounding the role of truth within judicial proceedings.

Based on the analysis conducted thus far, it can be affirmed that criminal proceedings maintain only a limited connection to the truth. The information available for establishing facts is often inadequate—both due to its relative reliability, which stems from the complex relationship between events and their evidentiary representation, and its inherently incomplete nature, as it relies on traces of the past that serve more as substitutes than actual correspondents. As a result, judgements derived from the evidentiary submissions of the parties will inevitably occur amidst uncertainty, a condition that persists even when the facts appear straightforward. Collectively, these considerations underscore the significance of the regime of the *Other*.

Nonetheless, the requirement of empirical substantiation for arguments advanced during proceedings ensures that the epistemic process remains anchored, in part, to truth. As previously noted, traces of the past serve as foundations upon which the judge substantiate a sentence. Consequently, knowledge derived from such traces possesses a basis in truth—though this alone is insufficient to confer upon it a definitive mark of identity—distinguishing it from fields devoid of comparable empirical rigour, such as literature. However, asserting an empirical referent does not fully resolve the inherent distance between present inquiry and past events; it is precisely here that the central aporia emerges, necessitating careful consideration to define the appropriate regime of truth within legal processes. The interplay between presence and absence, sameness and otherness, constitutes the core enigma whose resolution is essential to comprehending the status of truth as it pertains to historical realities.

As previously indicated, my effort to redefine truth within criminal proceedings is informed by the framework proposed by Rui Cunha Martins, who asserts that excluding the concept of truth would ultimately be detrimental. Nonetheless, this approach seems to have generated a tension between the *Same* and the *Other* that must be at least partially addressed before moving forward. This does not, however, entail yielding to the notion of corresponding truth—even in its relative form—as the operative standard within these proceedings. Indeed, a transformed criminal justice system demands a conception of truth that transcends the propensity for objectification of the truth-seeking process.

A key consideration arises here: rationalist scholars who favour the perspective of relative correspondence are distinguished from positivist proponents of absolute (real, material, substantial, etc.) truth in that they do not wholly reject the distinctness of the past. Confronted by this aporia, such authors ultimately reach an intermediary position between the notions of the *Same* and the *Other*: they embrace a relative or approximate interpretation of corresponding truth, which nevertheless remains grounded in the concept of the *Same* and ascribes to the knowing subject the ability to pursue absolute truth. The solution I put forward diverges sharply from this approach; as I have repeatedly emphasised, I reject both the search for truth and the notion of corresponding truth—even in its relative form.

To address my solution to this aporia, I again refer to Ricoeur's work. As he notes, "the historic representation is undoubtedly the image of the absent thing; but the absent thing is in turn divided into disappearance and existence in the past. Past things are abolished, but no one can make them not have been" (Ricoeur 2003: 374). Recourse to traces of the past imparts to the narrative representation of history a referential credibility that distinguishes it from other forms of narrative lacking this attribute, thereby rendering a complete disassociation from truth impossible. Nevertheless, as previously discussed, the corresponding truth has been—and remains—employed as a discursive strategy that legitimises the distortion of the preferred accusatorial structure within criminal proceedings.

Inquisitorial and positivist frameworks were clearly driven by an unrelenting ambition for truth. The epistemological foundation of evidentiary rationalism remains anchored in the correspondence principle, sustaining its commitment to the search for absolute truth in criminal proceedings. Therefore, it is imperative to seek advancement beyond this traditional approach to truth.

In this context, what constitutes an appropriate regime of truth for criminal proceedings—one that effectively guards against the epistemic risks associated with mistaken reliance on correspondence theories of truth as well as the dangers posed by relativism, that completely dismisses the notion of truth?

Ricoeur provides a clear response to this question by referencing "an expression common to both painter and historian: both seek to 'restore' a landscape, a sequence of events". The author notes that "'restore' reflects the intention to 'return what is due' to what is and what was" (Ricoeur 1997: 256). In a similar manner, a judge who drafts a conviction does so with the aim of justifying the decision through a narrative representation believed to be accurate and reflective of the elapsed time, drawing upon traces from the past. Ultimately, for the judge, the defendant's responsibility has been established. If responsibility had not been demonstrated, it is presumed that no conviction would occur.

I have identified a pivotal epistemic limitation by demonstrating that traces do not allow for a corresponding relationship, thereby highlighting the inherent uncertainty that defines the procedural regime of truth. Even the most seemingly unambiguous conviction—ostensibly closest to the correspondence ideal—cannot achieve absolute truth.

The sentence consistently aims to address the absence inherent in recounting a past event. Its function is primarily substitutive rather than directly correspondent. Evidentiary rationalism has sought to resolve this issue by linking correspondence within the sentence to the evidence presented during proceedings and not to the past event under judicial scrutiny—a self-referential cognitive structure that allows for the legitimisation of any decision, including those where the judge introduces evidence themselves. Suggesting that the temporal distance from the event is irrelevant may provide reassurance to the judge but ultimately reinforces the judge's cognitive privilege and grants them undisputed authority in criminal proceedings—an approach historically demonstrated to conflict with the protection of human rights.

What potential solution exists for addressing the challenge posed by the regime of truth in narrative representations of the past—one that moves beyond the correspondence theory of truth and establishes an epistemology of historical understanding capable of serving as a safeguard against excessive punitive power within a reimagined criminal justice system?

It is essential that judges remain cognisant of the persistent risk of error and wrongful convictions. An epistemological framework that prioritises human rights should emphasise harm reduction, rather than presuppose absolute authority or infallibility.

The convergence of political and epistemological implications in criminal justice is evident in the belief that judges possess cognitive privilege, which fosters an aspiration towards discovering truth. This perspective emphasises achieving factual correspondence with past events, presuming such alignment is possible, and consequently prioritising the pursuit of absolute truth as the principal aim of criminal proceedings. Although evidentiary rationalism may not contend that absolute truth is readily attainable, it asserts that truth remains absolute and must be pursued by the judge; while the judge's understanding of truth may be relative, the quest for truth continues to serve as the primary driver of proceedings rather than the protection of fundamental rights.

The attempted balance between the *Same* and the *Other* by evidentiary rationalism revitalises inquisitorial and positivist epistemology. Although the language used to articulate this may have evolved, the underlying theory of truth as correspondence continues to support an authoritative proceeding, reminiscent of nineteenth-century positivism. The adoption of evidentiary rationalism frameworks may risk promoting objectification and raises concerns regarding possible human rights violations. Furthermore, the principle of correspondence does not consider the ontological limitations inherent to the notion of the trace, thereby leaving the essential epistemological challenges unresolved.

Ricoeur endeavoured to advance the discourse concerning the nature of historical knowledge, extending beyond mere representation to introduce the notion of *representance*. He posits that the past is the *"face-to-face"* to which historical knowledge strives to represent appropriately, through the trace (Ricoeur 1997: 242).

In rendering a judgement, the judge engages in an act of reconstruction—producing a narrative account—and ideally seeks this reconstruction to reflect as closely as possible the reality of past events; that is, to ensure the conviction aligns with the defendant's actual guilt.

Ricoeur's philosophy provides a means to move beyond the view that the interplay between the *Same* and the *Other* results only in a model of relatively or approximately corresponding truth. For Ricoeur, attempts at correspondence with the past are inherently tied to the concept of representance—a debt to history that cannot be repaid. The notion of representance thus refers to the relationship between historiographical narratives and their object: a past that is simultaneously expired and preserved through its traces. Ricoeur asserts that this sense of representance denotes an enduring obligation to the past, one the historian can never fully satisfy (Ricoeur 1997: 175). He posits that representance offers the least inadequate means of honouring the reconstructive approach essential to historical truth, recognising its intrinsic limitations relative to the time it seeks to depict (Ricoeur 2003: 376).

Marrou describes the complexities inherent in the historian's experience, a perspective that is particularly relevant for judicial consideration. Regarding the work of the historian and the knowledge of facts, he points that

> It could not be described as the tranquil work of one, nor as the triumphant expansion of the other; it is something far more risky, tragic in a sense, from which we emerge breathless, humbled, somewhat defeated [...] there we are not alone, we find ourselves in the darkness with a mysterious Other, a reality that we feel at once terribly present and resistant to our efforts: we try to grasp it, to force it to submit, and it always ends up, at least in part, slipping away... history is a battle of the mind, an adventure and, like all human exploits, achieves only partial, entirely relative successes, which are not proportional to the initial ambition; as with any struggle with the disconcerting depths of being, man returns from it with an acute sense of his limits, his weakness, his humility. (Marrou 1978: 46)

If this is the case, it might appear that the sign of the *Other* most appropriately signifies knowledge pertaining to history. As Marrou notes, "History is what the historian manages to grasp of the past, but as it passes through their instruments of knowledge, that past has been so reworked, so transformed, that it is completely renewed and has become, ontologically, something quite different" (Marrou 1978: 49). The relevance of Marrou's insight increases further when one considers the inherent complexity of criminal proceedings—as discussed before, legal language adds different layers of meaning to past events and the truth in criminal proceedings relates to arguments presented by the parties.

Consequently, it is evident that the narrative truth produced by a judge is ontologically distinct from the historical events it attempts to represent; thus, only representance remains. Absolute truth is simply out of reach. Similar to the historian, the judge will inevitably remain indebted to the past.

Recognising this is essential—what implications does this concept have for criminal justice? The response thus far has been inadequate; historical uncertainty has prompted a persistent pursuit of truth, often reflected in judicial practice by the conscious or unconscious intention to confirm pre-established hypotheses regarding the accused's guilt.

The past remains fundamentally inaccessible, marked by an indelible difference that cannot be bridged. Our avenues for engagement are limited to traces of former realities, which serve more as substitutes than true representations, and are insufficient to resolve the inherent complexities of an object resistant to close approximation. This resistance transcends epistemological frameworks; it is ontological by nature, as the essence of the past lies in its irretrievability—what has occurred no longer exists and cannot be divested of its defining quality of pastness. Nevertheless, even with this temporal distance, past events persist through their traces, lending them a degree of endurance and ensuring that knowledge of the past retains some relevance, rather than rendering it entirely alien or *Other*.

The fundamental misunderstanding about the duality inherent to the past underpins epistemologies that may be harmful to human rights. Western criminal justice systems have often emphasised punitive measures, frequently relying on interpretations of past events informed by epistemological frameworks that prioritise the cognitive role of the judge. The dominant discourse situates this authoritative approach within objectives such as applying justice, establishing factual accuracy, and safeguarding societal interests.

These theories are based on a fundamental misunderstanding concerning traces of the past, which gives rise to three erroneous theoretical perspectives related to the regime of truth in legal proceedings. Each of these may potentially place the accused at a significant disadvantage.

The first two positions accept the corresponding notion of truth, though with somewhat distinct approaches: (a) the positivist approach: the belief that absolute truth is attainable and should be pursued unconditionally; and (b) the rationalist approach: the aspiration towards corresponding (absolute) truth, predicated on the judge's continued ability to seek the (relative) knowledge of the truth. Conversely, (c) the relativist approach: the third position wholly dismisses the concept of truth by claiming that the past is merely distant and entirely inaccessible, embodying an extreme form of sceptical relativism.

Notably, these three perspectives ultimately converge upon the same objectionable consequence: each enhances the discretionary scope of procedural decisionism. While the first two uphold a correspondence theory—relying on the search for truth and thereby empowering judicial protagonism—the third expands the realm of decisionism by denying the probative value of traces of the past, as will be addressed further.

As previously stated, this study does not endorse radical scepticism; rather, it supports the establishment of an appropriate truth regime to uphold the protection of human rights within criminal proceedings.

Resolving the aporia and transcending the aforementioned positions fundamentally depends on the notion of trace, which inherently leads to Ricoeur's notion of representance. It is based on the trace that I contend that the knowledge of the past should not be exclusively framed within the domains of the *Same* or the *Other*. When anchored in traces from the past, the narrative formulated by the judge should instead occupy a third ontological sphere: that of the *Analogue*. The term *Analogue* here encompasses both *Being-as* and *Not-being*; it describes a truth that is produced under persistent tension between revelation and concealment, ultimately analogically generated as a narrative artefact by the judge, who should be perceived as a being-in-the-world and not as an all-knowing entity. Thus, this form of truth is produced analogically through narrative—truth in criminal proceedings should be understood as an analogical narrative production of the past—distinct from notions of correspondence to events of the past. In this context, the term analogy is utilised as a current alternative for a reality that remains inaccessible. The judge's narrative does not precisely recreate past events; rather, it forms an ontologically independent account that functions as a replacement for the unavailable reality of what occurred.

In contrast to the epistemic excesses associated with the concept of corresponding truth, Ricoeur—drawing upon inspiration from Plato's "Sophist"—introduced the following categories: the *Same*, the *Other*, and the *Analogue*. According to Ricoeur, engaging with the reality of the past necessitates progressing through successive interpretive filters: first the *Same*, then the *Other*, and finally the *Analogue* (Ricoeur 1997: 258). Within this framework, the trace functions as the *Same* (since it represents a remnant of the past that now exists in the present), even as the past itself constitutes the *Other* (given that traces provide only partial access to what was once a greater whole, thus requiring recognition of the past's otherness). The interplay between the filters of the *Same* and the *Other* generates proof that may inform the narrative construction of the *Analogue*, understood as *Being-as* and *Not-being*. This approach deliberately avoids subscribing to a correspondence model of truth. Ultimately, a narrative artefact that seeks to represent the past in a substitutive manner may evoke the notion that "things must have happened *as* is said in this narrative; thanks to the tropological filter, the *Being-as* of the past event is brought into language" (Ricoeur 1997: 258). But *Being-as* should not be perceived as *Being equal to*—hence the idea of a surrogate for the past.

Evidentiary positivism and evidentiary rationalism commit a significant epistemological error by treating the signs of the *Same* (correspondent truth) and the *Other* (complete departure from truth) either in isolation or simply relativising the *Same* by recognising that the past in an *Other*. As previously noted, Heidegger recognised that a trace simultaneously signifies both presence and absence, necessitating an alternative regime of truth—one that incorporates the *Same*, the *Other*, and ultimately the *Analogue*: *Being-as* and *Non-being*. This approach does not reflect correspondent truth, nor does it entirely exclude truth; rather, it repositions truth to mitigate the epistemic excess inherent in its canonical form. Such a conception inspires caution, respect for human rights and harm reduction, contrasting with correspondence notions that may lead to assumptions of judicial omnipotence. Accordingly, evidentiary activity should be framed within this nuanced perspective, transcending the binary construct of truth/non-truth and the gradations of relative truth that often perpetuate abuses attributed to the perceived capacities of the knowing subject's pursuit of absolute truth.

In criminal proceedings, truth should not be understood strictly as the *Same* (real, absolute, material, or substantial truth) nor as the *Other* (untruth), nor should it be reduced to the rationalist reinterpretation of correspondent truth, which occupies an intermediary position between the *Same* and the *Other*, retaining the ideal of a search for truth. The inherent risks, uncertainties, limitations, and fallibility in reconstructing past events underscore that the regime of truth in criminal justice is better situated under the sign of the *Analogue*. Here, truth emerges from a dynamic tension between revelation and concealment, ultimately being analogically constructed as a narrative artefact by the judge, grounded in remnants of past events. Thus, the produced truth assumes an analogical and narrative form.

This perspective, rooted in philosophical hermeneutics and detached from consciousness-based philosophy, holds that truth is the analogical narrative production of the past rather than its mere correspondence. Adopting Coutinho's view, "Truth is in the whole" and if this totality is absent from the proceedings, then Truth itself is absent, leaving instead what may be referred to as "truth" with a lower-case "t" (Coutinho 2023). This "truth" is analogically generated within proceedings that should be governed by ritualised and regulated frameworks that define evidentiary limits and prohibitions, effectively rejecting the aspiration for absolute truth and favouring respect for human rights.

The "truth" produced by the judge serves as a surrogate for the unattainable totality of Truth, comprising a narrative anchored in the available evidentiary substratum and invariably subject to numerous errors—existing, perhaps unacknowledged, under the sign of uncertainty. Given that Truth, in its entirety, is not present in legal proceedings, conviction requires recourse to language (Coutinho 2023), whereby a narrative is formulated that, for procedural purposes, replaces unattainable Truth with an analogically produced "truth" in the verdict.

In the end, only representance will remain—the "truth" that the judge narratively produces is something ontologically distinct from the past he wishes to represent (Truth), thus, the judge will always be an insolvent debtor to a past (totality) that lies beyond human capacity. As Koselleck observes,

> Every source or, more precisely, every trace that becomes a source through our questioning refers us to a history that is always something more or less than the trace itself, and always something different from it. A history is

> never identical to the source that bears witness to it. If it were, every source that flows clear would already be the very history one seeks to know. (Koselleck 2006: 186)

Consequently, the "truth" that emerges within legal proceedings possesses an ontologically distinct nature and remains, at best, contingent—it might potentially coincide with Truth, but then again, it might not. A conviction is only justified if the due process of law has been rigorously observed, thereby enhancing efforts to minimise harm from wrongful convictions, as expected in a citizen-focused criminal justice system built upon the presumption of innocence rather than the pursuit of absolute truth. It is fundamentally flawed to adopt a positivist perspective based on "presence", suggesting that Truth exists within proceedings and can be located through mechanisms such as free conviction and the so-called principle of real truth. Similarly, adopting a concept which acknowledges "absence" and contends that procedural statements address factual matters, yet retains notions of 'objective' or "absolute" truth and insists it must be sought by judges actively managing evidence, is also erroneous. The ambition for truth persists and such arguments risk being appropriated to serve authoritarian ends under the guise of a rhetorical commitment to the "search for truth", "justice", "societal defence", and countless others.

These findings should lead to a profound reconsideration of the role of the judge and the very nature of criminal proceedings. Instead of seeking the truth—unattainable in the face of human limitations and the temporal distance from past evens—scholars should recognise the inherent limitations of reconstructing the past. The function of criminal proceedings, in this context, is not to faithfully reproduce the reality once lived in pursuit of a conviction, but rather, should there exist a robust evidentiary basis against the defendant, to construct a narrative grounded in the available traces, always under the aegis of constitutional safeguards and due process of law. Thus, the primary commitment is to the protection of the human and fundamental rights of the accused, preventing the proceedings from becoming an instrument of arbitrariness or a means of perpetuating historical injustices by reiterating the inquisitorial aim of objectification.

Should a judge prioritise an exhaustive pursuit of the truth when proof is only required for convictions, and reasonable doubt not only suffices but requires acquittal? This approach raises concerns regarding potential infringements on human rights. In this context, it is important to consider the constitutional and international human rights treaties that should guide evidentiary standards in criminal justice. The framework I propose here clearly aligns with upholding human rights, while evidentiary rationalism resembles perspectives aligned with criminal justice authoritarianism, such as inquisitorialism and evidentiary positivism.

Through adopting a comprehensive analytical framework that places the cognitive underpinnings of legal proceedings within the context of historical perspective, the conclusions presented here extend beyond those proposed by Ferrajoli. While Ferrajoli analyses the comparative roles of judge and historian, his approach does not integrate the ontological considerations addressed by Ricoeur. This study advances the discussion by moving past the notion of relative correspondence truth and placing greater emphasis on the safeguarding of human rights, favouring a harm reduction programme. The distinction from Taruffo—and thus Beltrán—is even more marked, as the findings here fundamentally diverge from their model, which is rooted in both political and epistemological aspects of modern rationality that are fundamentally authoritarian in nature, as will be explored below.

A Reassessment and Critique of the Political and Epistemological Foundations of Evidentiary Rationalism

Taruffo regards the pursuit of truth as a fundamental aspect of judicial impartiality and an epistemological necessity, consistent with the modern subject-object framework. He notes that: a) the parties may lack an inherent interest in uncovering the truth (Taruffo 2010: 202); and b) their dialectical engagement does not necessarily provide an effective means for establishing truth, which he considers the primary objective of legal proceedings (Taruffo 2010: 195). Taruffo emphasises the importance of enabling judges to actively seek evidence not introduced by the parties, explicitly to facilitate the ascertainment of truth—a prevailing tendency he identifies in contemporary legislation (Taruffo 2010: 197). He further clarifies that this approach does not transform judges into inquisitors acting to the detriment of the parties' rights and safeguards but rather endows them with ancillary and supplementary authority. This authority includes confirming that all relevant evidence has been submitted by the parties, and, when necessary, adopting an active role (Taruffo 2010: 199). This perspective is firmly upheld by Brazilian procedural scholarship influenced by rationalism (Badaró 2019: 260), which maintains that the pursuit of truth is compatible with the accusatorial system (Badaró 2019: 261).

The pursuit of truth is a central tenet of rationalism; however, this perspective conflicts with the impartiality expected of judges in the accusatorial system by granting them the authority to intervene directly in evidence management. Such theoretical developments indicate a shift that challenges the dispositive principle and provides further support for the truth-seeking ideology, potentially resulting in negative outcomes, including human rights violations, criminal selectivity and an increase in racially biased mass incarceration. Additionally, this approach encapsulates the fundamental rationale behind the objectification process integral to inquisitorial epistemology.

The rationalist approach closely resembles the inquisitorial mindset, which regards it as beneficial for the judge to independently ascertain all relevant facts, including those not specified in the accusation, due to their comprehensive authority over the proceedings at any stage. Consequently, the judge, operating outside adversarial processes and serving as the principal arbiter of evidence, seeks information primarily based on their interpretation or construction of the case facts (Coutinho 2018: 42).

It is crucial to recognise that even judges with the best intentions may inadvertently be influenced by unconscious biases, which can reinforce impressions outside of their awareness due to the complexities of consciousness and the potential for developing paranoid tendencies (Coutinho 2018). The persistent risk of a judge forming opinions beforehand should not be overlooked, as it could lead to confirmation bias when granted investigatory powers. Furthermore, issues related to cognitive dissonance require careful attention and are often intensified by such powers. Modern rationalist thought, shaped by a solipsistic and subjective perspective, tends to uphold the judge's cognitive privilege. As Streck notes, "The judge is not a scientist who, from the outside, observes reality from a privileged *locus* (as Taruffo believes)" (Streck 2016: 124).

Taruffo expressly disregards concerns about judicial engagement with evidentiary material introduced *ex officio* during the exercise of their duties (Taruffo 2010: 200). He contends that the central issue is not whether to address the judge's investigatory authority, but rather how to implement appropriate safeguards over its use. According to Taruffo, it is essential that parties retain the ability to challenge the relevance and admissibility of evidence introduced by the judge *ex officio* and are afforded the opportunity to present counterevidence. He asserts that the proper approach ensures the robust functioning of adversarial proceedings without invalidating the judge's investigatory powers (Taruffo 2010: 201–202). As Streck notes,

> It thus appears that the parties are underestimated, unable to assume the advantages and disadvantages of conducting their own (available!) interests in court, except under the tutelage of a supposedly impartial judge in pursuit of the truth. His truth, sought and constructed at his discretion. Afterwards, the parties may comment on this and produce counterevidence, with who knows what effect before a *biased* judge. (Streck 2016: 128)

Taruffo's proposal appears to challenge a core tenet of the accusatorial system: the restriction against judicial involvement in evidence management, as mandated by the dispositive principle (Coutinho 2018). This principle is intended to ensure the conditions necessary for an impartial judge, which Werner Goldschmidt identifies as fundamental to procedural fairness. In doing so, Taruffo's argument may overlook important distinctions between civil and criminal procedure, including their respective legal categories, underlying rationales, and the historical consequences associated with inquisitorial models—where judges manage or initiate evidence, potentially contravening the *ne procedat iudex ex officio* standard that underpins judicial impartiality.

Coutinho observes that such a system risks privileging deductive logic, a characteristic feature of Western jurisprudence, wherein the decision-maker selects a major premise beforehand and subsequently seeks supporting evidence, thus raising concerns about impartiality (Coutinho 2018: 43). Even though deductive reasoning may be formally rejected, similar tendencies can be discerned in Taruffo's doctrine of free motivated conviction; despite advocating intersubjective control, there remains an implicit acceptance of judicial discretion (Streck 2016: 131). Cavallone characterises Taruffo's position as reflecting a persistent advocacy for a proactive judiciary, drawing a parallel to the Prussian monarchy (Cavallone 2012: 33).

Regarding Ferrer-Beltrán, it is worth noting that, while adopting Taruffo's perspective—which overlooks the nuances of criminal procedure—the author designates the pursuit or ascertainment of truth as fundamental to the legal system. He evaluates possible conflicts between this "primary objective of law" and other potentially competing aims. Ferrer-Beltrán concludes that the value or purpose of determining the truth occupies a structurally distinct position relative to other objectives. He contends that the primary aim of legal proceedings must be the establishment of truth, as this is essential for the law to serve as an instrument for influencing compliant behaviour. According to Beltrán, only when legal consequences are consistently applied do individuals have reason to act in accordance with legal norms, thereby enabling the law to fulfil its conflict resolution function (Beltrán 2007: 82).

It is evident that the implications of these arguments for criminal proceedings are significant. Beltrán articulates his position clearly: proceedings can influence individuals' conduct to deter homicide only if they effectively serve their purpose of identifying the perpetrator and imposing the legally prescribed sanction (Beltrán 2007: 30). In another discussion, Beltrán suggests reconsidering the elevated evidentiary standards in criminal proceedings, noting that in recent decades, the use of criminal law as a tool for societal governance has expanded considerably, moving beyond its original role as an instrument of *ultima ratio*. Concurrently, the range of criminal sanctions employed to shape behaviour has also increased (Beltrán 2007: 140). Beltrán not only acknowledges but endorses this expansion; critiques of mass incarceration and penal selectivity are nowhere to be found in his work. His perspective stands in direct contrast to efforts aimed at reconceptualising criminal justice as a programme of minimal intervention and respect for human rights.

The perspectives on criminal law and criminal procedure presented by evidentiary rationalism underscore that the approaches of Taruffo and Beltrán in these fields are grounded primarily in political considerations rather than epistemological ones.

Their approach can be summarised thus: criminal proceedings serve as mechanisms for establishing factual truth, wherein judicial authorities are empowered to conduct investigations, identify violations of legal norms, and administer appropriate sanctions. The primary aim is to shape societal conduct by applying exemplary penalties—a prevailing approach within Western criminal justice systems that does not adequately consider international human rights treaties.

Upon closer critical examination beyond the surface-level discourse of rationality and objectivity, it becomes clear that evidentiary rationalism may promote objectifying practices that risk infringing upon human rights.

This prompts a brief shift towards examining what should be the meaning and purpose underpinning criminal law in contemporary times—a subject characterised by a multitude of differing perspectives. The criminal justice system that was first envisioned in the eighteenth century clearly emphasised social control, notwithstanding certain safeguards that served to legitimise it.

According to rationalist perspectives, criminal procedure is viewed as a mechanism designed to reinforce police selectivity, rather than as a process intended to constrain such discretion through adherence to due legal procedures. Taruffo and Beltrán demonstrate adherence to the prevailing punitive perspective and, to a considerable extent, do not integrate the humanitarian elements found in Beccaria's classicism. Instead, their approach reflects inspiration from Bentham's anti-formalist stance. It can be stated that the rationalist "epistemic engine" was primarily designed for punitive purposes rather than as a safeguard against authoritarian power.

In contemporary discourse, however, this perspective has been significantly challenged by recent theories, such as Zaffaroni's "marginal realism". His theory asserts that criminal law functions primarily as a safeguard against authoritarianism which establishes a series of prior requirements that must be met before the punishment can be imposed.

Zaffaroni conceptualises criminal law from a novel perspective, likening its role to that of the Red Cross during conflicts. He asserts that its primary purpose is to minimise harm and uphold the Rule of Law, distinguishing it from police state practices that may endanger civil liberties.

Based on his rationale, the criminal justice system ought to be reconceptualised to uphold human dignity and preserve the presumption of innocence. This principle is foundational to criminal law, functioning to limit punitive power—a fundamental criterion inherent to democratic societies. As Zaffaroni notes,

> Criminal law must programme the exercise of legal power as a *dike* containing the police state, preventing it from overwhelming the rule of law. However, the waters of the police state are always at a higher level, so that it tends to overflow the *dike*. To prevent this, the dike must allow a

> controlled amount of punitive power to pass, doing so selectively, *filtering* only the least irrational torrent and reducing its turbulence, through a complex system of sluice gates that prevents any one of them from breaking and, should this occur, provides others to ensure containment. (Zaffaroni et al 2003: 156-157)

Zaffaroni's dike metaphor underscores the necessity of redesigning the criminal justice system to constrain punitive authority. The legal simplification of past events should serve to prevent disproportionate punishment and selective law enforcement, leading to a reconsideration of the judiciary's role and legal discourse in alignment with democratic principles (Coutinho 1998: 145). Judges must refrain from adopting an inquisitorial approach motivated by an unchecked pursuit of truth, as such actions can compromise legality and potentially violate human rights. Legal-criminal terminology abstracts reality—that is, to a certain extent, something unavoidable. But its central objective should be the prevention of arbitrariness, not a relentless pursuit for absolute truth to enact exemplary punishments.

Accordingly, criminal procedure should not be exclusively directed towards the enforcement of criminal law through convictions; despite the allure of truth-seeking, it is essential that criminal justice operates to restrain, rather than advance, police selectivity. This perspective is consistent with the principles expected in a democratic state founded on the Rule of Law, where the protection of the accused's human rights remains a central priority.

Criminal law should be viewed as a mechanism that both defines and restrains the exercise of punitive power. The simplification inherent in legal language, while necessary for the administration of justice, must always be balanced against the imperative to safeguard human rights and dignity. Only by maintaining this balance can the legal system fulfil its role in a democratic society, providing protection against arbitrariness and ensuring that every individual is treated with respect and fairness.

From this perspective, it is apparent that, regarding Taruffo and Beltrán, the divergence extends beyond the epistemological matter of relative corresponding truth found in Ferrajoli's position. Instead, it fundamentally revolves around not only epistemological but differing political views on the judicial power to actively pursue absolute truth during legal proceedings—a notion rightly set aside by Ferrajoli.

The examination of traces and historical context presented here—including the identification of the *Same*, the *Other*, and the *Analogous*—has led to distinct conclusions than those of evidentiary rationalism. These findings reinforce the view that the largely analogical production of narrative truth in criminal proceedings demands attention to procedural safeguards and protection of human rights. Consequently, this highlights the necessity of maintaining a clear separation between prosecutorial and adjudicative functions and ensuring proper evidence management by the respective parties, as prescribed in accusatorial systems grounded in human rights principles.

While the procedural ramifications of my proposal require further analysis, the arguments presented suggest that this new approach acknowledges the epistemological significance of pastness and does not endorse the correspondence theory of truth or advocates for an unequivocal search for truth. Rather than promoting the pursuit of truth, it emphasises the need to recognise and manage the intrinsic uncertainty within criminal proceedings. It is accurate to assert that traces define both the potential and the limitations of our knowledge about the past. These potentials and constraints are not normative, but rather ontological in nature, and cannot be transcended by an epistemology grounded in the notion of corresponding truth. Consequently, as previously noted through the notion of trace, it is untenable to uphold an idea of procedural truth premised on the sign of the *Same*; a trace merely indicates—it endures as a remnant or fragment of an *Other*, the past event—enabling the construction of knowledge with an *Analogous* character, embodying both *Being-as* and *Not-being*. In this framework, narrative constructions serve as analogues for historical events in decision-making, underscoring that truth is always contingent and highlighting the considerable risk of judicial error and wrongful conviction.

As Carnelutti observes, the risk lies in becoming misled due to the fallibility of evidence; this risk is particularly severe when the reconstruction of the past influences a person's fate (Carnelutti 1965: 73). Taruffo also recognises this challenge, noting that errors, omissions, manipulations, and inaccurate reconstructions of facts are both prevalent and serious, and may result in significant mistakes and profound misunderstandings in the adjudication of disputes (Taruffo 2010: 49).

Nevertheless, Taruffo continued to attribute an epistemic role of truth-seeking to the judge. He argued that the concept of hypotheses taking precedence over facts relies on simplistic and largely unsubstantiated psychological assumptions, which suggest that individuals attempting to gather information about a fact immediately lose their capacity to accurately assess the content and reliability of the information obtained (Taruffo 2010: 210).

Taruffo promptly dismisses the risks associated with cognitive dissonance and unconscious confirmation bias, deeming them unworthy of serious consideration—yet another intricate topic left unexplored. Nevertheless, the issue he raised opens the door to a significant inquiry: if traces from the past serve as the foundation for constructing historical knowledge, does evidentiary rationalism correctly assert that judges ought to examine evidence beyond what the parties present? Would adopting such an approach lead to more informed decisions?

Is it appropriate for judges to possess the authority to proactively seek additional "traces of the past" (potentially ad infinitum)?

These arguments can be compelling, encouraging a shift towards antiformalism and a disregard for procedural safeguards. This perspective aligns with Bentham's rationale, echoed by modern evidentiary rationalists, who contend that exclusionary rules hinder epistemic objectives.

Conversely, my position holds that rules and principles establishing evidentiary boundaries should not be viewed as "counter-epistemic". Instead, they are fundamental to procedural epistemology, serving as a framework wherein power may be appropriately challenged and resisted.

Additionally, it is important to acknowledge another relevant factor. As discussed in the following section, the hallucinatory nature of evidence necessitates external assessment and adversarial processes—uncorrected evidence should not be accepted as proof (as a trace of the past). Taruffo's approach favours the hallucinatory character of evidence and increases the risk of wrongful convictions.

Contrary to Taruffo's viewpoint, I argue that it is not feasible for a judge to seek additional evidence objectively while maintaining an unbiased and impartial stance. This methodology risks significant errors by inadequately recognising the uncertainty intrinsic to criminal proceedings and the hallucinatory nature of the evidence.

Although Taruffo may not have addressed the implications of this uncertainty, choosing instead to emphasise the cognitive privilege of the judge, my approach here has been distinctly different. By emphasising the pastness of the past, I have underscored the unsurmountable uncertainty that afflicts criminal proceedings.

If taken as an absolute, an epistemology that recognises the pastness of past events may make condemnations impossible, due to the uncertainty of the knowledge obtained through evidentiary activity: traces serve as placeholders instead of providing a direct connection to historical fact.

Given these considerations, it is important to address a significant issue: if the meaning of legal proceedings is determined by the substantive law with which they interact, then the fact that the truth regime in criminal proceedings is organised around the notion of analogy has noteworthy implications. This is especially relevant as criminal law prohibits analogy except *in bonam partem* (Bitencourt 2009: 166–167).

If every condemnation is analogous to the past, if in every condemnation uncertainty and representance are all that remains, it is as if every condemnation is a form of analogy *in mala* partem. Ferrajoli similarly recognised uncertainty in his analysis, offering the following observation:

> Strictly speaking, if one were to think that the criminal judgment should reach "objective" truth and take the principle of *in dubio pro reo* literally, the irreducible margins of uncertainty that characterise procedural truth should entail the illegitimacy of any conviction and, therefore, the paralysis of the judicial function. (Ferrajoli 2002: 51)

Therefore, caution is warranted. It should be noted that I am not completely refuting the legitimacy of criminal jurisdiction. At this point in history—particularly if reconsidered—the criminal justice framework retains significant potential for regulating punitive authority, much of which remains untapped.

As mentioned before, my approach is reformist and grounded in a framework of immediacy. In this context, immediacy refers to the recognition that, although the implementation of non-punitive conflict resolution mechanisms is an aspirational goal for the future, current conditions necessitate a focus on harm reduction and the protection of human rights. I have adopted a stance of resistance accordingly.

My argument is not that all convictions are erroneous; rather, it is that the process of producing truth through analogy is inherently fraught with tension and uncertainty, rendering outcomes at best contingent. I have sought to make clear that the sign of the *Other* does not constitute an epistemic basis for historical knowledge. As Lopes Jr (2010: 541) aptly remarks, just as it would be unsophisticated to claim that judicial judgement is wholly falsehood, similar criticism of my stance would be both reductive and inaccurate.

According to Lopes Jr., "truth is thus contingent, and the legitimacy of a decision can only be achieved through the rigorous adherence to due process" (Lopes Jr 2010: 540). Within this framework, Lopes Jr. unequivocally rejects the notion that criminal procedure serves to attain truth or that truth is inherent in judicial judgement. The author clarifies, however, that while a judgement may coincidentally reflect actual events (truth as correspondence), this outcome cannot be attributed as the purpose or responsibility of the procedural system. "There remains no valid rationale for defending what cannot be justified, even under the premise that truth, though unattainable, should serve as an aspirational ideal" (Lopes Jr 2010: 540).

To assert that truth is contingent entails abandoning the pursuit of truth and adopting a new framework in which the judge must demonstrate a predisposition to acquit, following the presumption of innocence. Accordingly, the presumption of innocence should serve as the central and foundational principle guiding criminal proceedings—including the responsibilities and roles of the judge—thereby facilitating a departure from the prevailing inquisitorial, positivist or rationalist approaches focused on condemnations. Once again: to search for the truth is to search for evidence to substantiate a condemnation—proof is not required for acquittal.

The inherent limitations in achieving absolute truth—regardless of the chosen epistemological framework—inevitably result in an irreducible margin of uncertainty in every conviction. This reality underscores the need to urgently fortify safeguards against punitive power within a reimagined criminal justice system, one that upholds human rights and ensures protection for the accused against enduring objectification.

A critical implication of this discussion is the necessity to reframe the expectations placed upon criminal justice. Rather than aspiring to an unattainable absolute truth, the legal system must embrace procedural mechanisms designed to manage and contain the risks inherent in evidentiary uncertainties. This shift in perspective prioritises the protection of individual rights and the reduction of harm over the illusory pursuit of an objective historical truth.

In practice, this means that the legitimacy of criminal adjudication hinges not on the search for truth, but on the robustness of procedural safeguards, transparency, and the consistent application of the presumption of innocence. Such an approach acknowledges the inherent fragility of reconstructing past events and recognises that justice is best served not by the ambition for truth, but by the fair and respectful treatment of the accused.

By elucidating the concepts of the *Same*, the *Other*, and the *Analogous*, I am initiating an examination of the substantial risks inherent within criminal proceedings and highlighting the consequent necessity to move beyond a truth-seeking epistemology, as this approach tends to heighten those risks. As noted in the first chapter, redefining the parameters of truth in criminal proceedings underscores the importance of reinforcing the ritualised containment of punitive power. This reimagined framework for criminal justice will be further developed in the following section.

The objective is as follows: to highlight the necessity for stricter controls and to prioritise procedural safeguards. In doing so, this approach aims to move beyond an epistemological framework that may inadvertently perpetuate injustices against the accused and undermine the contextual realities inherent in criminal proceedings. While an epistemology of pastness may not entirely delegitimise criminal justice, it does demonstrate that criminal procedure can only be justified as a mechanism for restraining punitive authority, with a primary focus on harm reduction and the protection of human rights—objectives fundamentally at odds with the judge's independent search for truth.

Evidentiary Activity, Proof, and the Hallucinatory Character of Evidence

Having defined the notion of trace, I will now examine the procedural journey that an evidentiary element undertakes to have its status as a trace—serving as an analogue link to past events—verified, thereby authorising its recognition as proof and its utilisation as a cognitive tool by the judge. Proofs are not merely included in the proceedings for judicial review; rather, it is essential to assess which evidence submitted by the parties may be accepted as proof and acknowledged as traces, as indicative of past events.

The distinction between evidence and proof is essential within legal discourse. While the terms are often used synonymously in casual conversation, their meanings diverge in a legal setting and should be understood accordingly. Evidence encompasses information, data, or objects submitted to support a claim, whereas proof refers to evidence that has successfully undergone scrutiny for authenticity and reliability. Evidence functions to substantiate or reinforce an argument during evidentiary proceedings, but its acceptance as proof signifies confirmation of the assertion.

Accordingly, evidence serves as the foundational element, whereas proof denotes the affirmative outcome of judicial evaluation—namely, the legal acknowledgement that the material is not falsified or fabricated but constitutes a remnant of historical events (though such an assessment may be subject to error).

Accordingly, evidence can be defined as the foundation of evidentiary procedures, encompassing documents, indications, and testimonies, among others. Evidentiary activity refers to the process undertaken with the objective of establishing proof. Proof, in turn, is the affirmative outcome of evidentiary activity, which allows a piece of evidence to be formally accepted as proof within legal proceedings—as a record of past events from which the judge may produce truth in narrative form.

I support this tripartite classification because I believe that a clear understanding of the challenges in elevating evidence to proof requires a careful distinction between the two notions. Evidence refers to the material presented by parties during proceedings with the aim of supporting their arguments. For such material to be recognised as proof—meaning traces of the past—it must withstand the rigorous process of evidentiary scrutiny designed to address its potentially hallucinatory nature.

My understating represents a substantive departure from a long-standing tradition of knowledge that downplays the necessity of addressing the hallucinatory—and thus inherently inaccurate—characteristics of evidence. This is exemplified by the search for truth ideology in its positivist and rationalist manifestations: both approaches emphasise the judge's cognitive authority while often overlooking the potential unreliability of evidentiary material.

Fernando Gil offers a critical perspective, advancing the discourse on evidence by challenging traditional philosophies which treat evidence as inherently true and therefore exempt from evidentiary procedures by involved parties (Martins and Gil 2002: 17). Gil advocates for a rupture with the notion that evidence amounts merely to a judgement of fact, asserting that the presumption of immediate perceptibility and complete factual correspondence is fundamentally flawed.

The relationship between evidence and truth warrants careful consideration. As Cunha Martins notes, there is significant proximity between these two concepts, regardless of how their connection is configured (Martins and Gil 2002: 22). Nevertheless, the determination of truth should ultimately be shaped by the evidentiary activity, which seeks to transcend mere evidence; evidence itself may possess a hallucinatory nature. Gil observes that "the evidence of perception and language is transformed, through an unusual process, into conceptual evidence. This latter form is excessive in two respects: epistemologically, as it regards itself as intrinsically truthful, *index veri*" (Martins and Gil 2002: 19). Furthermore, Gil asserts, "unlike proof, evidence does not rely on external evaluative mechanisms because it serves as the unfolding of meaning in its own indication of truth, existing independently" (Martins and Gil 2002: 21).

Consequently, within an accusatorial system governed by democratic principles, it is inappropriate to equate evidence with truth. Due process necessitates that proof achieves a substantial level of reliability, exceeding the threshold of mere evidence. As noted by Gil, law represents one of the areas in which the theory of proof has reached its greatest sophistication (Martins and Gil 2002: 22–23). Accordingly, "the truth of evidence does not align with the concept of criminal proceedings, whereas the truth of proof does" (Martins and Gil 2002: 21). This distinction underscores that inquisitorial, positivist and rationalist epistemologies are defined by a cognitive framework that tends to favour the hallucinatory qualities of evidence, while accusatorial epistemology establishes mechanisms to constrain evidence and thereby enhance the probability of correcting this hallucinatory potential. Gil asserts that

> it is ultimately evidentiary activity that must work with truth in a non-hallucinatory manner; thus, evidentiary activity in some way exerts a corrective effect on this hallucinatory character; and it is also evidentiary activity that removes truth from the shelter of evidence, subjecting it to the scrutiny of the proceedings. (Martins and Gil 2002: 21)

Viewed from this standpoint, the potential transformation of evidence into proof—achieved through the evidentiary activities undertaken by the parties—establishes a robust basis for rendering judgements grounded in traces, thereby facilitating decisions supported by proof. Evidence consists of elements introduced during the evidentiary activity to substantiate the hypotheses put forth by the parties; only when this process yields positive results does evidence become proof, mitigating its inherent risk of unreliability. This approach allows for the assessment of an element's validity as an analogue trace of past events, while acknowledging that the possibility of error persists, though it is substantially diminished compared to epistemological frameworks that are primarily concerned with absolute truth.

The adoption of these premises serves to prevent convictions founded on speculative or illusory interpretations of evidence mistakenly regarded as reflections of past events. As previously outlined, the standard required for conviction must be met with substantive and tangible elements, rather than subjective beliefs about the truthfulness of evidence. Accordingly, when a fact is deemed proven, it signifies that the judge has confirmed the quality of an element as a credible trace of the past—where previously it was only considered as evidence. This process represents an advancement in procedural cognition, recognising that proof exceeds mere evidence by withstanding verification through the adversarial structure of legal proceedings. Consequently, once the trace is acknowledged by the judge as indicative of the past, it attains the status of proof.

This perspective stands in contrast to the simplified approach of factual judgement, which equates truth strictly with what is immediately apparent, or with its contemporary relativised form that assumes judges can independently overcome the potentially misleading nature of evidence. Both approaches tend to encourage authoritative and potentially misguided conclusions grounded in unexamined evidence, thereby increasing the risk of judicial error. Essentially, conflating evidence with truth constitutes an unacceptable epistemic overreach: as Gil observes, from this standpoint, "evidence now means the presentification of meaning and truth as self-sufficient and self-positing, as suggested by the expression *index sui*. A truth that is its own index is excessive by nature" (Martins and Gil 2002: 19). Consequently, the implementation of external evaluative mechanisms is essential to counteract the self-referential tendencies of evidence. Importantly, these mechanisms are jeopardised when judicial impartiality is abandoned and the judge adopts an inquisitorial role, unilaterally constructing truth—a process that ultimately potentially undermines the human rights of the accused.

Judgements derived from a judicial approach that prioritises active truth-seeking are susceptible to evidentiary contamination. If the status of evidentiary material as proof or trace is not sufficiently established, the resulting determination of truth may substantially deviate from historical events. Accordingly, criminal proceedings should function as a systematic framework to address the potential unreliability of evidence, thereby minimising the risk of wrongful convictions through rigorous examination of the prosecutorial narrative.

Evidence should be regarded as the material foundation that underpins evidentiary proceedings, while proof represents the positive outcome of this process—specifically, the confirmation of a trace within the proceedings that enables the analogical justification of a conviction or acquittal based on evidentiary grounds (noting that an acquittal may occasionally lack such a basis—*in dubio pro reo* is sufficient). In this context, evidence refers to the foundation upon which a party's hypothesis can be supported. Such evidence must be properly managed by the parties during the evidentiary phase—if accepted by the judge as trace of the past, it functions as a cognitive operator in an analogical framework.

A structured process that can exercise corrective authority over the reliability of evidence is necessary to minimise harm—the risk of wrongful conviction. Accepting lesser standards risks legitimising arbitrary decision-making, relying on reasoning that pursues absolute truth solely under the premise of the *Same* and increases the possibility of judicial errors.

In summary, the distinction between evidence and proof emerges not only as a theoretical requirement but as a practical safeguard for a reimagined criminal justice system. Recognising that evidence, by its very nature, cannot automatically be equated with proof reinforces the need for rigorous mechanisms of assessment and confrontation, ensuring that a judge has a more solid foundation for forming their conviction. Thus, the transition from evidence to proof should be seen as a dialogical process of confrontation between the parties, capable of mitigating the risks of arbitrariness and decisions in which hypotheses prevail over facts.

The rational subject's pursuit of absolute truth is frequently regarded as fundamental to the process of discovering truth. This approach, however, may foster an unrelenting drive for more evidence—ambition for truth—, potentially causing the judge to prioritise hypotheses over factual information, whether deliberately or inadvertently. This approach compromises the judge's impartiality.

Acknowledging the potentially hallucinatory nature of evidence prompts distinct conclusions. It is important to understand that evidence in isolation does not constitute proof. Evidence attains the level of proof only after comprehensive assessment and scrutiny—through rigorous argumentation by the parties involved—thereby serving as an informed indicator of a past event if the judge is satisfied with its authenticity.

Authoritarian perspectives prevail when criminal proceedings are viewed mainly through the lens of desired outcomes and supported by unverified evidence. Such an approach endorses an overly simplistic view of evidentiary epistemology, placing unchecked confidence in the judge's capabilities, which may result in various misapplications. It assumes that apparent evidence requires no rigorous scrutiny, treating its truth as self-evident and positioning the judge as an epistemic authority singularly focused on uncovering absolute truth.

This represents a fundamental error, as the judge's pursuit of truth may compromise the corrective framework intended to address the potentially hallucinatory character of evidence—an essential component of an accusatorial criminal procedure framed by democratic principles. By casting the judge in the role of an omniscient arbiter seeking absolute truth, criminal justice risks relying on unexamined evidence, unchecked by the dialogical confrontation structure set by procedural rules and incorrectly regarded as remnants of the past.

Ironically, an epistemology that is discursively aligned with the sign of the *Same* may ultimately result in convictions grounded in constructed perceptions and preconceived notions, where the resulting knowledge potentially aligns with the characteristics of the *Other*. This process is shaped by a framework prone to the primacy of hypothesis over facts that overlooks both the complexities of consciousness and the reality that the judge is a being-in-the-world.

As previously discussed, the absolute truth remains unattainable; however, erroneous convictions—stemming from the hallucinatory character of evidence—are likely to occur more frequently than anticipated, especially when the evidentiary framework is governed by the inquisitorial logic of objectification traceable to Eymerich.

In summary, this analysis demonstrates that the current dominant approach is fundamentally adverse to the rights of the accused. Consequently, it is essential to move beyond rudimentary epistemological frameworks and adopt a perspective that rigorously redefines the concepts of proof and evidence accordingly to their full complexity. Such a shift requires re-examining the foundational meaning of evidentiary processes and departing from traditional notions that may perpetuate inadvertently or not inquisitorial and positivist epistemology.

In this context, it is pertinent to consider what forms of evidentiary activity are best suited to address the hallucinatory character of evidence and align with the concept of trace as an analogue link to the past. Thus far, I have highlighted the necessity for mechanisms that mitigate the hallucinatory aspects of evidence and observed that the pursuit of truth may undermine adversarial proceedings. However, I have not yet specified which methods most effectively support the corrective function required in evidentiary activity. This issue will be examined further in the next chapter.

CHAPTER 7

The Lived Experience of Criminal Proceedings

The Meaning of Evidentiary Activity: Demonstration of Truth, Formal Establishment of Facts, Argumentative Rhetoric, or Psychic Capture of the Judge?

Within criminal procedure scholarship, at least four interpretations regarding the nature of evidentiary activity have been outlined. The first views it as an objective process for establishing truth within legal proceedings; the second considers it a means for the formal determination of alleged facts; the third integrates the notions of proof and truth into the domain of argumentation; and the fourth regards it as a process intended to psychologically persuade the judge.

I will now proceed with a comprehensive analysis of each specific conception.

(a) *The material orientation, which defines evidentiary activity as an endeavour to demonstrate the existence or non-existence of a fact, the truth or falsity of a statement*

Guasp and Aragoneses Alonso contend that, from this perspective, evidentiary processes are intended to establish the existence or non-existence of facts, as well as the veracity or falsity of assertions. While this framework

S. H. Khaled Jr., *Reimagining Criminal Justice, Search for Truth and Human Rights*, https://doi.org/10.1007/978-3-032-27227-0_7

is built on a robust theoretical foundation, they argue it is undermined by practical limitations, given that fully demonstrating such matters in legal proceedings is, both in theory and in practice, unattainable (Guasp and Alonso 1998: 300).

This conceptualisation of evidentiary practices is consistent with the correspondence theory of truth and the foundational principles of modern scientific inquiry—it dominates both positivist and rationalist perspectives.

Bettiol, a proponent of the real truth doctrine, illustrates this perspective by emphasising that the primary and relevant question regarding evidence lies in establishing the existence or absence of facts within their historical context (Bettiol 1973: 247).

As previously outlined, the ideal of correspondence remains unattainable within the scope of historical knowledge: irrespective of judicial protagonism—a notion inherently linked to this perspective—the corresponding truth cannot be established through evidentiary procedures. When the correspondence theory is integrated with empowering judges in the pursuit of truth, it provides a foundation for an authoritarian model of criminal procedure characterised by a distinctly inquisitorial epistemology. This approach fosters the generation of hallucinatory convictions based on evidence untested by the dialogical safeguards inherent to due process.

The issue extends beyond authors who advocate the possibility of fully achieving the modern ideal of knowledge through variables such as real, material, or substantial truth—as exemplified by Manzini and much of Brazilian criminal procedural scholarship. Lopes Jr. observes that rationalist scholars adopt the same understanding. These authors are unable to transcend the concept of truth as a justification for the evidentiary function in legal proceedings (Lopes Jr 2009: 536–537). Taruffo serves as a paradigmatic example of this position:

> It also seems evident that this scheme is the only one capable of giving a positive and non-evanescent meaning to the general concept of evidence as an instrument endowed with a specific function within the procedure. At the very least, this scheme constitutes the only analytical perspective in which the phenomenon of evidence is not immediately dissolved or placed in a dead end where everything is reduced to an indeterminate persuasion. Moreover, it should be emphasised that only within the conception of evidence as an instrument for achieving a true determination of the facts can a coherent confirmation be found of the ideology previously defined as the legal-rational ideology of judicial decision-making, together with all the safeguards associated with it. Indeed, it makes no sense to invoke

> values such as legality, correctness, and justice of the decision if one does not recognise that the truth of the facts is a necessary condition for the correct application of the norm. But all this is meaningless if one does not recognise that the proper and exclusive function of evidence is to provide elements for the rational choice of the version of the facts that can be defined as true. (Taruffo 2005: 86–87)

Taruffo recognises that "not even the definition of evidence as an instrument for seeking and establishing the truth of the facts in the process constitutes in itself a true and complete theory of evidence" (Taruffo 2005: 87). Nevertheless, he proceeds from this observation to assert that a more refined definition of the model is necessary, ultimately reaching conclusions that may be considered contentious. As previously indicated, Taruffo argues for a non-naive and critically developed version of the correspondence theory of truth (Taruffo 2010: 95). Based on this conceptual framework, Taruffo contends that the legal procedure serves an epistemic function, conceived as a structured set of activities intended to obtain true knowledge about facts pertinent to dispute resolution (Taruffo 2010: 155). Accordingly, he maintains that it is the judge who fulfils the primary epistemic role—the establishment of factual truth (Taruffo 2010: 196). To facilitate this purpose, Taruffo highlights the widely employed judicial technique of empowering judges to take evidence *ex officio* (Taruffo 2010: 197).

Taruffo's conceptual revisions, while nuanced and reconfigured to address the overt limitations of earlier frameworks, ultimately remain grounded in modern theoretical categories. By employing these foundational premises—a paradigm rooted in the philosophy of consciousness with a strong confidence in human ability to grasp the essence of reality—the potential persists for legitimising authoritarian judicial practices and reinvigorate inquisitorial approaches towards truth-seeking.

Ferrajoli's perspective on this matter fundamentally diverges from that of Taruffo, as he supports the concept of procedural truth. He regards procedural truth as a corresponding, relative, or approximate construct, shaped by adherence to procedural rules and safeguards for the defence. Within Ferrajoli's framework, legal truth operates alongside what he designates as historical truth—pertaining to actual past events—which is analysed using general epistemological principles, such as those applied in historiography. It is also noteworthy, as previously indicated, that Ferrajoli does not endorse the notion that judges should actively pursue truth, viewing this approach as characteristic of the inquisitorial system. While I concur with several aspects of Ferrajoli's arguments, I find his advancement on the issue insufficient, as he continues to engage with the correspondence theory of truth, albeit in a relativised manner, and occasionally utilises the expression *search for truth* (Ferrajoli 2002: 42–45).

As previously noted, an evidentiary process organised according to the principle of the *Same*—coupled with investigative authority granted to the judge—maximises the potential for decisionism. This approach increases the likelihood of convictions that fall within the scope of the *Other*, as it fails to address the potentially hallucinatory character of evidence. Nonetheless, while there may be grounds for critique, proponents of this framework demonstrate consistency with their underlying assumptions. Scholars who advocate for judicial initiative in evidence collection conceptualise evidentiary proceedings within the so-called material orientation.

(b) *The formal approach, under which evidentiary procedures are regarded as procedural mechanisms designed solely to establish the facts asserted within the proceedings*

While previous perspectives may mistakenly prioritise the tangible nature of evidence as a direct reference to historical events, the formal approach emphasises the procedural aspects, focusing on evidentiary processes carried out during legal proceedings and their distinctive characteristics. Under this view, evidentiary activities are considered to be strictly regulated, imposing a set of rules on both parties and judges that dictate their conduct. This distinction highlights a fundamental difference between legal evidentiary activity—which operates within a regulatory framework—and general evidentiary activity, which relies solely on epistemological principles.

From this perspective, it is not feasible to analyse the production of truth in legal proceedings through general epistemological criteria or criteria that focus on the pastness of past events. Procedural mechanisms sufficiently differentiate evidentiary processes to render such approaches unworkable.

Similarly, discussions concerning evidence and proof from disciplines such as history or philosophy are generally regarded as inappropriate for assessing criminal procedure frameworks. This viewpoint appears inadequate for a comprehensive evaluation of evidentiary activity.

This perspective implies that the "truth" generated within legal proceedings is inherently distinct from a more rigorous conception of truth, which alone should be regarded as genuine truth in its strictest sense. Guasp notes that formal truth does not necessarily correspond to actual events; as such, formal truth may represent either a false truth or, in effect, a non-truth (Guasp 1996: 338).

This approach typically prompts debate over formal truth versus material (or real) truth, a distinction that has historically yielded limited progress in discussions concerning the nature of truth within legal proceedings. In alignment with Badaró's perspective, it is appropriate to recognise that "it is high time to bury the worn-out dichotomy between formal truth and material truth, which has contributed far more to confusion than to valid constructions" (Badaró 2003: 36). Taruffo similarly challenges the validity of distinguishing between formal or procedural truth and *real truth*, asserting that the veracity of statements about facts hinges on the facts themselves, thereby precluding the existence of multiple kinds of truth (Taruffo 2010: 100–101). He further observes that "the distinction between formal truth and material truth is, however, unacceptable for several reasons that the less superficial doctrine has highlighted for some time. In particular, the idea of a judicial truth that is completely 'distinct' and autonomous from truth *tout court* merely because it is determined in the proceedings and by means of evidence seems untenable; the existence of legal rules and limits of various kinds serves, at most, to exclude the possibility of obtaining absolute truths, but is not sufficient to totally differentiate the truth established in the proceedings from that which is discussed outside them" (Taruffo 2005: 24–25). According to Taruffo, such limitations do not establish a category of procedural truth; instead, they indicate that procedural regulations may restrict access to all relevant evidence, resulting in a partial or incomplete truth, or, in more severe cases, the absence of any established truth. He contends that this issue pertains not to the concept of truth itself, but rather to the constraints imposed by legal processes upon its determination. Consequently, he characterises the resultant truth as corresponding, yet necessarily relative or approximate knowledge of the truth (Taruffo 2010: 100–101).

From an analytical perspective, it is not feasible to assess evidence purely from a formal standpoint, as the formal structure of criminal proceedings alone does not fully eliminate references to prior empirical reality. Such empirical reference is essential for understanding the production of truth within criminal proceedings, especially from the epistemological viewpoint of past events. To suggest otherwise would imply that a judge may make determinations based solely on procedure—while adhering to procedural regulations—without requiring analogical connections to the actual incident under adjudication. This approach risks removing the concept of truth from criminal justice entirely, potentially resulting in significant harm to the accused, since convictions would not necessarily be anchored in perceived traces of the past but could be justified by formalistic criteria alone.

While Taruffo similarly rejects the concept of formal truth, my critique diverges significantly from his, due to my focus on the pastness of the past. This perspective precludes the notion of relative corresponding truth as a viable alternative. According to Taruffo, absolute truth is unattainable and truth should not be considered formal, thus leading to an approximative model. However, his solution constitutes a false alternative that endorses the ongoing pursuit of truth.

Both the approach that seeks to demonstrate material (or actual) truth and the formalist orientation are ultimately inadequate and, paradoxically, can produce comparable results. The former is underpinned by corresponding truth under the notion of the *Same*, thereby discursively legitimising decisionism through the pursuit of truth. The latter, may distance the process from truth altogether, dangerously placing it under the notion of the *Other*, which can also lead to decisionism. Such outcomes are unacceptable for a framework that should restrain punitive power and uphold human rights.

Accordingly, as previously noted, it is important to reconsider the complexity of truth production in criminal proceedings beyond the dichotomy of absolute truth versus non-truth while simultaneously rejecting the false alternative to them, relative truth. This involves moving past both an exclusive focus on the search for absolute truth and the disregard for truth, while also avoiding the compromise represented by relative corresponding truth, which remains confined within the parameters of the *Same*.

If evidentiary procedures are oriented towards achieving material or factual truth, this approach endows judges with the authority to actively pursue such truth, which inherently increases the potential for decisionism. Conversely, when the pursuit of truth is set aside and evidence is treated solely as a formality, any outcome may be considered valid as long as procedural criteria are satisfied, regardless of reference to past events—an approach that may also broaden the discretion afforded to the decision-maker. It is clear that basing evidentiary activities exclusively on either substantive truth (in any form) or formal truth is inadequate for addressing the cognitive aspects of legal proceedings or advancing a model of criminal justice centred on human rights protection. Both perspectives ignore or do not emphasise that the judge must adopt a receptive approach and refrain from evidence management.

(c) *Narrativist or semiotic conceptions, structured around argumentation*

The manifestation of the sign of the *Other* within constructions regarding evidentiary meaning in legal proceedings is not confined solely to the notion of formal truth. This also appears in semiotic and narrative frameworks, wherein traditional concepts of evidence, proof and truth are subsumed within the broader idea of argumentation. While it is acknowledged in such approaches that the judge serves as the recipient of evidence, these perspectives ultimately reduce evidentiary activity to a process of argumentation, viewed primarily as an effect of persuasion. I find this reduction problematic; argumentation should be regarded as one contributory aspect rather than the defining criterion for evidence and proof within criminal proceedings.

Approaching evidentiary activity solely as a rhetorical pursuit limits criminal proceedings to an oratorical framework, with minimal consideration given to historical evidence that could analogically reference past events. While this perspective differs substantially from others, it might also lead to authoritarian judicial practices.

The first approach is characterised by an insufficient epistemological framework that overlooks the practical realities of criminal proceedings and prioritises the pursuit of absolute truth. Conversely, the second approach disregards considerations of truth, focusing exclusively on procedural mechanisms and neglecting the analogical links to historical events that can be established through traces of the past.

The third approach also leads to problems: the narrativist or semiotic perspective sets aside the notion of truth, instead framing it within the broader context of narrative constructs—a perspective that may also favour decionism. Ferrajoli notes that adopting a theoretical decisionist stance—whether driven by scepticism or political conviction—tends to promote legal systems characterised by diminished legality and criminal models that are discretionary and lack safeguards (Ferrajoli 2002: 52).

Argumentative persuasion is an integral aspect of procedural dynamics. As will be elaborated later, my understanding of evidentiary processes—those aimed at persuading the judge through what may be described as "psychic capture"—is rooted in this dimension. Cordero (2000: 16) rightly notes that the speaker employs strategic appeals to achieve such influence over the judge. Nevertheless, when rhetoric is taken to its extreme, legal proceedings risk devolving into purely rhetorical gamesmanship, where the pursuit of persuasion supersedes all other considerations. This approach, focused solely on convincing without regard to ethical means, would elevate the potential for harm to an unacceptable level within a system intended to regulate punitive power and uphold democratic principles. The narrative element cannot ignore factual occurrences; empirical referentiality remains essential, as judges are required to justify decisions based on proof from past events. Consequently, procedural rules mandate that judicial decisions rest upon probatory foundations.

In response to the concerns posed by argumentative relativism, it is pertinent to advocate for a restoration of the accurate definition of *rhetoric*, which can serve to mitigate procedural decisionism. This reconsideration is intrinsically linked to the value assigned to proof as a fundamental element in shaping judicial conviction. Accordingly, it is essential to recognise that Aristotelian rhetoric is rooted primarily in proof. In examining Aristotle's rhetoric, Cunha Martins observes that

> when he includes the idea of proof within the argumentative sphere, he does so precisely in the name of truth; moreover, he does so with the aim of eliminating from this truth those elements that might associate it with persuasion achieved through emotion, similar, after all, to what is typical today of the media spectacle. (Martins and Gil 2002: 23)

Consequently, rhetoric should not be viewed as a mere collection of techniques aimed at persuading the audience at any expense. Aristotle posits that the core element of rhetoric is the art of proof (Aristotle 2000). For him, proof is the only aspect that genuinely relates to the Art, while everything else is secondary (Aristotle 2000: 29). Gil also addressed this matter, highlighting that, due to its rhetorical roots, significant focus has been placed on argumentation in connection with legal proof. However, he argues that the effort to merge the concept of proof with that of argumentation is entirely unacceptable and does not reflect any reality (Martins and Gil 2002: 23). In this regard, Gil asserts that "in Aristotle, rhetoric is also concerned with truth; it is not merely a compilation of persuasive effects" (Martins and Gil 2002: 23). Ferrajoli further observes that the notion of a trial as a dispute or controversy is linked to the paradigm of *disputatio* established by the classical rhetorical tradition and passed down through the English experience to the contemporary accusatorial procedure (Ferrajoli 2002: 490).

Consequently, while the integration of argumentation and rhetoric into evidentiary processes cannot be disregarded, it is imperative to maintain a careful balance that safeguards the foundational role of evidence and proof. This equilibrium ensures that persuasion operates within the bounds of empirical referentiality, thus preventing the proceedings from descending into mere rhetorical contest or arbitrary discretion. The emphasis must remain on substantiating claims with verifiable traces from the past, so that the persuasive dimension complements, rather than supplants, the probatory basis upon which judicial decisions are justified. In this way, the legitimacy of the evidentiary process is preserved, and the risk of procedural arbitrariness is mitigated.

Consequently, truth cannot be entirely disregarded without risking another extreme—an intensified relativism—that is neither a viable procedural approach nor without significant repercussions, as it may legitimise arbitrary decision-making. In this context, Cordero describes trials as retrospective mechanisms designed to determine the occurrence of events and establish responsibility; parties advance hypotheses, while judges select the most probable based on established rules and empirical knowledge, rather than relying on conjecture or intuition (Cordero 2000: 7). Thus, Cordero's conceptualisation of historical judgement consistently operates within boundaries set by normative standards, which fundamentally aim to counteract arbitrary, substantive judgements that could otherwise justify unauthorised realms of discretion.

Taruffo correctly notes that narrating events in evaluative rather than descriptive terms results in a fundamentally different narrative—one that falls outside the realm of proof (Taruffo 2010: 71). Placing undue emphasis on argumentative aspects may, in fact, render evidentiary discussion meaningless. It is therefore proof that forms the foundation of the legal system and establishes the conditions for ascertaining possible truths. Abandoning reliance on proof creates an environment in which *a priori* judgements concerning the implausibility of the defence's arguments may proliferate, often supported by persecutory notions such as social defence; more problematically, the very nature of evidence within judgement may be distorted, allowing unexamined evidence to be organised arbitrarily so that only elements supporting a preconceived hypothesis are accepted as valid, as will be discussed further below.

Given the misleading dichotomy between the sign of the *Same*—whether absolute or relative—and the sign of the *Other*—whether defined by formal criteria or the dissolution of truth through argumentation—it is crucial to recognise that both viewpoints present significant risks: the supremacy of hypotheses over facts or the ascendancy of persuasive rhetoric. The considerable resources available to state apparatuses highlight the hazards inherent in moving away from party-managed evidence, regardless of direction. At both extremes of distortion within the accusatorial model, punitive aims tend to predominate. Lopes Jr. aptly observes that "respect for the rules of the game creates the conditions of possibility for a balance between sceptical relativism and the mythological real truth" (Lopes Jr 2010: 542). A notable challenge with these distortions is that models seldom appear in their pure forms, making clear identification feasible only in exceptional circumstances, such as the relentless pursuit of truth during the Inquisition. More commonly, subversion of the accusatorial system occurs subtly. As Lopes Jr. further explains, "this is the case with the Brazilian system, clearly inquisitorial in its essence, even if adorned with some 'accessories' that usually help to dress up the accusatorial system (but which in themselves do not transform it into an accusatorial one)" (Lopes Jr 2005: 174–175).

It is therefore possible to assert that decisionism may exhibit two distinct characteristics: on one side, judicial arbitrariness, where decisions are rendered solely on personal belief, disconnected from traces of the past and disregarding the link between proof and rhetoric; and on the other, a relentless pursuit of absolute truth that serves only to justify unrestricted exercise of authority, thereby favouring the hallucinatory character of evidence due to monological rather than dialogical deliberation. As will be further discussed, a monological perspective favours the judge's belief, whereas a dialogical perspective favours the judge's conviction.

Based on the preceding analysis, it can be argued that while truth may not serve as the sole guiding principle in procedural contexts, it should not be disregarded entirely. The total exclusion of truth could result in judicial proceedings becoming reliant solely on rhetorical strategies aimed at influencing the judge.

On one hand, disregarding the epistemological and ontological issues related to truth has lent legitimacy to authoritarian inclinations; on the other, prioritising persuasion above truth increases the likelihood that rhetorical strategies and procedural mechanisms overshadow substantive analysis, ultimately leading to decisionism.

Both the relentless pursuit of truth and its complete neglect each entail specific limitations. This challenge is not adequately addressed by merely embracing the notion of relative or approximate truth. In alignment with Cunha Martins, I recognise the significance of defining the appropriate function of truth in criminal proceedings (Martins 2010: 81).

Accordingly, the fourth conception presents itself as the most suitable framework, though it should be assessed in conjunction with the other perspectives, particularly since some advocates of relative corresponding truth also endorse this approach. In summary, while the earlier conceptions correspond to the notions of the *Same* (material conception) and the *Other* (formal and narrativist conceptions), the fourth conception—Psychic capture—is most accurately described as aligning with the *Analogous*, as will be further demonstrated below.

(d) *Psychic capture of the judge: the evidentiary activity is aimed at achieving the psychological conviction of the judge or court regarding the veracity or falsity of the alleged facts*

Aragoneses Alonso argues that demonstrating the existence of a fact is virtually impossible, and that the formal establishment of alleged facts within proceedings cannot serve as a reliable foundation for criminal procedure. Instead, he suggests that evidentiary activities are focused on achieving the psychological conviction of the judge (Alonso 1986: 283). Guasp and Aragoneses Alonso propose that both material and formal conceptions can be surpassed by viewing evidentiary activity as an activity aimed at substantiating facts—not simply establishing them formally, but with the express purpose of convincing the judge of their existence or non-existence. Consequently, the truth or falsity of data is determined by the adjudicator's psychological conviction; evidentiary activity thus comprises the procedural acts intended to secure the judge's conviction regarding the logical data relevant to the proceedings (Guasp and Alonso 1998: 300–301). Ultimately, evidentiary activity entails persuading the judge that a particular element presented by one party—an item of evidence—is genuinely connected to a past event. Cunha Martins asserts, "to prove is, to a large extent, to convince" (Martins 2010: 8), a notion consistent with Gil's perspective, which, drawing inspiration from Wittgenstein, maintains that there is no knowledge or proof without a recipient; the essence of evidentiary activity lies in generating conviction (Martins 2010: 8). This approach seeks to mitigate the hallucinatory character of evidence, emphasising that evidentiary constraints favour conviction over belief, though it is not possible to eliminate belief entirely, as will be further discussed.

This perspective reorients evidentiary procedures towards the judge's persuasion—a fundamental aspect of procedural cognition frequently overlooked by other frameworks, that instead opt to assign an active role to the judge. Importantly, this definition retains certain elements of earlier approaches, albeit with modifications: evidentiary activity is conceptualised as a demonstrative process conducted through procedural acts, which still involves reference to the truth, given its retrospective nature. However, the determination of truth or falsity is now evaluated in relation to the evidentiary activity's recipient—the judge—whose persuasion is crucial for accepting a particular element introduced in the proceedings as proof. As Guasp (1996: 344) asserts, when a judge must declare the truth of a fact—meaning its alignment with past reality—the law ultimately defers to the judge's conviction formed during the proceedings. This conviction results from various influences, some of which extend beyond purely psychological factors; for example, in evaluating uncertain circumstances, the judge must weigh and select between conflicting arguments offered by the parties. Thus, the judge engages in a deliberate act of choice (Guasp 1996: 344). Likewise, Mora (2006: 83) rejects the pursuit of absolute truth; particularly in complex factual circumstances, he contends that the prevailing factor is the conviction regarding what transpired, shaped by the persuasiveness of conflicting accounts. As Huertas Martin notes, evidentiary activity aims to achieve the judge's psychological conviction regarding the existence or absence of the facts (Martin 1999: 28).

Goldschmidt also observes that the actions of the parties are designed to persuade the judge regarding the veracity of factual assertions. Procedural evidentiary activity pertains to facts and is intended to convey sensory perceptions to the judge (Goldschmidt 2010: 860). Truth is not simply derived from facts as tangible events introduced into the proceedings. Rather, within the criminal proceedings, statements are constructed by multiple parties who engage with each other and the judge, inherently introducing a subjective dimension that is challenging to regulate—both in representations of fact and in the resultant decisions and their justifications.

A review of the different conceptions of evidentiary activity historically established in procedural criminal law indicates that the psychic capture of the judge is most compatible with an accusatorial system and constitutional principles. From an epistemological standpoint, this approach addresses issues that evidentiary models based solely on the demonstration of truth cannot resolve: it acknowledges the complexity inherent in the cognitive aspect of proceedings and maintains the judge's impartial role as a third party and recipient of evidence. Consequently, the judge's involvement in evidentiary activities should be confined to ensuring procedural rules are observed. This perspective also grounds criminal proceedings in actual lived reality by requiring convictions to be based on proof rather than persuasive rhetoric or mere formal compliance with normative obligations. As such, it offers a means to moderate the prevalent voluntarism and decisionism in judicial practice and to limit the expansion of subjective interpretations that support the pursuit of absolute truth, mitigating potential harm to the accused's rights.

The psychic capture framework enables a critical reassessment of evidentiary processes that extends beyond traditional inquisitorial objectives by posing questions that enhance the interpretive significance of concepts such as event, trace, and evidence. It emphasises the judge's position as the recipient of evidence, thereby acknowledging the uncertainties inherent in judicial decision-making. This encourages reflection on the relationship between belief and conviction, the complexities of consciousness, the influence of historical traditions on judicial perspectives, and the possibility for narrative reinterpretation of past traces. As a result, this approach highlights the fundamentally analogical nature of narrative truth production within legal proceedings—a theme explored further in the following chapters.

The subsequent section will explore the relationship between evidence and its recipient, underscoring that the central issue lies not within the modern misconception of certainty, but rather in the dynamic between belief and conviction—showing that conviction aligns more closely with uncertainty than with certainty. As Cunha Martins aptly observes, "to be convinced is not the final stage of an unblemished epistemic journey" (Martins 2010: 9).

Certainty, Belief, and Conviction

Some scholars link the concept of psychic capture of the judge to the principle of certainty. However, as this section will examine, certainty is not merely a construct confined within modern frameworks; it has also historically served as a foundation in the pursuit of absolute truth.

It is not my intention to provide an exhaustive list of authors who associate evidentiary activity directed at persuading the judge with the concept of certainty; rather, my aim is to outline this argument and explain why I find it unconvincing. According to Montero Aroca, current limitations in achieving metaphysical and physical truth are shifting the focus of evidence towards establishing certainty in relation to the parties' factual assertions, which is to be accomplished through adversarial proceedings (Aroca 2006: 243).

Although this viewpoint shares certain aspects with my advocated position, notable differences remain. As noted earlier, Montero Aroca recognises the judge's proactive efforts in fact-finding. Therefore, employing the term "certainty" may be misleading, since the judge's assumption of an inquisitorial role can undermine adversarial proceedings—a framework effective only when the parties retain control over evidence management.

The idea that a judge may search for personal certainty instead of absolute truth through the management of evidence can result in similar or potentially greater issues, as it appears to openly place undue emphasis on subjective considerations. The judge is expected to remain impartial and primarily receptive, intervening actively only to ensure adherence to the principles of due process.

Similar reasoning is found among other scholars employing this category, such as Gimeno Sendra and Roxin, both of whom concede the judge's involvement in evidence gathering and invoke the notion of certainty. Gimeno Sendra posits that the objective of evidentiary activity is to establish the court's conviction regarding the existence of a punishable fact and the author's participation, encompassing all relevant circumstances as they transpired in historical reality prior to the proceedings (Sendra et al. 1996: 372). Therefore, evidentiary acts are intended to ascertain the certainty of the facts or provide sufficient elements to form the court's conviction regarding the existence of the facts and the accused's involvement (Sendra et al. 1996: 372). Roxin similarly asserts that to prove means to persuade the judge of the certainty surrounding the existence of a fact (Roxin 2003: 185).

The issue highlighted here is that these scholars conceptualise the judge as the recipient of evidence but use certainty almost interchangeably with truth. This approach effectively reinforces a logic focused on the search for the truth, allowing the judge to pursue certainty regarding absolute truth. Consequently, scholars adopting this perspective inadvertently refer back to positivist notions of evidentiary activity by replicating its correspondence ideals under a different term—Manzini's reference to "certainty of material truth" (Manzini 1951: 260–261) is illustrative. This results in the loss of nuanced meaning from viewing evidentiary activity as the judge's psychological apprehension, thereby diminishing its potential contribution to the accusatorial and regulated framework necessary to limit punitive power within a democratic system.

To clarify the challenges associated with the concept of certainty, it is beneficial to examine Carnelutti's influential work. Drawing from Heidegger, Carnelutti revised his original stance—where he had argued for formal truth stemming from the pursuit of substantial truth within legal proceedings—by positing that genuine truth exists only in its entirety, which, as Coutinho notes, remains beyond our complete grasp. For Carnelutti,

> Truth is, and can only be, one: what I, like others, used to call formal truth is not the truth. Nor did I know at that time what it was, or why, above all, neither through the proceedings nor by any other means, can truth ever be attained by man. [...] a rose is a rose [...] because it is not some other flower [...] to truly know the rose, that is, to reach the truth, it is necessary to know not only what the rose is, but also what it is not. Therefore, the truth of a thing eludes us until we can know all other things and, thus, we can only ever achieve a partial knowledge of that thing. And when I say thing, I also mean a man. In short, truth lies in the whole, not in the part; and the whole is too much for us. (Coutinho 2002: 174–175)

Carnelutti redirects attention from truth towards certainty, suggesting that his methodological approach—which initially regarded legal proceedings as a search for truth—should instead prioritise the pursuit of certainty (Coutinho 2002: 175). He explains that certainty originates from the Latin *cernere*, meaning not merely to observe, but to choose, implying a process of selection or exclusion. Since choice is inherently tied to interpretation, achieving certainty necessitates interpretative decision-making. This realisation enabled Carnelutti to discern both the genuine significance of his conceptual framework and the inherent complexities of legal proceedings. According to Carnelutti, absolute truth remains unattainable; instead, only certainty, arising through evaluative judgement and deliberate positioning, can be reached. Consequently, an important inquiry presents itself: while the author's argument for moving away from absolute truth—and consequently, from corresponding theory of truth—is compelling, does substituting it with certainty constitute an effective alternative?

Carnelutti's perspective demonstrates an advancement over the positivist conception of the automaton judge, as it acknowledges that judges are human beings who must render decisions extending beyond mere factual evaluation. However, questions arise regarding whether certainty—a fundamentally modern concept—may present challenges analogous to those associated with truth. Badaró asserts that "evidence will never provide the judge with certainty, but only a greater or lesser approximation to certainty regarding the facts" (Badaró 2003: 31). Moura asserts, "it is clear that subjective certainty is not to be confused with the objective truth of things. And, since the human mind is fallible, the certainty obtained in judicial decisions is not absolute, nor does it claim to be" (Moura 1994: 97). Badaró argues that

> This does not mean, however, that the judge should abdicate the search for a "certainty": the possible certainty. That certainty which can be reached, with the epistemological limitations to which any judgement based on a historical reconstruction is subject, and to which must be added the procedural restrictions on the discovery of "truth". (Badaró 2003: 31)

The central issue concerns the implications of employing the term certainty within frameworks that recognise the judge's pursuit of truth. In this context, the quest for certainty effectively replicates—albeit under a different guise—the enduring search for the truth in criminal procedure.

While the move towards certainty does not imply that absolute truth can be achieved, it underscores the importance of striving for it to maintain a high degree of certainty. This endeavour may inadvertently give rise to similar issues associated with the search for absolute truth, as the ongoing pursuit of truth—perhaps concealed or reframed as certainty—continues to justify the judge's management of evidence.

It is in this sense that Cunha Martins points out that the pursuit of an unblemished conviction, capable of meeting the expectations of truth traditionally associated with criminal adjudication, ultimately neglects the necessary forms of control to constrain judicial conviction; as a result, the role of the judge within the proceedings is expanded and alternative zones to adversarial proceedings are permitted as means of constructing proof (Martins 2010: 24). In clear opposition to the insufficient shift represented by the argument of certainty, Cunha Martins reflects that

> instead of a linear process extending between two poles, conviction corresponds to a process of successive tangencies and overlaps, complex and dense, within which the different components of the path interrelate and mutually summon each other, contaminating their respective positions, meanings, and effects. (Martins 2010: 21)

The author describes a process of conviction formation that diverges significantly from Cartesian certainties and demonstrates a complexity of meanings to be further examined within the hermeneutic tradition. At this stage, it is feasible to outline the scope of possibilities surrounding the development of conviction and to assert that judicial protagonism may result only in an illusory certainty, whose connection to truth is notably debatable, given that standard mechanisms for rectifying evidentiary misperceptions are fundamentally challenged. This simplified notion of certainty appears suitable for justifying procedural decisionism from two distinct angles: firstly, one oriented towards the pursuit of certainty—either as a replacement for, or in conjunction with the search for truth—and secondly, one that potentially overlooks truth entirely, a concern acknowledged even by advocates of relative correspondence theories of truth.

Taruffo contends that statements suggesting a conviction is warranted only when the judge possesses absolute certainty of the accused's guilt or must attain moral certainty regarding the facts in question, result in two fundamental errors. Firstly, such approaches disregard the concept of truth, excluding the requirement for decisions to be rooted in an accurate determination of facts. Secondly, they accept as the foundation of judicial decisions the degree of subjective persuasion achieved by the judge (Taruffo 2010: 103–104). Taruffo maintains that, while a judge's knowledge is inherently relative, judicial conviction should not stem from personal preferences but instead be justified by objective reasons derived from evidentiary cognitive data (Taruffo 2010: 100). According to Taruffo, truth is an objective quality contingent upon the reality of the facts under consideration, whereas certainty represents a subjective psychological state, reflecting the intensity of an individual's conviction. A statement may be true irrespective of anyone's belief in it, and strong conviction does not necessarily equate to truth (Taruffo 2010: 102). Taruffo is cautious about employing the term "certainty" even within a framework based on the subject-object scheme such as the one he employs.

As discussed earlier, Taruffo adopts a material orientation in his understanding of evidentiary activity. It is coherent for him to reject both the psychic capture of the judge and the notion of certainty, but his vision of proceedings as a laboratory where unequivocal and objective demonstrations of truth can be found is fundamentally naïve and mistaken.

My perspective diverges from his. The notion of psychic capture of the judge extends beyond theoretical discourse; it encapsulates the practical realities of criminal legal proceedings. Carnelutti's observation remains pertinent: by engaging in evaluative judgement and intentional positioning, the judge is compelled to make a decision—one that may potentially be erroneous. This subjective dimension is inescapable and must be acknowledged to establish appropriate boundaries. In this context, the pursuit of certainty can become counterproductive. Rather than anchoring the judge as a passive recipient of evidentiary contributions, it instigates a quest for certainty that may ultimately be more prejudicial to the accused than the pursuit of truth itself. Such an environment risks fostering unchecked confirmation bias and creates conditions that hinder efforts to mitigate the hallucinatory nature of evidence.

Some scholars advocate for the notion of relative certainty, suggesting that judges should pursue this standard. Within this framework, introducing the category of certainty becomes redundant, as it does not represent a meaningful departure from foundational discourses on truth and its pursuit. Simply substituting or supplementing truth with certainty does not adequately highlight the unpredictable and uncertain nature of criminal proceedings, nor the impossibility of perfectly reconstructing past events.

Frequently, the concepts of truth and certainty are closely linked; for example, in the explanatory memorandum to the 1941 Code of Criminal Procedure, Francisco Campos refers simultaneously to both the elucidation of truth and the judge's moral certainty (Campos 2010: 352). Confronted with this discursive limitation, I maintain that a genuine break with the pursuit of truth requires dismissing notions of relative, approximate, or probable corresponding truth, as well as the idea of certainty that perpetuates the same misunderstandings as the corresponding theory of truth.

Certainty—much like correspondence truth—serves as a framework that can reinforce the centrality of the judge, who may pursue not absolute truth, but a degree of certainty regarding the facts or the veracity of those facts. Carnelutti allows for such an interpretation, albeit without explicitly advocating it. I concur with Lopes Jr., who argues that Carnelutti's suggestion to abandon the pursuit of truth is appropriate, yet his attempt to substitute truth with certainty is problematic, given that certainty is equally challenged by the epistemological shift towards uncertainty. Morais da Rosa observes that "judges feel (and need to feel) innate members, guardians of the *truth* linked to *certainty*: a Cartesian substitution that filled the void left by True Truth without relinquishing its foundational role" (Rosa 2011: 48). Thus, the logic of certainty remains aligned with the philosophy of consciousness, sustaining a model of knowledge based on the protagonism of the rational subject—a paradigm that must be re-examined to reveal the numerous challenges present in judicial decision-making. Lenio Streck cautions that, "[…] even under the full force of the 1988 Constitution, the outcome of proceedings is determined by the judge's conscience, as evidence management is not governed by intersubjective criteria filtered through due process, but rather by the inquisitorial discretion of the judge. Conscience, subjectivity, the inquisitorial system, and discretionary power all represent facets of the same principle" (Streck 2010: 26–27).

The preceding evaluation of certainty as an alternative or supplementary category to truth demonstrates the myriad problems it brings into play. Given this analysis, it becomes apparent that the introduction of certainty as an alternative or supplement to absolute truth does little to resolve the enduring tensions inherent in criminal proceedings. Instead, it risks perpetuating the very dilemmas it seeks to address, as the judge's conviction—no matter how robust—remains shaped by subjective processes and epistemological limitations. The reliance on certainty as a procedural ideal may therefore obscure the complexities and uncertainties that necessarily inform the adjudicative process.

For a model designed to mitigate inherent harms to be effective, it is essential to move beyond the logic of correspondence theory of truth and recognise that truth can only emerge analogically in criminal proceedings. This shift inevitably results in an acknowledgement of the uncertainty in criminal proceedings, something that is only partially recognised by evidentiary rationalism.

Badaró acknowledges that at the conclusion of proceedings, the judge experiences uncertainty due to the inability to achieve absolute factual knowledge (Badaró 2003: 20). Similarly, Ferrer Beltrán recognises uncertainty; however, he remains anchored to the concept of correspondence truth. Beltrán contends that, given the uncertainty present in judicial decision-making regarding evidence, it is reasonable to relativise the truth value assigned to resulting conclusions. He clarifies that he is not suggesting it is impossible to ascribe truth value to propositions established as proven within the proceedings; rather, he intends to highlight that the evidentiary record permits only a certain degree of confirmation or probability concerning the veracity of such propositions (Beltrán 2007: 26–27).

Taking a step beyond this observation—though a substantial one—would involve moving past the discursive boundaries that tie contemporary criminal justice to the modern reestablishment of inquisitorial epistemology. However, authors working within the framework of evidentiary rationalism are unable to make this transition.

Reimagining criminal justice requires moving beyond discourse grounded in certainty and advancing a substantive shift towards embracing uncertainty. As previously noted, the notion of certainty prevailed in science for centuries; however, scholars such as Prigogine (1996) have argued for a renewed appreciation of complexity and unpredictability. Relativity theory (Einstein 2002) challenged established certainties, and one of the most significant insights of the twentieth century is that science does not guarantee absolute certainty (Morin 1996). Furthermore, Popper (1991) contends that determinism is flawed, thereby underscoring the contingent nature of human experience.

It is important to recognise that even judges who are mindful of the receptive attitude required by a democratic system must acknowledge that the *iter*—the process leading to a decision—remains a representation, as observed by Coutinho. More accurately, it is characterised by representance, meaning it is inherently insufficient in relation to the past it aims to depict. This understanding introduces an unavoidable degree of uncertainty into judicial decisions. Such uncertainty persists because the *iter* necessarily involves choices based on evidence presented through narrative representations intended to persuade. Even if this evidence may later be viewed as traces of historical events, an element of uncertainty will always remain in the decisions made. In this Carnelutti's intuition was also right: the trace is only part of a whole that eludes us.

Calamandrei proposed the concept of a judgement of verisimilitude concerning *res judicata*, which Carnelutti eventually endorsed (Coutinho 2002: 183). Carnelutti observes that, after examining evidence, hearing arguments, and evaluating both, the judge ultimately encounters an irreducible doubt that cannot be eliminated (Coutinho 2002: 185). Nevertheless, despite thorough precautions, the judge is compelled to make a decision—to convict or acquit—a choice that remains inherently distressing. This illustrates the presence of uncertainty in Carnelutti's reasoning, a quality he could not satisfactorily connect to epistemological dimensions. He notes, "it is said that the judge is also a historian; and everyone agrees with this definition; but making history is only part of his task; and perhaps the least difficult; it is certainly the least tormenting" (Coutinho 2002: 190). Here lies the boundary that even Carnelutti's intellectual prowess could not surpass. As Coutinho remarks, Carnelutti endeavoured to preserve the idea of truth, albeit under a different designation.

My perspective does not preclude a certain degree of subjective certainty on the part of the judge when issuing a conviction. For a judge to render a conviction, their sense of certainty must meet the high threshold of being beyond a reasonable doubt. But this level of certainty remains a subjective perception and should not be conflated with the truth about past events, which inherently contain an element of uncertainty. Uncertainty in this context does not refer to a subjective state but to the knowledge of the past, that will always be uncertain. This uncertainty is not merely subjective but represents an inherent limitation in the ability to fully reconstruct the past, as knowledge inevitably captures only a fragment of what has been irretrievably lost. Representance is all that remains.

The judge will always be an insoluble debtor to the past he seeks to narratively represent in the sentence. It is essential to recognise this in order to reduce the risk of wrongful convictions.

Nevertheless, it is the responsibility of the judge to render a decision. At times, this duty includes issuing a conviction. This authority is both a function and a burden of their office. However, the necessity for a judicial decision should not imply that a judge must pursue certainty during proceedings. In accusatorial proceedings, each party submits evidence with the intention of obtaining the psychic capture of the judge, who is required to maintain an impartial and independent stance above the interests of the parties involved.

This interpretative approach shifts the epistemological framework of criminal proceedings, correcting misconceptions regarding the judge's role and their cognitive authority. Impartiality is no longer viewed as a personal quality of the judge, but rather as a systemic requirement imposed by the accusatory system, wherein judges refrain from managing evidence in pursuit of truth. Similarly, the notion of the judge's subjective certainty—often associated with the search for truth—is regarded as an unavoidable element that must nonetheless be regulated to prevent the unchecked proliferation of the hallucinatory character of evidence. Such regulation necessitates that evidentiary processes are managed exclusively by the parties involved and acknowledges that knowledge of past events will always contain elements of uncertainty, thereby requiring the adoption of strategies to minimise judicial errors.

The widely praised transition from an emphasis on truth to a focus on certainty appears to offer limited protection against authoritarian tendencies. Instead, it is preferable to encourage a shift towards acknowledging uncertainty. Even when supported by evidence evaluated and accepted as proof, the judgement will only be *Analogous* to past events, situated within the context of "*Being-as*" and "*Not-being*". Consequently, some degree of uncertainty remains, even after the decision is formally articulated.

The introduction of uncertainty has important implications for efforts to reinforce regulated containment structures of punitive power and to reimagine criminal justice. Certainty supports confidence in the rational subject's cognitive abilities to understand reality, whereas uncertainty highlights the risks and potential harms intrinsic to criminal proceedings. Consequently, uncertainty contributes meaningfully to challenging the pursuit of truth that leads to the objectification of defendants within criminal justice processes. The relationship between belief and conviction—which will be discussed further below—underscores the concept of the *Analogous*, demonstrating that conviction, by its very nature, resides within the realm of uncertainty.

As previously referenced through Cunha Martins at the conclusion of the preceding section, the development of conviction does not represent a flawless epistemic progression; rather, it constitutes an intellectual process that inherently highlights uncertainty. Cunha Martins notes that criminal proceedings typically regard conviction with caution, prompting the implementation of various control mechanisms—such as adherence to the adversarial principle. Nonetheless, the author highlights that these same criminal procedures appear disinclined to adopt such reservations comprehensively, even in instances where the accusatory model, inspired by constitutional frameworks, is applied (Martins 2010: 24).

To elucidate this statement, I refer once again to Cunha Martins and Gil, who examined the relation between conviction—conceived as the outcome of evidentiary investment—and belief.

The idea of a strong conviction appears to encompass the potential for constraining the hallucinatory aspects of evidence and thereby establishing a conviction that is grounded in proof, specifically in traces of the past whose analogical nature would be reliably determined.

However, the authors argue that the formation of conviction does not occur in such a straightforward manner. As Cunha Martins asserts, conviction can serve as a platform for various insinuations generated by epistemic regimes of evidence (Martins 2010: 22). He cautions that the distinction may be merely one of degree, given that the influence of evidence on conviction is prevalent; the intermingling of conviction with belief is intrinsic to both constructs (Martins 2010: 9). Gil further notes, "there is also a hallucinatory aspect present in belief, which conviction strives to dispel, though it never fully succeeds" (Martins and Gil 2002: 20). In light of these insights, should we consider conviction to simply be an intensified form of belief? According to Gil,

> Yes. But despite this, they are two different instances, that is: both evidence and conviction are, in part, indistinguishable from belief, but they are not reducible to it. Otherwise, everything would be belief. In all this, where is the truth? It is obtained, as we have just said, through operators and constraints imposed on an essentially devouring evidence. (Cunha and Gil 2002: 23)

Their argument underscores the importance of implementing operators and constraints designed to minimise—even partially—the hallucinatory nature of evidence. This does not imply that truth is irrelevant in criminal proceedings; rather, the assertion that evidentiary processes aim to establish conviction, or strong belief, pertains to the acceptance of a hypothesis advanced by the parties. Ultimately, the judge's conviction must be founded not only on argumentation but also on material presented and scrutinised through adversarial proceedings, particularly when the outcome is a guilty verdict. The central claim here is that forming a strong conviction—surpassing mere belief—demands appropriate mechanisms to regulate the evidence, ensuring that persuasion rests on proof—tangible traces of historical events. As Gil observes,

> in proof, evidence and belief are extremely constrained, restricted. Firstly, to recognise a proof, I must determine, by means of criteria that can only be epistemological and objective, that the content of the knowledge being proved is not an illusion, a fabrication, a hallucination; it must be established as an "objective fact", in accordance with rules that belong neither to the realm of proof nor of conviction. Secondly, proof is defined by the procedures that underpin it. The condition of assent is therefore limited by the others—in which, at least in principle, there is no place for belief. (Cunha and Gil 2002: 22)

Accordingly, the required condition for assent pertains to what has been established during proceedings, subject to the constraints of a regulated framework designed to maximise conviction and minimise mere belief, thereby preventing the emergence of condemnations based on hallucinations. In this context, it is clear that granting judges the authority to directly pursue the truth (or certainty) contravenes the intended objective. Such an approach fosters the reinforcement of belief at the expense of mechanisms best equipped to mitigate, albeit not eliminate, the potentially hallucinatory character of evidence: namely, adversarial proceedings grounded in dialogue, strict separation of prosecutorial and adjudicative functions, and party-driven evidentiary management.

When evidentiary activity is viewed as a process primarily focused on influencing the judge's psychological perception, it signifies a step beyond regarding evidence solely as a means to ascertain truth. Regardless of how profoundly convinced a judge may be about the facts, such conviction does not necessarily correspond to absolute truth or modern standards of certainty, given the inherent difficulty in distinguishing belief from conviction. As a result, uncertainty remains an intrinsic aspect of judicial proceedings. The risk persists that a judgement may be shaped more by subjective belief than by traces of the past, potentially attributing a hallucinatory quality to the formation of conviction. Even if it were feasible to systematically validate all evidence presented and thereby eliminate the risk of misguided conviction, the inherently analogical nature of traces from the past would still preclude a definitive realisation of truth under the notion of *the Same*.

The persistent uncertainty inherent in criminal proceedings affects not only the epistemological basis for conviction but also necessitates procedural safeguards to uphold fairness and legitimacy. This ongoing uncertainty shapes the roles of all participants, calling for procedural frameworks that stress rigorous evidentiary standards and acknowledge that the pursuit of certainty may introduce challenges similar to those encountered when seeking truth. The importance of robust adversarial mechanisms is underscored, as they constrain subjective interpretations and help prevent arbitrary judicial actions. Ultimately, the relationship between belief, conviction, evidence, and proof highlights the contingent nature of truth in legal settings, indicating that evidentiary processes must account for the possibility of error in judgement.

Further highlighted the inherent uncertainty and risk present within criminal proceedings. As such, it is essential to emphasise the implementation of rules designed to limit potential arbitrariness in the criminal justice system, thereby framing truth as a contingent element within its structure and focusing on harm reduction.

Narrative Representations in Conflict: The Uncertainty of Procedural Legal Situations

Building upon the rejection of a monological conception of truth and recognising the importance of delegating evidence management to the parties, the dynamics of representation become an essential facet in the interpretation of evidence. Evidence is introduced into proceedings via narrative representations crafted by the parties involved. Accordingly, it is necessary to examine argumentative intentionality within criminal proceedings, relating it to the notions of evidence and trace, while avoiding sceptical-argumentative relativism. To analyse the notion of representation, I reference Ricoeur's definition, which underscores the dual significance of the term: on one hand, there is the evocation of an absent entity through the use of another element that serves as its default representative; on the other hand, there is the presentation of a presence, wherein the visibility of what is present tends to obscure the process of substitution that constitutes an actual replacement of the absent (Ricoeur 2003: 305).

Consequently, the concept of representation involves an inherent logic that obscures its fundamental distinction from what it aims to depict. Its role as a substitute is to assume the position of the represented entity, thereby establishing itself as authentic in the perception of the observer. The mechanisms of representation create an intricate interplay between presence and absence. The scenario outlined by Ginzburg clearly illustrates this dynamic:

> In the humanities, much has been said, and for a long time, about "representation"—a phenomenon undoubtedly owed to the ambiguity of the term itself. On the one hand, "representation" stands in for the reality it represents and thus evokes absence. On the other, it renders the represented reality visible and therefore suggests presence. Yet this opposition can easily be reversed: in the first case, the representation is present, albeit as a substitute; in the second, it ultimately refers, by contrast, to the absent reality it seeks to represent. (Ginzburg 2001: 85)

In legal proceedings, evidence is not simply objectively presented for the judge's analysis; rather, it is strategically structured into narratives that support particular hypotheses, aiming to guide the judge's perception towards accepting certain assertions as true or disputing the claims made by the opposing party. This process effectively attempts to equate an event from the past with its narrative representation, or conversely, to challenge the accuracy of the adversary's account relative to actual occurrences. The prosecution's narrative endeavours to make the absence of a past event present before the court, while simultaneously obscuring distinctions between the narrated account and historical reality. Conversely, the defence's narrative primarily seeks to counteract the influence of the prosecution's case, potentially introducing evidence that specifically refutes the prosecution's hypothesis, though there is no strict obligation to demonstrate innocence. In this context, my perspective diverges from those who emphasise the judge's independent pursuit of truth.

Proponents of this approach contend that the judge should be dedicated above all to uncovering the truth, including seeking information beyond parties' submissions. However, this reasoning subtly reintroduces inquisitorial principles, as the necessity for judicially determined "truth" is inherently linked to a guilty verdict—a concept at odds with accusatorial and democratic criminal procedures predicated on the presumption of innocence.

The narrative representations presented by the parties are inherently selective; they utilise evidence insofar as it effectively bolsters the judge's confidence in their account of events. Consequently, selection is exercised from the initial introduction of evidence into proceedings, where it is transformed into a potential source of knowledge that may be recognised as a proof or trace of the past. Within this framework, the adversarial principle assumes a significant role, which will be examined in further detail subsequently.

In sum, it can be asserted that the processes of appropriation, analysis, and interpretation of evidence by a representation characterised by narrative intentionality introduce an additional layer of complexity to the issue of truth production—thus further illustrating the limitations inherent in the prevailing correspondence regime of truth.

Rationalist frameworks face challenges in comprehensively recognising and addressing the complexities inherent in evidentiary procedures, particularly where parties construct representations and arguments based on selectively gathered evidence. Rationalist scholars often view this critically, contending that such parties may not prioritise uncovering the truth. The recommended approach—granting judges enhanced authority over evidence management to promote truth-seeking and expand the scope of available information—has been criticised for potentially increasing the risk of wrongful convictions.

This dynamic should be thoroughly examined within a framework specifically designed to limit, rather than expand, punitive authority. Evidence is not simply assessed through an analytical or objective process intended to verify its status as a trace; instead, it is integrated into a narrative structure built around an argumentative hypothesis advancing a particular thesis, aiming to shape the adjudicator's perspective. This cognitive approach differs markedly from the "laboratory of history" model typical of the modern paradigm, which relies on correspondence truth and the certainty of the knowing subject.

As previously indicated, evidentiary activity fundamentally pertains to assertions about factual circumstances rather than past events themselves. This does not preclude a connection between proof and historical occurrences, as proof is established through evidence refined by the adversarial process. However, it underscores that any legal determination results from a procedure that systematically reorganises and transforms such evidence; accordingly, whether evidence truly represents a trace of the past remains subject to scrutiny even after procedural evaluation. There is no infallible mechanism for eliminating the potential unreliability of evidence. It is within legal frameworks of argumentation that evidence attains the status of proof in a procedural context—a process that fundamentally must obey certain rules but does not guarantee the correction of the hallucinatory character of evidence.

Rationalism confronts uncertainty through the "epistemic function" of judicial truth-seeking, an approach that may increase the risk of wrongful convictions. An alternative methodology is required to establish a procedural framework focused on harm reduction. Rather than perpetuating the cognitive advantage of judges, it is necessary to conduct a comprehensive epistemological and political review of criminal proceedings, accompanied by an explicit acknowledgement of their inherent risks.

Consequently, the connection between the refinement of evidence and the realm of proof warrants thorough analysis, as it enables the exploration of numerous matters pertinent to producing truth within legal proceedings.

The primary concern raised by these preliminary observations relates to the context in which parties formulate their narrative representations, as well as the process wherein evidence may be transformed into proof through judicial determination.

From this perspective, it is important to emphasise again the inherent uncertainty that defines legal proceedings. Lopes Jr., referencing James Goldschmidt, observes that "the proceedings—just like war—are shrouded in a cloud of uncertainty" (Lopes Jr 2007: 47). To illustrate his dynamic understanding of legal proceedings, Goldschmidt utilises a political analogy: during periods of peace, the relationship between the State and its subjects remains static, forming an intangible dominion. However, when conflict arises, every aspect is subject to change; even the most intangible rights may shift into expectations, possibilities, or liabilities, and any right may be lost due to missed opportunities or overlooked obligations. Conversely, conflict may enable the victor to claim rights to which they otherwise would not be entitled. This analogy can be appropriately applied to the substantive rights of the parties and their circumstances within legal proceedings (Goldschmidt 2010: 842).

Evidence is introduced into proceedings amid conflict and uncertainty, shaped by the narrative representations provided by the parties. This occurs within a framework where time serves as a crucial component, often in subtle ways: Lopes Jr. identified that proceedings possess a dual temporal character, stating, "proceedings do not escape time, for they are rooted in their very conception as a concatenation of acts that unfold, endure, and are carried out within a specific temporality" (Lopes Jr 2005: 92). Accordingly, proceedings are influenced by the passage of time in two respects: first, through their function of historical verification, and second, as sequential stages governed by distinct temporalities and directed towards defined objectives. The judge, seeking knowledge while confronting uncertainty, encounters a temporal paradox—simultaneously reflecting on the past and anticipating future outcomes, all from the vantage point of the present. As Carnelutti observes, this perspective further elucidates the concept of uncertainty.

> The *present*, the most problematic aspect of the most problematic of concepts, that is, time, is nothing more than the illuminated zone before a man walking with a lantern. So does the judge; he tries to illuminate as much as possible the path that unfolds before him. So does anyone who must form a judgement. While the judge asks questions, he tries to expand the present. But at a certain point, he stops questioning. The present extends to the limits of the possible. And then? The judge cannot remain there. He has heard the accused. He has listened to the witnesses. He has seen the footprints of the crime. But not the crime itself. The former are in the light, the latter in darkness. And yet the judge must proceed. Judgement is, therefore, a leap from the known to the unknown: from the judge's past to the accused's past, and then to his future. Now, its unitive nature begins to reveal itself: the function of judgement is essentially to unite, through the present, the past and the future. A superhuman task. (Carnelutti 2001: 55–56)

Carnelutti reflects that "men, who do not have the time necessary to judge, nonetheless have the need to judge. I know of no more tragic aspect of life. We cannot know what is good or evil; and yet, we must do good and not evil" (Carnelutti 2001: 28). This is not to mention the judge's own standpoint, himself irredeemably subject to historicity, which further deepens the uncertainty and risk that are characteristic of proceedings, as will be discussed later. For Goldschmidt, uncertainty is consubstantial with proceedings, since the outcome can never be predicted with certainty (Goldschmidt 2010: 832). According to Lopes Jr., the sphere of legal proceedings is characterised by instability; as such, it is not feasible to assert the presence of security, certainty, or stability in matters concerning reality, which inherently involves risks. Consequently, proceedings are marked by uncertainty and insecurity (Lopes Jr 2007: 47).

This presents another area of divergence between positivist and rationalist perspectives on legal proceedings—based on principles of stability, predictability, and security—and viewpoints acknowledging that legal processes are frequently marked by risk and uncertainty. To briefly address this topic within the boundaries of this study, it is useful to highlight the distinction between Oskar von Bülow's concept of legal relationship and Goldschmidt's notion of legal situation. Bülow's theoretical framework, initially developed for civil proceedings, played a significant role in criminal proceedings as well, particularly in advancing the judge's cognitive privilege (Streck 2020: 110).

In brief summary, Bülow established the concept of legal relationship and developed its characteristics, describing it as autonomous (independent of the substantive legal relationship), public (given the presence of the State, holder of jurisdiction to whom the action is addressed), and complex (due to its dynamic and transformative nature), whose content (rights and obligations) develops in motion (through the various stages of the proceedings), under the concept of unity (Ferrer 2006: 12).

The principal contribution of this theory, with respect to criminal proceedings, lies in its acknowledgement that the accused is not simply an object of prosecution by the state but has instead been accorded the position of a party within the proceedings. As noted by Lopes Jr., the argument that proceedings involve a party exercising subjective rights, particularly with the capacity to require the judge to grant the requested judicial relief by way of resistance (defence), is persuasive. Equally compelling is the notion of a legal relationship that obliges the judge towards the parties, who, through the final judgement, possess the right to attain an authentic environment of legality and the *restoration* of "social peace" (Lopes Jr 2010).

Conversely, Lopes Jr. asserts that Bülow's contributions laid the groundwork for erroneous concepts regarding security and equality, stemming from the so-called relationship of established rights among parties and between parties and judges. The author underscores that the principal error was to assume an actual legal relationship existed in criminal proceedings, characterised by a genuinely party-driven procedure (Lopes Jr 2010). It is important to reiterate that Bülow himself did not contend his theory extended to criminal proceedings but rather suggested it might occasionally offer utility (Bülow 1964). Additionally, while procedural autonomy represented progress at its inception, the relationship between criminal law and criminal procedure has since been reevaluated. This revaluation frames their connection not through subordination but through interrelation, as Coutinho proposes (Coutinho 1998: 145). According to Coutinho, criminal procedure should be established using categories appropriate to its unique characteristics, necessitating a departure from civil procedure frameworks that fail to capture the distinctiveness of criminal procedural mechanisms. As Coutinho observes, the general theory of civil procedure, riding on the general theory of procedure, penetrates our criminal procedure and, instead of providing it with a general theory, reduces it to a poor relation, a mere segment, a slice of the general theory. In short, the general theory of procedure is a deception; the true general theory is that of civil procedure, and from it, the others are derived (Coutinho 1998: 122–123).

Coutinho observes that there are few dissenting voices regarding the so-called general theory of procedure, but that it is necessary to establish the proper place of civil procedure discourse, which cannot be fully applied to criminal procedure, as this ignores the difference in semantic reference and leads inevitably to the legitimisation of the *status quo* (Coutinho 1998: 123). For him, in this vacuum, the law of power prevails, as Cordero reminds us, and thus an epistemological rupture is required, in the sense proposed by Bachelard. Coutinho refers to the overcoming of sclerotic causalism by finalism within criminal law (and the consequent legislative changes) as an example of the shift that is necessary (Coutinho 1998: 124).

Coutinho's statement aptly encapsulates several key objectives underlying this study: reinforcing the procedural framework designed to restrain power, establishing an epistemological break from discourses centred on corresponding truth, and emphasising the importance of criminal procedural dogmatics in assuming a critical and innovative function. These elements collectively serve to strengthen safeguards against excessive punitive authority.

Adopting this approach, the realisation of accusatory and democratic epistemology within a re-envisioned criminal justice system necessitates conceptualising criminal procedure through categories aligned with its structural principles, wherein crime is not treated as a legal transaction and individuals are not regarded as *res*, as articulated by Coutinho. In this context, Goldschmidt's theoretical framework most effectively captures the intricacy of criminal procedure and the significant risks it entails, thereby underscoring the imperative to safeguard the rights of the accused against the possible exercise of punitive authority. It was Goldschmidt who advanced the most persuasive theoretical account for interpreting and justifying the multifaceted nature of criminal proceedings (Lopes Jr 2010: 40). As Lopes Jr. notes,

> Goldschmidt first attacks the assumptions underlying the legal relationship, then denies the existence of procedural rights and obligations—that is, the very content of the relationship—and finally, definitively regards the prevailing doctrine in contemporary procedural systems as static or metaphysical. (Lopes Jr 2010: 40–41)

Goldschmidt's principal critical contribution centres on his critique of the perceived security inherent in viewing legal procedure as a fixed legal relationship (Lopes Jr 2010: 41). Lopes Jr. notes that Goldschmidt emphasised the dynamic nature of criminal proceedings, illustrating how the certainty associated with substantive law is supplanted by the procedural uncertainty typical of judicial activity (Lopes Jr 2010: 41). The divergence between Bülow and Goldschmidt is apparent in their contrasting perspectives on stability and risk, or security and uncertainty. In this context, Goldschmidt introduces an additional dimension to the evolving understanding within criminal proceedings, aiming to move beyond the paradigm of corresponding truth towards a criminal justice system grounded in respect for human rights.

Goldschmidt formulated a set of distinctive categories that highlight the dynamic nature of legal scenarios, conceptualising criminal proceedings as contests over rights. His perspective clearly shifts criminal proceedings theories from abstract dogmatics to lived experience. Lopes Jr. notes, "Proceedings, seen as evolving situations, generate expectations, prospects, chances, burdens, and releases from burdens. The utilisation or omission of these chances results in burdens or benefits" (Lopes Jr 2004: 155). Goldschmidt asserts that these procedural categories represent legal circumstances—specifically, an individual's position concerning their rights relative to the anticipated judicial decision, as prescribed by law (Goldschmidt 2010: 768).

He further observes that the expectation of procedural advantage, the prospect of a favourable judgement, relief from procedural burden, and the opportunity to achieve such positions via procedural action constitute rights in the procedural sense. However, these are not rights in the strict legal sense but rather states that may be described using the French term *chance* (Goldschmidt 2010: 829). Consistent with Goldschmidt's view, Lopes Jr. maintains that when presented with a *chance*, a party may fulfil a procedural obligation and thereby progress towards a favourable judgement (expectation), or fail to do so, which increases the likelihood of an unfavourable outcome (perspective). Consequently, parties are considered to hold a procedural possibility or chance whenever they have the capacity, through their actions, to secure a procedural advantage and, ultimately, a favourable judgement. Examples of exercising such opportunities include presenting evidence, contesting an allegation, or submitting documents within prescribed deadlines (Lopes Jr 2004: 156).

According to Lopes Jr., parties are not bound by obligations but are instead subject to procedural burdens, which involve undertaking actions to avoid an adverse judgement. These acts primarily consist of substantiating their claims and taking advantage of opportunities presented during proceedings. Goldschmidt notes that procedural situations arise from procedural acts—defined as actions performed by either the parties or the judge—which serve to create, alter, or extinguish expectations, possibilities, or procedural burdens, or to release parties from such burdens (Goldschmidt 2010: 769). In the context of criminal proceedings, the burden of proof rests exclusively with the prosecution. This is due both to its responsibility for formulating the indictment and the principle of the presumption of innocence (Lopes Jr 2007: 45).

Accordingly, the accusatory narrative must explicitly define its hypotheses to allow the accused an opportunity of a proper defence. The judge does not hold the burden of proof; within the accusatorial framework, the judge's role regarding evidence remains receptive rather than investigative. As Goldschmidt notes, evidence is always contingent upon a claim requiring substantiation—specifically, the assertion made by the interested party—while the judge's official responsibility, in terms of evidentiary procedure, is limited to receiving evidence, underscoring a fundamentally receptive function (Goldschmidt 2010: 778).

Goldschmidt's perspective fundamentally diverges from a truth derived through judicial authority wielded with extensive powers in pursuit of factual accuracy. Within inquisitorial approaches to epistemology, a judge's conviction develops independently: proceedings are conducted unilaterally towards a predetermined result, and the absence of mechanisms for evidentiary correction often leads to convictions influenced by personal beliefs. Conversely, in an accusatorial epistemology founded on democratic principles, the judge's conviction is constructed through dialogue. Here, it is the parties who introduce and articulate evidence, manage its presentation, and assume responsibility for its organisation, while the judge's principal role is to ensure due process and to base their judgement on evidence that has endured adversarial examination, being recognised as proof. Drawing upon this proof, the judge may analogically produce the truth, narratively expressing a conviction shaped by past traces—an idea that will be further examined in subsequent chapters.

According to Goldschmidt's concept of accusatorial epistemology, elevating evidence to the status of proof constitutes the realisation of an opportunity: it enables the prosecution to fulfil its evidentiary burden and supports the anticipation of a favourable judgement. Consistent with the democratic principles underpinning a reformed criminal justice system, accusatorial epistemology maintains that the responsibility for discharging burdens rests with the prosecutor; the defendant is not obligated to prove their case but may choose to produce evidence or challenge the prosecution's submissions as part of the adversarial process. Lopes Jr. describes this as the presence of an "assumption of risk"—the negative consequences that may arise when a party fails to support their own position or refute the arguments presented by the opposition. In the absence of contestation, evidence transitions into proof, heightening the likelihood of an adverse outcome. Consequently, the defence risks losing opportunities both to present evidence and to prevent the prosecution's submissions from attaining probative value. Therefore, rather than bearing a formal burden, the defence assumes risk, such that the prosecution carries the burden of proof while the defence manages associated risks (Lopes Jr 2007: 45). According to Lopes Jr.,

> The expectation of a favourable judgment or the prospect of an unfavourable judgment always depends on the seizing of opportunities and

> the discharge of burdens. At no point is there certainty that the judgment will be upheld. The prosecution and the defence may be truthful or not; a witness may or may not tell the truth, just as the decision may be correct or not (just or unjust), which clearly highlights the risk inherent in the proceedings [...] the view of the proceedings as a battle underscores the reality that the victor (the one who obtains a favourable judgment) is the one who fights best, who best knows how to seize opportunities to free themselves from procedural burdens or to reduce risks. (Lopes Jr 2007: 47)

Within an accusatorial epistemology informed by democratic values, the basis for any conviction is verification—specifically, the identification of evidence that can be elevated to concrete proof. This process involves discharging evidentiary burdens or mitigating risks when such evidence is recognised by the judge as a tangible trace of past events. Accordingly, the judge must adhere to the narrative presented in the case file and determine whether it contains evidence that, after procedural validation, qualifies as proof due to its demonstrable connection to historical facts. As Lopes Jr. observes, "the criminal procedure is an instrument for correcting the hallucinatory character of evidence" (Lopes Jr 2005: 269).

Although this corrective function is entrusted to the trial process, it can only partially achieve it, operating primarily through harm reduction—an approach extending beyond modern assurances of security and predictability to truly safeguard human rights. Crucially, this function is only fulfilled if the process eschews the inquisitorial pursuit of truth that prioritises the quantity of evidence over its substantiation, and belief over conviction.

Accordingly, this proposal introduces a framework aimed at regulating punitive authority, with the objectives of minimising harm and constraining judicial discretion to mitigate the routine abuses associated with decisionism in epistemological systems focused on establishing truth, often to the detriment of the accused. Within a democratic accusatorial system, the accused is not positioned as an enemy. Thus, the structure formulated by Goldschmidt and further developed by Lopes Jr. facilitates harm reduction by requiring the prosecution to meet evidentiary burdens, in accordance with the principles of *in dubio pro reo* and the presumption of innocence, and crucially, in observance of the human rights afforded to the accused.

It is important to reiterate that an accusatorial epistemology intended to minimise the hallucinatory character of evidence should not be regarded as absolute. Such an approach cannot guarantee absolute truth by perfectly correcting evidence or eradicating judicial errors. As Lopes Jr. notes, efforts to address the hallucinatory aspects of evidence must be guided by harm reduction principles. As Cunha Martins observes,

> The problem, however, is that of the effectiveness of its performance. It is, in some sense, a mission doomed to failure—not only do none of these operators achieve total regulatory satisfaction, but there is also a tendency for their "contamination" by the register of evidence. (Martins 2010: 4)

Although unpredictability may be inherent, a reimagined criminal justice system—one not dominated by an all-powerful judge—possesses a strong capacity to regulate evidence with the aim of reducing harm, as adversarial proceedings foster corrective oversight between involved parties. This mechanism ensures that narratives presented are rigorously scrutinised before being accepted as factual. Additionally, it emphasises the importance of numerous legal provisions that exclude evidence that infringes upon fundamental rights, aligning with the democratic principles and constitutional safeguards required for procedural integrity. These restrictions create boundaries by designating certain evidence as inadmissible, primarily to protect essential rights. In this context, there is a marked departure from the rationalist approach espoused by scholars like Laudan, Taruffo and Beltrán, who support broadening evidentiary standards in pursuit of truth and view such exclusionary rules as detrimental to epistemic objectives.

Dialogical Adversarial Proceedings as a Structure for Constraining the Hallucinatory Character of Evidence

The recognition of the hallucinatory character of evidence underscores the importance of a rigorous evidentiary framework. Adversarial proceedings support this rigour by offering a structured platform for parties to contest opposing evidentiary narratives. Within this framework, the adversarial model enables comprehensive scrutiny of the hallucinatory character of evidence. The process of evidentiary constraint is inherently non-neutral, influenced by arguments shaped by the narrative intentionality inherent in representation. Accordingly, the procedural architecture should facilitate the implementation of corrective constraints on evidence throughout the proceedings. As Gil notes, "guarantees-based law is another system of constraints imposed on evidence. The meaning of rationality is always this, in science as in law" (Martins 2002: 23). According to Cunha Martins,

> constraint, understood as a form of safeguard against the impulse of evidence, defines, in principle, a procedural aesthetic committed to the accusatorial system with a democratic-constitutional foundation, whereas the deliberate absence of constraint will, by the same logic, characterise a process aligned with the inquisitorial tradition and rooted in an authoritarian background. (Martins 2010: 23)

Accusatorial epistemology plays a pivotal role by maintaining a clear separation between prosecutorial and judicial responsibilities, as well as assigning evidence management to the appropriate parties. This framework promotes robust adversarial proceedings, thereby upholding essential evidentiary standards and enabling the fulfilment of burdens or mitigation of risks, with a strong emphasis on controlling the recognition of evidence as proof. Within this context, the insights provided by Cunha Martins are particularly noteworthy:

> What is called *evident* is that which dispenses with proof. A simulacrum of self-referentiality, a claim to justification centred on itself, evidence corresponds to a satisfaction that is all too rapid in the face of mere plausibility indicators. In some way, evidence establishes a *lovelessness of adversarial proceedings*. Endowed with such a set of values, it would be expected that its participation would be shielded in any critical or procedural mechanism intended to serve as a safeguard against arbitrariness. (Martins 2010: 3)

From this standpoint, Fazzalari's analysis is particularly relevant; as a proceduralist focusing on adversarial principles, he contends that this element is fundamental to defining what constitutes a legal procedure, to the extent that it may preclude classifying inquisitorial procedures in the same category. According to Fazzalari, the core of any legal proceeding resides in its adversarial character, distinguishing it from mere administrative procedures, such as applying for a hunting licence. He underscores that "something more is required; something that the archetypes of the legal procedure allow us to observe: the dialectical structure of the procedure, that is, precisely, the adversarial principle" (Fazzalari 2006: 119). Fazzalari further notes that "it is necessary, therefore, to identify the proceedings, that there be a set of rules (and acts, and legal positions) that refer to the recipients of the effects of the decision, establishing between them an adversarial parity" (Fazzalari 2006: 121). As Lopes Jr. points out, the adversarial principle "is indispensable to the very existence of the dialectical structure of the legal procedure" (Lopes Jr 2010: 188).

Accepting Fazzalari's position, the existence of a comprehensive and effective adversarial proceeding must be regarded as essential. This requirement becomes even more pronounced within criminal proceedings, where the judiciary possesses the authority to impose penalties. Accordingly, it is vital to highlight the necessity for "symmetrical parity among adversaries" (Fazzalari 2006: 123).

If, as Fazzalari contends, the thorough application of the adversarial principle defines the nature of judicial proceedings, then the risk posed by discretionary decision-making spaces—that permit or accept the unchallenged acceptance of evidence—becomes evident and results in an unjustifiable absence of adversarial safeguards, as Rui Cunha Martins notes. Lopes Jr. further observes that, from a contemporary standpoint, the adversarial principle incorporates not only the parties' right to present arguments before the judge but also requires judicial engagement—not to be mistaken for inquisitorial conduct or investigative authority on the part of the judge. The judge must respond appropriately to petitions and requests, provide explanatory reasoning for all decisions, including interlocutory ones, and avoid actions taken *ex officio* or that may take the parties by surprise. When rendering a judgement, it is imperative to respect the balance between prosecution, defence, and the final ruling (Lopes Jr 2010: 190). As Lopes Jr. (2010: 190) articulates, "the adversarial principle should be viewed primarily as the right to participate, to maintain a counter-position relative to the accusation, and to be informed of all actions taken throughout the procedural sequence".

Adversarial proceedings, in which evidence is presented via the narrative accounts of the respective parties, are essential to criminal proceedings. This method enables comprehensive scrutiny by all participants and reduces the potential for subjective bias that may arise when evidentiary matters are primarily directed by the judge.

Cunha Martins asserts that the Democratic Rule of Law achieves greater legitimacy and adherence to its foundational principles when mechanisms intended to uphold these values are minimally affected by undue reliance on evidentiary expressions (Martins 2010: 4). Accordingly, Martins contends that prof, conviction, and procedural safeguards each function to impose necessary boundaries that restrain excessive emphasis on evidence itself (Martins 2010: 4). Similarly, Calamandrei notes that judges are not granted discretion to arbitrarily favour any party but are obligated to rule in favour of the party who, through appropriate legal methods, most convincingly demonstrates the correctness of their position (Calamandrei 1999: 223). This perspective underscores the fundamental importance of a comprehensive and effective adversarial process.

> The judge must be impartial, standing above the litigants; but lawyers are made to be partial, not only because the truth is more easily reached if attacked from both sides, but because the partiality of one is the impulse that generates the counter-impulse of the adversary, the stimulus that provokes the reaction of the opponent and which, through a series of almost pendular oscillations from one extreme to the other, allows the judge to grasp, at the point of equilibrium, what is just. (Calamandrei 1999: 126)

This possibility is attainable only within an accusatorial system, characterised by conflict and uncertainty, but governed by rules designed to minimise harm—rules which must remain uncompromised as a fundamental requirement of democracy. In this context, multiplicity, imbalance, and the adversarial principle should not be regarded negatively within procedural epistemology; rather, they should be seen as contributing positively to the evidentiary process. As Ricoeur observes,

> A philosophical theory of justice thus finds its first foundation in the assertion that the self only constitutes its identity within a relational structure, which gives precedence to the dialogical dimension over the monological dimension that a tradition of reflective thought would be tempted to privilege. (Ricoeur 1995: 12)

This is the truly dialogical character that must mark the process of judicial conviction, entrusted "to the exposure of accusatory hypotheses to falsification by the defence, that is, to the free development of the conflict between the two parties in the proceedings, who hold contrasting viewpoints precisely because they are bearers of opposing interests" (Ferrajoli 2002: 488). Carnelutti reflects that

> it is common sense that everything the prosecution and the defence, that is, the search, demand in terms of drive and passion, the decision requires in terms of calm and serenity; there is no better way to represent the difference than to contrast stillness with movement: prosecutor and defender are and must be two combatants, whose reciprocal efforts the judge, without participating, observes with full attention, limiting himself to ascertaining which of the two ultimately prevails. (Carnelutti 2004: 236)

The receptive approach advanced by Goldschmidt is once again referenced here, this time reflected in Carnelutti's position: such an attitude is presented as optimal for judges operating within a criminal justice framework that prioritises human rights. Conversely, from a civil procedure standpoint, Taruffo offers a contrasting argument, maintaining that adversarial exchanges between parties are not an effective means for discerning the truth (Taruffo 2010: 195).

As previously indicated, this line of reasoning leads Taruffo to the assertion that judges must undertake a fundamental epistemic role, serving as the principal agents responsible for determining factual accuracy. While Taruffo does not explicitly acknowledge it, his discourse is clearly influenced by inquisitorial and positivist principles, as he remains tethered to the practice of judicial management in the quest for absolute truth. As Carvalho observes, from the standpoint of the inquisitorial tradition, as revitalised by Enlightenment-era scientific discourse, the magistrate is tasked with delivering a definitive determination of the truth. This responsibility requires the decision-maker to adopt an active role in the proceedings, which may extend beyond the conventional boundaries separating the judge from the parties, particularly during the evidentiary phase. Within this framework, restrictions on the judge's investigative authority are viewed as challenges to be addressed in pursuit of the ideal of truth (Carvalho 2008: 74).

It is not unexpected that the logic employed by inquisitorial, positivist and rationalist epistemologies results in a "truth" that effectively enacts monological violence against both the accused and the pastness of past events. The emphasis lies solely on fulfilling an ambition for truth, which serves as the basis for criminal proceedings focused on confronting the perceived enemy of society and setting exemplary punishments. As Ferrajoli notes,

> the truth sought and pursued by the inquisitorial procedure, being conceived as absolute or substantial, and therefore *unique*, does not admit the legitimacy of contrasting viewpoints whose conflict should be arbitrated by a third-party judge. (Ferrajoli 2002: 487-488)

Taruffo addresses this issue from a perspective that differs significantly from the evidentiary correction model via adversarial proceedings advanced here. According to Taruffo, the notion that the judge must select between the narratives presented by the parties aligns only with a procedural ideology that disregards the pursuit of truth (Taruffo 2010: 222). In contrast to Taruffo's perspective, my approach is not unconcerned with the truth; instead, it is founded on a thoughtful appreciation of its complexity, a position that differs significantly from an ideology driven by the intent to determine absolute truth.

Taruffo contends, on the basis of this rationale, that judges should pursue the truth. He asserts that the central concern lies not in debating the scope of judicial investigative powers, but in implementing effective controls over these powers. According to Taruffo, it is crucial that parties retain the ability to challenge the relevance and admissibility of evidence introduced by the judge *ex officio*, as well as to present counterevidence. He maintains that the proper approach is to uphold the full operation of adversarial proceedings, rather than to abolish judicial investigative authority (Taruffo 2010: 201–202).

Taruffo's arguments are unconvincing: the proper functioning of adversarial proceedings depends on the presence of an impartial judge who remains receptive and unbiased. In contrast to Taruffo's position, I present the insights of another esteemed civil proceduralist, who has continually emphasised the unique aspects of criminal proceedings. As Calamandrei notes,

> The best evidence of the purifying effect that the debate between two opposing lawyers has on the judge's conscience, destined to absorb from the air all polemical excesses and leave the judge isolated in an atmosphere of serenity, is provided by the institution, in criminal proceedings, of the Public Prosecutor. In this, the State has created a kind of official antagonist to the defence lawyer, whose presence prevents the judge from engaging in

> polemics with the latter and, unconsciously, from taking a position adverse to the accused. (Calamandrei 1996: 127)

Calamandrei clearly highlights the necessity for judicial impartiality within the accusatorial model, emphasising the explicit division between prosecutorial and adjudicative functions to ensure thoroughly adversarial proceedings and the dialogical development of knowledge, in contrast to the unilateral imposition of truth. The integrity of adversarial proceedings is sustained only by preserving judicial impartiality throughout the evidentiary process; any suggestion that a judge may participate in this adversarial engagement, as Taruffo posits, is untenable. Therefore, it is essential to regard adversarial procedures as a foundational criterion of validity: only evidence presented before the judge and initiated by the parties—having been subjected to rigorous dialogical scrutiny—can legitimately be evaluated as proof. Calamandrei's insights in this regard remain particularly instructive:

> Thus, in criminal proceedings, where the interests of the party might have been satisfied with a single lawyer, the State felt the need to appoint two, as a matter of public interest—to counterbalance the natural partiality of the defence with a kind of artificial partiality, intended to disinterestedly fuel the debate upon which the judge relies to rise above it. (Calamandrei 1996: 127)

This reflects a considered preference for the highest standard of proof, which is appropriate for a system designed as a safeguard against excessive punitive authority and that does not operate on an epistemology intent on treating defendants as enemies or objects. Accordingly, it is essential to move away from the inquisitorial approach and its positivist reinterpretation based on a philosophy of consciousness, which clearly demonstrates authoritarian tendencies. The central concern is adopting an epistemological framework that accurately addresses the complexities of criminal proceedings—a complexity that should not be overlooked by explanatory models that seek to diminish it, thereby enabling arbitrary use of punitive power. In short, acknowledging uncertainty necessitates a greater focus on procedural safeguards, not an epistemic function of truth-seeking undertaken by the judge. Ultimately, the divergence stems from differing expectations of criminal justice, particularly in contrasting views of whether criminal proceedings serve as an instrument of social control focused on deterrence.

This perspective is exemplified by Ferrer Beltrán, who suggests that the higher evidentiary standard in criminal proceedings warrants reconsideration, especially given the diminishing role of criminal law as an *ultima ratio* in recent decades and the introduction of pecuniary sanctions (Beltrán 2007: 140). It follows that an author who interprets criminal proceedings primarily through a deterrence framework may advocate for this position, reflecting a punitive approach focused on social control, not human rights (Beltrán 2007: 30). Conversely, my understanding of criminal justice emphasises its function as a guarantee against excessive punitive power, which logically leads to my recommendation for adopting the highest possible standard of proof before rendering any conviction.

In addition, convictions must not be influenced by deterrence or negative general prevention methods that objectify individuals as examples to intimidate others. Accepting such premises introduces utilitarian aims that can undermine offence-based criminal law, permitting sentencing decisions to rely on factors unrelated to the offence itself. Assigning this function to the criminal procedure effectively creates an enemy criminal law structure—a concept rooted in Roman law, revived during the Inquisition, and incorporated throughout modern political theory, with prominent figures such as Hobbes, Locke, Rousseau, Kant, Fichte, and most recently Gunther Jakobs, who advocates for this approach.

Importantly, an enemy criminal procedure is incompatible with democratic principles and the rule of law, which are fundamentally based on human dignity. Such incompatibility requires a reconsideration of both procedural frameworks and the underlying purpose of criminal jurisdiction. Therefore, a criminal procedure centred on human dignity upholds the presumption of innocence as its core principle, while a procedure focused on pursuing the "enemy" prioritises the ambition for truth above all else. Ultimately, in the former, judges approach cases with a predisposition towards acquittal; in the latter, they are inclined towards conviction, motivated by an unwavering commitment to confirm what they believe to be the truth.

The choice is unequivocal: a criminal justice system that upholds human rights versus one that objectifies defendants. Consequently, any relaxation or relativisation of the standard of proof or the judge's impartial stance is inadmissible under the pretext of metaphysical protection of legal interests, societal defence or any similar rationale. Evidence cannot be recognised as valid unless it has undergone thorough scrutiny through a genuine adversarial process, in alignment with democratic principles. Such principles require an equal footing for all parties and promotes the dialogical correction of evidence within judicial proceedings.

I must reiterate that my argument is not that the adversarial process reveals absolute truth; rather, it reduces the likelihood of wrongful convictions and furthers harm reduction objectives. The inherently uncertain nature of evidence can be moderated but not entirely eliminated. This point warrants clear understanding. As Cunha Martins observes, "things do not proceed in such a linear fashion. From the outset, due to the high degree of porosity characteristic of the forms of constraint on evidence that we find in regimes of proof and truth" (Martins 2010: 3). Accordingly, Martins' caution suggests that despite rigorous safeguards, the adversarial process cannot guarantee the veracity of findings, given the complex nature of evidentiary materials. Thus, even comprehensive adversarial proceedings may fail to prevent improper acceptance of evidence as proof, mistakenly regarded as definitive indicators of past events. Martins further contends that the adversarial process remains susceptible to subtle shifts in evidential interpretation (Martins 2010: 18).

In concluding this chapter, I emphasise that decision quality is intrinsically linked to the calibre of proof: specifically, its ability to shape judicial conviction through dialogical processes and adversarial scrutiny. Subsequent analysis will expand upon the concepts explored thus far.

CHAPTER 8

Criminal Procedure and the Complexities of the Late Modern Era

Acceleration, Risk, and the Rules of the Game

In the preceding chapters, I have advocated for reimagining criminal justice and moving away from the pursuit of truth characteristic of inquisitorial, positivist, and rationalist epistemologies. Such a shift necessitates departing from longstanding traditions and embracing innovative perspectives, an approach to which legal scholars have generally been resistant.

However, this is only one component of the broader challenge. The integration of novel viewpoints into the epistemological foundations of criminal justice is further complicated by various factors, many of which originate outside the domain of law.

These external influences are particularly significant because criminal justice operates within—and is shaped by—the wider societal context. Judicial practices are unavoidably affected by complex social dynamics, which can profoundly influence the effectiveness and functioning of the criminal justice system, often resulting in a tendency towards authoritarian and punitive measures.

In the context of late modernity, rapid social change and epistemic uncertainty significantly influence the operation of criminal justice systems. As societal rhythms accelerate and the frameworks that once anchored collective understanding begin to dissolve, legal institutions likewise face mounting pressure to adapt quickly. This urgency often

S. H. Khaled Jr., *Reimagining Criminal Justice, Search for Truth and Human Rights*, https://doi.org/10.1007/978-3-032-27227-0_8

manifests in calls for expedited proceedings and harsher penalties, underpinned by a desire for immediate responses to perceived threats. However, such tendencies risk undermining the deliberative qualities essential to just adjudication, as the complexity of contemporary life resists reduction to straightforward, mechanistic solutions.

The very notion of risk has become central in this environment: it is not only an object of legal regulation but also a lens through which uncertainty is managed, sometimes with problematic consequences. Criminal justice, therefore, becomes entangled with societal demands for reassurance and control, which may, paradoxically, erode the foundational safeguards designed to protect individual rights. This chapter will explore how these dynamics challenge the balance between efficiency and fairness, and why a renewed commitment to procedural integrity is more crucial than ever.

There is a significant connection between the persistent support of dogmas such as correspondence truth and the rapid acceleration that, in recent decades, has contributed to the depletion of various convictions and perspectives. By the late twentieth century, this accelerating vector of transformation reached unprecedented levels, leading to diminished points of reference and a decline in the certainties that previously offered stability amid changing social dynamics. Consequently, prevailing sentiments have shifted towards anxiety and nostalgia for conditions once perceived as secure and familiar.

The end of the twentieth century witnessed the apparently definitive collapse of the grand explanatory narratives. As Gauer observes, currently, time no longer serves as a fundamental principle of intelligibility, as demonstrated by the concept of progress, which previously suggested that later developments could be understood through earlier ones. This notion diminished in significance following widespread conflicts, totalitarian regimes, genocidal actions, and the dissolution of overarching narratives. The major interpretative frameworks, which once aimed to explain the progression of humanity collectively, ultimately lost their relevance in the contemporary era (Gauer 1998: 20).

Lyotard posits that legitimising narratives are in decline, rendering the notion of universal consensus increasingly untenable. Consequently, all discourses—including those considered scientific or philosophical—may now be viewed as perspectives (Lyotard 2002: 129). Such developments mark a society without a clear horizon of expectation, confronted by a future perceived as increasingly precarious and uncertain. As Gauer notes, the consensual logic underpinning truth is disrupted by rapid experiential change and shifts in temporal regimes (Gauer 2004: 13).

Some scholars argue that modernity has been superseded by postmodernity—a period marked by uncertainty, where established lessons from the past appear less instructive, and the future no longer guarantees aspirations for progress. Irrespective of whether the term "postmodernity" is fully appropriate, contemporary society faces significant ambiguity due to the decline of prevailing paradigms and comprehensive explanatory frameworks, which now struggle to account for growing complexity. This is evidenced by Morin and Prigogine's work, *A Society in Search of Values*.

The extent to which the current era may be characterised as postmodern remains subject to debate. Western institutions and prevailing worldviews continue to exhibit key modern features, indicating that modernity has not been fully transcended. Consequently, it is most appropriate to conceptualise this apparent transitional period as late modernity. As Ferrell, Hayward, and Young (2019: 92) suggest, "the contemporary world is, in fact, a shifting combination of modern and postmodern characteristics, which, for the sake of conciseness and clarity, we refer to as late modernity".

In late modern times, a decline in optimism regarding the future has contributed to the perception that society is becoming increasingly present-oriented. This tendency towards presentism, characterised by accelerated rhythms of human experience and a diminishing sense of continuity, complicates our ability to navigate a world perceived as increasingly complex and potentially hostile. Noted commentators, including Paul Virilio, have observed this shift; Virilio describes the "presentification" of history, whereby the immediacy of the present supersedes considerations of both past and future. He further conceptualises this development as an "amputation of the volume of time" emphasising his belief that time possesses dimensionality and that individuals exist within the three chronological dimensions of past, present, and future (Virilio 2000).

The consequences are notably diverse. In many respects, the future appears devoid of hope, as utopian visions have been thoroughly depleted. Some analysts contend that the collapse of utopias signifies the demise of the future itself, which aligns with various ideologies focused on the "end" of history. Lopes Jr. observes, "the future is genuinely contingent and indeterminate; each moment exists independently, without a foreseeable or prescribed progression. Ambitions and commitments—the Promethean drive—become irrelevant. The result is compounded uncertainty" (Lopes Jr 2005: 52).

Consequently, only the past remains—a past that no longer exists in a tangible sense and, therefore, can no longer provide meaning or guidance for the present. This situation creates a disquieting condition. According to Gauer, this reflects a profound conflict between a modern understanding of time and "the speed with which we must readjust our classifications, our emotions, as a result of the very demobilisation of the past itself" (Gauer 1998: 21).

The prevailing uncertainty and diversity surpass what modern thought can readily encompass, resulting in a sense of concern that extends beyond academic contexts. Consequently, the characterisation of a crisis arises, as presentism appears insufficient to provide reference points for restoring "normality".

Consequently, while the past and future no longer offer reliable guidance, addressing the increasing dominance of the present poses a significant challenge, as it constitutes only a fleeting moment that vanishes immediately. Ost (2001) notes that a rupture in the ordinary experience of time has occurred, rendering the instant truly instantaneous and lacking any predictable sequence, thus diminishing the meaning of projects and promises.

This reorientation of temporal experience has significant implications for the administration of criminal justice. As the anchoring effects of tradition wane and the certainty provided by established narratives diminishes, legal actors are increasingly confronted with the challenge of operating in a context where the future is opaque and the past offers little reliable precedent. The result is a heightened reliance on the present moment as the primary reference point for action and decision, which, in turn, intensifies the drive for immediate outcomes and swift resolutions.

These circumstances create an environment where caution and careful deliberation may be disregarded in favour of expediency, a perspective closely associated with the enduring emphasis on the pursuit of truth in criminal proceedings. The legal process, which ought to be based on systematic evaluation of evidence and thorough analysis of arguments, now faces expectations influenced by the accelerated pace of contemporary society—requiring not only the pursuit of truth, but its prompt attainment.

This tension between the demands of speed and safeguarding human rights lies at the heart of the contemporary crisis facing criminal procedure, raising critical questions about the capacity of criminal justice to safeguard fairness and uphold the rule of law amidst persistent uncertainty.

Within this increasingly uncertain environment, many individuals rely on the perceived stability provided by specific modern frameworks. Notably, confidence in the cognitive abilities of the knowing subject remains widespread; when applied to the legal system, this belief underpins the authority granted to judges in their pursuit of truth.

The reliance on judicial cognition, rooted in the enduring faith in the subject's capacity to discern and interpret facts, persists even as the structural supports of certainty erode in the broader social context. Judges, therefore, are frequently cast as arbiters of truth in an environment where the coordinates of that truth are increasingly unstable and contested. This reliance, while offering a semblance of stability, also exposes the judiciary to heightened pressures and expectations to deliver clarity and resolution amid pervasive ambiguity.

The increasing pace of lived experience in late modernity has placed additional demands on criminal justice systems. The prevalence of acceleration, characterised by an intensified focus on the present and diminished attention to past and future contexts, has led to speed becoming the standard; in such an environment, delays are considered unacceptable at all levels, including within intellectual pursuits. Referencing Virilio, it is important to note his assessment that speed can generate significant negative consequences. He argues that "the logic of the race, divesting from the earth and the world, and progressively investing in the vector, promotes a true assault on human nature" (Virilio 1996: 12).

Consequently, hyper-acceleration exerts significant influence and necessitates a careful, deliberate adjustment process. When responses lack due consideration, there is a risk that the criminal justice system may expedite proceedings to an extent that diminishes and relativises the rights of the defendant, potentially undermining the integrity of evidentiary assessment. It is important to recognise that certain processes are inherently incompatible with the rapid pace demanded by efficiency; when such speed becomes embedded in legal reasoning, it can profoundly affect punitive measures, effectively permitting judges to prioritise not only the pursuit of truth, but also its attainment in a "swift" and "efficient" manner.

The focus on adversarial proceedings may serve to restrict, to some degree, the emergence of decisionism that results from illegitimate demands for expediency in criminal justice. In this context, Cunha Martins discusses the concept of a procedural "machinery of expectations", suggesting that when criminal proceedings are subjected to pressures for rapid resolution, these pressures stem from external influences that risk introducing contaminated evidence. Such conditions advocate for a criminal procedure prioritising social control, which is characteristic of authoritarian regimes (Martins 2010: 55). As Morais da Rosa observes, a conception of proceedings as adversarial procedure "entails a cost in time and money incompatible with the logic of efficiency, in the name of which the exclusion of the defence and witnesses is justified, thus resurrecting an understanding of Substantial Truth, hitherto buried" (Rosa 2011: 96).

Criminal proceedings should not be influenced by unrealistic expectations of swift resolution, as adequate deliberation is essential to ensure guilty verdicts are supported by minimal assumption and are at least partially refined through evidentiary safeguards. These mechanisms, however, as previously discussed, are not wholly sufficient for their intended purpose; inevitably, elements of subjectivity will persist in the material upon which judicial decisions are based. The underlying issue is that certain procedural logics may amplify this subjective aspect in the development of judicial conviction, a practice that warrants reconsideration. As Gil observes: "Truth has no definitive standard. Or, if you prefer, its only standard is carefully considered conviction" (Martins and Gil: 2002).

Therefore, it is essential to move away from cognitive frameworks that support unfounded beliefs and instead embrace models that emphasise rigorous evaluation of evidence. This approach aims to reinforce safeguards against the overreach of punitive authority, while acknowledging that these protections must function within a harm reduction paradigm.

The issue arises from the continual demand for increasingly rapid responses from the judiciary as a result of social acceleration. Lopes Jr. highlights concerns regarding the potential erosion of the rights of the accused, citing a paradox created by presentism: "a society accustomed to the speed of virtuality does not want to wait for criminal proceedings, hence the passion for pre-trial detention and the visibility of immediate punishment" (Lopes Jr 2005: 27). Consequently, the hyper-acceleration described by Virilio may prompt adjustments in judicial processes that should not be implemented without careful consideration. The pace required for criminal proceedings is inherently at odds with the demands for speed, as evidentiary procedures function as counterbalances that necessitate time distinct from broader societal dynamics (Martins 2020).

Speed, often described as the lever of the world by Virilio, does not align with the cognitive requirements inherent in knowledge acquisition, nor does it adequately respects the human dignity of the accused. Conversely, the right to be tried within a reasonable timeframe is also paramount, as unwarranted delays may result in undue anxiety, hardship, and social stigma for individuals under prosecution (Lopes Jr and Badaró: 2006). Consequently, it is essential to establish a judicial pace that upholds the fundamental human rights of defendants. Achieving this balance, particularly in a contemporary context marked by risk, presents notable challenges. As Timm de Souza and Gauer observe, "life is, without doubt, movement inscribed in a socially constructed time. If life is movement, the balance we can find within movement is essentially dynamic" (Gauer and Souza 2004: ix).

Lopes Jr. observes that "we live in a complex society, where risk is everywhere, in all activities, and affects everyone indiscriminately" (Lopes Jr 2005: 49). The sociology of risk is exemplified by Beck, who argued that the contemporary world faces a new category of risk—unpredictable, transcending spatial and temporal limitations, and lacking effective safeguards. Examples include environmental degradation; ecological repercussions following nuclear accidents such as Chernobyl; the dissemination of chemicals into ecosystems; and genetically modified organisms, whose long-term effects remain uncertain. These risks contribute to significant insecurity, making it challenging to attribute causality or responsibility, especially given their transgenerational nature. Beck also introduces the concept of glocality, describing risk phenomena that simultaneously exhibit global and local characteristics, owing to the indeterminate scope of their impact (Beck 2002).

Consequently, contemporary society is characterised by rapid change and a reliance on short-term frameworks. According to Lopes Jr. (2005: 49), this acceleration increases elements of risk, uncertainty, and insecurity, all of which are prominent features of the present era and necessitate a legal response. Nevertheless, the law frequently remains anchored in traditional constructs—such as the correspondence theory of truth—that function primarily to legitimise discretionary punitive authority. As Lopes Jr. further observes, "the conflict between social and legal dynamics is inevitable, once again highlighting the failure of scientific monologue in the face of the complexity imposed by contemporary society" (Lopes Jr 2005: 49).

In environments marked by rapid change, elevated risk, and widespread uncertainty, individuals often encounter difficulties adapting to new information and shifting standards. As a result, any source providing even minimal certainty is typically retained and valued. Within this context, the correspondence theory of truth serves as a perceived anchor amidst ambiguity—a framework that addresses concerns over challenges to established beliefs, which strive for continuity and are frequently used to legitimise the exercise of authoritative power.

Advocates of truth-oriented judicial practices frequently invoke the ongoing climate of uncertainty characteristic of late modernity to support enhanced criminal prosecution, positioning it as a response to increasing societal demands for security amid escalating risks.

Given the prevailing context characterised by risk, uncertainty, insecurity, and particularly rapid change, it becomes essential to establish a framework of minimum guarantees that criminal procedure must uphold (Lopes Jr 2005: xxiv). Nonetheless, the trend often observed is the opposite: in an environment lacking clear reference points, neoliberal thought tends to gain traction, resulting in both a reduced role for the state and an expansion of criminal law, guided by a distinctly inquisitorial epistemology. This development is problematic, as Lopes Jr. observes, because "a social order cannot be built solely on repression" (Lopes Jr 2005: 29).

Conversely, issues stemming from the development of an exclusionary society contribute to an increase in violent crime. This escalation often serves to justify, in the perspective of some, the implementation of more stringent penal measures, thereby undermining the objective of minimal social control—criminal justice is repeatedly tasked with addressing violence, yet it can offer only limited solutions; violence should not be viewed as an external affliction easily removed from society, but rather as an indicator of deeper, intrinsic societal challenges.

In situations marked by urgency and perceived threats, there arises an increasing expectation for repressive action within the criminal justice system—interpreted primarily as an exercise of power—which in turn pressures judges to assume roles that may conflict with established legal principles and could ultimately render judicial decisions instruments of violence. Therefore, it is imperative to resist dynamics that undermine the possibility of effectively regulating punitive authority.

Within this context of uncertainty and potential harm, Ferrajoli's perspective is pertinent: in the absence of a robust theory of truth, verifiability, and procedural verification, essential safeguards may be compromised. If developing a theory that comprehensively addresses the complexity of the issue proves unfeasible, it is necessary to at least establish a model suited to the matter at hand.

This consistently suggests an accusatorial epistemology aligned with democratic values. Such an epistemology appears best equipped to mitigate the hallucinatory character of evidence, though it is limited to damage reduction rather than complete resolution, as elimination remains unattainable. Despite these advantages, there will always be a risk of judicial error stemming from inherent uncertainties within procedures influenced by life's complexities and the challenge of addressing past events. Underlying the issue of evidence are the ontological boundaries of traces, which serve merely as indicative and substitutive elements; this uncertainty further underscores the persistent risks and potential for harm.

In this context, Calamandrei presents insights on the legal process that facilitate a more nuanced examination of its intrinsic risks. The author notes that

> in order to obtain justice, it is not enough to be in the right. The old Venetian proverb, among the necessary ingredients for success in litigation, certainly places " *being right* " first, but immediately adds that it is also necessary to "*know how to present it* ", "*find someone who understands* ", and "*find someone willing to grant it* ", and finally, "*a debtor who is able to pay*". (Calamandrei 1999: 223)

This argument presents a highly realistic perspective, underscoring the inherent uncertainty of legal proceedings. Even well-defined criteria for hypothesis verification and burden discharge do not render outcomes predictable, as decisions ultimately rest on judicial discretion. As Calamandrei observes, a judge's deliberation is not "one of those automatic machines into which you simply insert a coin on one side and a card with the answer comes out the other" (Calamandrei 1999: 223). The author further indicates that, for a claim to succeed,

> it must be filtered through the mind of the judge and must succeed in making itself understood and persuasive: the outcome therefore depends on the interplay of these individual psychologies and the persuasive force

> with which the claimant's arguments are able to resonate and elicit sympathy in the judge's conscience. (Calamandrei 1999: 223)

Calamandrei highlights the risks associated with the process of forming conviction, emphasising that narrative and argumentative persuasion strategies play a significant role and that outcomes are not determined exclusively by concrete evidence presented during adversarial proceedings. His observations further underscore the strong connection between belief and conviction, as previously outlined. Consequently, it becomes apparent that such processes possess a considerable capacity for harm, as Calamandrei noted:

> The judgment is therefore not the automatic product of applying the law to the facts, but rather the psychological result of three forces at play, two of which, each trying to pull the third in its own direction, engage in a fierce competition, which is not only about good arguments, but also about the technical skill in making them prevail. It is a fortunate coincidence when, between two litigants, the more just is also the more skilful: but even in certain cases (and I wish to believe they are rare) when this coincidence does not occur, it may happen that the proceedings, instead of being an instrument of justice created to favour the more just, becomes an instrument of technical skill, created to grant victory to the more astute. (Calamandrei 1999: 224)

Calamandrei highlights a significant area of tension, noting that legal procedure incorporates aspects reminiscent of both warfare and regulated competition. Although the evidentiary process is governed by established rules, the narrative strategies employed to influence judicial perception are inherently tactical, introducing an element of risk that is frequently overlooked. Consequently, Calamandrei cautions that there exists the potential for legal proceedings to devolve into mere contests focused on victory (Calamandrei 1999: 224).

The potential for an accused individual's outcome to hinge upon the proficiency of either the prosecution or the defence presents a significant concern. Recognising the influence of this factor—one that further underscores the inherent uncertainties within evidentiary processes—may be vital in formulating guidelines to mitigate the unpredictable and potentially detrimental aspects of legal proceedings. Lopes Jr. notes that, although judicial decisions are limited by the narrative presented in the case file, technical expertise is crucial for safeguarding rights and achieving favourable litigation outcomes given the intrinsic risks of procedural actions (Lopes Jr 2007: 51).

Accordingly, Calamandrei draws attention to the considerable risks inherent in procedural dynamics, which are marked by an environment of conflict and uncertainty—a point also emphasised by Goldschmidt. Given these circumstances, such uncertainty necessitates the creation of transparent procedural rules that uphold the formal rigour required by due process. As Calamandrei notes:

> The procedure is not merely a series of acts that must follow a certain order established by law (*ordo procedendi*), but also, in the performance of these acts, an orderly alternation of various persons (*actus trium personarum*), each of whom, in this sequence of acts, must act and speak at the precise moment, neither before nor after, just as in the performance of a play each actor must know when to "enter" for their intervention, or in a game of chess the players must alternate regularly in moving their pieces. (Calamandrei 1999: 225)

Ultimately, strict adherence to procedural rules is essential for criminal proceedings to align, at least in part, with the standards of justice expected within accusatory and democratic frameworks. Accusatory formalism requires unwavering compliance with established procedures, as such formality—though not without limitations—serves as a safeguard against arbitrariness. Within this context of risk, the central challenge concerns ensuring respect for due process and, preceding that, adherence to rules aligned with constitutional principles. This involves advocating for a system of fundamental safeguards. The focus should not be on reviving the illusion of security, or the search for truth, but rather on recognising the inherent risks and establishing an irreducible framework of formal safeguards. Security (as safeguard) must be redefined through the acceptance of risk; that is, acknowledging that a safeguard can only exist when the possibility of absence is recognised (Lopes Jr 2007: 55).

In this context, criminal procedure serves to delineate the boundaries of the state's punitive authority while safeguarding the rights of those subject to it. The criminal justice system must retain prosecutorial and punitive capacities but should be balanced by a set of procedural and individual guarantees (Lopes Jr 2007: 56). This approach recognises the inherent limitations within the system, aiming for the reduction rather than the complete elimination of harm—an objective acknowledged as unattainable in practice. Even with procedural frameworks designed to strengthen evidentiary standards and minimise misinterpretations, achieving fully satisfactory outcomes remains elusive due to the inherently interpretive nature of reconstructing past events. Such challenges are unavoidable, given the uncertainties that underpin procedural developments. As Calamandrei notes,

> despite the fixed forms of procedure, there are no two proceedings that are identical, just as in chess there are no two games alike. The procedure is born and develops in each case, move by move, shaped in unforeseen and unpredictable ways by the often disconcerting combinations of opposing forces that cross within it. (Calamandrei 1999: 227)

If the objective is to minimise harm, a framework aligned with this purpose should not confer upon judges the authority to conduct proceedings based on their preliminary assumptions. History indicates that such methods are not advisable. While this approach might seem to foster control, security, and predictability in line with late modern expectations to curb uncertainty, it frequently results in errors arising from prioritising hypotheses over factual analysis. Historically, inquisitorial and positivist epistemologies have been known to intensify harm rather than mitigate it. The same can be said of the reinvigorated search for truth ideology that underpins evidentiary rationalism. Accordingly, I underscore the essential role of judicial impartiality within accusatorial epistemology, drawing on Calamandrei's reflections:

> The scales are the traditional symbol of justice because they seem to materially represent that interplay of psychological forces which makes the proceedings function. For the judge, after some oscillation, to settle on the truth, it is necessary for the dispute between two opposing theses to intervene, just as the two pans of the scales must bear weight at the end of each arm in order to balance each other. (Calamandrei 1996: 122)

Drawing on Goldschmidt's categorisation, Fazzalari's emphasis on adversarial proceedings, and Calamandrei's insights regarding the risks inherent in legal contests, it becomes clear that certain assumptions should be reconsidered—most notably, the notion that a judge can straightforwardly ascertain the truth and thereby guarantee justice through procedural means. As Lopes Jr. observes, such assumptions may obscure a deeper understanding of the underlying dynamics of adversarial processes (Lopes Jr 2007: 55).

The guiding principle in criminal justice should prioritise the containment rather than the maximisation of harm. Consequently, maintaining a clear separation between prosecution and adjudication functions, as well as ensuring that parties manage evidence appropriately, are fundamental procedural safeguards. Such measures serve to limit arbitrariness and procedural decisionism within a framework specifically designed for this purpose. It is not suggested that the concept of truth be abandoned altogether; rather, it is crucial to acknowledge the specific form of "truth" that legal processes can yield, without conflating its role with objectives incompatible with a ritualised structure aimed at constraining punitive authority.

As previously discussed, assigning the judge the duty of truth-seeking demonstrates substantial trust in human capacity to understand reality, a notion rooted in nineteenth-century scientific paradigms. Within this epistemological framework, the judge may select evidence based on personal discretion and convert it into proof without mechanisms for review or correction of their own assumptions. As a result, the conclusive nature of such proof remains ambiguous, given its unilateral formation and potential to contribute to erroneous convictions.

An accusatorial-democratic epistemology recognises the historical context of events and resists the contemporary demand for expedited processes, emphasising the importance of acknowledging uncertainty and risk. Its fundamental attributes include a commitment to rigorous correction and scrutiny of evidence, as well as comprehensive adversarial procedures that ensure thorough verification of information presented. This methodology promotes harm reduction and limits punitive authority by upholding strict evidentiary standards, thereby protecting human rights.

Conversely, it is recognised that risk is an inherent aspect of procedural legal contexts and their evolving nature; such risk may only be mitigated, not eliminated. The epistemological approach presented here does not purport to eradicate belief as an essential component of conviction. This might be desirable, but it is simply not possible. Accordingly, the emphasis is placed on adherence to procedural rules—most notably, the delineation between prosecutorial and adjudicative functions and the management of evidence by the parties involved. This approach represents a departure from models grounded in inquisitorial truth-seeking logic.

Acceleration and risk are not the only late modern factors influencing criminal proceedings; recent authoritarian tendencies in the Brazilian criminal justice system have led to the emergence of a new type of criminal procedure—one that intertwines criminal justice, politics and culture wars. This new development challenges traditional boundaries between criminal proceedings and broader societal dynamics.

The following section will expand on the earlier case study of chapter three to demonstrate the shifting dynamics of procedural authoritarianism within contemporary late modern contexts.

The Advance of Authoritarianism in the Peripheral Late Modernity and Criminal Procedure as a Cultural Phenomenon

This section focuses on conceptualising criminal procedure primarily as a cultural phenomenon. While this approach does not disregard normative and epistemological considerations, its primary objective is to analyse how meaning is constructed within criminal procedure and to explore the processes by which intricate procedural legal contexts are subject to mediated reconstruction or amplification of meaning. This analysis is particularly attentive to the ways in which discourses emerging from criminal procedure are disseminated externally and consumed by the broader population as cultural products.

The interplay between criminal procedure and expectation requires reconsideration in light of the developments stemming from Operation Lava Jato, as detailed in the case study concerning proceedings against Lula in chapter three. It is widely acknowledged that criminal procedure should not function solely as a mechanism for confirming preconceived expectations; rather, it must establish boundaries and uphold a regime of truth that mitigates the hallucinatory character of evidence (Martins 2010: 37). Within a criminal justice system that respects human rights, procedural confrontation should occur through distinct narrative representations designed to persuade the judge, where the prosecution carries the burden and the defence manages risk. The inherent uncertainty of legal-procedural situations ought to be addressed by implementing safeguards that ensure fairness, protect the accused, and guide the judge according to accusatorial epistemology (Goldschmidt 2010: 778). This framework supports a regime of truth informed by analogy, embracing epistemologies characterised by an acknowledgement of pastness and acceptance of the limitations inherent in knowledge derived from historical traces.

Achieving this objective requires the establishment of both normative and epistemological boundaries. While the Constitution outlines normative limits, these are frequently overlooked; epistemological boundaries often go unacknowledged entirely. However, it is precisely these limits that can protect the accused from authoritarian tendencies and inappropriate conflation of the regimes governing proof, evidence, conviction, and belief.

Criminal proceedings risk becoming objectifying when judicial decisions are made through solitary deliberation, with evidentiary support sought only afterward. Such circumstances often arise when dialogic processes are replaced by the monologic practices characteristic of inquisitorial systems, which may overlook adversarial procedures and potentially legitimise methods aimed primarily at achieving a predetermined result.

The recent rise in authoritarian practices in Brazil reflects a persistent inquisitorial culture that appears largely unaffected by constitutional principles. This tradition has enabled an ideological transformation whereby legal proceedings often become authoritative monologues that supplant adversarial proceedings. During Operation Lava Jato, such monologues were presented as assertive public discourse, particularly within the context of late modernity and the evolving landscape of social networks. This marked a notable departure from previous frameworks that operated mostly in secrecy and distant from the public eye.

Inquisitorial systems are often characterised by the production of truth within confidential settings, where the judge plays an active role in managing the evidence. These processes typically do not favour transparency. However, during Operation Lava Jato, such systems moved away from traditional secrecy, functioning as instruments of authority and symbolic influence that both responded to and shaped public expectations, reflecting a complex dynamic of arbitrariness.

In this scenario, the procedural hiatus no longer functioned as a counter-majoritarian tool of resistance; instead, it operated as a mechanism that cultivated public desires and raised expectations. Criminal proceedings were consumed symbolically by the public much like commodities. In this context, the legal process shifted its focus away from the criminal case, prosecutorial claims, or the pursuit of truth, and instead aimed to shape the public perception of the accused. This approach frequently transformed the proceedings into punitive practices that prioritised destroying reputations and inflicting personal harm over genuine engagement with the relevant events, as the specific facts at issue were sometimes reduced to pretexts for targeting individuals for imprisonment.

It has been noted that criminal proceedings can function as a form of punishment in and of themselves, significantly impacting the social standing of the accused, sometimes irreversibly. Traditionally, such consequences have been regarded as incidental, resulting from the stigmatising effects inherent in criminal prosecution, rather than as deliberate objectives. During the height of Operation Lava Jato, however, criminal procedure became central to sociopolitical debates, with its aims sometimes being influenced by animosity towards groups identified as enemies. Consequently, this development contributed to heightened political polarisation, promoting a binary mode of reasoning within society. Rather than serving as a principled procedural safeguard against public hostility, criminal proceedings have, in some cases, delineated subjective boundaries that reinforced division, thereby challenging the normative framework necessary for a criminal justice system grounded in respect for human rights.

In Brazil, prejudice proliferated during periods marked by ontological insecurity and relative deprivation. Discontent is frequently channelled towards those advocating for the expansion of citizenship—groups whose objectives are legitimate, yet who are often viewed as recipients of misapplied social and identity-based public policies (Young 2002). When strategically influenced, this discontent evolved into opposition from privileged sectors against Black, feminist, and LGBTQ movements. Such dynamics manifested both directly towards these groups and towards political allies, generating punitive attitudes and facilitating the politicisation of criminal justice proceedings. The penal system played a significant role in this process, as seen in the phenomenon of lawfare: targeted outrage regarding corruption—exemplified by Operation Lava Jato's actions against the left, particularly Lula—serves as a key context for understanding these developments.

The rise of authoritarianism in peripheral late modernity profoundly impacted the cultural dimensions of criminal procedure, revealing how criminal justice is shaped by—and shapes—social narratives. As authoritarian practices encroached upon democratic institutions, criminal justice was increasingly wielded by Operation Lava Jato not merely as a mechanism for adjudication, but as a tool for constructing and disseminating meaning. The interplay between legal frameworks, public opinion, and mediated representations underscores the transformation of criminal procedure into a site of both symbolic production and contestation.

Within this context, criminal procedure came to be influenced by punitive expectations, which emerged not only from acts of violence but also from the sensationalist depiction of crime as a commodity in societies with high crime rates. When these punitive expectations were transformed into symbolic capital, they served to legitimise the judiciary's perceived role as a social avenger, reflecting societal demands for prioritising certain rights over others. This phenomenon occurred at both individual and institutional levels: the discourse affected the perspectives of judges who were influenced by paradigms such as those established by Sérgio Moro, and it was echoed by Supreme Federal Court justices during the most prominent periods of Operation Lava Jato, particularly between 2014 and 2018.

Understanding criminal procedure as a cultural phenomenon involves recognising it as a dynamic space where social control and resistance intersect. It is essential to appreciate that criminal procedure operates within a permeable and evolving context, continuously subject to change, adaptation, and contestation. This space is historically shaped and reshaped, functioning as an authoritative domain maintained through rhetorical discourse that often obscures its inherent potential for violence. Criminal justice remains vulnerable to punitive influences and has, particularly in recent history, been reframed as a pivotal mechanism in national reform efforts, driven by agents and institutions pursuing what they interpreted as the nation's salvation.

Contemporary Brazilian criminal procedure progressively adopted elements of coercion, compliance, and negotiation, particularly due to the uncritical integration of plea bargaining from common law systems. This shift has, in certain respects, reframed criminal prosecution as an issue of public interest and undermined human rights, introducing considerable challenges to procedural protections.

Currently, a comprehensive understanding of criminal procedure necessitates consideration of these aspects; otherwise, the analysis risks remaining abstract and disconnected from broader interpretive frameworks. Operation Lava Jato both demonised the accused and dramatised the proceedings, shaping public perception through a constructed account that may be critically described as fictional: the focus extended beyond alleged actions to include the capacity of individuals or behaviours to reinforce the overarching narrative of corruption.

The narrative in question was commercialised in various evident ways. An industry developed around it, generating profits from ghostwritten biographies of judges and prosecutors as well as numerous films and series. The individuals at the centre also leveraged their institutionally established positions to command substantial fees for speaking engagements. As a result, contemporary criminal procedure became an integral aspect of public life, often followed by audiences as though it were both a reality show and a continuing series.

During this period, criminal procedure began to function as a mediated event disseminated by the media, serving as a source of entertainment, consumption, and information as well as misinformation. This approach proved effective for certain forms of social control, integrating into the logic of global capitalism and paralleling other mechanisms that reframe individuals as consumers and emotions as commodities (Hayward and Ferrell 2012). This form of cultural capitalism, emphasising the manipulation of meaning and visual appeal, commodifies all aspects of society and shapes individual subjectivities towards market-oriented conformity (Hayward and Ferrell 2012). As power is increasingly exercised through symbolic and mediated representations, debates over image, meaning, and cultural interpretation become central to contemporary social negotiation (Hayward and Ferrell 2012). The ideology disseminated and amplified by mainstream media played a significant role in what is described as the mass impoverishment of subjectivity (Casara 2017).

Nonetheless, opportunities for subversion remained. Public spaces of resistance provided forums where meanings were contested, potentially redirecting processes of symbolic subjection and offering alternative discourses on crime and justice that challenge official narratives (Hayward and Ferrell 2012). For example, in Brazil, numerous academics have contributed to collaborative works addressing and critiquing the authoritarian developments following the 2016 *coup d'état* (Proner et al. 2016) and the conviction of Lula (Proner et al. 2017).

Participants often remarked that Lava Jato should continue indefinitely, a statement suggesting a timelessness reminiscent of fairy tales and aligning with the operation's vague spatial and temporal boundaries, as was demonstrated by the broad jurisdiction exercised by Sérgio Moro. Although Lava Jato has concluded and its unlawful actions have come to light—most notably Moro's lack of impartiality—leading to the annulment of Lula's initial conviction—the impact was significant. Its authoritarian legacy endures, having permanently influenced the standards deemed acceptable within Brazilian criminal procedure.

The enduring influence of Lava Jato and its transformation of criminal procedure has not only shaped institutional practices but has also affected the everyday experience and perception of justice in Brazil. This legacy is observed in the ongoing debates about the legitimacy and fairness of judicial processes, the persistent tension between authoritarian impulses and democratic ideals, and the challenge of restoring public trust in the legal system. The cultural and symbolic dimensions of criminal justice continue to be contested, as new movements and voices seek to redefine the terms of engagement and imagine alternative futures for law and society. In this climate, the role of media, public discourse, and collective memory remains pivotal, underscoring the importance of critical reflection and advocacy for procedural safeguards that protect human rights and promote genuine accountability.

Given the diminishing constraints on the exercise of authoritarian power (Casara 2017), the development of a counter-discourse that considers criminal justice from a democratic perspective has become increasingly important. Accordingly, this study seeks to foster critical examination and reveal the various ways in which interpretations of legal reality are constructed. Re-envisioning criminal justice calls for both a thoughtful commitment and a willingness to challenge established narratives and the prevailing inquisitorial, positivist and rationalist frameworks focused on truth-seeking.

However, even with strict adherence to the framework proposed here, there are inherent limitations to addressing the hallucinatory nature of evidence. This becomes particularly apparent when examining issues related to perception, memory, and testimony, as will be discussed further below.

Excursus: The Complex Interweaving of Perception, Memory, and Testimony

Contrary to common assumptions, human sensory perception offers only a limited understanding of the surrounding environment. In other words, reality is not inherently comprehensible to the observer, even through direct observation. As Merleau-Ponty observes, noting that the eye lacks the necessary conditions to perceive the world and a painting lacks the requisite means to represent it, "after all, the world is around me, not in front of me" (Merleau-Ponty 1969: 76). According to the author,

> The thought of vision operates according to a programme and a law it did not set for itself; it is not in possession of its own premises; it is not a thought wholly present, wholly actual; at its centre there is a mystery of passivity. This, then, is the situation: everything that is said and thought about vision makes it a thought. (Merleau-Ponty 1969: 69)

According to Carnelutti, "to observe reality is something we cannot do, unfortunately, except to a very limited extent. Our field of vision is insuperably narrow. However much we try to broaden it, we are always in the position of someone looking at a house through the keyhole" (Carnelutti 2004: 58). In a classic passage, the author offers the following reflection:

> Beautiful word! *Aliquid jacet ob.* Something lies ahead. The object refers to the subject; and we have already had occasion to see that, for this reason, man deserves the name of subject as long as he is observing. What, then, is it that lies ahead? The world, one might answer. True. But the world is too vast to be seen in its entirety. Human senses are like the windows of a house, through which the whole world cannot enter. The scene presented before the window: that is the object. (Carnelutti 2001: 36–37)

In this excerpt, Carnelutti highlights the inherent limitations of the subject-object framework, which are frequently disregarded. Human beings, constrained in their cognitive capacities, are unable to fully comprehend the vastness of reality, perceiving only isolated segments rather than the entirety. The assembly of these parts continually results in new components, rendering the complete whole unattainable. This observation indicates that the concepts of "whole" and "part" point towards a redefinition of our ability to apprehend reality. According to Peter Gay,

> Perception is largely projective and motivation is decisive for the outcomes. Every perception is an interpretation. The simplest observation is already a theory. Pressures from the social context or cultural assumptions, contingencies of time, space, and kinship create the mental frameworks that act as distorting lenses. To observe and to reflect is, at the same time, to act. (Gay 1990: 175)

The concept that perception inherently entails an element of projection is especially insightful, as it underscores the limitations associated with understanding reality. Merleau-Ponty notably refers to this as a remarkable revelation—one long recognised by painters—that

> there are no visible lines in themselves, that neither the outline of the apple nor the boundary of the field and meadow is here or there, that they are always on this side or that of the point from which one looks, always between or behind what is being gazed at, indicated, implied, and even most imperiously demanded by things, without themselves being things. (Merleau-Ponty 1969: 91)

It is essential to re-evaluate the degree to which reality resists the limitations of human sensory perception. As Lopes Jr., referencing Merleau-Ponty's scholarship, observes,

> man's verticality prevents him from knowing totality, for "the world is around man and not in front of him". There is a silent historicity, advancing through the labyrinth by detours, transgressions, usurpation, and sudden pressures, which prevent the painter (and witness) from portraying [...] this does not mean [...] that the painter does not know what he wants, but rather that he falls short of the goals and means... due to the impossibility of apprehending the whole. (Lopes Jr 2005: 263)

Gadamer clarifies that his assertion, "every being that can be understood is language", signals the view that "what is, can never be fully understood" (Gadamer 1992: 323). Language thus establishes an inherent limitation; it serves as the principal medium through which the world is accessed and mediates all consciousness and knowledge. Consequently, our encounter with the world is fundamentally shaped by linguistic processes, meaning that "given" reality cannot be separated from its interpretation (Gadamer 1992: 327). According to Gadamer, "The truth is that we are as intimately embedded in language as in the world" (Gadamer 1992: 148), indicating that human existence is intrinsically situated within language.

Certeau observes that the scope and substance of reality are determined solely through discourse (Certeau 1982: 32). Furthermore, Gauer's analysis of the relationship between time and speed illustrates how velocity inhibits the stabilisation of images, causing them to disperse as a result of its fluid nature (Gauer 1998: 26). According to Gauer and Timm de Souza, the accelerated world, marked by its illusions, represents only a limited perspective of visible phenomena: it projects an apparent completeness that is, in fact, partial and contingent upon the observer's standpoint (Gauer and Souza 2004: xi). Consequently, speed obscures the conditions necessary for clear visibility.

According to Merleau-Ponty, "it is true that vision depends on movement. One only sees what one looks at" (Merleau-Ponty 1969: 33). He posits that "vision is not a certain mode of thought or of presence to oneself: it is the means by which I am given to be absent from myself" (Merleau-Ponty 1969: 99), further stating that "it is characteristic of the visible to have a lining of the invisible in the strict sense, which it renders present as a certain absence" (Merleau-Ponty 1969: 103).

These perspectives underscore the importance of recognising the inherent limitations and imperfections within human perception, necessitating a revaluation of the concept of *flagrante delicto*.

Flagrante delicto, defined as an expression of apparent evidence, is rooted in its inherently hallucinatory quality and therefore requires critical scrutiny. As Lopes Jr. observes, situations where an individual is found committing an offence or immediately thereafter are described as instances of visibility—a visual certainty derived from direct observation. Such certainty may lead to questions about the necessity of due process and whether *flagrante delicto* justifies immediate adjudication or even imprisonment (Lopes Jr 2010: 91).

However, the situation is often complex, and visual certainty may remain elusive due to perceptual limitations, particularly in incidents involving violence. During traumatic events where a firearm is present and a threat is perceived, victims or witnesses frequently concentrate their attention on the weapon itself rather than the assailant's features. This phenomenon poses considerable difficulties in ensuring the accuracy of later identification of the perpetrator.

Considering these arguments, it is clear that *flagrante delicto* should not be deemed sufficient on its own; the evidence obtained in such circumstances may be unreliable and requires careful assessment in accordance with established procedural legal standards.

While perception already poses significant challenges, memory introduces an additional layer of complexity. Ricoeur (2003: 304) asserts that the act of remembering entails both an ambition and a claim—the aim to provide an accurate representation of the past. Memory is characterised by the desire to retrieve a perception from a bygone moment. However, as previously discussed, the inherent limitations of perception mean that reality is seldom entirely accessible or intelligible to the observer, particularly when interpreting the significance of events within the continuum of life. As Marrou observes,

> When it was present, that past was like the present we are living in now—something dusty, confused, multifaceted, unintelligible: a dense web of causes and effects, an infinitely complex field of forces, which human consciousness, whether as actor or witness, is necessarily incapable of grasping in its authentic reality (there is no privileged vantage point—at least not on this Earth). (Marrou 1978: 39)

Given these constraints, one must consider how to adequately transpose past observations into accounts that faithfully represent the original event. Human limitations in apprehending reality become evident not only in direct observation but are further amplified when recollection relies on memory, introducing a complex array of conceptual challenges.

Lopes Jr. observes that narratives about the past depend on the narrator's memory, with any omissions often supplemented by other experiences—even those pertaining to other events (Lopes Jr 2005: 263). Cordero adds that memories deteriorate physiologically and once reactivated by a stimulus, are inevitably transformed; each act of reconstruction both recovers and reshapes recollections according to contemporary expectations (Cordero 2000: 60). Similarly, Cunha Martins asserts, "we have concrete proof that whenever we recall a given object, face, or scene, what emerges is not an exact reproduction but rather an interpretation—a new version reconstructed from the original" (Martins 2004). Finally, Catroga characterises memory as an inherently selective process of reconstruction:

> It can never be a mere *record*, for it is an *affective representation*, or rather a *re-presentation*, constructed from the present and within the three-dimensional tension of time. Here, the future is linked to the past by a *totalising* and *teleological* thread. That is, every recollection tends to be objectified in a coherent narrative which, in retrospect, domesticates the random, the accidental, the perverse effects of the real-past, when it was present, acting as if, along the way, there were no black holes left by forgetting. In a certain sense, it is a prediction in reverse. (Catroga 2001: 46)

Substantial theoretical attention has been devoted to the study of memory, with influential contributions from thinkers such as Bergson, Proust, Husserl, Ricoeur, and Halbwachs. Notably, Halbwachs' framework posits the absence of purely individual memory, suggesting instead that all recollections are fundamentally social constructs (Halbwachs 1990). Halbwachs' perspective adds another layer that significantly enhances the complexities inherent in testimony. He maintains that even seemingly personal memories are intrinsically linked to group contexts. While individuals retain recollections personally, they are continually engaged with society, its groups, and institutions. Consequently, memories emerge within these relational spheres, as individual remembrance is intertwined with the collective memories of the various groups to which one belongs.

From this standpoint, what is typically regarded as individual memory is deeply influenced by the memories of those within our social environment. Even in the absence of others, both our recollections and our interpretation of our surroundings are shaped by an intricate network of shared experiences, which we may perceive as a singular, personal construct. In essence, memory involves reconstructing the past through the lens of current social frameworks (Seixas 2002: 97). Memory attains authenticity only to the extent that it is anchored in such frameworks, which endow recollection with legitimacy, making it inherently dependent on external factors (Seixas 2002: 100).

According to Halbwachs, it is society that remembers—recollections are mediated by present ideas and representations provided by *cadres sociaux*. Consequently, "individuals only remember their pasts to the extent that they position themselves from the perspective of one or more currents of collective thought" (Santos 2003: 35). The group's collective memories—the "affective community"—nourish individual recollections. It is uncommon, in Halbwachs' analysis, for individuals to recall outside these frames of reference, underscoring the pivotal role of the social context in both memory construction and recollection. For Halbwachs, memory does not equate to reliving the past; rather, it entails its reconstruction based on external influences (Seixas 2002: 102). Thus, the past is continually reconstituted in the present, and this reconstructed version is the only past that meaningfully "exists". The sole margin for individual agency lies in one's ability to adopt the perspectives of various groups, which, according to Halbwachs, accounts for the so-called "individual" memories that are nonetheless defined by social structures.

Halbwachs' sociological perspective on memory is closely connected to the influence of mass media in shaping collective memory in contemporary society—a role of substantial importance. Gil observes that media language often diverges from evidentiary truth, focusing instead on persuasion through emotive and stimulating content, achieved by rhetoric in its less favourable sense (Martins and Gil 2002: 24).

However, the issue extends well beyond this. Television programming, cinema, media coverage, and social media narratives have significant implications for testimonial evidence and may even blur the line between fiction and reality. The distinction between realistic and fictional scenarios is fading (Appadurai 1996: 35). The interplay between actual events and their media representations is reciprocal, rendering the boundary between virtual and real experiences increasingly ambiguous (Hayward and Young 2012). Given the pervasive influence of media and technology in daily life, it is becoming progressively challenging to distinguish "crime" from "images of crime". Criminal acts, their portrayals, and perceptions are in constant interaction and mutually shape one another. If the term "real" is understood to encompass tangible consequences and effects, then contemporary crime culture is equally as substantive as crime itself; the two phenomena may be converging (Hayward and Young 2012).

Mediated representations play a significant role in shaping public understanding and may also impact witness behaviour, as individuals can unconsciously align themselves with perceived societal expectations regarding punishment. The interaction between media portrayals and witness testimony carries considerable implications, including the possibility that media spectacle could influence statements made by witnesses. Scholars have expressed concern over a contemporary form of colonialism perpetuated by mass culture disseminated through various media platforms. For instance, Octavio Paz criticises television and radio for exacerbating the divide between speaker and audience.

> the true foundation of all democracy and authentic socialism is, or should be, conversation: people face to face. Such media reinforce non-communication: they distort interlocutors, magnify authority, make it inaccessible—a divinity that speaks but does not listen—and thus deprive us of the right and pleasure of reply. They suppress dialogue. (Paz 1993: 81)

Clarification, which is fundamental in democratic debate, is often overshadowed by the notion that information has become a commodified product. This shift enables sensationalist marketing practices that may distort events to attract uninterested audiences, driven by economic and political motives (Lopes Jr 2005: 188). While a free press is indispensable within a democratic system, its influence can sometimes exceed appropriate boundaries, resulting in what Ramonet describes as the "tyranny of communication" (Ramonet 2001). Lopes Jr. acknowledges the historical contribution of the press to democracy but argues that it should now operate under defined democratic constraints, given its current state of "super-freedom", which approaches media domination (Lopes Jr 2005: 191). Within this framework, the subjective treatment of criminal cases by the media—which often achieve national significance—can create symbolic anticipatory convictions, depriving defendants of the possibility of a fair trial by constructing their guilt discursively in an almost irreversible manner. The potential for witnesses to unconsciously align with these constructed narratives poses significant risks. As Gil notes, "the media are, certainly, outside the realm of proof. Outrageously so" (Martins and Gil 2002: 24).

Accordingly, it may be tentatively concluded that witness testimony does not constitute a straightforward replication of past events and cannot be likened to the replication of results under controlled scientific conditions typical of the natural sciences. Consequently, this raises important questions regarding the veracity of testimonial evidence.

Leone (1963) defines testimony as a statement concerning a specific fact pertinent to the proceedings, provided by an individual who is not a party to the matter. However, this definition does not fully capture the complexity of testimony. As Gil observes, testimony embodies "the idea that it substitutes for, or reveals without distortion, the direct experience of the facts, as if these were reporting themselves" (Martins and Gil 2002: 26).

The term *witness* originates from the Latin *superstes*, denoting an individual who has undergone an event and is thereby qualified to provide testimony regarding it. This concept implies authority established through direct presence: "I saw, I was present, I bore witness". However, it remains necessary to consider whether this condition alone fulfils the requirement of accurately representing past events. Based on the foregoing discussion, it appears that this criterion may not be sufficient.

A thorough evaluation of testimony requires consideration of several factors: the witness's capacity to perceive events; whether observational conditions support the credibility of their statements; the extent to which the circumstances enabled accurate retention of observations; the witness's competence, based on faculties and experience, not only to perceive but also to organise complex information; potential influences on perception and memory, such as suggestion or unconscious bias; and the witness's genuine intention to provide truthful statements (Döhring 1986: 93).

Beyond the initial assessment, testimony serves as a transitional structure linking memory to the cognitive framework of legal proceedings. Testimony necessitates careful safeguards because, as previously noted, sensory perception offers only a limited grasp of reality. As Cordero observes, rules governing testimony assume that the sensory apparatus captures events objectively and that memory preserves them much like recorded images or sounds. However, Cordero critiques these assumptions as overly simplistic; from the standpoint of internal psychological processes, recollection appears intricate and unpredictable, with little objective content remaining upon analysis. Cordero further highlights that sensory channels are inherently selective due to the perceptual system's limited capacity. When confronted with multiple stimuli at once, individuals perceive what aligns with their sensory adaptation, heavily influenced by their emotional state. Sensory data, therefore, are not direct perceptions but are subjected to an automatic and unconscious classification process (Cordero 2000: 59–60).

A pertinent question arises regarding the pursuit of truth through the inherently constrained perceptions of past events, which are accessible only via the memories recounted by witnesses. Crime exists within the realm of history, and the knowledge of the past sometimes depends entirely on the recollections of witnesses. In instances where memory is incomplete, the witness employs imagination or creative faculties to supplement these gaps, drawing upon authentic experiences derived from other events. Imagination thus influences memory by incorporating additional associations. This concept can be illustrated by the classic example of a cube: while only two or three faces are visible simultaneously, the complete representation of all six faces exists solely in the mind's eye. Therefore, imagination does not simply reproduce images but rather alters the practical representations provided by perception (Lopes Jr 2005: 263).

Reconstructing historical events poses a considerable challenge, as testimony frequently represents the most reliable resource available for determining whether an incident occurred. In the absence of tangible evidence to guide the inquiry, the confrontation of testimonies becomes crucial for establishing facts. As Aragoneses Alonso observes, with the exception of certain offences, documentary evidence typically holds limited significance in criminal proceedings (Alonso 1986: 302). Testimonial evidence remains essential, particularly since it is often the sole form of evidence provided by the accused or third parties (Alonso 1986: 303). Consequently, its role in criminal proceedings is substantial. It has been noted that, whereas civil proceedings prioritise documentary evidence, criminal proceedings rely heavily upon testimony (Alonso 1986: 302). However, this reliance also underscores the potential risks associated with placing undue trust in a restricted form of cognition, which may inadvertently jeopardise the interests of the accused—especially if witnesses feel compelled to meet perceived expectations.

Historians recognise the complexities inherent in interpreting testimony. As Hartog notes, the historian transcends the role of witness and can only assume the historian's perspective by establishing critical distance from any witness, including themselves (Hartog 2001: 11). In this context, Bloch's observation is instructive: testimonies are manifestations of memory, and thus subject to perceptual errors that may be compounded by the mutable nature of recollection—what one jurist previously described as "fertile" memory (Bloch 2001: 103). Hobsbawm further elaborates that memory serves less as an objective recorder and more as a selective filter, with selection itself remaining highly variable (Hobsbawm 1998: 221). Consequently, even direct comparison of testimonies does not resolve the critical challenge: determining reliability in the absence of corroborating evidence (Hobsbawm 1998: 221). Bloch addresses the scenario of conflicting accounts, suggesting that when discrepancies arise, one account must be discredited in accordance with the principle of contradiction, which precludes the coexistence of mutually exclusive events (Bloch 2001: 110). While this approach may benefit historical inquiry, it does not eliminate the necessity for the historian to engage actively with contradiction; moreover, the presence of contradiction alone does not guarantee the veracity of either account, as both could be independently erroneous. Bloch further asserts that evaluating the credibility, falsehood, or error within each testimony leads to judgements that may seem almost conclusive but are inevitably characterised by significant uncertainty in different contexts (Bloch 2001: 110). Ultimately, testimony should be viewed as an inherently imperfect and constrained account of actual events. This limitation poses a significant challenge to epistemological frameworks that heavily rely on witness statements.

Direct testimony constitutes a significantly more pivotal component in judicial proceedings than in historical analysis, as evidentiary activity frequently relies solely on testimonial accounts. Nevertheless, there exists a marked disparity between one's lived experience and the capacity to articulate it within testimony, a gap influenced notably by the individual's perspective. As Heller observes, in contrast to works of art, which are intentionally created as meaningful objects and therefore serve as carriers of meaning, historical events derive their significance, or lack thereof, from the perspectives of the various individuals involved. The same event might manifest as the fulfilment of one individual's will while appearing as an inexplicable occurrence to another; it can also be interpreted as the outcome of multiple competing intentions, ultimately resulting in an objective that is not attributable to any single person (Heller 1993: 199).

Furthermore, a witness's belief in the truth of their statement does not necessarily guarantee its accuracy. Bloch asserts, "it remains evident that many witnesses, despite acting in good faith, are mistaken. Consequently, historians should utilise insights from recent developments in the psychology of testimony, which has emerged as a valuable discipline" (Bloch 2001: 102–103). Similarly, Aragoneses Alonso underscores the inherent uncertainty of testimonial evidence by emphasising that psychological factors introduce risks of fallibility. The author refers to the complex mental processes involved in providing testimony, thereby reinforcing earlier observations on this subject:

(a) The sensory perception of things or events, which varies according to individuals or the conditions in which they find themselves.
(b) Memory, a complex process that requires perfect coordination of a variety of circumstances for the witness to truly respond with the truth in its strict sense, not to mention the possibility of its voluntary alteration.
(c) The statement or communication of recollections to the authority responsible for collecting them, as a final assessment intended to inform the judge (Alonso 1986: 303).

When addressing procedural matters, a judge is presented with narrative accounts from the parties regarding past events. The judge must determine, using various methods such as witness statements, which version is more plausible and offers a more reliable depiction of what transpired. Frequently, the judge encounters conflicting testimonies, differing assertions concerning the same facts, and expert evidence that may be ambiguous or contradictory. In such cases, it is incumbent upon the judge to evaluate the credibility of each witness in order to assign appropriate evidentiary value. Within this context of uncertainty, even when a witness appears credible and their testimony seems truthful, it remains necessary to compare these statements with those provided by other witnesses to form an informed understanding of the facts (Mora 2006: 83). This requirement does not imply that the judge should assume the role of examiner; rather, as has been recently highlighted, the judicial function is primarily receptive. The judge should only intervene directly to clarify ambiguities in testimony. The responsibility for producing evidence must rest exclusively with the parties, and in a democratic criminal proceeding, it is the prosecution and defence who are tasked with questioning.

Paul Ricoeur identifies testimony as inherently characterised by a continual tension regarding its credibility. This dynamic juxtaposes two conditions: trust and suspicion. Testimony relies on the concept of a guarantee, which is encapsulated in the declaration "I was there". Ricoeur explains that this assurance emerges through a function of self-designation—specifically, the use of the first person singular, the verb's past tense, and the reference to a location in contrast to the present ("there" in relation to "here") (Ricoeur 2003: 214). Testimony serves to affirm, before an audience, the reality of an event observed by the witness, who may have participated as an agent or victim but, during the act of testifying, occupies the position of a third party relative to the principal actors involved.

According to Ricoeur, "this dialogical structure of testimony immediately highlights its fiduciary dimension: the witness asks to be believed. He does not merely say: 'I was there'; he adds: 'believe me'" (Ricoeur 2003: 214). Cordero further observes that the narrator anticipates being trusted, asserting that the content holds significance only to the extent that the audience accepts it as credible, with outcomes influenced by factors related to emotional states (Cordero 2000: 4). For the author, persuasion is ultimately achieved through an act of faith.

Roxin asserts that every witness has a duty to convey the truth (Roxin 2003: 222). However, aside from an ethical perspective, the matter of accurately representing the truth is not necessarily pertinent for the witness. Serving as a witness entails more than merely observing an event; it involves declaring that observation and agreeing to report the experience in consistent terms. Consequently, both the veracity of the event and the credibility of the witness are subject to evaluation. Testimony, therefore, is accepted on the basis of belief rather than certification. According to Ricoeur, the focus regarding testimony transitions from the adequacy of the statement relative to what transpired, towards the fiduciary relationship and the credibility of the testimony. Testimony resides in the realm of trustworthiness and reliability, rather than in that of definitive proof or established fact. As Carnelutti notes, witnesses in criminal proceedings are essential, yet their role carries significant risks. It is crucial not merely to have witnesses, but to ensure their testimony is truthful. The court's responsibility is twofold: to identify honest witnesses and to guarantee the accuracy of their statements (Carnelutti 2004: 292).

Therefore, the issue should be examined through the lens of the trust/suspicion dichotomy. As Ricoeur (2003: 212) observes, suspicion operates through a series of stages beginning with the perception of an event, followed by its retention in memory, and culminating in its narration and restitution. Similarly, Döhring (1986: 89) notes that scepticism is essential when evaluating a witness's account. According to Cordero, this process amplifies potential risks, as there is no standardised method for determining the credibility of witnesses. Cordero argues that while a witness may claim to recount facts based on personal perception, they simultaneously reference their own actions. For those who consider neuropsychic factors, the objectivity required by evidentiary rules appears unattainable; perceptions are shaped by individual experiences and memories, which can be especially variable when recollection is prompted rather than spontaneous, as often occurs in testimony. Once articulated, these mental representations are presented as factual statements. This complex cognitive and semantic process, susceptible to numerous variations, underscores the challenges in fully trusting testimonial evidence (Cordero 2000: 55).

The potential for suspicion facilitates adversarial proceedings, where differing testimonies can be directly compared. Testimony inherently involves the acceptance of scrutiny, which may lead to contradictions or confrontations. A testimony must be capable of repetition and consistency in the presence of doubt. Nevertheless, as noted by Badaró, confrontation seldom produces the desired outcome. If an individual has acted in bad faith and intentionally provided false information, it is improbable that such confrontation will result in a changed narrative (Badaró 2008: 256).

According to Ricoeur, testimony relies fundamentally on trust in another's word, thereby establishing it as an institution. This climate of trust may be compromised when corrupt political structures foster an environment of surveillance and denunciation, diminishing confidence in linguistic exchanges (Ricoeur 2003: 218). Extending beyond Ricoeur's analysis, it is pertinent to examine whether the media also contributes to undermining the foundational conditions for testimony. There is support for this notion; for instance, excessive publicity and the stigmatisation of accused individuals are notable examples (Lopes Jr 2005: 186). Consequently, testimony faces a crisis of belief, prompting consideration of its dynamics from a perspective grounded in suspicion.

Further complications arise from limited perception and the inherent value judgements within any assessment of actions, underscoring the complexities involved in relying on testimony. It follows that assertions regarding the possibility of attaining objective truth about past events through testimony are questionable, as access typically occurs via statements rather than direct evidence. Ibañez emphasises the emotional factors that influence witnesses, third parties who possess moral interests in trial subjects. He notes that these impressions are generally formed spontaneously throughout life, often without the critical detachment characteristic of scientific inquiry, where objectivity is actively pursued (Ibáñez 2005: 51). As Chiovenda observes, a witness is an individual who is separate from the parties involved in the proceedings and is called to provide the judge with their personal observations of events pertinent to the case. This testimony may encompass both the immediate impact those events, witnessed firsthand, had on the witness's senses, as well as any logical conclusions they formed based on those impressions. In all instances, the observations offered by the witness are presented as subjective facts—unique to the individual—and are not intended to represent objective conclusions regarding the consequences of certain facts, which remains the distinct responsibility of the expert (Chiovenda 1998: 131).

Even when adopting an accusatory epistemological framework that allows for the contestation of claims, the findings of such inquiries do not necessarily imply that the truth is readily or unequivocally obtainable through witness testimony. The account provided by a witness offers only indirect access to past events, constrained by the limitations of individual perception and memory; as previously noted, all perception entails some degree of projection and, consequently, illusion—and memory not merely reconstructs it also reinvents past events. As Carnelutti highlights, legal professionals often categorise witnesses with documents under the umbrella of evidence, overlooking the fact that, unlike documents, witnesses are individuals possessing unique physical and psychological characteristics, personal interests and vulnerabilities, varying memories and lapses, disparate levels of knowledge and education, as well as courage or apprehension. These individuals are placed in challenging and sometimes precarious positions during proceedings, removed from their daily activities, subjected to interrogation, and potentially regarded with suspicion (Carnelutti 1965: 77).

In this context, the narrator's subjectivity necessitates an examination of intimacy, which further complicates inquiries into the attainability of truth through narrative assertions. Employing Bachelard's imagery proves valuable in this regard. As Bachelard asserts, there exists a genuine intelligence inherent to the concept of hiding place (Bachelard 1960: 72). This notion aligns with the interplay of trust and suspicion described by Ricoeur. Certain memories are so embedded within the sphere of intimacy that effective communication becomes unattainable. According to Bachelard, the intimate dimension consists of chests. Some, as previously mentioned, are sealed so thoroughly that opening them is impossible, whereas others allow for at least partial access. In this context, the concept of trust becomes apparent: upon opening, the safe implicitly requests belief. Nonetheless, such sincerity cannot be assumed, as a dialectic persists between the exterior and interior. It is owing to this dialectic that Bachelard references the following image: at the moment the safe is opened, all dialectical opposition ceases. The distinction between the interior and exterior is immediately removed; everything appears renewed, unfamiliar, and unexpected. External factors lose their significance. Notably, as a final paradox, spatial dimensions are rendered irrelevant, since the act introduces a new dimension—that of intimacy (Bachelard 1960: 75).

This issue is of considerable importance, as the opening of the intimate dimension results in a valorisation of the contents by the container (Bachelard 1960: 75). As Bachelard notes, "we never reach the bottom of the safe. How better to express the infinity of the intimate dimension?"

(Bachelard 1960: 75). Thus, a closed safe contains more than an open one; the intimate dimension remains fundamentally inscrutable.

It is evident that the intimate dimension encompasses a richness of experience beyond the capacity of any single testimony to fully capture. Furthermore, even an extensive collection of testimonies does not equate to a comprehensive account of an event. A narrative fragment, when detached from its human context, represents only an incomplete depiction of lived reality, distinct from the actual moment itself. As Ricoeur observes, "The stories of lives are so entangled with one another that the narrative each person gives or receives of their own life becomes a segment of those other narratives which are the narratives of others" (Ricoeur 1995: 31). As highlighted earlier, testimony may be credible and trustworthy, but this remains insufficient for meeting the probatory standards required for judicial conviction. According to Lopes Jr., for procedural truth to be realised, evidence must undergo rigorous scrutiny within the legal proceeding, persisting only if it demonstrates that it is not illusory, fabricated, or hallucinatory. Consequently, criminal procedure must attain a high standard of correcting for the potential hallucinations intrinsic to evidentiary material (Lopes Jr 2005: 270).

Given this objective, testimony presents a significant challenge. Evaluating the reliability of testimonies remains inherently subjective, exceeding the corrective scope of adversarial procedures. Ultimately, belief in testimony depends on trust, without concrete reference points comparable to those provided by physical traces. The term *trace* is only marginally applicable to testimony. Brazilian criminal procedure relies heavily on witness statements; a greater emphasis on technical evidence derived from analytical rigour would foster a stronger connection with past events, aligning better with the requirements of an epistemology of pastness. However, this ideal is not reflected in current practice.

In this regard, I once again affirm my complete divergence from Taruffo's perspective. Taruffo asserts that interviewing individuals familiar with the facts represents an epistemologically sound approach for establishing factual truth, necessitating the judge's active involvement in truth-seeking (Taruffo 2010: 178). Ultimately, Taruffo aligns with the modern ideal of rationality, positing that a rational actor who adopts an active role in pursuit of the truth can achieve it—a stance that appears questionable, as procedural uncertainty cannot be resolved solely through such efforts, and may indeed result in erroneous convictions. The judge is not—and should not be—akin to a detective depicted in crime fiction, despite the persistence of this image in Western cultural imagination.

Accordingly, I consider it both necessary and timely to re-examine the judge's role, an issue that will be addressed extensively in the following chapter. However, prior to that discussion, it is essential to first present several reflections on the concept of truth-seeking and the complex discursive strategies that support it.

The Myth of the Search for Truth

Engaging with the concept of myth involves delving into a topic that has prompted extensive scientific debate for decades, often without definitive resolution. Certain theoretical schools within anthropology even question the validity of a distinct category that aligns with the commonly accepted notion of myth.

A comprehensive examination of these discussions falls beyond the scope of this text and would necessitate a dedicated study. Nevertheless, it remains beneficial to regard the ideology of the "search for truth" as a form of mythic discourse within the legal domain.

This understanding enables contemporary judicial practices to be contextualised within wider cultural frameworks, acknowledging that truth-seeking is influenced by ritualistic and symbolic factors, even in systems considered rational. By understanding the search for truth accordingly—as an exercise of power—, one can better analyse how these mythic elements shape the perception and administration of justice, frequently concealing underlying uncertainties and ideological influences in judicial processes.

Although inquisitorial and positivist epistemologies may not attain absolute truth, the pursuit of this ideal continues to yield significant effects. Rationalism's reinvention of truth-seeking can lead to the objectification of the accused during criminal proceedings. Therefore, it is essential to analyse how myth theory's components might inform the foundations of truth-seeking and assess their contribution to understanding the persistent nature of this ideology.

Accordingly, the primary focus is not on establishing coherence among various authors—particularly given the limited consensus on this topic—but rather on introducing arguments that favour a critical examination of the myth under consideration. The objective here is one of analysis and clarification, akin to the methodical deconstruction commonly associated with myth debunking.

The association between the dogma of truth-seeking and myth is supported by Paz, who asserts that "our myths have changed form and are now called political, technological, erotic utopias" (Paz 1993: 58). Consequently, myths transcend understandings attributed solely to tribal societies or those often disparagingly considered "primitive".

To further elucidate the mythic qualities inherent in the search for truth, it is crucial to recognise that legal discourse often adopts ritualistic forms which reinforce its authority and perpetuate its symbolic power. The invocation of truth as an ultimate objective serves not only to legitimate judicial practices, but also to mask the inherent limitations and uncertainties embedded within the legal process. This ritualisation imbues the proceedings with a sense of inevitability, encouraging participants to accept the outcomes as manifestations of a higher, almost sacred, order. In turn, such dynamics cultivate a climate in which the myth of truth operates as a stabilising force, shaping perceptions of justice and reinforcing the prevailing legal framework.

Eliade describes myth as an exemplary narrative that establishes human norms and procedures (Eliade 2002). The myth concerning the pursuit of truth, originating from Eymerich's inquisitorial systematisation, offers a definition and explanation of the foundational structure for criminal proceedings. It legitimises and justifies this framework to the point that any deviation from its primary objective—uncovering the truth—is categorised as heretical.

Eliade observes that myths consistently function as narratives with exemplary and instructional purposes, a principle that also extends to the myth surrounding the pursuit of truth (Eliade 2002). Myths establish behavioural models and provide justification for the authority of specific social groups; for instance, the myth of the judge's infallibility legitimises the judge's role in uncovering facts related to historical events. This perception is further supported by the rituals and ceremonies accompanying the exercise of jurisdiction, which impart a characteristically sacred quality to what is, in essence, a secular process (Thums 2006: 192). Indeed, myth is intrinsically linked to ritual. Here, ritual refers to a culturally embedded system of symbolic communication, consisting of organised and standardised sequences of words and actions, manifested in various forms and exhibiting different levels of conventionality, rigidity, unity, and repetition. Ritual practices and their embodiments—the rites—are dynamic and evolving, accommodating numerous adaptations over time.

To deepen this exploration, one must consider how myth and ritual intertwine within the legal sphere, creating a narrative that both legitimises and perpetuates judicial authority. The invocation of myth serves as a powerful tool to reinforce the perceived objectivity and inevitability of legal outcomes, thereby shielding judicial processes from scrutiny and fostering a sense of communal acceptance. This dynamic is further complicated by the ongoing evolution of mythic discourse, which adapts to changing societal values while retaining its core function of supporting established power structures. By critically examining these mechanisms, it becomes possible to reveal the underlying tensions between the ideals of truth-seeking and the realities of judicial practice, highlighting the importance of reimagining criminal justice.

Ricoeur asserts that "if one were to contrast *myth* and *ritual*, one could say that myth *expands* ordinary time (as well as space), whereas ritual *brings* mythical time closer to the profane sphere of life and action" (Ricoeur 1997: 181). Rituals position individuals within a sacred context of time and space, thereby imbuing their actions in everyday time and space with significance. According to Mauss, a ritual attains its significance only when its underlying meaning is understood—that is, the concepts and beliefs that have shaped and continue to inform its foundation. A myth can be fully explained by demonstrating its connections to particular movements, rituals, and the practices it dictates. Without association with specific cultic applications, myth possesses minimal substance; likewise, a ritual holds little importance if it does not embody certain established beliefs (Mauss 1979: 103–104).

Ritual and myth, therefore, operate in tandem to sustain the illusion of certainty within legal proceedings. The integration of ritualistic elements, such as ceremonial language and formal procedures, not only reinforces the authority vested in judicial figures but also obscures the constructed nature of legal truths. These practices foster an environment where the boundaries between the sacred and the secular are blurred, allowing the myth of truth to flourish and retain its persuasive influence over both participants and observers.

The significance of the judicial robe merits attention, as it has been largely discarded elsewhere but remains integral within the judiciary, as noted by Garapon (Garapon 1997: 73). The robe functions as a symbolic barrier and positions its wearer above ordinary status, facilitating a form of discursive authority while reinforcing the magistrate's elevated role relative to involved parties (Garapon 1997: 85). Additionally, it allows judges to separate their personal accountability from their judicial decisions, as the robe operates as a mask encapsulating the broader symbolism of judicial power (Garapon 1997: 86). In this context, it is not merely the individual who dons the garment; rather, the institution itself manifests through the attire. Judgement is thus rendered by an entity vested with a quasi-sacred status, which substantiates and legitimises the judge's authority.

The enduring interplay between myth and ritual within the legal domain underscores the profound influence these constructs exert on both the perception and administration of justice. By embedding mythic narratives and ritualistic practices at the heart of judicial proceedings, the legal system cultivates an atmosphere in which the pursuit of truth is elevated to a near-sacrosanct ideal. This elevation, however, frequently obscures the contingent and constructed nature of legal outcomes, rendering the process less susceptible to critical examination. As a result, participants and observers alike are inclined to accept verdicts and procedures as embodiments of an immutable order, rarely questioning the legitimacy or origins of such authority.

It is within this context that myth serves not merely as a narrative device but as an essential mechanism for legitimising and perpetuating institutional power. Through the careful orchestration of symbolic acts and ceremonial language, the judiciary reinforces its status and authority, ensuring the continued acceptance of its role within society. The myth of truth, therefore, operates as both a shield and a catalyst—protecting the institution from scrutiny while simultaneously defining the meaning of criminal justice. This dual function highlights the necessity of ongoing critical engagement with the myths underpinning criminal procedure, to favour a harm reduction programme.

Ultimately, recognising the mythic and ritualistic dimensions of legal discourse invites a more nuanced understanding of the complexities inherent in truth-seeking. It reveals how the invocation of myth and the performance of ritual not only shape the contours of criminal justice but also sustain the illusion of certainty that is so central to the perceived legitimacy of legal proceedings that potentially objectify the accused. By interrogating these dynamics, one can better appreciate the underlying tensions and contradictions that define the criminal justice system, paving the way for meaningful reform and the reimagining of its foundational principles.

As is characteristic of myths, the narrative surrounding the search for truth often obscures its own origins. Eliade notes that, although myths are created by humans, they take on an inherent quality that transcends their initial creation. Consequently, myths function within their unique temporality—often referred to as the time of "once upon a time…"—and intentionally conceal their beginnings while leveraging tradition to sustain their relevance.

The pursuit of truth is regarded as a fundamental principle in criminal proceedings; however, its associations with the Inquisition and authoritarian regimes are often omitted, either deliberately or inadvertently. This omission indicates that classifying the search for truth as a myth is justified and further suggests that arguments supporting its importance are rooted in political and ideological perspectives. Oliveira (2005: 281) notes that "the unwavering conviction that the State could genuinely attain truth led to the notion that its urgent pursuit should be the primary objective of criminal proceedings".

Myth serves to relieve institutional authorities from the ongoing necessity of asserting their legitimacy, as it provides a foundation rooted in the sacred, thereby requiring laypersons to accept this legitimacy. As Thums observes, "the judge needs to convince the litigant that the State is capable of providing a response based on truth, which must be accepted as dogma" (Thums 2006: 192).

In this regard, Ginzburg's findings are highly informative. Unlike Eliade, Ginzburg addressed the concept of myth through political and social lenses. By examining the operation of myth from the standpoint of Greek philosophy, Ginzburg established that Plato did not object to myth itself, but rather to its use as a means of disseminating falsehoods. He notes that in some sections of the *Republic*, Plato explicitly permitted rulers to employ untruths for the benefit of society. Furthermore, Ginzburg identifies in Socrates the recognition that myth constitutes a deliberate falsehood intended for the collective good, though within the Greek context, such prerogatives were conferred solely upon civic leaders and withheld from private citizens (Ginzburg 2001: 61). With respect to Aristotle, Ginzburg observes that for the majority, who were governed by passion and ignorance, order could only be maintained through religious belief or myths devised by wise individuals "to enforce compliance with the law and for reasons of utility" (Ginzburg 2001: 64–65).

An early connection can thus be identified between myth and power, as well as between myth and the mechanisms that uphold social order and define societal models. The myth of pursuing an absolute truth serves as a foundational element in shaping inquisitorial and authoritarian models of criminal procedure. Nevertheless, this notion persists due to a form of utilitarianism that can be used to justify almost any action as necessary. As a result, much of the literature on criminal procedure continues to support this approach, legitimising the exercise of authoritarian state power within a democratic-constitutional framework, even though such a context inherently calls for the limitation and oversight of state authority.

Similarly, Ginzburg referenced a competition held in 1777 by the Royal Prussian Academy of Sciences and Letters on the topic, "Is it useful to deceive the people?" One of the winners, Frederic de Castillon, contended that deception could serve a purpose: "It may prove useful for the people to be deceived both in matters of politics and in matters of religion". He further observed that whether the populace is misled into new errors or affirmed in their existing misconceptions, this may ultimately benefit the greater good. However, Castillon cautioned that if this principle were widely known, it would lose its effectiveness (Ginzburg 2001: 72).

A further pertinent citation from Ginzburg's essay, attributed to Nietzsche, notes: "the State itself knows of no unwritten laws more powerful than the mythical foundation" (Ginzburg 2001: 83). Consequently, proponents of procedural authoritarianism cannot forgo myth—whether consciously or unconsciously—as it functions as a unique mechanism of social coercion, including at the symbolic level.

This intertwining of myth and legal authority invites a reconsideration of the frameworks through which legitimacy is constructed and maintained. It is not merely the explicit statutes or codified rules that confer power, but the subtle, often unspoken narratives and symbols that underpin the system. The persistence of these myths, even in the face of rational critique, demonstrates their profound adaptability and capacity to shape collective beliefs. As such, efforts to reform criminal procedure must also address the symbolic and mythic dimensions, acknowledging their role in sustaining the structures of legal power.

In this manner, the narrative surrounding the pursuit of truth and judicial infallibility serves to provide discursive legitimacy to a legal structure of power and repression that may conflict with the defence of human rights. Despite these observations, this narrative persists within legal thought; therefore, it is important to examine the persuasive mechanisms that continue to justify its endurance.

Jean-Pierre Vernant asserts that, in Western thought—shaped by the traditions inherited from Greek philosophy—myth is typically characterised by its opposition to reality, being seen as fiction, and to rationality, being regarded as absurd (Vernant 1992). Nevertheless, Vernant emphasises that such binary distinctions oversimplify the complexity inherent within myth; it possesses a distinct intelligibility. Myth persists due to its capacity for continual semantic renewal, which underpins its considerable persuasive influence and enduring presence, even amidst historical discontinuities. Vernant's perspective provides valuable insight into the argument concerning the renewal of the inquisitorial pursuit of truth by modern reason, underscoring that the evolving definitions of truth still relate fundamentally to the same intrinsic drive for discovery.

Within this intricate interplay between myth, legal authority, and rational discourse, it is possible to observe that the structure of procedural legitimacy is not merely a matter of formal rules or institutional mechanisms. Instead, it is profoundly shaped by the symbolic narratives that continue to exert persuasive force even in contemporary contexts. The mythic underpinning of truth-seeking in criminal procedure endures, not only because of tradition, but due to its adaptability and resonance with collective values and anxieties. These myths are rejuvenated through their capacity to absorb and reinterpret new challenges, cloaking contemporary authoritarian practices in the enduring language of necessity and justice.

As society contends with emerging threats and challenges to prevailing concepts of criminal justice, the narrative of truth within criminal proceedings is repeatedly reframed to legitimise both the extension and application of state authority.

The myth is embedded in an implicit historical context, often not readily apparent to those who perpetuate it discursively. Octavio Paz, drawing on Levi-Strauss's analysis of myth, observes that symbolic systems are self-perpetuating: myths generate further myths through processes of opposition, permutation, mediation, and renewed opposition. Each iteration presents a subtle variation from its predecessor, resulting in myth evolving in a spiral manner—each new version simultaneously alters and reiterates the original (Paz 1993: 31).

The strategy of repetition and readaptation operates as a highly effective persuasive mechanism, accounting for the sustained influence of its exemplary narrative. In this context, Vernant identified that myth employs a form of language defined by mimetic processes (*mimēsis*), which aim to engage the listener, as well as emotional participation (*sympatheia*), which facilitates the listener's integration into the discourse.

Vernant contends that the concept of *logos*, as a form of thought articulated through written discourse, serves distinct purposes. For instance, he references historiography, which prioritises establishing truth through proof-based argumentation rather than captivating or enchanting an audience. Thus, myth operates as a means of emotional persuasion, whereas *logos* functions as rational persuasion. In this context, Leenhardt observes that "myth is experienced and internalised prior to being comprehended and explicitly formulated. Rather than constituting a rigid narrative, it manifests as speech or emblem; as gesture, it defines the event within the individual's core, eliciting an emotional response comparable to that of a child" (Leenhardt 1987: 87–88).

If this reasoning is extended beyond the dichotomy established by modern thought—which often separates emotion from reason—it becomes feasible to recognise that both persuasive mechanisms can mutually reinforce one another. Myth, therefore, should not be viewed as irrational; rather, it possesses its own distinct rationality while still appealing to emotional foundations. In this context, Leenhardt maintains that myth and rationality are complementary forms of knowledge and essential components of the human mind. Although myth functions primarily as an affective mode of understanding, it does not negate rationality but instead complements it (Leenhardt 1987: 87–88).

This close association allows authoritarian arguments to merge ostensibly rational claims—such as increasing crime rates—with a constructed solution, namely the pursuit of absolute truth and behavioural motivation through punitive measures. However, these measures do not address the problem as it is presented; rather, they serve to reinforce the persistence of an authoritarian framework where the discretionary use of punitive power remains unchallenged. Consequently, this cycle perpetuates itself indefinitely. According to Octavio Paz,

> The interpretation of one myth is informed by another. Each myth derives its significance from reference to others, which themselves evoke further myths, establishing a continuous chain of meaning. Collectively, these

> interrelated allusions construct a textual fabric—a grouping or lineage of myths. This assemblage in turn refers outward to additional texts, creating a network not characterized purely as discourse but rather as a dynamic system in constant transformation: a language in perpetual evolution (Paz 1993: 32). However, the myth operates with language as if it were a pre-significative system: what the myth says *is not* what the words of the myth say. (Paz 1993: 23)

Consequently, an implicit narrative regarding responses to violence is conveyed in a persuasive manner—language now operates within the accelerated dynamics of the media environment. The pursuit of truth and accountability is often articulated through media discourse, which can influence public perception by presenting dramatic narratives that may unconsciously foster acceptance of authoritative perspectives.

The intertwining of myth and rational discourse within criminal procedure not only shapes the legal landscape but also influences how society perceives justice and authority. The persistence of mythic narratives, even in an ostensibly rational and evidence-driven environment, reveals the depth at which cultural traditions inform legal practices. This dynamic is particularly evident when myths are leveraged to justify the expansion of state power, framing contentious measures as necessary safeguards for societal order. Such narratives, though cloaked in the language of necessity, often obscure the underlying motivations and consequences, allowing for the perpetuation of established structures without critical scrutiny. Ultimately, the myth of truth-seeking remains a powerful instrument for legitimising authoritative practices.

This discourse has the potential to impinge on individual freedoms and reinforce established power structures, reaffirming inquisitorial approaches. Its persuasive nature can affect judicial decision-making, allowing extrajudicial expectations to permeate legal proceedings. This phenomenon highlights the importance of educational reform, as critical thinking is seldom emphasised in traditional legal training.

An additional perspective on the persuasive influence of myth lies in its status as a form of truth. The myth is distinguished by its capacity to provide answers without explicitly articulating the underlying questions. It conveys a certain kind of truth—one communicated indirectly—which sets it apart from science and philosophy. As Paz observes, "in myth a logic develops that does not confront reality and its coherence is merely formal; in science, theory must submit to the test of experimentation; in philosophy, thought is critical" (Paz 1993: 31). Vernant further explains, "it is in this sense that the mythical symbol can be said to be tautegorical: it does not represent something else; it posits and affirms itself" (Vernant 1992: 201). For him, if myth serves as both the foundation upon which a culture develops and as an element whose authenticity appears unacknowledged by that culture, this is likely because its primary role, function, and significance are not immediately evident to those who use it. Furthermore, these aspects do not primarily exist at the level of its written form (Vernant 1992: 189).

The enduring notion of the judge's pursuit of truth persists largely because its meaning is not always immediately evident—even to those who perpetuate it—and its adaptability ensures its continued relevance. As Vernant observes, "myths may vary from one version to another, without the balance of the overall system being affected" (Vernant 1992: 109). In this manner, myth upholds the continuity of the inquisitorial approach to truth-seeking, reinforced by misconceptions associated with the mixed system and the insufficient scrutiny of authoritarian principles. This leads to repeated implementation of an exclusionary model of criminal procedure, wherein the accused is ultimately treated as an object. Despite variations, the myth surrounding the pursuit of truth remains fundamentally unchanged.

Chaui posits that a founding myth continually discovers new avenues of manifestation—be it through different languages, values, or ideas—such that its apparent transformation merely reinforces its intrinsic repetition (Chaui 2001: 8). The seeming adaptability of the myth ultimately serves as a continuous reaffirmation of its tautological "truth". In this context, it is evident that the pursuit of absolute truth functions as a foundational element within inquisitorial and authoritarian criminal procedure, a premise left largely unchallenged by rationalist conceptual frameworks that still enable such practices. The doctrines and rituals characteristic of authoritarian judicial practice are thus closely interconnected and substantiated by these principles. Thums observes that "the real truth, despite the conceptual ambiguity of the term—which conflates truth with reality—is considered by traditional legal scholarship and Supreme Court jurisprudence to be a 'postulate'. The dogma that justice determines truth, distinguishing the guilty from the innocent, provides the legitimising structure for all rules within the criminal system" (Thums 2006: 195).

Within this framework, the intertwining of myth and legal tradition acts as a powerful mechanism through which authority is justified and perpetuated. The narrative fabric constructed by myth does not merely serve as an abstract cultural reference; it becomes an operative force within the legal system, shaping both the structure and rationale of judicial practice. As criminal procedure evolves, myths are repurposed to suit contemporary discourses, sustaining their relevance while obscuring the boundaries between rationality and inherited belief.

The myth is articulated across a tradition that sustains the inquisitorial element it supports, though the association may not be immediately evident. Paz observes, "myths have no author and exist only as embodied in a tradition" (Paz 1993: 51). While tradition is frequently regarded favourably, it should be subject to critical examination, as certain traditions are capable of fostering dynamics of dominance and power. Tradition can perpetuate exclusionary relationships that must be addressed, as such patterns impede the development of a democratic society. This phenomenon is particularly notable within the inquisitorial tradition, which tends to adopt a dogmatic character reminiscent of religious structures, as illustrated by Geertz's explanation of what a religion is:: (1) a system of symbols which acts to (2) establish powerful, pervasive, and long-lasting moods and motivations in men by (3) formulating conceptions of a general order of existence and (4) clothing these conceptions with such an aura of factuality that (5) the moods and motivations seem uniquely realistic (Geertz 1989: 105).

According to Geertz, religion encompasses both intellectual and emotional aspects, drawing upon culturally constructed notions of reality and systems of moral valuation (Geertz 1989: 104). He posits that religion, through its symbols, creates a persuasive worldview and a coherent way of life, presenting itself as both an ontological and moral necessity. In this context, religious symbols shape dispositions within a cosmological framework, embedding them with ideas of transcendental truths that define the fundamental nature of reality.

While this comparison may appear audacious, it is important to recognise that the fundamental impetus for the pursuit of truth is inherently influenced by religious traditions. Secularisation did not substantially challenge these attributes; instead, it repositioned the objective of prosecution upon scientific foundations for uncovering the truth. As a result, the integration into a tradition with religious undertones follows logically from the very nature of the discursive system of prosecution as originally designed. This observation holds true even if the perpetuation of such myths is not entirely deliberate, as noted by Paz: the social group responsible for developing the myth does not possess an understanding of its significance; those who recount a myth are unaware of its implications, simply repeating segments of a broader narrative or reciting lines from a poem without knowledge of its beginning, end, or central theme. This lack of awareness extends to both their audience and the audiences of other myths. Collectively, there is no recognition that these narratives are components of an extensive poetic tradition: myths interact with one another through individuals, often without their conscious awareness (Paz 1993: 33).

Some legal scholars may inadvertently perpetuate inquisitorial principles, reflecting a distinct disconnection from the defence of human rights, with the 1941 Code of Criminal Procedure often serving as a key reference. The veneration of this code poses significant barriers to reforms aimed at fully eliminating inquisitorial elements in Brazilian criminal procedure. In practical terms, the persistent influence of the "sacred book" can lead to procedural distortions that conflict with democratic-constitutional standards, subtly fostering an objectifying criminal procedure within a system that should ensure regulated exercise of punitive power. Many judges continue to rely on the explanatory memorandum of the Code as their primary guide for judicial practices. Consequently, social practices within the legal system are frequently shaped by mechanisms not consciously recognised by those involved.

It is important, therefore, to analyse how myths circulate in the legal sphere. As Paz (1993: 32) notes, "the meaning of a myth depends on its position within the group and, therefore, to decipher it, it is necessary to take into account the context in which it appears. The myth is a phrase in a circular discourse, and its meaning is constantly changing: repetition and variation".

Given judicial concerns regarding the removal of powers that allow judges to ascertain the "real truth", it is evident that the persistence of this notion is closely linked to maintaining judicial authority. This authority is reinforced by a specific understanding of truth—one that, although inherently constructed, is presented as truth revealed through judicial determination. The judge is thus seen as the guardian of an established order, whose perceived reliability derives from the doctrinal foundation of their role. According to Thums, dogmatic legal thought, often upheld by conservative groups, contributes to maintaining the law's association with myth—that is, reasoning founded on institutional beliefs which may introduce a degree of arbitrariness to fundamental legal norms.

This concept is considered metaphysical rather than scientific. A similar form of arbitrariness can be observed in religious dogmas (Thums 2006: 194).

The application of implicit rhetoric contributes to the pursuit of truth in criminal proceedings, even as questions persist regarding the capacity of authoritarian criminal procedures to fulfil the security objectives first established in modernity. As Lopes Jr. notes, this debate is best framed within the context of the burden-benefit relationship. It prompts critical considerations: What cost are we willing to bear for a form of "security" that remains largely symbolic and reassuring rather than truly effective, and that inevitably retains a considerable degree of uncertainty or lack of control? Furthermore, how much individual liberty are we prepared to surrender in favour of increased state oversight? (Lopes Jr 2005: 67).

Chaui posits that, from an anthropological perspective, myth functions as an imagined resolution to tensions, conflicts, and contradictions that remain unresolved in reality. The persuasive capacity of such representations becomes apparent when observed in practice—specifically, when they address genuine tensions through imaginative means and obscure underlying contradictions (Chaui 2001: 8–9). The concern arises when individuals accept the illusory assurances of security provided by an authoritarian model of criminal justice; this ultimately fosters a symbolic relationship of subjugation between authorities and their subjects. Chartier describes symbolic domination as the mechanism through which the dominated either accept or resist imposed identities designed to secure and perpetuate their subordination (Chartier 2002: 12).

The pursuit of absolute truth serves as a narrative framework that is both exemplary and instructional, illustrating the concept of judicial infallibility and, by extension, suggesting an absence of checks on judicial authority. This perspective legitimises the power vested in those responsible for uncovering historical truths—an outlook that aligns closely with the inquisitorial tradition, something that is recognised by many judges. According to Carvalho, by legitimising the judge's broad initiative in evidence gathering, the inquisitorial system permits the adjudicator to perform the roles of both defender and prosecutor in proceedings they ultimately resolve. This framework allows the judge to determine a central thesis—deemed to be the definitive truth—and pursue its substantiation without limitation. Consequently, the logic inherent in the inquisitorial approach, as applied to case resolution, results in the continued pursuit of the so-called "myth of real truth" within a democratic state governed by the rule of law (Carvalho 2003: 186).

A criminal procedure based on the premise of pursuing absolute truth may be viewed as perpetuating a fallacy; its quest for so-called persecutory truth not only aims to eliminate perceived enemies of society but also fundamentally upholds the authority vested in judges. Gerber, discussing the inquisitorial system, observes that "the continuation of such a structure can only be rationalized in societies where the Divine presence is perceived as 'real', thereby granting its representatives inherent and unquestionable knowledge" (Gerber 2004: 228).

The defining characteristics of myth, as an explanatory structure with significant depth of meaning, are complex. Paz (1993: 58) observes that "myth is neither poem, nor science, nor philosophy, although it coincides with the first in its processes (poetic function), with the second in its logic, and with the last in its ambition to offer us an idea of the universe". The integration of these three dimensions results in a narrative structure equipped with highly effective persuasive mechanisms, which accounts for the considerable influence and widespread acceptance commonly associated with myths.

In summary, the mythic structure underlying the pursuit of truth in criminal proceedings continues to exert a profound influence on legal reasoning and practice. This myth not only shapes judicial expectations but also frames the collective understanding of justice, imbuing legal processes with a sense of inevitability and authority that is often accepted uncritically. The enduring power of such narratives demonstrates how deeply entrenched beliefs can persist, even as legal systems evolve towards more democratic and adversarial models. Recognising the mythic dimension is, therefore, essential for critically engaging with the assumptions that underpin judicial roles and the administration of justice.

To achieve this, it is essential to recognise that judges are not embodiments of the sacred; they are individuals subject to human limitations. Like all members of society, judges are beings-in-the-world and should be regarded accordingly. The subsequent chapter will address this topic in detail.

CHAPTER 9

The Analogical Production of Truth in Narrative Form

The Hermeneutics of Facticity: Judicial Decision-Making as an Existential Activity

The evidentiary process ultimately culminates in the decision of the judge, who bears the responsibility of rendering a verdict. The crucial question concerns the foundation of this decision: whether it is derived from narrative accounts substantiated by thoroughly examined evidence, recognised as proof through adversarial proceedings; from the rhetorical abilities of the parties, whose persuasive arguments may not always be grounded in factual history; or from the judge's own isolated deliberation, where even the most well-intentioned judge may be influenced by unconscious biases. As noted by Coutinho, it is essential to recognise the role of subjectivity within judicial proceedings. By incorporating perspectives from psychoanalysis, the author aims to shed light on the cognitive mechanisms underlying judicial decision-making in criminal cases and to address issues related to the limited formation of judges. This approach provides judges with greater awareness of potential influences on their reasoning, thereby underscoring the significance of establishing the judiciary as a guarantor of rights (Coutinho 1998).

A revised approach to criminal justice views criminal procedure as a structured process designed to regulate the exercise of punitive authority. This perspective necessitates that judges recognise their specific functions

S. H. Khaled Jr., *Reimagining Criminal Justice, Search for Truth and Human Rights*, https://doi.org/10.1007/978-3-032-27227-0_9

within this framework, which involves moving beyond the traditional notion of pursuing absolute truth.

The judge serves as the principal figure entrusted with safeguarding due process and delivering the final judgement. Achieving this equilibrium requires overcoming several significant challenges, including the persistence of inquisitorial attitudes, the conception of jurisdiction as an absolute authority, the positivist view of the judge as merely a conduit for the law, and modern scientism characterised by the separation of subject and object. Furthermore, it is crucial to move beyond the assumption that the adjudicator must search for the truth. As Morais da Rosa states, "the process of desubstantializing the judge's position does not depend on procedural change, although this may assist. It fundamentally depends on an attitude, and that is what is expected" (Rosa 2011: 131).

In a criminal justice system dedicated to upholding human rights, it is necessary to reconceptualise the judge's role accordingly. This section presents an analytical proposal that rethinks the judge's role through the framework of philosophical hermeneutics. Having previously established that evidentiary procedures are oriented towards shaping the judge's conviction and discussed the uncertainties inherent in such processes, the current discussion now turns to the formation of conviction from the perspective of philosophical hermeneutics.

It is important to clarify that hermeneutics does not seek to prescribe a method for interpretative practices, whether in daily life or academia. Misinterpretation may arise from the title of Gadamer's seminal work "Truth and Method"; however, unlike Heidegger's "Being and Time", where being is equated with time, Gadamer's volume might aptly be titled "Against Method" or "Beyond Method". His focus rests on the pre-understanding that both enables and constrains any interpretive technique. Thus, Gadamer addresses the very dynamics of understanding, rather than providing a mechanism for distinguishing between valid and invalid interpretations (Outhwaite 1985: 24). As Palmer notes, "the title of Gadamer's book is ironic: method is not the path to truth. On the contrary, truth mocks the methodical man" (Palmer 1997: 168).

Hermeneutic reflection has the potential to enhance our comprehension of interpretative processes and the dynamics of understanding. Furthermore, it can assist us in addressing the inherent limitations within the human sciences (Soares 2004: 32). According to Gadamer, the objective of hermeneutic reflection is to address the traditional *querelle des anciens et des modernes* without aligning with either the moderns' progressive outlook or adopting a stance of mere emulation of the ancients. This entails, firstly, critically examining the biases inherent in privileging self-consciousness and in treating methodological scientific certainty as an absolute standard, and secondly, being vigilant against the converse bias: assuming it is possible to wholly disregard the influence of the Christian era and modern science (Gadamer 1992: 291).

Accordingly, my approach to hermeneutics does not entail its use as a paradigmatic solution. Hermeneutics neither claims to resolve all epistemological issues nor seeks to establish a novel framework from an absolute starting point; rather, it aims to achieve equilibrium and clarify the processes by which knowledge emerges through the act of understanding. It is also essential to recognise that hermeneutics encompasses a variety of perspectives—not merely a singular method—with particular emphasis in this study on hermeneutics as both a phenomenology of existence and existential interpretation (as articulated by Heidegger and Gadamer), as well as cultural hermeneutics informed by Ricoeur's contributions to philosophy (Palmer 1997: 43). Consequently, the present inquiry does not attempt a comprehensive review of every school within hermeneutics but instead seeks to define a field of reflection stimulated by this tradition in relation to the issue at stake, drawing upon the works of Heidegger, Gadamer, and Ricoeur.

As previously discussed, viewing the judge solely as an instrument of the law does not fully account for the fact that the judge operates within a context shaped by their own experiences, which differs significantly from the position of a physicist in relation to the physical world. Consequently, the issue of impartiality assumes a distinct character for the judiciary. Additionally, it has been demonstrated that the notion of truth as mere correspondence, determined by rational judgement, warrants critical examination. As Morais da Rosa notes, modernity introduced a decision-making framework based on logical premises and metaphysical distinctions—such as the division between principle and rule or findings of fact and findings of law—that does not align with the hermeneutic complexity developed in the latter half of the twentieth century. The inherited model, prominent in legal literature, assumes that heightened rationality can provide complete certainty about empirical facts. This perspective overlooks advances that move beyond the philosophy of consciousness and relies on traditional metaphysical thinking. Therefore, it is necessary to move past the modernist framework and its comprehensive approach (Rosa 2011: 58).

In order to move beyond modern frameworks, it is essential to adopt a novel perspective on decision-making that acknowledges the judge as an entity situated within the world. Drawing on Heidegger's insights, the principal focus should not be directed towards theories concerning the conceptualisation of history, historical knowledge, or the epistemology of historical events as objects of scholarly enquiry. Instead, priority should be given to interpreting the nature of being that is inherently historical in its own historicity (Heidegger 2005: 37).

Such an approach aims to move beyond the assumption that a judge can achieve a corresponding notion of truth—an assumption that ultimately leads to granting powers for its pursuit, with the risk of objectifying the accused. Heidegger contends that "the characterisation of truth as 'concordance', *adaequatio* is, indeed, all too empty and universal" (Heidegger 2005: 283). He argues that the traditional understanding of the essence of truth, as well as the prevailing opinion based on this mistaken definition, embody the following characteristics:

a) The "*locus*" of truth is the proposition (the judgement).
b) The essence of truth resides in "concordance"—between the judgement and its object.
c) Aristotle, the father of logic, not only indicated the judgement as the original *locus* of truth but also popularised the definition of truth as concordance.

According to Heidegger, truth as correspondence denotes the idea that a judgement achieves complete adequacy in relation to its object. Heidegger subsequently poses the following question:

What is it, in whose perspective, that those things which are related in the *adaequatio* are in agreement? In clarifying the relation of truth, one must also consider the specificity of the members of the relation. In what perspective do *intellectus* and *res* agree? Do they, in their mode of being and essential content, provide something in whose perspective they can agree? If equality between them is impossible, because they do not belong to the same kind, is it not possible that both (*intellectus* and *res*) are similar? Nevertheless, any knowledge must "give" the thing *as* it is. "Concordance" has the character of the "as" relation. How does this relation become possible as a relation between *intellectus* and *res*? From these questions it becomes evident that, in order to clarify the structure of truth, it is not enough simply to presuppose this whole relational structure; rather, the inquiry must be redirected to its ontological context, which sustains this whole as such (Heidegger 2005: 283–284).

Heidegger expresses his perplexity at the impasse thus established, when he asks whether "it is mere chance that this problem has remained unresolved for more than two millennia? Or does the misdirection of the question lie in its starting point, that is, in the ontologically unclarified separation between the real and the ideal?" (Heidegger 2005: 284).

According to general opinion, only knowledge is true. To know, however, is to judge. In every judgement, one must distinguish the act of judging as a *real* psychic process and the content judged as *ideal* content. Of the latter, it is said to be "true". In contrast, the real psychic process is simply given or not. The ideal content of the judgement is, therefore, what is found in a relation of concordance. And this concerns a connection between the ideal content of the judgement and the real thing *about which* one judges. In its mode of being, is concordance real, ideal, or neither? *How should the relation between the ideal entity and the simply given real be apprehended ontologically*? This relation subsists and consists in factual judgements not only between the content of the judgement and the real object, but also between the ideal content and the real act of judging; and here, is the relation not manifestly "intrinsic"? (Heidegger 2005: 284).

He adds: "is it not the case that the reality of knowledge and judgement is split into two modes of being or 'layers', whose suture will never reach the mode of being of knowledge?" (Heidegger 2005: 285). For Heidegger,

> When does the phenomenon of truth express itself in knowledge itself? Undoubtedly, when knowledge shows itself *as true*. It is the very act of self-verification that assures its truth. In the phenomenal context of this verification, therefore, the relation of concordance must become visible. [...] The proposition *is true* means: it discloses the being itself. It proposes, indicates, "let's see" the entity in its being and being-uncovered. The *being-true (truth)* of the proposition must be understood in the sense of *being-uncovering*. Truth, therefore, does not possess the structure of correspondence between knowledge and object, in the sense of an adequation between one entity (subject) and another entity (object). (Heidegger 2005: 285-286)

Heidegger not only rejects the traditional understanding of the concept of truth but also denies the attribution to Aristotle of this notion of correspondence. According to him,

> Aristotle never defended the thesis that the original "place" of truth was the judgement. In fact, he says that *logos* is the mode of being of presence, which can be uncovering or concealing. This *dual possibility* is what is remarkable in the being-true of *logos*, for this is the comportment that *can also conceal*. [...] The thesis that the genuine "place" of truth is the judgement is not only wrongly attributed to Aristotle but, in terms of its content, constitutes a misunderstanding of the structure of truth. The proposition is not the primary "place" of truth. *On the contrary*, the proposition, as a mode of appropriation of discovery and as a mode of being-in-the-world, is founded upon the uncovering or *openness* of presence. The most original "truth" is the "place" of the proposition and the ontological condition of possibility for the proposition to be true or false (to be uncovering or concealing). (Heidegger 2005: 295)

Heidegger proposes to overcome the idea of truth (a concept constructed as correspondence) by the idea of removing from its concealment the entity about which one speaks and letting the entity be seen as something unveiled. In short, to discover (to be true).

Truth, in this context, refers to the act of uncovering or revealing by removing veils or coverings. This interpretation allows for the continual questioning of established certainties and the discovery of previously unrecognised connections; it presents truth as inherently problematic, contrasting with a form of truth imposed through force upon the reality one aims to understand. Gadamer notes that Heidegger proposed conceiving of truth as both revelation and concealment simultaneously (Gadamer 1992: 398).

Heidegger's critique of the correspondence theory of truth fundamentally challenges the assumption that truth is a static relation between judgement and object. Instead, truth emerges as a dynamic process of uncovering, deeply rooted in the ontological structure of being. This means that what is judged to be true is not merely a matter of matching statements to facts but rather involves an act of revealing or discovering the entity itself, which may simultaneously conceal other aspects. Thus, truth is never purely objective nor entirely subjective but is situated within the unfolding context of understanding and interpretation.

The implications of this perspective are profound, especially when applied to areas such as law and decision-making. Rather than relying on a rigid framework of correspondence, the evidentiary activity should be understood as an ongoing endeavour, shaped by historical, temporal, linguistic, and contextual factors. In this sense, the uncovering of truth is inseparable from the interpretative activity of *Dasein*, whose existence is bound up with time and historicity. Consequently, any claim to truth must acknowledge both its revelatory and concealing dimensions, recognising that understanding always occurs within a horizon shaped by tradition and prior experience.

This perspective helps clarify the inherent uncertainty present in both the knowledge of the past and the process of decision-making. Furthermore, conceptualising persuasion through the simultaneous processes of revelation and concealment effectively reflects the dynamic between belief and conviction previously outlined. As Heidegger observes, truth may be obscured or even distorted—a phenomenon particularly relevant to the dialogical dynamic typical within adversarial proceedings. This notion of truth as both revelation and concealment extends far beyond the reassurances and certainties that a simplistic notion of corresponding truth might provide.

As previously noted, the notion of truth as correspondence ultimately perpetuates, albeit subtly, the epistemological framework characteristic of inquisitorial proceedings, distorting the accusatory structure of due process.

My perspective is fundamentally distinct from that of Ferrajoli and Taruffo, both of whom interpret truth as correspondence, understood in an approximate or relative manner. As I have reiterated on numerous occasions, it is essential to move beyond this perspective and consider alternative conceptions of truth, as the traditional notion perpetuates in a veiled way the underpinnings of inquisitorial epistemology.

To move beyond the concept of correspondence theory of truth, it is essential to approach truth as the possibility of disclosure, while also recognising the ongoing tension associated with potential concealment. This perspective aligns more closely with the inherent uncertainty that characterises procedural legal contexts and the narrative accounts presented by opposing parties within the adversarial framework of legal proceedings.

According to Heidegger, to deceive in the sense of concealing is to place one thing in front of another (to let and make see) and thus present it as something it is not. That is, "Precisely because 'truth' has this meaning and *logos* is a determined mode of letting and making see, *logos* cannot be pointed to as the primary 'place' of truth" (Heidegger 2005: 63). Therefore, judgement cannot be considered the privileged locus of truth, in the sense of *adaequatio*. According to Heidegger,

> *All truth is relative to the being of presence insofar as its mode of being essentially possesses the character of presence.* Does this relativity mean that all truth is "subjective"? If one interprets "subjective" as that which "lies within the subject's discretion", certainly not. For, in its most proper sense, uncovering removes the proposition from "subjective" discretion and leads the uncovering presence towards the entity itself. And only *because* "truth" as uncovering is a *mode of being of presence* is it withdrawn from the discretion of *presence*. The "universal validity" of truth is also rooted simply in the fact that presence can discover and free the entity itself. Only thus can this entity in itself be connected to each possible proposition, that is, to his own demonstration. Is truth, when properly understood, compromised by the fact that, ontically, it is only possible within the "subject", and depends on the being of the subject? (Heidegger 2005: 296-297)

Heidegger maintains that it is not: for him, "to assert 'eternal truths' and to confuse the 'ideality' of *Dasein*, grounded in phenomena, with an absolute and idealised subject belong to the remnants of Christian theology within philosophical discourse, which have long failed to be radically purged" (Heidegger 2005: 299). In other words, "the being of truth is found in an original nexus with *Dasein*. And only because *Dasein* is, as that which is constituted by openness, that is, by understanding, is it possible to comprehend being and for an ontological understanding to occur" (Heidegger 2005: 299).

According to Gadamer, Heidegger was not the first to discover that *aletheis* properly means unconcealment. But he has taught us what it means for the conception of being that truth must be wrested from a state of concealment and covering up. Concealment and covering up are correlative. Things remain hidden by nature; "nature tends to hide itself", Heraclitus is said to have remarked. Likewise, covering up is characteristic of human action and language (Gadamer 1992: 53).

Heidegger's insights lead to the recognition of the historicity inherent in all forms of understanding, a perspective that stands in stark contrast to both the *tabula rasa* concept (Bacon) and Cartesian principles underpinning the philosophy of consciousness. Heidegger firmly establishes the historicity of being through its pre-understanding, shaped by the tradition in which it exists; for him, being is fundamentally intertwined with time. Consequently, a persistent temporal aspect is present, and Heidegger maintains that all understanding emerges and unfolds within the context of time.

This is what Heidegger means when he states that "*time* is the starting point from which *Dasein* always implicitly understands and interprets being [...] *time as the horizon for the understanding of being from temporality, as the being of Dasein, which is fulfilled in the movement of understanding being*" (Heidegger 2005: 45). Therefore, according to Heidegger, "every investigation, and not only the investigation that moves within the central question of being, is always an ontic possibility of *Dasein*. The being of *Dasein* finds its meaning in temporality" (Heidegger 2005: 47). The historicity of *Dasein* seeks to show that this entity is not "temporal" because it "finds itself in history", but rather, that it only exists and can only exist historically because, at the core of its being, it is temporal.

Understanding, therefore, is not a task of the mind; it is *Dasein* itself and, thus, to be in the world is to understand. According to Gadamer, what Heidegger points out is that "understanding no longer means a mode of human thought among others that can be disciplined methodologically and shaped into a scientific method but rather constitutes the basic movement of human existence" (Gadamer 1992: 105).

From a hermeneutic standpoint, the development of conviction should be understood not from an abstract rationalist starting point, but rather from a contextually grounded position, which will inevitably interpret meaning in its own distinct manner.

Understanding occupies an ontologically primary position, preceding any act of existence, and consistently functions within a framework of preinterpreted relations constituting a relational whole. As Palmer notes, Aristotle had already highlighted that interpretation precedes logical analysis; this recognition addresses a fundamental misunderstanding in modern thought, which "tends far too quickly to fix interpretation automatically at the moment of logical analysis" (Palmer 1997: 33).

Consequently, understanding inherently involves self-understanding, as human beings exist temporally, alongside the world they seek to comprehend. There is, therefore, no privileged or transcendental vantage point that permits one to transcend historicity and achieve absolute objectivity in discerning truth. Gadamer asserts that Heidegger resolves the dichotomy between subject and object through the concept of being-in-the-world, employing his transcendental analytic of *Dasein*: similar to how using a tool entails engaging with it rather than objectifying it, understanding—enabling *Dasein* to know itself both in its being and its context—is not simply a relation to objects of knowledge, but constitutes being-in-the-world itself (Gadamer 1992: 320). Accordingly, Heidegger conceptualises understanding as the capacity to apprehend the various possibilities of one's own being within the context of the lifeworld each individual inhabits (Palmer 1997: 135).

The concept of corresponding truth becomes untenable for comprehending criminal proceedings when one takes into account the ontological presuppositions inherent to understanding. It is not feasible to achieve understanding without incorporating aspects of one's own perspective, which strenghtens the conclusion that truth regarding past events is not discovered but rather analogically produced.

In this regard, Heidegger's approach to the relationship between understanding and interpretation is especially significant, as he asserts that understanding serves as the foundation for interpretation:

> In understanding, *Dasein* projects its being towards possibilities. This *being towards possibilities*, constitutive of understanding, is a potentiality-for-being that reflects back upon *Dasein* the possibilities as openings. The act of understanding inherently possesses the potential to be developed into forms. We refer to this development as *interpretation*. In interpretation, understanding appropriates what it comprehends. Through interpretation, understanding becomes itself and nothing else. Interpretation is existentially grounded in understanding, not the other way around. To interpret is not to become aware that one has understood, but rather to elaborate the inherent possibilities of understanding. (Heidegger 2005: 204)

Understanding constitutes the foundation upon which interpretation takes place. Heidegger asserts that interpretation is never a presuppositionless apprehension of something previously presented; this stands in direct contrast to the modern view that ideal knowledge is constructed through the pursuit of corresponding truth. Consequently, this perspective challenges the notion of an objective search for truth and contests the confidence in the methodological capabilities of the rational subject to achieve it. According to Heidegger,

> Interpretation is always grounded in a *fore-sight*, which "delineates" what has been assumed in the fore-position, according to a particular possibility of interpretation. What is understood, established in a fore-position and viewed with "fore-sight", becomes a concept through interpretation. Interpretation may draw concepts belonging to the entity to be interpreted from the entity itself, or else impose concepts against which the entity may resist in its mode of being. In any case, interpretation has always already decided, definitively or provisionally, upon a particular conceptualisation, for it is founded on a *fore-conception* (Heidegger 2005: 207.

From this perspective, understanding can only occur from a situated position, defined by temporality and independent of assertions of objectivity, detachment, or neutrality. Understanding does not initiate from an absence seeking *adaequatio*, but rather emerges from what is already present, serving both as potential and constraint. Accordingly, Palmer observes, "the hope for an 'unprejudiced' and 'presuppositionless' interpretation has recently disappeared, in light of the way understanding operates. What appears of the object is what we allow to appear; it is what the thematisation of the world, operative in understanding, brings to light" (Palmer 1997: 141). As Soares further emphasises, there is no Archimedean point, external to languages and paradigms, equidistant, neutral, a solid platform for fully rational discernment. Every decision, by definition, entails the burden of a prior commitment to some horizon, from which questions and alternatives gain intelligibility and are hierarchised (Soares 2004: 58).

It is essential to recognise that Heidegger conceptualises understanding and interpretation as preceding any potential dichotomy between subject and object (Palmer 1997: 141). These reflections prompted Heidegger to examine the origins of understanding, which led to the incorporation of the notion of tradition into the category of historicity, a concept that he maintains is neither inherently positive nor negative. According to Heidegger, tradition exists prior to *Dasein*. Consequently, it is at the intersection of tradition and *Dasein* that projection emerges—specifically, the initial hypothesis concerning the object, which is fundamental to the reciprocal movement characteristic of the hermeneutic circle. The following passage, where Heidegger critically addresses tradition as a limiting factor, serves as an illustrative example:

> In a certain way and to a certain extent, *Dasein* immediately understands itself from tradition. This understanding opens up and regulates the possibilities of its being. Its own past, and this always means the past of its "generation", does not *follow* but precedes *Dasein*, anticipating its steps. [...] Tradition deprives it of the capacity to guide itself, to question and choose itself. Ultimately, the same can be said of understanding and its possibility of construction, which takes root in the very being of *Dasein*, that is, in the ontological. Tradition, thus predominant, tends to make what it "bequeaths" so inaccessible that, in most cases and at first approach, it conceals and hides it. (Heidegger 2005: 48-49)

According to Heidegger, "if the question of being is to acquire transparency regarding its own history, it is necessary, then, to shake the rigidity and hardening of a petrified tradition and to remove the accumulated debris" (Heidegger 2005: 51). Consequently, existence in the world is inseparable from understanding; every act of reflecting upon oneself or one's environment constitutes a distinct comprehension of both. In Heidegger's perspective, "world" signifies an individual's experienced reality rather than an objective entity, distinguishing it from the universe as examined by a scientist seeking factual correspondence.

This ontological turn prompts a reconsideration of the judge's role—not as a detached arbiter applying static principles, but as a participant whose interpretative stance is shaped by the interplay of tradition, lived experience, and the particularities of each case. In this light, legal decisions are not simply the output of deductive logic or mechanical application of rules; instead, they are the result of an interpretative process that both reveals and is conditioned by the horizon within which the judge operates. Such a perspective foregrounds the importance of reflexivity and openness in judicial reasoning, allowing for a more nuanced engagement with the complexity of human affairs.

It is essential to recognise that these observations extend beyond merely overcoming paradigms. The intent here is not to suggest that a judge should act according to a specific paradigm; rather, it is to highlight that when a judge embraces the modern methodological framework, their starting point is shaped by an established investigative tradition. This tradition will influence their interpretation of reality in a manner unique to its context. Such an interpretation is not exclusive, nor does it represent a purely scientific or neutral methodological perspective. Consequently, it will not lead to absolute truth, as every viewpoint is inevitably influenced by adherence to a particular tradition.

The core issue concerns traditions that engage in dialogical exchange with phenomena—adopting a receptive approach to their inherent complexity—and those that tend towards subjugating them; this distinction aligns with Nietzsche's critique regarding the malice embedded within certain forms of knowledge. In other words, knowledge is inevitably metaphorical to some degree, as it cannot transcend the confines of language and conceptual frameworks. However, not all concepts function equivalently: some are robust and attentive to the profundity of reality, whereas others are reductive, oversimplifying reality to the point where one must question whether reality remains part of the interpretive process or is overshadowed by the subject's unilateral perspective. Concepts characteristic of the inquisitorial tradition—revitalised in modern thought—fall into the latter category. A similar critique applies to evidentiary rationalism.

It is important to acknowledge that conceptual frameworks may not provide a sufficient pathway to understanding reality. Consequently, one must strive to engage with reality despite the persistent influence of concepts, which, due to ingrained Western classificatory habits, frequently impede our efforts to "return to the things themselves" and exert considerable persuasive power (Souza 2004: 29). As Timm de Souza notes,

> it is necessary to attribute to concepts (especially generalising concepts, so dangerous in their seductive power) only the force that is proper to them and nothing more, without considering them as analytical tools so powerful that they end up becoming the reality they indicate or symbolise. The confusion between these dimensions is extremely common in science and, unfortunately, equally common in philosophy, which ought to be more cautious in dealing with the various layers of reality. It is possible that the hypertrophy of the concept—or of a set of particular concepts transformed into a key to the world—has decisively contributed to this confusion, which, at bottom, is also the confusion between a *part* and an *aspect* of a given reality, which allows one to think that, by enumerating and intellectually analysing aspects of something, we are reconstructing it, in a more perfect, better articulated and meaningful way, within the universe of our intellect. (Souza 2004: 37)

The process of understanding is inherently shaped by the interplay of tradition and conceptual frameworks, which both enable and constrain our access to reality. This dynamic underscores the necessity for critical engagement with inherited concepts, particularly given their persuasive influence and capacity to obscure the nuances of lived experience. Therefore, the challenge lies not simply in rejecting tradition, but in cultivating an awareness of its effects and striving to enter into a more authentic dialogue with phenomena, unburdened by the seductive power of generalising concepts and the illusions of methodological rigour.

Heidegger's hermeneutics of facticity significantly alters the perception of judicial decision-making, shifting it from a strictly technical or methodological approach, characteristic of legal positivism, to an existential and ontological process. Within this framework, judges are not merely tasked with the application of fixed legal rules to factual situations; rather, they interpret law in the context of a dynamic "world" of meanings informed by lived experience.

The Hermeneutic Circle and the Processes of Interpretation

Philosophical hermeneutics is grounded in assumptions that conceptualise knowledge through frameworks distinct from those of modern epistemology. A central contribution of hermeneutics is its recognition that interpreters are inherently situated within the hermeneutic circle. Interpretation emerges from an individual's tradition and pre-judgements, which must always be considered. In this context, Gadamer asserts that it is pre-judgements, not simply judgements, that constitute our being. Consequently, the meaning assigned to pre-judgement by modern science—as something to be discarded in pursuit of truth—does not align with its understanding in hermeneutics. Pre-judgements are not necessarily unfounded or erroneous, nor do they inevitably distort truth; rather, the matter requires reframing, as our historical existence endows pre-judgements with the status of prior orientation for all experiential capacity (Gadamer 1992: 218). These pre-judgements shape the tradition in which interpreters are embedded and from which they engage in the hermeneutic process. Belonging to a tradition constitutes an existential condition, shaping pre-judgements that enable understanding. As Lopes Jr. observes,

> the judge is a being-in-the-world, and thus his understanding of the criminal case (and the application of the norm) is the result of an immense complexity involving the subjective factors that affect his own perception

> of the world. There is no possibility of a *zero point of understanding*, given the range of values, prejudices, stigmas, pre-judgements, subjective aspects, etc., that converge in the act of judging, and thus, in feeling and selecting meanings. (Lopes Jr 2010: 344)

As noted earlier, the prevailing modern intellectual framework was characterised by confidence in the capacity to separate preconceptions, thereby circumventing perceived distortions arising from them. It is pertinent to illustrate the fallacy embedded in this assertion. According to Heidegger, scientific knowledge.

> demands the rigour of a well-founded demonstration. Scientific proof must not presuppose that which it is to establish. If, however, interpretation always already moves within what is already understood and must draw from it, how can it produce scientific results without moving in a circle, especially if the presupposed understanding is articulated in common knowledge of man and world? According to the most elementary rules of logic, however, the circle is a *circulus virtuosus*. With this, however, the task of historical interpretation is *a priori* banished from the field of all rigorous knowledge. Unless this circle is abolished from understanding, historiography must be content with less robust possibilities of knowledge. It is permitted, in a certain way, to make up for this lack by means of the "spiritual meaning" of its "objects". According to the opinion of historians themselves, the ideal would be to avoid the circle and that there was hope of creating, for the first time, a historiography as independent of the observer's perspective as knowledge of nature is presumed to be. (Heidegger 2005: 2010)

Heidegger presents a critical examination of the notion of truth as mere correspondence to the past, characterising this perspective as reductive. He disagrees with the idea that knowledge of history can be grounded solely in scientific parameters. He challenges not only the feasibility of achieving truth through historiography but also addresses the prevailing nineteenth-century historical paradigm. This is exemplified by Ranke—the eminent German historian—who articulated the ideal: "I would like to be able to erase my own self, giving voice only to things that manifest themselves through powerful forces" (Koselleck 2006: 164).

The concept of self-annihilation as a method for achieving neutrality, thereby facilitating the pursuit of truth, is intertwined with the modern dichotomy between reason and emotion. It presupposes that a rational individual is capable of acquiring knowledge by excluding emotional influences. Ranke's inclination towards self-effacement parallels the approach of a judge who asserts neutrality when establishing facts to support his own reasoning. Nonetheless, it is essential to recognise subjectivity in order to identify and address potential pitfalls; as Coutinho noted, disregarding these areas of subjectivity can lead to significant negative consequences.

This recognition should compel legal scholars to confront the limitations inherent in any claim to pure objectivity, particularly within the context of legal adjudication and historical analysis. The aspiration towards a neutral standpoint, free from the influence of tradition and subjectivity, ultimately proves illusory; instead, it is through the conscious engagement with their own pre-judgments and the interpretative horizons they establish that genuine understanding becomes possible for judges. In this way, the process of interpretation transforms from a quest for absolute truth into a reflective exercise that acknowledges the inescapable interplay between the interpreter and the phenomena under consideration.

Adopting a perspective grounded in strict rationality and objectivity establishes a framework for understanding that primarily perpetuates inquisitorial epistemology. This approach risks divorcing theory from practical reality, as hypotheses are seldom subjected to rigorous testing in accordance with hermeneutical principles. Cordero's articulation of the precedence of hypotheses over facts aligns with contemporary rationalist views on cognitive processes: the notion that facts can be simply discovered by a rational subject is untenable and challenges fundamental tenets of comprehension.

Despite advances in legal thought, many practitioners continue to adhere to the confines of contemporary scientific paradigms, maintaining faith in the absolute neutrality of legal science. As Coutinho observes, "today, dogmas such as Kelsen's isolation of law are a thing of the past, the neutrality of jurists is almost legal archaeology, and their impartiality is only imaginable with much discourse to support it" (Coutinho 2002: 175–176).

In line with this perspective, Gadamer contends that those who endeavour to detach themselves from their own individuality, as Ranke attempted, remain products of their time and culture (Gadamer 1992: 27). Thus, it is imperative to reconceptualise cognitive activity through alternative parameters—moving beyond a limited understanding of science that fails to reflect the complexity of reality and persists, albeit in attenuated forms, that merely relativise the authority of rational subjects, diminishing their omnipotence but still regarding them as quasi-demigods in pursuit of truth.

Gadamer identifies an undue dominance arising from the application of natural science methodologies to the human sciences. He distinctly opposes the pursuit of objectivity, as defined by historical knowledge within the paradigm of the natural sciences, asserting that this approach is inappropriate given the differing subject matter involved. Gadamer's criticism could well be directed at the use of the theory of truth as Tarski's correspondence by evidentiary rationalism.

As Soares (2004: 46) observes, the human sciences address material that is fluid and irregular, reflecting the unpredictability and complexity of social life and history. Gadamer argues that modern metaphysics neglects the historical context of its own assertions, endeavouring to extricate itself from tradition and its inherent historicity. He categorically rejects the universality attributed to modern scientific methods. According to Gadamer, modern science is the science born in the seventeenth century, founded on the idea of method and the methodological guarantee of progress in knowledge. It has radically changed our planet by privileging a form of access to the world that is neither the only one nor the most complete that we possess (Gadamer 1992: 183). For the author, science has distorted the phenomenon of understanding (Gadamer 1992: 184).

Hermeneutics offers an alternative approach in which understanding, guided by intent, does not merely aim to confirm prior assumptions but instead strives to recognise and regulate them, thereby attaining a more profound comprehension of the subject matter. This methodology seeks to avoid simply reaffirming one's own hypotheses and expectations. Within hermeneutics, there exists a tendency towards a problematic truth intrinsic to its meaning, which facilitates addressing challenges arising from subconscious opacity and the influence of tradition.

It is evident that a hermeneutic orientation offers greater resilience against the risks highlighted by Cordero. This approach is exemplified in Heidegger's hermeneutics, where understanding is consistently shaped by both the anticipatory framework of pre-understanding and a sense of belonging to tradition. Nonetheless, the preliminary assumptions that emerge must undergo continual reassessment. Thus, objectivity resides in the progression of prior judgements through ongoing engagement with reality, rather than in an uncritical quest for confirmation under the guise of pursuing absolute truth or certainty.

Ranke's aspiration for self-annihilation is unattainable; it cannot be realised. The idea of escaping historicity and utilising an analytical tool that ensures absolute neutrality and objectivity, thereby legitimising the pursuit of truth, overlooks the reality that such tools are themselves shaped by specific historical contexts. These contexts inevitably reflect a distinct approach to constructing knowledge rather than representing a universal method. Consequently, this issue should no longer require further debate. As Fazzalari notes,

> The work of the interpreter, like all human endeavours, inherently possesses a historical dimension; the outcomes produced stem from circumstances that, however persistent they appear, are never permanent and evolve through methods and conditions that are themselves subject to change. Furthermore, it should be noted more broadly that every discourse—including those outside legal contexts, along with the associated signs, concepts, and theories—is shaped by its historical context and is fundamentally relative. (Fazzalari 2006: 59)

Accordingly, it is essential to consider the perspective from which interpretation occurs and the manner in which understanding evolves. As Heidegger observes, "it is only from the mode of being of history, historicity, and its rootedness in temporality that one can conclude how history can become a possible object of historiography" (Heidegger 2005: 180). The central issue involves acknowledging the interpreter's position within the interpretive process, as they are inherently part of this dynamic. As discussed previously, the fact that evidentiary activities aim to persuade the judge introduces complex dynamics all of which merit thorough examination.

In contrast to assumptions made by modern scientific approaches, the interpreter's involvement in the hermeneutic circle—shaped by their own tradition—should not be regarded as a limitation but as an essential aspect of knowledge formation. The hermeneutic circle is integral to the process of understanding itself, rather than serving merely as a methodological tool; it characterises the very manner in which comprehension unfolds. However, as Gadamer (1992: 258) notes, respect for tradition does not entail uncritical acceptance, undue privileging of the traditional, or subordination to its authority. For Heidegger,

> *to see in this circle a flaw, to seek ways to avoid it, or even to "feel" it merely as an inevitable imperfection, is a fundamental misunderstanding of what understanding is.* It is not a matter of equating understanding and interpretation with an ideal of knowledge, which, determined in itself, is nothing but a degeneration and which, in the proper task of grasping simply given being, has lost itself in a misunderstanding of its essence. To fulfil the fundamental conditions of a possible interpretation, one must not ignore the essential conditions of its realisation. What is decisive is not to escape the circle but to enter it in the right way. This circle of understanding is not a constraint in which any kind of knowledge moves. It expresses the *pre-structure* of existence, proper to *Dasein*. The circle should not be reduced to a *vitiosum*, even if only tolerated. Within it lies the positive possibility of the most original knowledge, which, indeed, can only be authentically grasped if interpretation has understood that its first, only, and last task is not to be guided, in its preconceptions, pre-views, and preconceptions, by naïve concepts and "guesses". In developing its preconceptions, pre-views, and preconceptions, it must secure the scientific subject matter from the things themselves. Because understanding, in its existential sense, is the being-possible of Dasein itself, the ontological presuppositions of historical knowledge fundamentally exceed the idea of rigour found in the most exact sciences. Mathematics is not more rigorous than history. It is only more restricted, in terms of the scope of existential foundations relevant to it. (Heidegger 2005: 210)

Consequently, the issue does not pertain to methodological rigour, but rather to the ontological assumptions underlying historical knowledge, which, as Heidegger argues and as previously outlined, fundamentally transcend the framework established by modern reason and its *ésprit géométrique*. This is, in part, attributable to the inherent historicity of being. In the humanities, understanding remains inherently historical, linguistic, and dialectical.

The implications of this hermeneutic perspective are significant for legal practice and judicial reasoning. Rather than aspiring to an illusory detachment or striving for an unattainable methodological neutrality, the judge is called upon to embrace the interpretative nature of their task. This requires an honest engagement with the traditions, assumptions, and horizons that shape one's understanding, fostering a critical and reflective approach to the evaluation of evidence and legal argument. In this way, the process of judging becomes an ongoing negotiation between inherited meanings and the particularities of the case at hand, always conditioned by the judge's own historicity.

This approach underscores the necessity for humility in the face of complexity and ambiguity. It invites the judiciary to recognise that truth in legal proceedings is not a static endpoint to be uncovered by mechanical application of rules, but rather a product of dialogical engagement and open-ended interpretation. Ultimately, the hermeneutic method offers a path towards a more nuanced and human-centred justice, one that acknowledges the limitations of knowledge while remaining committed to the pursuit of fairness and reasoned judgement, upholding safeguards to protect human rights.

This transition necessitates adopting a new perspective—one grounded in an awareness of existential boundaries rather than driven by ambition for dominance.

Gadamer, following Heidegger, regards understanding as an existential phenomenon; therefore, it transcends the mere formulation of an epistemology or theory of knowledge, since knowing fundamentally involves being-in-the-world. In this framework, pre-judgements are not considered impediments to knowledge but rather constitute the very conditions that enable the intelligibility of the past. Accordingly, Gadamer posits that the reality of the world is constituted through dialogue and temporality, emerging from collective engagement. Human reality is continually shaped by the dynamic interplay with the tradition of reflective experience. Consequently, culture within a tradition develops through an ongoing dialogical and temporal process, realised in the acknowledgement and transmission of civilisational principles.

According to Gadamer, the basis of understanding is rooted in the interpreter's affiliation with a specific tradition. Tradition provides the context within which individuals exist, often operating implicitly. Consequently, some pre-judgements facilitate insight while others restrict perception and thought. Understanding emerges when interpreters consciously engage their own prej-judgements in the interpretive process, thereby establishing temporal perspectives through which the past may be meaningfully understood.

However, it is essential to acknowledge that pre-judgements shape our experiential framework and, accordingly, should be critically examined. Ignoring this reality and presuming that one can begin from an entirely abstract position without acknowledging inherent assumptions may lead to knowledge that imposes unintended consequences; in the context of criminal proceedings, such an approach could prove especially detrimental.

This hermeneutic insight thus reframes the role of the interpreter—specifically, the judge—not as a neutral arbiter detached from the influences of history and tradition, but as an active participant whose preconceptions and situatedness inevitably shape the process of understanding. The challenge is not to eradicate these influences, but to become aware of and critically engage with them, allowing for a more authentic and transparent approach to interpretation. Such engagement requires that the judge adopt a posture of openness and reflexivity, recognising that their interpretative acts are always embedded within a particular horizon that both enables and limits understanding.

These pre-judgements constitute the interpreter's horizon and represent the tradition within which they are situated. Consequently, the complete eradication of pre-judgements is unattainable. As Soares observes, without nurturing the positivist dream of completely eliminating pre-judgements, it is for the author of a hermeneutic endeavour to extend as far as possible (indefinable *ex ante*) the critical awareness with which the 'object' will be received, so as to understand—and make explicit the consequences in each case—the partial nature of all understanding, which is a fusion of horizons (Soares 2004: 36).

In practical terms, this means that judicial reasoning must remain vigilant against the risks of unexamined assumptions and strive for a deliberate and iterative process of self-questioning. The judge's task, then, is to negotiate between the inherited meanings of tradition and the unique circumstances of each case, fostering an interpretive environment in which competing perspectives may be acknowledged and thoughtfully considered. Through this dynamic, the pursuit of justice becomes a process of critical dialogue and responsible judgement—one that is not driven by a relentless ambition for truth.

Any methodological approach necessitates an awareness of one's position within a particular tradition and is shaped by its inherent pre-judgements. Gadamer notes that "time is not primarily a gulf to be bridged because it separates and distances, but rather the basis of the event in which understanding is rooted. Therefore, temporal distance is not something that must be overcome" (Gadamer 1992: 68). This hermeneutic perspective introduces the concept of effective history, which is attuned to life's contingencies and oriented towards processes of co-determination. It acknowledges and accepts the tragic elements of existence, as well as the enduring nature of both social belonging and human finitude—concepts Soares identifies as interconnected aspects (Soares

2004). As Gadamer observes, it is essential to remain cognisant of one's own limitations and historical context in scholarly research, and to avoid the self-glorification characteristic of the Enlightenment (Gadamer 1992: 48).

Understanding occurs within a pre-existing horizon of meanings and intentions. This presupposed context, known as (pre-)understanding, informs the tradition in which the interpreter operates and defines their perspective; consequently, understanding emerges from a fusion of horizons, forming what is called the hermeneutic circle. Such an approach requires prior familiarity with the horizon under consideration; without it, communication is not possible. A reciprocal movement is necessary, as the interpreter must enter the subject's horizon and situation, engaging fully with the text both cognitively and affectively (Palmer 1997: 36). The intricate interplay between interpretation and the merging of horizons encapsulates the hermeneutic challenge, making interpretation dependent on the questions posed by the interpreter (Palmer 1997: 75).

In procedural dynamics, the scope of inquiry is initially defined by the indictment; however, this initial question gives rise to myriad possibilities that require the judge's open-mindedness. As previously observed, the criminal procedure may begin with a binary issue, yet, when addressing real-life events, it engages with an intricate universe of complexity. Such complexity can only be partially addressed through a tradition that acknowledges the richness of potential meanings, rather than narrowing them in pursuit of an unbounded desire for truth.

The challenge, then, lies in cultivating a judicial mindset that is not only critically aware of its own pre-judgements but also actively seeks to engage with the plurality of meanings inherent in every legal narrative. This requires a deliberate openness to the unfamiliar and a willingness to revisit initial assumptions as new evidence and perspectives emerge. By embracing this iterative process, the judge fosters a more nuanced and equitable approach to interpretation, ultimately serving the broader aims of justice.

It is essential for judges to recognise their own biases and continually assess them in light of the specific situations they encounter. Acknowledging the existence of a hermeneutic circle enables an approach that distinctly departs from the notion of absolute certainty in forming judicial convictions. This mindset is arguably more conducive to the objective and reflective disposition required when judges form opinions within procedural legal contexts. With this perspective, judges remain conscious of their inevitable initial hypotheses—a natural aspect of human reasoning—yet avoid steering proceedings towards affirmation of those views. Instead, judges maintain a receptive attitude, as advocated by Goldschmidt, attentively considering the evidence provided by the parties. Procedurally validated evidence may reveal new opportunities, alleviate burdens, or reduce risks. Such an orientation fundamentally differs from knowledge imposed by force and aligns with the principles of accusatory epistemology, where evidentiary management is entrusted to the parties involved.

While hermeneutics does not prescribe a definitive method for interpretative practice, it elucidates the complexities inherent in the process of understanding. This perspective suggests that a hermeneutic approach can inform interpretative strategies that avoid construing knowledge as inherently coercive. As Soares observes, meaning in the hermeneutic circle emerges from the interplay between parts and whole, realised through a reflective, comprehensive, and imaginative trajectory: given that an interpreter's initial engagement with an object is unavoidably tangential, partial, and fragmentary, it becomes necessary to address interpretative challenges by formulating provisional interpretations of accessible segments—serving as initial hypotheses concerning the full context of the object. The significance of each part is fundamentally relational and determined by its position within the entirety, depending on the concurrent apprehension of all components. Consequently, preliminary interpretations of a segment presuppose an anticipatory grasp of the overall meaning (Soares 2004). Palmer further highlights that the hermeneutic circle entails a conceptual "leap", wherein one endeavours to comprehend both the whole and its constituent parts simultaneously, a process that relies, in part, upon intuition (Palmer 1997: 94). Thus, there is no repudiation of subjectivity and its associated risks, as is often characteristic of modern philosophical thought.

The process of tentatively seeking to comprehend the entirety necessitates minimal prior knowledge, enabling an initial conceptual leap essential for dialogue—an element central to hermeneutics. As Soares (2004) notes, the effort to interpret a part as understood within a hypothetical whole is subsequently evaluated upon consideration of further segments. It is probable that this phase will demand reassessment of the preliminary meaning assigned to the whole, particularly when subsequent parts do not align with the initial hypothesis. Iterative refinements thus lead to anticipations supported by more substantial partial understandings, fostering corrective interplay between parts and whole until a comprehensive, well-founded interpretation emerges—one that is relevant, reasonable, plausible, and acceptable to potential interlocutors. This approach is especially appropriate for the dynamic context of procedural legal situations, where the inherent complexity of the relationship between part and whole is not overlooked but embraced as a fundamental aspect in the development of conviction.

Taruffo noted that the foundational principles of hermeneutics are applicable to the interpretation of legal narratives, particularly procedural narratives. He highlighted that the meaning of individual narrative elements can only be ascertained in relation to the narrative as a whole, while the overall significance of the narrative is accessible only through its constituent parts (Taruffo 2010: 79). Nevertheless, although Taruffo acknowledged the promise of hermeneutics, he made only limited reference to Gadamer's philosophical hermeneutics and did not address the challenge that hermeneutics poses to his ideal of truth, given that it is incompatible with the modern conception of the knowing subject's methodological pursuit of absolute truth.

From a hermeneutic standpoint, knowledge assumes a nuanced and non-violent meaning: it signifies an effort towards approximation rather than equivalence, acknowledging the interpreter's subjectivity and suggesting mechanisms to manage it. This process involves continually comparing initial assumptions with the subject matter itself and demonstrating openness to differing perspectives. Such a mindset stands in contrast to modern approaches and appears better suited to the judicial role within frameworks designed to restrain punitive authority, discouraging the pursuit of absolute truth as conceptualised by modern thought. Notably, this methodology excels in its ability to dismantle traditional dichotomies—such as universal versus particular, identity versus difference, part versus whole, subject versus object, belonging versus detachment, reason versus emotion, and neutrality versus commitment.

Although not formally classified as a methodology—and arguably its strength lies precisely in refraining from purporting to disclose absolute truths—hermeneutics offers a more productive approach to understanding reality and pursuing knowledge than that proposed by the subject/object dichotomy. Its merits in informing the process of judicial conviction formation, particularly when evaluating narrative accounts presented by parties, are evident. Hermeneutics stands in contrast to approaches in which an authoritative subject seeks to exhaustively penetrate an object in pursuit of its underlying essence. As Morais da Rosa observes with irony, this relentless pursuit may be misguided:

> Nothing escapes the judge when pronouncing the Truth; note that this truth is not just any truth, but the Whole Truth. Thus, paranoid by definition—it imagines itself as possessing total knowledge, of all facts, hearts, and minds. Indeed, not without reason, for the fantasy of being the divine chosen one, the Elite Squad of the Heavens, fertilises the judicial imagination. (Rosa 2011: 126)

Adopting a truly hermeneutic stance requires openness to other perspectives, characterised by ongoing reassessment and adjustment of hypotheses in response to the complexity of phenomena that cannot be fully comprehended or controlled. Reality inherently presents resistance, as previously noted, and when engaging with the past, this resistance is heightened due to temporal distance. Consequently, it is necessary to set aside the pursuit of absolute truth. In his discussion of Rosenzweig, Timm de Souza observes that.

> the meaning of discourse— *of any discourse* —does not, in its profound sense, consist in the supposed coincidence with the essence of what is said, but rather in the *approximation* of the *sense of reality of that about which something is being said.* [...] here we are at a fundamental turning point in philosophical thought. Abandoning the nostalgia for essences does not mean falling into some absolute scepticism or philosophical nihilism: it means having to handle other, quite different tools, in dealing with reality. *To a reality which does not correspond to the mere intellectual images we are capable of forming of it, one must be faithful in another way;* one must be flexible enough to accommodate the multiplicity of meanings the world entails. (Souza 2004: 74)

Acknowledging this complexity marks a significant departure from the principles of modern scientific thought and the Cartesian assertion rooted in rational underpinnings, which purportedly facilitated access to reality. When approached from the judicial standpoint, it is essential to recognise that interpreters are inherently influenced by tradition—a narrative structure conveying a worldview, body of knowledge, and explanatory frameworks, both scientific and ethical, which in turn shape interpretation (Ricoeur 1997: 443).

Nevertheless, overcoming such conditioning requires interpreters to remain open to alternative perspectives, accepting that their conceptualisations may not reflect objective truth. Consequently, absolute truth remains unattainable due to the inherent limitations of language, which serves as the fundamental medium through which we access the world and articulate consciousness and knowledge. The reality presented is thus intrinsically linked to its comprehension and subsequent interpretation, shaped by prevailing traditions. These traditions ultimately influence the significance afforded to evidence during the drafting of a judgement, a topic I will address in greater detail subsequently.

It is important to note, however, that understanding does not originate solely from tradition; rather, it emerges through a dialectical process encompassing the interplay between an individual's self-perception, their perspective, their environment, and new experiences. Thus, understanding should be regarded not merely as a human action, but as an event occurring within the individual. From this standpoint, understanding shifts away from mere contemplation of objects and is better conceived as an act that transforms the context to which those objects belong, moving beyond the notion of corresponding truth. In this framework, truth is conceptualised not as something discovered, but as something produced.

This reconceptualisation of truth, grounded in hermeneutics, highlights the dynamic and productive nature of legal understanding. Within adversarial proceedings, the judge's role transcends the passive reception of evidence or the mere verification of facts against a fixed reality; instead, the judge actively participates in weaving together the narratives presented, infusing them with their own situated perspective and creative engagement. As such, the process of forming a judicial conviction is not a mechanical application of rules to facts, but an interpretative act shaped by tradition, context, and the judge's existential horizon.

This hermeneutic stance not only embraces the inherent pluralism of meaning but also acknowledges the inevitable uncertainty and provisionality that characterise all attempts at understanding. The truth produced in the legal judgement is, therefore, not a mirror of the past but a new narrative construction—a unique synthesis that both references and transforms the traces of what has been. This approach rejects the notion of finality, promoting thoughtful and accountable engagement with the complexities inherent in law and human experience, and is grounded in a steadfast commitment to the protection of human rights—one that is not found in evidentiary rationalism's reproduction of the subject-object schema.

The deliberate invocation of a "web" surrounding the event is not coincidental; it is intended to underscore its narrative dimension. It is important to note that hermeneutics adopts an especially broad definition of text. Beyond the life narrative in which the event is situated, adversarial proceedings bring forth competing narrative accounts. Through contestation within a context of conflict and uncertainty, these narratives aim to persuade the judge by demonstrating that the evidence they present serves as traces of the past that substantiate their respective positions.

The intricacies of this dynamic emerge clearly when considering that the judge must evaluate not merely two, but three distinct narratives from their receptive standpoint. In addition to methodically listening to the parties' accounts and arguments, the process of forming a judgement necessitates careful scrutiny of the potential evidentiary core they present. It is within this evidentiary foundation that relevant elements may be found, guiding the judge in constructing their own narrative—the judgement—based on traces of past events and enabling analogical reasoning. Beyond persuasive strategies, the evidentiary core demands the judge's attention; if it does not sufficiently substantiate the accusatory hypothesis, acquittal is warranted, aligning with principles rooted in the presumption of innocence.

This approach plays a critical role in countering decisionist tendencies. The capacity to navigate and engage with the complexities of narrative otherness, without reducing its intricacies, is essential; the breadth of meaning cannot be fully understood through the conventional subject-object dichotomy prevalent in modern traditions. A superficial impartiality is inadequate—an interpretative stance is necessary to address this tripartite narrative framework while constructing judgements. The iterative process of hypothesis revision, characteristic of the hermeneutic circle, is vital in this context.

The question therefore emerges: Is all experience inherently narrative? In certain respects, this may be affirmed; as previously stated, any entity that can be comprehended is fundamentally expressed through language. Language, history, and existence are not simply interconnected but profoundly interwoven, making knowledge inherently metaphorical. Morais da Rosa asserts, "Each interpretation is subjective, situated within specific temporal and spatial contexts, and invariably traverses signifiers that elude definitive grasp. The absolute truth, a concept inherited from the philosophy of consciousness that lies beneath the text's surface, ultimately cannot endure the linguistic shift" (Rosa 2011: 43). Timm de Souza further observes, if it is necessary that there be representations, images, concepts, figurations, categories—and they exist, and occur, whether we wish it or not—at the very least, let them be acutely aware, so as not to continually generate self-illusions regarding their own strength, their own limits, their provisional meaning, their shifting course, their always precarious position (Souza 2004: 41).

Consequently, what implications might arise for the process of conviction formation from embracing a hermeneutic attitude and abandoning the inquisitorial pursuit of absolute truth?

While the initial effort to interpret an event originates from its legal context, establishing an appropriate understanding relies on the ability to comprehend, to a certain degree, the complexities of real life. This involves understanding the intricate circumstances surrounding the event, each emerging from a broader narrative that must be examined within the framework of adversarial proceedings. Such proceedings are designed to test and correct the hallucinatory character of evidence and should fix the judge in an impartial position, mitigating the possibility of confirmation or previous hypotheses. The hermeneutic approach, therefore, invites the judge to become a participant in a process of ongoing negotiation between inherited traditions, legal norms and the unpredictable realities of each case. Rather than seeking to impose a singular, definitive meaning, this disposition encourages a continual reassessment of interpretations as new evidence and perspectives are introduced. In this way, judicial reasoning becomes a collaborative and dialogical endeavour, where the aim is not to reach an unassailable truth but to arrive at a plausible, reasoned understanding that is responsive to the complexities of human experience. Such an attitude not only enhances the quality of legal interpretation but also upholds the ethical imperative to treat all parties with fairness and dignity.

The Role of the Judge as a Being-in-the-World

Heidegger was extremely critical of the subject-object dichotomy, rejecting the "assumption, so prevalent today, of knowledge as a 'subject-object relation', as 'true' as it is futile" (Heidegger 2005: 98). With his characteristically provocative spirit, he questions.

> how this subject who "knows" leaves their internal "sphere" and reaches an "other" sphere, the "external" one? How can knowledge have an object? How should the object itself be conceived so that the subject finally comes to know it, without having to risk the leap into an "other" sphere, the "external" one? [...] What is perceived and determined can be expressed in sentences and maintained and preserved in this quality of *proposed*. The perceptual maintenance of a proposition about... is, in itself, a mode of being-in-the-world and cannot be interpreted as a "process" through which a subject creates representations of something for themselves, in such a way that these representations, thus appropriated, are kept "inside" so that only then is it possible, at times, to ask how they are to "correspond" to reality. (Heidegger 2005: 99-101)

Heidegger simply dismantles the category of subject through his notion of *Dasein*. According to him, "*Dasein*, as being-in-the-world, has the tendency first to bury epistemologically the 'external world' in a negative nothingness, so that it may then be resurrected by means of proofs" (Heidegger 2005: 273).

According to Gadamer's perspective, the act of understanding is defined by the reciprocal relationship between the interpreter and the object of interpretation, rendering traditional subject-object distinctions no longer applicable. Consequently, historical knowledge should not be interpreted within the framework of the philosophy of consciousness' subject-object schema, but rather as an expression of the fundamental mode of human existence. Gadamer's hermeneutics distinctly rejects the subject/object dichotomy prevalent in mainstream modern philosophy. As Soares observes,

> Within the hermeneutic process, subject and object are interdependent, eliminating distinctions as separate entities. Consequently, interpreters must avoid treating their object with undue naivety, refraining from considering it autonomous or detached from themselves—the reflexive subject—before inadvertently adopting one of two approaches: the essentialist perspective, which attempts to discern the object's inherent content, or the subjectivist route, which results in cognitive limitations by failing to acknowledge the object's otherness and thus rendering it inaccessible. (Soares 2004: 69)

Within Gadamerian hermeneutic philosophy, the subject is understood as that which moves towards the object to comprehend it, with both the subject and object engaging in a reciprocal dynamic. The subject does not function solely as the active agent, nor is the object entirely passive; rather, the subject's constitution emerges from its directedness towards the object and its definition through objectivity. This relationship reflects the influence of tradition, which establishes a sense of belonging, combined with the creative capacity for reflection and imaginative thought. As Marrou (1978) notes, knowledge of man by man, history is an apprehension of the past by—and in—a living, committed human thought; it is a complex, an indissoluble mixture of subject and object.

It is noteworthy, as Ricoeur observes, that despite the pursuit of historical objectivity, questions regarding objectivity in history still persist (Ricoeur 1994: 252). In this context, Gadamer asserts that "the true historical object is not an object, but the unity of the one and the other, a relationship in which consists both the reality of history and the reality of historical understanding" (Gadamer 1992: 170).

Accordingly, a degree of creative imagination is inevitably involved; such imagination reorganises and reinterprets the remnants of the past in order to understand the complexities surrounding particular events. Consequently, the narrative articulation of conviction necessarily assumes a poetic quality, functioning as a form of interpreted life and an effort to discern essential truths.

It follows that when a judge articulates their conviction in the form of a judgement, this act generates something fundamentally new that surpasses a simple alignment with a presumed objective truth. Truth, in this context, cannot be reduced to a mere correspondence between subjective judgement and its object, whether absolutely or relatively defined. Rather than functioning solely as an analytical instrument that objectively renders factual determinations—thereby achieving truth or certainty, which are often considered synonymous—the judge operates as a subject situated within a broader legal tradition of evaluating such objects. This process is further shaped by the judge's individual perspective, resulting in the formulation of a fundamentally new hypothesis, even as it relates to and contrasts with the relevant object. Accordingly, creative imagination should be regarded not as the replication of a pre-established reality, but as an approach where representation transcends mere duplication of presence (Ricoeur 1994: 76). This conception aligns closely with the notion of representance—an ongoing engagement with an irreconcilable debt to the past that one endeavours to represent.

The existential aspect of the judge introduces an additional layer of unpredictability to the determination of truth within legal proceedings—a phenomenon noted by several esteemed scholars. Ferrajoli (2002: 46) points out that, regardless of the judge's commitment to objectivity, they are invariably influenced by their surrounding circumstances, personal emotions, preferences, and ethical–political values. Similarly, Taruffo (2010: 67) observes that narratives are the result of complex and sophisticated creative processes on the part of their authors; consequently, these narratives actively construct the facts they present. This process is not a passive, abstract, or neutral account, but rather one in which the author's perspective shapes the constructed reality—something that Taruffo does not acknowledge.

Ferrajoli and Taruffo overlooked that, given such findings, the corresponding model of truth—even when considered in an approximate sense—constitutes an epistemic excess. The proceedings generate something fundamentally novel, despite maintaining a referential connection to prior events. Accordingly, the concept of corresponding truth becomes untenable, since the formation of conviction always relates to an existential context that introduces its own perspective when recounting the narrative, even if this is grounded in traces of the past. As Pozzebon notes, the judge.

> will be using his feelings, his emotion, his reason, his pre-understanding of things, his values, his history, his worldview, and even his unconscious in the decision; he will always reflect something of himself. The subjectivity relegated to the parties in the proceedings is also present in the judge. The activity of evaluating evidence and even that of subsumption involves choosing between hypotheses and legal provisions available to the judge and the outcome the adjudicator wishes to reach. (Pozzebon 2006: 234)

Consequently, even when grounded in proof and structured according to appropriate normative standards, a judgement remains fundamentally an act of belief, as Lopes Jr. observes (Lopes Jr 2007: 45). As previously noted, no conviction can completely eradicate this element of faith. Gadamer asserts that historical vision or understanding is never entirely objective but always contextualised by present consciousness influenced by inherited prejudices. Thus, in terms of historical comprehension, the past cannot be regarded simply as an isolated object; it is invariably connected to our current and future perspectives. The imperative of decision-making accentuates this concern for judges. According to Timm de Souza,

> *The understanding of reality does not primarily occur through comprehension, but through the relationship we are able to establish with it*—and only subsequently can it, eventually, be reconsidered in terms of "understanding"—if by understanding we do not mean its reduction to some intellectual representation of itself. This tendency towards reduction—congenital to thought—can only be corrected by reiterating the temporality that emerges and re-emerges from relationships. (Souza 2004: 82-83)

The cognitive process involved in forming judgements is guided by creative imagination, which fulfils a schematic role rooted in tradition. This process results in a form of understanding that integrates the theme of historical narrative with an intuitive grasp of situational factors. The underlying schematism draws upon tradition, not as a static legacy, but as an active dynamic shaped by the interplay of innovation and sedimentation, as described by Ricoeur (1994: 107).

The development of conviction is inherently complex in relation to tradition. Tradition establishes boundaries within which judicial actors must operate, and these confines are mandated by legal norms rather than being optional or discretionary. Nevertheless, the matter remains unresolved at the normative level, as varying interpretations—shaped by differing traditions—can give rise to fundamentally different epistemological frameworks, such as accusatorial versus inquisitorial systems. Consequently, it is possible to identify two distinct orders of truth that reflect separate traditions: one that is characterised by the potential for both revelation and concealment, and another that pursues truth through objectification, potentially resulting in adverse consequences for the accused.

Traditions give rise to paradigms, which, in turn, establish rules subject to modification under the influence of new advancements, yet often exhibit resistance to change due to sedimentation processes (Ricoeur 1994: 104). Nonetheless, opportunities for innovation persist, as the development and articulation of conviction always yield distinctive narratives. Each narrative is inherently singular, forming its own unique context, even while maintaining necessary references. However, innovation remains guided by established rules; imaginative work draws upon existing traditions and does not emerge in isolation.

Accordingly, it should be emphasised that the dynamic relationship with tradition operates along a spectrum ranging from strict adherence to intentional divergence, encompassing various levels of regulated modification (Ricoeur 1994: 109). Ultimately, such deviations are constrained by the boundaries established by law. As Lopes Jr observes,

> it is necessary to seek in constitutional hermeneutics the instruments required to effect constitutional filtering, the conformity of ordinary law to the Constitution, but without this descending into absurd relativism. Considerable scientific maturity is required to make an honest effort in reading the Constitution (and ordinary legislation, provided it is filtered, of course) in order to reach an interpretation that is not always to our liking, without this implying a position of naïve conformism. (Lopes Jr 2010: 348)

In this sense, excessive variation, whether by contesting the principle of concordance–discordance (a conviction not supported by proof) or by exceeding the limits of regulated deformation (admission of illegal evidence), can—and should—signify the demise of the narrative itself.

The interplay between adherence to tradition and the necessity for innovation requires a careful balancing act in judicial practice. Judges must not only operate within the boundaries set by established legal norms, but also remain receptive to evolving interpretations and contexts, thereby fostering a dynamic yet regulated environment for the development of conviction. This equilibrium is essential to maintain the integrity of the judicial process, ensuring that neither rigid conformity nor unchecked divergence undermines the pursuit of justice and the protection of human rights.

Considering the points raised in this section, it is essential to acknowledge the mechanisms underlying the process of understanding and remain receptive to the possibility that reality may surpass the scope of any initial hypothesis. The formulation of hypotheses should be grounded rather than arbitrary, incorporating insights offered by differing perspectives. The act of hypothesising is a fundamental aspect of human cognition and inquiry; however, these hypotheses must be rigorously tested against real-world evidence, bearing in mind the uncertainty inherent in forming convictions regarding past events. As Lopes Jr. (2005: 77) observes, "beyond independence, only a judge who is conscious of his role as guarantor and, above all, has doubt as a professional habit and as an intellectual style, is worthy of the power conferred upon him". The judge's approach should be anchored in the presumption of innocence, and if any doubt persists, acquittal becomes obligatory.

Cultivating doubt as an intellectual practice fosters a productive interplay between strangeness and familiarity, situating the hermeneutic approach within this intermediary space. This orientation enables the critical examination and temporary suspension of pre-judgments through deliberate questioning. Such inquiry is characterised by genuine engagement, which requires openness to the subject matter and authentic consideration of uncertainty. To inquire is to pursue understanding with the recognition that knowledge is incomplete, thereby remaining receptive to revising initial assumptions. The process by which hypotheses are continually reassessed—central to forming judicial conviction—is grounded in the production of evidence. Adherence to evidentiary requirements and procedural rigour establishes clear parameters that the judge must not exceed, thus defining both the manner and foundation upon which judgements may be rendered.

The judicial process should be marked by an inherent openness to doubt and the provisional nature of knowledge. This disposition, far from weakening judicial authority, reinforces it by fostering intellectual honesty and humility. By acknowledging the limits of knowledge and the potential for error, the judge cultivates a climate in which fairness is pursued through careful deliberation, rigorous evidentiary standards, and a steadfast commitment to the presumption of innocence. Thus, the pursuit of justice is maintained not through rigid adherence to dogma, but by embracing an interpretative *ethos* that values dialogue, scrutiny, and the continual reassessment of convictions.

In accusatory epistemology, the judge's responsibilities extend beyond solely restrictive duties; a distinct sphere of action is allocated where the concept of otherness is fundamental. Lopes Jr. describes this as a special capacity: the ability to simultaneously fulfil the roles of both judge and judged, necessitating that the judge refrain from perceiving the accused as a mere societal enemy to be condemned. This process involves an exercise in abstraction and altruism, respecting diversity and adopting the perspective of others, which is essential for judicial practice (Lopes Jr 2005: 80).

This attitude involves respect for otherness, requiring that the accused be presumed innocent until proven otherwise, and obliging the judge to safeguard their rights against State power until a final verdict is reached. The accused inherently occupies a disadvantaged position, as the exercise of power is directed against them. With this understanding, the judge can maintain their role as impartial arbiter within the adversarial process while also acting as a guarantor of fundamental rights. Moreover, should a conviction occur, the establishment of truth must surpass mere evidence. As Lopes Jr. notes, his conviction must be sought from what is brought before him and not from what he seeks, for the judge was ontologically conceived to be an "ignoramus"; he is ignorant of the facts and the evidence, and this is fundamental to the structure of the accusatory proceedings, with it being the parties' responsibility to provide him with information and elements of conviction (Lopes Jr 2010: 528).

Accordingly, it is principally the responsibility of the judge to form a reasoned conviction and render a decision based upon the evidence presented by the parties, which must be subjected to adversarial scrutiny. This approach seeks to ensure that an element introduced into the proceedings can only be regarded as indicative of past events if it results from the proper alleviation of a burden or mitigation of risk. The judge is required to maintain impartiality in the assessment of evidence while also overseeing the propriety of its production. As the accused benefits from the presumption of innocence, there is no obligation placed upon them to provide proof of innocence; rather, it falls to the prosecutor to attempt to refute this presumption through appropriate evidentiary means—a process in which neither the defendant nor the judge is actively involved. The judge's role does not include the production of evidence, thereby avoiding undue self-reliance and upholding the essential openness to ongoing hypothesis revision demanded by judicial duties.

In an accusatory epistemological framework that upholds human rights, it is not the responsibility of the judge to produce evidence; instead, the judge has other significant duties aligned with maintaining judicial impartiality. This impartiality does not equate to passivity: the judge acts as an arbiter rather than a passive observer. In this capacity, the judge must safeguard due process, remaining vigilant regarding both the development of evidence and the methods by which it is obtained, as procedural integrity is essential—deviation from established procedure may result in nullity. It is concerning that some perspectives argue for requiring proof of harm resulting from procedural invalidity before recognising nullity, as this contravenes fundamental principles supporting a criminal procedure that should be grounded in the presumption of innocence and the doctrine of *in dubio pro reo*. Likewise, the assertion that the accused bears the burden of proving a causa of justification such as legitimate defence is misguided, as it erroneously shifts the burden of proof from the prosecution, which must establish the absence of justification in each case.

Accordingly, the judge should maintain an active role, though this does not entail a "pursuit of absolute truth". While interpretation is involved in this process, such an approach is not inherently problematic. Rather than embracing objectivity as defined by modern neutrality, the judge's role is characterised by a specific engagement with the subject matter—one that resists conventional categorisation, as previously noted.

To interpret within a genuinely adversarial model entails ensuring robust defence mechanisms for the accused when confronted by prosecution. This requires setting clear and appropriate constraints on the exercise of state power against individuals facing potential punitive measures. Consequently, interpretation must adhere to constitutional safeguards, maintaining both rigour and fairness. As Cunha Martins notes, evidence should be held to stringent standards of accuracy. This approach involves interpreting within legally defined boundaries and functions, as mandated by an accusatorial system aligned with a democratic-constitutional framework. The central issue is not the mere existence of interpretation, but rather determining which interpretation is applied, from what perspective, and for what intended purpose.

This methodology should underpin the formation of judicial conviction. The dialectical structure of question and answer within adversarial proceedings facilitates an integration of perspectives. Such integration emerges from the adversarial process itself, through the narrative accounts submitted by the parties in the inherently uncertain and contentious context of trial, informed by evidence that may or may not be deemed proof, and governed by principles of regularity and legality. It entails adopting an open and receptive approach as advocated by Goldschmidt.

Nonetheless, even with an open and receptive stance, the process of understanding invariably generates something new. As Gadamer notes, all acts of knowledge are inherently hermeneutic, involving interpretative engagement. This distinction sets interpretative understanding apart from knowledge pursued for purposes of domination: interpretation requires active involvement and the establishment of a relationship with the subject matter. Consequently, as previously mentioned, interpretation is always a creative act—speculative and original by nature—since each instance of understanding occurs in a unique manner (Gadamer 1984: 368).

By adopting a hermeneutic approach, a judge effectively avoids the risks associated with prioritising hypotheses over facts—risks that arise from metaphysical frameworks allowing for a strict separation between subject and object and bestowing unchecked authority upon the subject in the search for absolute truth. Individuals who remain committed to such metaphysics may perceive the adversarial process and the distinction between prosecutorial and judicial functions as counterintuitive; however, the contrary is valid. The most reliable method for correcting the hallucinatory character of evidence is to implement robust adversarial proceedings consistent with due process requirements. Through such proceedings, evidence pertaining to a complex and intricate reality can be meaningfully interpreted, potentially serving as analogical markers for past events.

Accordingly, the proper approach to forming judicial conviction, in contrast to the nineteenth-century scientific paradigm, is primarily interpretative. The concept of absolute neutrality during the act of decoding—particularly in the creation of a third, historical moment through narrative—is fundamentally flawed. Judicial interpretation is inevitable, whether conscious or unconscious, and judges must acknowledge this reality to maintain an appropriate degree of control over their own subjectivity. Furthermore, judicial practice is inherently interpretative; it requires active engagement with the material at hand. The development of judicial conviction is mediated by adversarial proceedings, understanding, and interpretation, which necessarily involve adopting a position distinct from simple fact-finding or the pursuit of absolute truth as conceived in modernity and still defended by evidentiary rationalism. Only through accurate interpretation, as required by democratic principles, can judges uphold due process and achieve the balance and impartiality essential to accusatorial epistemology.

Jurisdiction within a reimagined criminal justice system encompasses not only the concepts of authority and duty but also functions as a safeguard: it guarantees the assignment of a natural judge and ensures due process of law. The judge's role is therefore fundamental in upholding the rights and core protections afforded to the accused in criminal proceedings (Lopes Jr 2005: 75). To perform this function effectively, judicial independence is essential, enabling the judge to remain uninfluenced by political pressures and to act with impartial conviction (Lopes Jr 2005: 73).

However, such independence must be balanced; absolute discretion could result in arbitrary decisions—judicial decisions must be carefully justified and based on evidence that has been rigorously assessed and verified as proof, which constitutes an essential foundation for sustaining convictions. This matter will be discussed in greater detail below.

Free Motivated Conviction: Decisionism and the Control of Improper Spaces of Subjectivity

The judicial verdict effectively terminates the conflict, formally concluding the dispute and determining the prevailing party. As Gössel notes, the issue arising from multiple perspectives is addressed by adopting the viewpoint of the judge (Gossel 2007: 24). According to Nassif, a criminal judgement is the process by which a qualified judge formally documents and evaluates all relevant circumstances and emotions, guided by constitutional safeguards of due process, in relation to an act defined as a crime requiring state intervention. Its purpose is to confirm or annul allegations, assign legal penalties, or uphold the presumption of innocence for the accused (Nassif 2004: 215).

Primarily, it should be noted that the approach presented here is focused predominantly on convictions. In such cases, establishing the truth is essential, as a coherent probatory foundation is required for the imposition of punishment. However, this does not imply that acquittals do not warrant justification; not all acquittals are due to insufficient proof. In certain instances, indicators of innocence may outweigh the allegations brought forth by the prosecution, and this must be appropriately reflected in an acquittal narrative that acknowledges the defendant's innocence.

Conversely, an acquittal based on insufficient proof is not required to establish factual truth. The presumption of innocence ensures that proof of non-culpability is unnecessary; simply lacking incriminating proof or the presence of reasonable doubt suffices for acquittal under the principle of *in dubio pro reo*. This characteristic fundamentally distinguishes legal narratives from those of historians. As Gimeno Sendra observes, both evidence and its evaluation serve as tools for the adjudicating body to conduct its historical judgement. Since conviction is permissible solely when a positive determination is reached—hypothetical reasoning cannot form its basis—the issue then concerns either a complete absence of evidence or inadequate evidentiary support to resolve judicial uncertainty. In the first scenario, acquittal results from the presumption of innocence; in the second, it follows the *in dubio pro reo* principle (Sendra et al. 1996: 604–605).

Taruffo posits that, where available evidence fails to meet the legally mandated standard for a positive determination, the judge formulates a negative narrative, indicating that relevant case facts have not been established and statements pertaining to those facts cannot be treated as true (Taruffo 2010: 67). However, Taruffo's analysis presents an unresolved question regarding the epistemic role exercised by judges during truth-seeking: what criteria determines when this process concludes, thereby prompting the construction of negative narratives instead of entailing an endless search for the absolute truth?

As noted by Lopes Jr., the rationale underpinning judicial decisions is fundamental to ensuring both effective adversarial proceedings and demonstrating that sufficient proof exists to rebut the presumption of innocence (Lopes Jr 2010: 201). Consequently, it is imperative to provide detailed justification and substantiation, particularly in cases resulting in conviction. The Brazilian Code of Criminal Procedure (Article 381, III) stipulates that reasoning entails articulating the factual and legal foundations of a decision. This requirement is further enshrined in the Constitution (Article 93, IX, CF/88), mandating clarity and logical consistency. According to Lopes Jr., reasoning serves as the

> crucial point of the judgment, in which the judge must analyse and address all (on pain of nullity) the arguments of both prosecution and defence, demonstrating the reasons that lead to one decision or another. Reasoning operates on two levels: factual and legal. In the first, the judge evaluates the evidence and the facts, reserving for the second the reasoning concerning the legal arguments raised but rejected. Finally, if the judgment is a conviction, the judge must rule on the defendant's civil liability, setting the minimum amount for compensation for the damage caused by the offence, taking into account the losses suffered by the victim. (Lopes Jr 2010: 398)

Accordingly, the sentence serves as a justificatory discourse that clearly outlines the judge's decision-making process. This narrative addresses the specific facts of the case, considering both parties' positions. At this stage, as previously outlined, the judge relies on the analogical value of proofs to underpin the reasoning behind their decision in guilty verdicts. Thus, legal reasoning functions as a means of representing past events through narrative form. This methodology is not only a logical result of the adversarial and uncertain nature of legal proceedings but also underscores the act of judicial writing as an expression of existence and creative agency.

In this initial phase of analysing the construction of narrative decisions, I will first examine the prevailing interpretations within procedural literature. Subsequently, I will present a new interpretative framework that addresses the complexity inherent in constructing narrative decisions and, by extension, the analogous production of truth.

Firstly, the requirement for reasoning in conviction judgements serves to constrain punitive authority and mitigate potential harm. As Ibáñez notes, "the initial emergence of the duty to provide reasons primarily corresponds to political demands: the search for a safeguard against arbitrariness" (Ibáñez 2005: 43). Lopes Jr. further emphasises that "only through reasoning is it possible to assess whether rationality prevailed over power in the decision, especially whether the rules of due criminal process were observed" (Lopes Jr 2010: 201). According to Pozzebon,

> The need to provide reasons for an act is not limited to a technical safeguard of the procedure, but is rather seen as a principle of political order, that is, as an essential safeguard for the administration of justice in a Democratic State governed by the rule of law. Through reasoning, it is possible to assess the exercise of judicial activity, examining the choices and selections made by the judge in establishing the criminal fact, the observance of the rules of full adversarial proceedings and, above all, the factual circumstances drawn from the case file which formed the judge's "truth". (Pozzebon 2006: 242)

For Gomes Filho, "unlike authoritarian power, which is exercised in an absolute and also *concealed* manner, the exercise of power in a democratic state requires *publicity* and *transparency*, which presupposes the ongoing *explanation of the reasons* for state action" (Filho 2001: 77). According to Calamandrei,

> The reasoning of judgments is certainly a major guarantee of justice, when it succeeds in accurately reproducing, as in a topographical sketch, the logical path followed by the judge to reach his conclusion. In such cases, if the conclusion is mistaken, it will be easy to discover, through

> the reasoning, at which stage of the process the judge lost his way. (Calamandrei 1996: 175)

According to Ibañez, the obligation to provide reasoning is intended to regulate the probatory discourse of the judge, thereby aiming to ensure, as much as possible, the rationality of judicial decisions within the confines of legal rationality (Ibáñez 2005: 85). Lopes Jr. asserts that this constitutes a fundamental safeguard, whose efficacy and observance confer legitimacy upon the authority exercised through decision-making acts. Within a constitutional-democratic framework, power does not derive its legitimacy from itself; rather, it requires adherence to the principles of due legal process. Among these is the obligation to provide reasoned decisions, which serves as an essential safeguard (Lopes Jr 2010: 201).

Sampaio (2010: 167) states that judicial decisions, accompanied by their reasoning, aim to offer a procedural account of the facts, thereby serving as a legal rationale to legitimise and rationalise outcomes. Guasp and Alonso (1998: 486) contend that judgements should not merely recount facts deemed proven but must also adequately and logically clarify the process by which conclusions regarding historical matters are reached. This includes emphasising the inadmissibility of evidence obtained through violations of fundamental rights and freedoms, while allowing for the assessment of other valid evidentiary sources within the case file. Taruffo (2010: 267) further asserts that the duty to provide justification is especially pertinent to the evaluation of factual findings.

Consequently, the sentence must be historically accountable, substantiating its reasoning through documented proof within the case file. This requirement stems from the principle of freely motivated conviction, which recognises the judge as an individual entrusted with evaluating evidence and issuing judgements concerning the accused. The judge is therefore mandated to articulate the rationale and delineate the processes that informed their conclusion (Mora 2006: 85–86). Nonetheless, as will be discussed later in this section, freely motivated conviction does not resolve the issue of decisionism; it permits the formation of decisions prior to evidentiary review, thereby frequently serving as a rhetorical pretext for authoritarian practices (Streck 2010), despite its frequent identification as a remedy for judicial arbitrariness. As Ferrajoli notes,

> Unlike any other legal activity, the judicial activity of a state governed by the rule of law is, in addition to being practical or prescriptive, a theoretical

> activity; or rather, it is an activity that necessarily requires a *motivation* that is wholly or partly cognitive [...] criminal judgments, therefore, by virtue of the safeguards of strict legality and strict submission to jurisdiction, require reasoning that must also be based on cognitive arguments of fact and re-cognitive arguments of law. (Ferrajoli 2002: 436)

It is frequently asserted that the necessity for judicial reasoning lies in its ability to provide satisfaction both to society and to the accused (Filho 2001: 80–81). Leone observes that the articulation of judicial reasoning marks a critical juncture for the criminal judiciary, as it not only delineates the logical process undertaken by the judge in reaching a decision but also communicates the foundation of that decision to society (Leone 1963: 374).

Accordingly, it is essential to account for both factual and legal grounds, informed by statute and judicial interpretation. Moreover, this requirement facilitates the exercise of the right to appeal, as it enables parties to comprehend the judge's rationale and thereby formulate grounds for contesting the decision before a higher court, thus ensuring the possibility of subsequent review (Taruffo 2005: 435). Gössel emphasises that a judgement can only be considered just if its underlying factual assumptions have been thoroughly assessed for their truthfulness (Gössel 2007: 134). This scrutiny is imperative because, as Fazzalari notes,

> even when reference is made to the judge's 'free conviction' regarding the evidence and the facts, it is certainly assumed and required that the judge employ the instruments and verified propositions previously mentioned, without which conviction would be left to arbitrariness and whim, and could not even be formed. (Fazzalari 2006: 461)

The significance of the issue increased markedly following the abolition of the concept of legal proof. As Taruffo observes, "the evaluation of evidence is removed from the domain of legal rules when it is assigned to the judge rather than the legislator; consequently, it becomes clear that the phenomenon of evidence cannot (or can no longer) be subsumed within the rules that regulate it" (Taruffo 2005: 23). Ferrer Beltrán asserts that the free assessment of evidence is "free" only in the sense that it is not governed by predetermined legal rules. This process involves evaluating the empirical support provided by evidentiary elements for a particular hypothesis, guided by general principles of logic and rationality (Beltrán2007: 45). The author emphasises that the reasoning presented by the judge or court should justify the fulfilment of a standard of proof for the hypothesis deemed proven and explain why other hypotheses failed to meet this threshold (Beltrán 2007: 151). According to Ibañez, criminal judgement as an exercise of state authority requires that any imposed penalty be preceded by a cognitive process and a standard sufficient to ensure that the facts deemed proven are considered to have actually occurred. In essence, it must be substantiated that the accused committed the act for which they are being convicted (Ibáñez 2005: 113). Lopes Jr. further notes, "reasoning concerning factual matters demonstrates the knowledge that legitimises power, since punishment may only be imposed on individuals who can—rationally—be considered the perpetrator of the alleged criminal act" (Lopes Jr 2010: 202).

The issue of truth in criminal proceedings is once again brought to the forefront. As previously discussed, if this requirement were strictly applied, the inherently analogical nature of truth emerging from such proceedings would ultimately invalidate all convictions and result in the paralysis of criminal jurisdiction.

It has already been established that there is no mechanism capable of correcting the hallucinatory aspects of evidence to ensure a conviction aligns with absolute truth; the best attainable structure focuses on harm reduction, specifically minimising wrongful convictions. Even traces cannot guarantee corresponding truth due to their analogical character and persistent uncertainty, meaning conviction will always involve an element of belief, influenced by the irreducible margins of discretion within decision-making. Accordingly, as argued before, truth in this context remains contingent.

However, this does not mean that reasoning does not have a fundamental role to play, one that is closely related to the question of truth. As Lopes Jr. observes,

> under the constitutional model, no penalty may be imposed: without the commission of the offence; without it being previously defined by law; without the necessity of its prohibition and punishment; without the conduct's effects being harmful to others; without the external or material character of the criminal conduct; without the author's imputability and culpability; and without all this being verified through empirical evidence, presented by the prosecution to an impartial judge in a public, adversarial trial, with full rights of defence and by means of a legally pre-established procedure. (Lopes Jr 2010: 202)

It is no coincidence that Cunha Martins observes, "the fundamental problem of truth concerns the disproportion of its canonical place and not the usefulness of the competences it ensures" (Martins 2010: 88). Indeed, concepts such as the presumption of innocence and *in dubio pro reo* would be rendered meaningless within a system that entirely neglected the concept of truth.

It is undeniable that the complete exclusion of truth would undermine the foundation of reasoning itself, inevitably resulting in unchecked discretionary power—an outcome fundamentally opposed to the principles underlying the regulated exercise of punitive authority. Therefore, a cognitive obligation is imposed upon the judge: although evidentiary procedures are intended for the judge's psychic capture, judicial discretion over the acceptance of narrative accounts presented during proceedings is not without limits. Accordingly, the evaluation of reasoning permits scrutiny into whether improperly obtained evidence—derived from inherently monological investigative actions—has been used. Such evidence cannot be regarded as grounds for conviction if obtained during police inquiries without full adherence to due process (Lopes Jr 2010: 205).

Consequently, once the judge reaches a decision to condemn, the judgement must be thoroughly justified by the evidence and historical context upon which his conviction is founded. As stated by Muñoz Conde,

> The necessity for judicial decisions to be reasoned, understood as intersubjective argumentation, communicable through language, and rationally verifiable in terms of the reasons that led to a particular assessment and, consequently, to a decision based on it, is thus the logical consequence of a criminal procedure that respects the fundamental freedoms and rights of the citizens involved. (Conde 2003: 115)

Viewing the matter through the lens of upholding the fundamental rights of the accused and establishing safeguards against excessive punitive power, Gomes Filho's observations introduce a significant point for reflection. The author notes that.

> by enabling scrutiny of the logical path followed by the judge to reach a decision, the reasoning fulfils the important function of ensuring the effectiveness of adversarial proceedings, revealing whether the various choices made along that path resulted from a positive assessment of the evidence and arguments presented by the parties or, on the contrary, are the product

> of the solitary deliberations of the decision-maker, without regard for what was brought forth in procedural dialogue. (Filho 2001: 100-101)

If the author's reasoning is followed to its logical end, notable conclusions emerge, particularly when a direct connection is established between robust adversarial proceedings and the necessity of judicial reasoning. In this context, the judge's search for absolute truth exemplifies the solitary deliberation criticised by the author, producing a monological conception of truth that should be considered inadmissible in criminal proceedings.

This line of reasoning strongly supports the intent to regulate the discretionary nature of judicial decisions, as a reformed criminal justice system should not permit the formation of unilateral convictions that predetermine case outcomes based on a pursuit of absolute truth rooted in an objectifying logic. Calamandrei presents a comparable critique, which closely parallels the analyses provided by Cordero:

> although it continues to be repeated that a judgment can be schematically reduced to a syllogism in which, from the given premises, the judge draws the conclusion solely by virtue of logic, it sometimes happens that the judge, in forming the judgment, inverts the normal order of the syllogism; that is, they find the conclusion first and then the premises that serve to justify it. (Calamandrei 1996: 176)

Reasoning serves a crucial role by enabling the analysis and deconstruction of the factors that shaped the judge's production of the truth. This analytical process is intended to ensure adherence to the procedural norms established by the democratic-constitutional order. In this context, reference is made again to Cunha Martins, whose perspectives challenge the primacy of truth within legal proceedings:

> from this perspective, the element of "truth" present in any procedural provision will correspond, in terms of its systemic functionality, to that which I can *de-compose*, to that which allows me to recognise the procedurally constructed character underlying what, at a given moment, is taken as "truth". (Martins 2010: 91)

In summary, the function of reasoning is to ensure control over the regulated formation of conviction within a framework designed to correct the hallucinatory character of evidence. This approach seeks to guarantee that convictions are grounded in substantiated facts rather than subjective belief. The process of analysis allows for verification that the conviction is indeed supported by proof—specifically, indications that refer analogically to past events. If this verification fails, the resulting judgement exceeds acceptable thresholds of distortion within a system guided by democratic principles, producing a scenario that must be rectified. Cunha Martins observes that.

> whenever this operation is denied to me, I am no longer operating within that functional framework. I will, clearly, be at the level of evidence, to which the complexity of decomposition is alien and which relies entirely on an authoritarian truth, stolen from its intra-systemic co-production; and, by that very route, I will be faced with a drift into illegitimacy by a "truth" suddenly misaligned with the system's governing principle, which, as we know, cannot itself be established indiscriminately and in disregard of the legitimising vectors provided by the constitutional environment, of which it is a subsystem [...] The operability of this truth, like that of the other procedural components, depends on its capacity to express democratic and constitutional values. And, as we all know, there is no better constraint on evidence than a Constitution. (Martins 2010: 91)

Cunha Martins thus situates the issue within the domain of normativity, adopting a perspective aligned with my own. The inherent margin of contingency in the analogical production of truth during proceedings attains legitimacy only through rigorous adherence to the procedural norms established by democratic principles.

Nonetheless, while it is undoubtedly desirable to regulate the scope of judicial discretion, such regulation will invariably be incomplete, even when procedural rules are strictly observed. It is essential to recognise and accept this limitation, which underscores the potential risks inherent within the system and highlights the necessity for robust oversight mechanisms. Chief among these is the management of evidence by the parties, which limits unilateral narrative control and mitigates the risk of discursive imbalance. This area of discretionary authority appears to have been overlooked by Taruffo and Beltrán, either intentionally or inadvertently.

Taruffo's examination of judicial reasoning does not address this specific issue. He does not consider it inconsistent to advocate both for limiting judicial discretion and for permitting judges to introduce and manage evidence; his analysis continues to prioritise the epistemic function focused on truth-seeking. Taruffo argues that.

> The conception of reasoning as the rational justification of the judgment, generally valid also for many other reasons, finds particular support in the need for control arising from the judge's discretion in the use and assessment of evidence: thus conceived, reasoning fulfils precisely the function of controlling that discretion, obliging the judge to justify his own choices and making possible a subsequent review of them, both within and outside the proceedings. (Taruffo 2005: 436)

Taruffo may not explicitly acknowledge this point; however, it represents a crucial aspect of the matter: assigning judges an "epistemic function of truth-seeking" expands the scope of discretionary power that the reasoning requirement is intended to regulate, thereby considerably diminishing its effectiveness as a safeguard. As will be discussed in the subsequent section, the narrator can emulate a form of absolute freedom in shaping the judicial sentence, which enables the use of various techniques to obscure the inherent weaknesses of a probative core constructed monologically on unchallenged evidence. This leads to an additional argument challenging reliance on the investigative capacity of the judge, as it remains unclear how unrestricted authority to search for and substantiate evidence could support the ritualised framework designed to restrain punitive power—a framework that fundamentally should underpin the purpose of contemporary criminal proceedings.

Consequently, the issue of the narrator's discretion warrants comprehensive examination, as it further underscores the potential risks associated with conferring nearly unrestricted authority upon the judge during proceedings. As Lopes Jr. observes,

> The reasoning of decisions, based on proven facts (cognitivism), refutable and on valid legal arguments, is a limiting factor (even if not an immuniser) of moral judgments. This is an improper space of subjectivity that will always be present (there is no neutral judge), but which the system of safeguards must constantly seek to unveil and limit. (Lopes Jr 2010: 527)

There is, therefore, an inherent space for subjectivity that allows for excessive discretion. Accordingly, it is important to prioritise procedural rules that, while acknowledging their limitations, can at least partially mitigate decisionism and the associated risks. This approach recognises potential hazards and intentionally supports the establishment of frameworks designed to reduce them. As Calamandrei notes,

> It is well known that the reasoning of the judgment, which logically should arise as a premise for the operative part, is often constructed afterwards, as an *a posteriori* justification of a will already fixed previously for moral or sentimental reasons. Something similar can be said of the evidence: it often serves the judge not to persuade him, but to cloak with apparent reasons a conviction already formed by other means. (Calamandrei 1999: 247)

Essentially, when a judge begins drafting a decision, the outcome is often predetermined; while this may be unavoidable, it is not necessarily optimal. Consequently, the judgement is guided by the obligation to conclude, which originates from the necessity for structured reasoning: "if this corresponds with 'truth', so much the better. It is essential to acknowledge that 'truth' is contingent rather than foundational [...] the final result does not always represent (nor must it represent) the truth but rather reflects the judge's conviction" (Lopes Jr 2010: 541). Therefore, a measure of oversight is required regarding the development of such conviction, recognising that an element of creativity will invariably be present. As Almeida Prado notes, acknowledging both thought and emotion is crucial, along with understanding the creative dimension intrinsic to judicial responsibilities (Prado 2003: 13). This concept closely parallels the previously discussed idea of creative imagination. According to Calamandrei,

> The premises, despite their name, are often constructed afterwards—in judicial matters, the roof may be built before the walls. This is not to say that the operative part arises blindly and that the reasoning serves only to present as the result of rigorous reasoning what is in reality the product of arbitrariness; it is merely to say that, in judging, intuition and feeling often play a much greater role than it appears to those observing from the outside. It is not for nothing, one might say, that the judgment derives from feeling. (Calamandrei 1996: 177)

It is important to approach this observation with critical consideration rather than interpreting it as an endorsement for judges to "decide according to their conscience", which could introduce undesirable subjectivity into judicial decision-making (Streck 2010). Gössel acknowledges that a judge's personal conviction regarding the justice of a particular case extends beyond mere fact-finding and clarification (Gössel 2007: 26). Similarly, Ibáñez observes that judges might be surprised by the epistemological depth and significant complexity inherent in the logical processes underlying even routine legal reasoning (Ibáñez 2005: 48). According to Lopes Jr., "the legitimacy of judicial decisions results from strict adherence to the rules of due process. These procedural safeguards are essential in protecting against both unchecked decisionism and its opposite—rigid adherence to the dogma of legal completeness and paleopositivism" (Lopes Jr 2010: 350).

Gomes Filho approaches this line of reasoning and acknowledges the existence of spaces for undue discretion, considering that.

> By requiring the judge to set out in the reasoning the grounds for their decision, the law seeks nothing other than to ensure that the *reasons* are taken into account in the *decision*; while it is true that, in practice, judges often decide based on personal impressions and only later present other grounds, the value of the legal duty to provide reasons lies precisely in ensuring the overcoming of this asymmetry (Filho 2001: 114)

For Ferrajoli, the judge "is not *bouche de la loi* even in the theoretical and ideal model; and even less so in practice, where the law grants the judge more or less broad scope for discretion" (Ferrajoli 2002: 439). According to Ibáñez, it is in the reconstruction or establishment of facts that the judge is most sovereign, but at the same time least subject to control, making this the aspect in which the judge has been, and on more than a few occasions remains, most arbitrary (Ibáñez 2005: 47).

This tension between judicial subjectivity and procedural safeguards reveals the ongoing necessity for reforms that address the imbalance. While legal frameworks strive to impose constraints, the persistence of subjective influences within the reasoning and formation of judgements underscores the limits of regulation. It is therefore imperative to continuously refine procedural mechanisms, ensuring greater transparency and accountability in judicial decisions, while maintaining respect for the complexity inherent in legal interpretation.

In recent years, decisionism has seen significant growth within Brazilian criminal proceedings, with an increase in subjective approaches that often operate without sufficient oversight. This development has resulted in a considerable expansion of judicial discretion. The emergence of new paradigms—such as those associated with Operation Lava Jato—has led to shifts in the exercise of punitive power, influencing legal processes and aligning them more closely with the political aims of figures like Judge Sérgio Moro.

Within this context, the scope of judicial discretion greatly expanded. The desired outcomes were explicitly articulated, resulting in proceedings that appeared to pursue predetermined conclusions—a pattern that became normalised and was frequently emulated by numerous judges across various cases. Consequently, convictions have tended to rely predominantly on the discretion exercised by the judge. Thus, the principle of freely motivated conviction—which historically provided limited assurance and was closely linked to the pursuit of absolute truth—has evolved into a rhetorical device, conferring apparent legitimacy upon decisions that may be arbitrary and reflective of individual moral judgements. Furthermore, purportedly noble objectives, such as fighting corruption, have at times been invoked to justify departures from procedural rigour, particularly within the framework of Operation Lava Jato, thereby contributing to the erosion of Brazil's developing democratic institutions.

Ideally, the boundary should be distinctly delineated: it is not simply free conviction, but rather freely motivated conviction, which obliges the judge to articulate the rationale for the decision and specify the probatory basis underlying judicial sentences. Nonetheless, the obligation to provide reasons has not effectively countered arbitrariness or authoritarianism. In fact, the notion of free conviction has often served as a rhetorical facade for authoritarian tendencies. Geraldo Prado observes that "the complexity of contemporary criminal jurisdiction, coupled with the expansion of the scope for criminal solutions that do not require factual knowledge as the empirical foundation for decisions, reveals a reality where the acceptance of a thesis is shaped by criminal policy choices and media influence" (Prado 2014: 19). Coutinho further asserts that "the ongoing challenge is the complete possibility of manipulation of the law by legal professionals—against which purely legal control mechanisms have failed, starting in procedural law—and especially in criminal procedure—with the principle of free conviction: a judgment can be shielded with carefully crafted rhetorical requirements, allowing judges to decide at their discretion, always invoking 'legal certainty', 'truth', and other essentially vague concepts. Instead of serving as immutable and sacrosanct principles, these should be continually supplemented and adapted to the realities of life; they must not provide merely apparent legitimacy, nor should they be accepted as such" (Coutinho 2013). The author cautions that "Ultimately, the key issue is to have a judge who recognises their own limitations (or temptations), thereby guarding against possible prejudices—not because they are a judge, but due to their inherent humanity" (Coutinho 2000).

This context underscores the persistent tension between judicial discretion and procedural safeguards. While the principle of freely motivated conviction officially aims to ensure transparency and rationality, its practical application often falls short, permitting subjective elements to influence outcomes. As such, the challenge lies in developing mechanisms that genuinely promote accountability and minimise arbitrariness, thereby strengthening democratic values within criminal justice.

Lenio Streck observes that a considerable portion of legal dogmatics does not sufficiently interrogate free conviction, the discretionary evaluation of evidence, or related issues such as the absence of a comprehensive theory of judicial decision-making (Streck 2015). Coutinho highlights that, "For judicial reasoning, constraints on any solipsistic action are grounded primarily in the Constitution of the Republic—particularly in the notion of Free Conviction (which requires nuanced understanding despite its misleading designation) and in Due Process of Law. In Brazil, this is shaped by the adoption of the Fazzalari adversarial procedure theory. Admittedly, this is limited. Nevertheless, lacking a robust theory of judicial decision-making, it represents progress compared to the virtually lawless circumstances prior to the 1988 constitutional framework [...]" (Coutinho 2015). The author underscores: "It must be stressed that the principle of free conviction should not legitimize arbitrary evidentiary assessment by the judge. It is crucial to acknowledge the potential for manipulation of this principle, which necessitates vigilance to enable appropriate oversight and thus uphold constitutional safeguards" (Coutinho 2000).

The principle of motivated free conviction appears to have been misapplied, resulting in criminal proceedings being subject to authoritarian perspectives and inquisitorial traditions. Geraldo Prado asserts that "Criminal proceedings should not constitute a mere formal ritual or protocol, simply serving as a precursor to punishment predetermined by political interests, including members of the Judiciary" (Prado 2014: 17). Coutinho further notes that when efforts are made to privilege imagination over democratic values, two appropriate responses emerge: first, to avoid succumbing to persuasive but simplistic reasoning that undermines citizens' fundamental rights in favour of repressive ideology; second, to consistently oppose such tendencies, thereby reinforcing that arbitrary actions, especially those contravening the Constitution, cannot be tolerated (Coutinho 2013).

Lenio Streck accurately notes that free motivated conviction creates a hermeneutic fraud, wherein a judge may reach a decision prior to examining supporting evidence. Geraldo Prado succinctly encapsulates the complexity of this issue: "A criminal procedure governed by the presumption of innocence must exercise meticulous oversight regarding evidentiary procedures, through the implementation of stringent epistemic controls aimed at curbing decisionism, identified in the text as 'the possibility of arbitrary decision, depending solely on the possibility of deciding'" (Prado 2014: 12).

These considerations highlight the delicate balance required in judicial reasoning, where the motivation for a decision must not only satisfy procedural requirements but also genuinely reflect the judge's intellectual journey. The provision of reasons is not a mere formality; it is intended to serve as a safeguard against arbitrariness and a means of fostering public trust in criminal justice. Nevertheless, the persistence of subjective influences and the potential for rhetorical manipulation demonstrate the necessity for ongoing critical reflection and reform. Ultimately, the legitimacy of criminal judgements hinges on the transparent articulation of their foundations, coupled with vigilant scrutiny to ensure that the principles of justice and human rights are not undermined by unchecked discretion or the allure of expedient outcomes. Calamandrei further observes,

> A well-reasoned judgment does not always mean a just judgment, and vice versa. Sometimes, a negligent and summary reasoning indicates that the judge, when deciding, was so convinced of the correctness of his conclusion that he considered it a waste of time to demonstrate the obvious; just as, at other times, a prolix and meticulous reasoning may reveal in the judge a desire to conceal from himself and others, by means of logical arabesques, his perplexity. (Calamandrei 1996: 180-181)

Calamandrei once again addresses the intrinsic risks associated with the unpredictable nature of legal proceedings—a topic previously discussed. As he observes, "how often is the reasoning a faithful reproduction of the path that led the judge to that conclusion? How often is the judge able to perceive with precision, himself, the reasons that induced him to decide in that way?" (Calamandrei 1996: 175). Calamandrei further reflects that:

> The judgment is academically represented as the product of a pure logical game, coldly carried out on the basis of abstract concepts, linked by an inexorable concatenation of premises and consequences; but, in reality, on the judge's chessboard, the pieces are living men, who radiate invisible magnetic forces that find resonances or repulsions, illogical but human, in the judge's feelings. How can a reasoning be considered faithful if it does not reproduce the subterranean meanderings of these emotional currents, to whose magical influence no judge, not even the strictest, can escape? (Calamandrei 1996: 175-176)

As Pozzebon observes, "impartiality should not be mistaken for neutrality, as judicial activity is inherently creative; in rendering decisions, judges inevitably contribute their own perspectives. The 'truth' presented in the case file does not equate to an objective reality, but rather represents a constructed, narrative truth" (Pozzebon 2006: 240). Accordingly, this narrative construction remains a central issue to be addressed, synthesising the topics previously discussed, as will be further examined below.

The Moment of Truth Production: The Sentence as a Narrative Analogous to the Past

Formulating a theory of decision-making is a pressing necessity given the current historical context. This endeavour demands both dedication and ambition, and its complexity extends beyond the scope of this work. Nonetheless, it remains feasible to offer insights that elucidate the intricate processes inherent in decision-making, with particular emphasis on the narrative externalisation of the judge's conviction. Consequently, the discussion undertaken herein reaches the juncture at which the concept of narrative aligns with the investment of meaning previously associated with the trace, thereby supporting my understanding that truth is analogically produced by the judge. The focus on the transposition of conviction into narrative is deliberate, as it represents a less-explored aspect of the production of truth within criminal proceedings. By analysing narrative structures, it becomes possible to identify the risks associated with the discretionary spaces they often create and potentially provide significant foundations for the development of a comprehensive theory of decision-making.

A thorough examination of the limitations inherent in the correspondence theory of truth has been conducted, leaving only the task of articulating how judgement is narratively constructed with respect to the analogical production of truth in legal processes. By analysing the narrative context of judgements, I introduce the final component necessary to support the argument that truth is produced analogically through narrative rather than found as a correspondence within criminal proceedings.

The judicial sentence further underscores the inherent challenges in achieving either relative or absolute truth within criminal proceedings. The complexities previously outlined now extend to the task of drafting judicial decisions, which demands significant diligence to fulfil the legal standards for substantiating judgements and safeguarding against arbitrary exercise of punitive power. It is erroneous to perceive this responsibility as straightforward; rather, it is arguably among the most sophisticated aspects of the judicial process.

The analysis of the judicial sentence prompts consideration of the nature of its narrative representation and the structural mechanisms underpinning its persuasive function. The judicial sentence, inherently a text intended for readership, presents an argument designed to persuade its audience. In its reasoning section, the judicial sentence operates as a present reconstruction of a past event, substituting direct experience with analytical reflection. Additionally, it synthesises aspects such as institutional context (including educational background, professional recruitment, and occupational identity), methodological approaches (encompassing established knowledge and epistemological frameworks), and textual form (as narrative). As a linguistic and cultural artefact, the judicial sentence fulfils the role of representing historical events for the purpose of enabling the application of punitive authority. Its intrinsic opacity requires careful and methodical examination to elucidate its characteristics.

There is a prevailing view regarding the narrative phenomenon. This perspective considers narrative as a neutral medium, inherently effective for the description of events. Specifically, narrative is seen as a form of discourse employing ordinary language to recount or explain a sequence of occurrences. Accordingly, it presents an account of real events—those that have actually transpired—which simply need to be drawn from existing evidence for their veracity to be immediately and intuitively acknowledged. In this context, descriptions of verified events are evaluated based on their accuracy to the factual record as well as their coherence and clarity. Consequently, the resulting judgement is regarded as the embodiment of corresponding truth, reflecting the judge's conviction as an assessment of adequacy between the narrative and past events.

The insufficient understanding of what constitutes a narrative presents a significant barrier to moving beyond the correspondence theory of truth. A narrative transcends its commonly ascribed meaning, incorporating elements and devices that construct a cohesive plot—encompassing characters, objects, and situations—and rendering them into an integrated whole. Additionally, each historical narrative relies on a referential framework that imparts coherence to elements which, though originally fragmented, come to be perceived as unequivocal and factual. Engaging with a narrative means progressing through contingencies and developments amid an anticipation that is ultimately resolved in the story's conclusion. This resolution is not strictly derived from preceding premises; rather, it serves as a definitive endpoint. The conclusion provides the vantage point from which the narrative retrospectively demonstrates how and why prior episodes converge upon it. Such a conclusion may not always be predictable, but it must be acceptable as consistent with the assembled episodes (Ricoeur 1994: 105).

Ricoeur (1998) observes that life narratives are inherently complex, exhibiting a form of concordance–discordance. This observation is relevant not only to the structuring of life events but also to adversarial contexts prevalent in criminal proceedings, where conflict and uncertainty often dominate. The process of narrative construction, which seeks to make sense of temporal events, serves as an operation of intelligibility, necessitating the elucidation of intricacies within these accounts. This process involves a notable reversal: the temporal direction is inverted, requiring the investigation to proceed retrospectively so as to substantiate past occurrences. In order for the judge to be persuaded of the defendant's responsibility, it is necessary to overcome temporal barriers—at least to a degree sufficient for attaining pertinent knowledge about prior events.

According to Ricoeur, synthesising heterogeneous and contradictory realities requires an operation of intelligibility that allows discontinuous, diverse, and complex elements to attain meaning and unity through narrative. Consequently, the sentence must impose order on the inherent chaos present in legal environments marked by conflict and uncertainty. However, this structuring may lead to the imposition of a decisionist meaning, introducing a level of subjectivity that can be challenging to regulate, despite frameworks intended to restrain punitive authority.

Resolving heterogeneity, as described using Ricoeur's framework, involves synthesising concordance and discordance through an argumentative and interpretative process, effectively restructuring disorder into a coherent narrative. In the context of historical narratives, this transformation must be based on analogical proof from traces of the past. The clarification of complex historical phenomena emerges from interpreting these traces, which facilitates understanding, and constructing arguments that provide explanations. This approach fosters a dialectical relationship between episodic succession and interpretive configuration, whereby the sequence of events is mediated by compositional methods that convert discordance into concordance, ultimately resulting in a unified meaning.

Within criminal proceedings, the narrative construction of judgement is not merely a technical exercise but a profound act of meaning-making. The process entails the careful ordering of disparate and often contradictory elements into a cohesive account that serves both to justify conviction and to render past events intelligible in the present. This act is inherently fraught with interpretative challenges, as the judge must navigate the uncertainties and complexities embedded within the evidence, all while maintaining fidelity to legal standards and avoiding the pitfalls of arbitrariness.

The narrative, therefore, emerges as a dynamic mechanism through which the past is analogically reconstituted, and truth is produced not as a direct mirror of reality but as a synthesis shaped by the interplay of institutional, methodological, and textual factors. The judge's role as narrator involves an ongoing negotiation between the demands of coherence and the realities of discordance, with the ultimate aim of achieving a persuasive and legally sound resolution that withstands scrutiny. In this context, the analogical production of truth underscores both the creative and the constraining aspects of judicial writing, highlighting its significance within the broader framework of decision-making theory.

According to Ricoeur, a successful narrative achieves a temporal synthesis of heterogeneous elements, rendering diverse events meaningful and comprehensible. However, this process requires the careful and provisional construction of a highly complex plot that is often obscured by time and accompanied by an inherent uncertainty. In this context, referring to proof merely as expressions of truth within a judgement can be seen as a means of labelling what ultimately remains incomprehensible. As Morin notes, "knowledge is nothing more than a translation, a reconstruction. We do not know the essence of external things" (Morin 1996: 252).

Although the criteria of validity—the proof—may indicate whether a narrative meets the referential foundation necessary to justify a conviction, its nature remains analogical and cannot fully correspond to past events. This is due not only to the inherent analogical limitations of traces but also to the narrative's connection with the writer's lived experience, which inevitably influences the formation of conviction. Consequently, the writing does not originate from an objective standpoint; instead, its persuasive strategies are shaped by cultural and historical conditions and power relations, varying according to the tradition with which the judges are associated.

Furthermore, it is important to recognise that reasoning extends beyond merely presenting a plot. The primary aim of any form of argumentation—including judicial narratives—is persuasion, which relies on a variety of strategic approaches. Argumentation inherently requires a foundational basis upon which it rests. Whether appropriate or not, the concept of reasoning is not limited to proof alone but also includes numerous elements external to the process of forming and demonstrating conviction. Accordingly, the argumentation that imparts coherence and meaning to otherwise fragmented information may employ additional persuasive strategies that do not directly pertain to the central event. This process involves attributing significance through references drawn from disciplinary bodies of knowledge—such as normative, jurisprudential, and academic sources—which, while distinct from the particulars of the criminal case, substantially enhance the perceived credibility of the narrative. However, it is crucial that this investment of meaning serves to substantiate, rather than obscure, the probatory foundation; otherwise, the narrative risks becoming an instrument of distortion rather than clarification.

The sentence inherently creates something novel; therefore, I reiterate that truth should be understood as being analogically produced in relation to the past. The act of judging is, thus, not simply a matter of recounting events or aligning facts with legal categories; it is a creative endeavour that weaves together disparate threads into a tapestry that aims to persuade, legitimise, and withstand critical examination. This process is profoundly shaped by the interplay between evidence, interpretative frameworks, and the cultural-historical situatedness of the judge, making each judgement an artefact of both constraint and creativity.

In this light, the analogical approach to truth in legal narratives does not seek to reproduce reality in its entirety but strives to construct a plausible and compelling account that resonates with the standards and expectations of the legal community and safeguards human rights.

The narrative form, with its capacity for integrating contradiction and ambiguity, becomes a tool for rendering the past intelligible, accountable, and actionable within the present. However, this very power necessitates ongoing vigilance to ensure that the persuasive strategies employed do not eclipse the probatory foundation, maintaining the integrity and legitimacy required by due process.

When applying creative imagination, the author utilises an established set of legal components that provide meaning, ensuring coherence in judicial reasoning and presenting an appearance of unity. This practice, however, carries inherent risks. Unlike literary or cinematic narratives—which may disrupt chronological order to build suspense or mystery—a judicial sentence must rigorously maintain chronological sequence due to its foundational role in establishing truth. Narrative structures derive their strength from chronology, which enables the integration of contrasting elements into an ostensibly unified whole. Consequently, anomalous details may be interpreted as exceptions or random occurrences; sources of conflict might be repositioned within the timeline; and irrelevant or absent details can be omitted or incorporated with minimal impact on the overall meaning.

As Dohring notes, there is an inventive aspect to constructing the overarching narrative: only through imaginative synthesis can one clarify complex relationships among evidentiary elements (Döhring 1986: 407). Nevertheless, judges should apply this creativity judiciously to avoid unfounded speculation lacking factual basis. When appropriately utilised, imagination empowers legal practitioners to connect seemingly unrelated facts by synthesising ideas in a way that elucidates the case. This approach orders discrete events into a coherent, logical, and meaningful framework (Döhring 1986: 407). Still, while Döhring emphasises the constructive potential of such methods, the possibility for misuse remains significant.

Building on the initial problematisation, it is pertinent to ask: What is produced when a judge assumes the role of author, departing from established evidence or constructing an evidential foundation independently—especially when such evidence has not been subjected to adversarial examination and may therefore be considered speculative?

A judicial sentence, viewed as a narrative, enables multiple layers of meaning to be imposed, with its distinctive chronological structure standing out prominently. This form of writing begins at the conclusion, as the author has reached their decision beforehand and then constructs the narrative to provide justification. Despite this, the sentence's narrative framework obscures its retrospective approach by presenting an ostensibly strict temporal sequence.

The narrator constructing a sentence seeks to establish a present moment that signifies the culmination of a process, creating within the narrative a temporal boundary encompassing the referenced event. The narrative commences at an author-defined origin point and concludes with the manifestation of a typical, unlawful, and culpable act, thereby invoking punitive authority and framing intelligibility through the lens of normativity. Since readers cannot directly experience proof when engaging with a judgement, this lack of verifiability is compensated by an enhanced authoritative stance, which serves to offset any perceived deficiency in rigour, structured around the concept of the typical, unlawful, and culpable act. Consequently, establishing this narrative zero point confers a near-transcendent authority, operating within a quasi-mythical temporality reminiscent of "once upon a time". This temporal delineation so distinctly isolates the event from its broader context—its underlying structures, antecedents, and ramifications—that legitimate questions arise regarding the coherence and justifiability of attributing meaning or punishing in the absence of these connections.

The narrative zero point thus marks a critical juncture in legal storytelling, wherein the boundaries of the event are artfully delineated to facilitate the imposition of meaning and the attribution of culpability. This approach, while effective in establishing a clear temporal framework, may inadvertently isolate the event from its broader socio-historical context, raising concerns about the legitimacy of the judgement rendered. The resulting narrative, imbued with authority, risks presenting a constructed coherence that overshadows the inherent complexity and ambiguity of real-life occurrences.

To some degree, this situation is unavoidable due to the inherent linguistic framework governing the legal analysis of real-world phenomena. However, this framework may also support the development of certain decisionist strategies, as the very "closure" it provides can lead to an unwarranted attribution of coherence within the narrative. This effect gives the impression that the narrative was constructed by an omniscient narrator—one who possesses complete knowledge and awareness, with a perspective comparable to that of an all-seeing observer.

A narrative approach may replace traditional cognitive processes, potentially obscuring the limitations of probatory foundations and diminishing the significance of traces in establishing conviction. As a creative act, decision-making narratives can be crafted to generate self-referential arguments, which may become difficult to challenge if articulated effectively. Such narratives often draw upon doctrine, case law, and statutory law, providing an impression of collective authority. Written discourse can employ scientific reasoning to address non-scientific subjects, invoking diverse arguments that strengthen its decision-making purpose. The language used supports the overall presentation, attributing a sense of realism and legitimacy through cited sources. Consequently, the text gains cultural and traditional credibility while concealing the author's personal perspective under the authority of legal expertise.

However, the inherent pastness of events, fixed in a time that has already elapsed, resists easy interpretation. It is important to acknowledge that reality remains an intrinsically heterogeneous whole, often contrasted against the relatively homogeneous frameworks developed by the methods of scientific disciplines. This principle holds true for methodologies that attempt to suppress such diversity through narrative construction, as well as those willing to honour its complexity. The distinction is that approaches attuned to complexity admit their own limitations, while those claiming absolute authority usually disregard elements that challenge their assumed comprehensiveness.

Consequently, the narrative may appear comprehensive, as it eliminates gaps that could undermine its coherence. This generates a perception of truth through a text that adopts a symbolic, didactic, and authoritative tone, thereby reinforcing unchecked punitive power. The discourse misleads, as its structure creates a reader who becomes indoctrinated, positioned as a layperson in relation to privileged knowledge. In this context, the narrative functions as a performative text, producing symbolic subordination. Given the genuine possibility of such outcomes, it is crucial to re-evaluate the significance of the report within the judgement, ensuring that the perspectives and arguments of both parties are accurately represented and mitigating the risks associated with "free motivated conviction".

As previously analysed, within rationalist perspectives the issue of truth concerns the degree to which decisions are justified; a decision is valid insofar as it is rationally substantiated, with the judge articulating their reasoning on the basis of the evidence that informs their conclusion. It follows that the expectation should not be for the judge to render the singularly correct decision, but rather any number of decisions that can each be justified—each holding validity if grounded in evidence. Therefore, so long as these decisions are acceptable—and recognising the considerable overlap between the free conviction and argumentative theories—the concept of judicial error is arguably less significant, since all reasoned decisions remain valid. This position is only defensible if one accepts that free conviction equates to comprehensive judicial discretion: in acquiring, evaluating, and justifying evidence. Accordingly, freedom of evidence serves as an expansive receptiveness to informational materials within proceedings, and free conviction operates as the "freedom" to assess such evidence, whereby the judge attributes "probative weight" to each element, aligned with the institutional objective of achieving correspondence with absolute truth.

In light of these considerations, it becomes imperative to recognise the dual nature of judicial narrative: while it serves to organise and clarify the evidentiary basis for a decision, it also possesses the capacity to shape perception and meaning in ways that may transcend the factual record. The judge, positioned as both adjudicator and narrator, crafts a story that not only resolves the dispute but also constructs a version of events imbued with authority. This process inherently involves choices about which facts to emphasise, how to frame legal principles, and the manner in which the narrative's coherence is achieved.

The challenge, therefore, lies in balancing the persuasive power of narrative with a commitment to procedural fairness and evidentiary integrity. By acknowledging the narrative's influence, legal practitioners can strive to maintain transparency and ensure that the judgement reflects not only the formal requirements of law but also the underlying realities of the case. Ultimately, the legitimacy of judicial decisions depends on the careful navigation of this interplay between narrative construction and production of truth.

It is evident that a judgement transcends mere narration; it is not simply the transcription of an unequivocal conviction devoid of personal belief. Even without a relentless pursuit of truth, the narrator must evaluate why certain factors carry more weight within the text's structure.

Although this evaluative process appears in other narratives, it does not serve as part of an argumentative strategy directed towards decision-making. As noted by Ricoeur, while the poet creates, the judge both constructs and substantiates. The judge effectively advocates for their own judgement (Ricoeur 1994: 252). As Fazzalari observes,

> Indeed, the judge can and must be "impartial" at the moment of forming their own conviction regarding the existence of the obligation, the right, the harm; and in the subsequent ruling; but once convinced of such existence, and having issued the judicial command, the judge can no longer be, and is no longer, impartial. [...] In short, the judge, in the end, can do nothing but lay down the scales and take up the sword. (Fazzalari 2006: 489)

These dynamic necessitates a suitable approach to problematisation that enables the narrative process—serving both to construct historical context through adversarial proceedings and to convey meaning and coherence via narrative chronology—to be imbued with renewed significance.

The judgement concludes the dispute between the parties; through the construction of the narrative, an otherwise complex past is transposed, accessed via evidence, which, once verified, was formally recognised as proof. This process enables an analogical reconstruction of events that occurred in a previous era. After the judge's conviction is reached—which inevitably contains elements of belief—the drafting of the judgement commences. Here, the judge aims to demonstrate he comprehended the matter at hand. This produces an effect of truth, allowing the present to revisit and reinterpret the past to the extent of forming knowledge.

In this context, engaging with a narrative involves more than understanding its overarching meaning; it entails perceiving each episode as a progression towards the conclusion. In narratives such as those found in judicial sentences, the chronological structure conveys an impression of authenticity, since there is neither recapitulation nor disruption of temporal order—an order that, while constructed, is presented as if through equivalence. This mechanism underpins the "magic" of corresponding truth, anchored by the truth effect that narrative can generate.

It is essential to establish explicit rules supported by a clearly defined axiological framework and to maintain the precedence of a robust probatory foundation—developed through adversarial proceedings between parties—over any persuasive argumentation. The effectiveness of narratives stems from imaginative constructs that shape the process, as narrators contribute unique perspectives. This dynamic illustrates how judicial "truth-seeking" can become a basis for convictions rooted in pure decision-making, enabling the creation of a comprehensive discourse that may prove difficult to contest in appellate review. In such cases, the narrative is systematically developed to achieve a predetermined outcome, potentially influencing readers with a powerful impression of truth.

Elements of decisionism may also manifest within the narrative realm. The narrative rendering of a judge's conviction inherently seeks to achieve an effect of truth, which incorporates persuasive strategies even when accusatorial epistemological standards are observed. Initially, the judge reaches a conviction based on evidence that has been thoroughly scrutinised and accepted as proof; subsequently, the process of articulating this conviction in narrative form aims to persuade the anticipated reader through the construction of a perceived truth—an effect inherent in this genre of narrative. According to Cordero, the term "motivation" can be interpreted in two senses: in the narrower sense, it refers to the cause underlying the decision, satisfied when fact and norm align; in the broader sense, motivation constitutes a dialectical act in which the reasoning addresses an ideal audience, elucidating the rationale behind the decision. In this context, the operative section embodies authority, while the articulation of reasons serves to persuade (Cordero 2000: 289). As noted by Gomes Filho,

> The ideas of *persuasion* and *conviction* presuppose, on the one hand, the existence of an *audience* to whom the justificatory argument is addressed; on the other, they imply the adoption of a certain type of reasoning to be used in each context; above all, the *persuasiveness* or *effectiveness* of the justification will depend on the appropriateness of the reasons presented at each moment to a given audience. (Filho 2001: 117)

Within the intent to persuade lies a notable paradox: although the event's pastness is acknowledged through verb tense usage, this temporal distance is effectively negated by claims of corresponding truth intended to legitimise the conviction before an ideal audience. This phenomenon arises because narrative transposition encompasses more than simply the act of writing; it culminates in the moment of reading. The acceptance or rejection of the narrative representation of a bygone time occurs during this act, as perceived by individuals other than the author. According to Ricoeur, it is here that the final transformation of time into narrative is achieved. Consequently, the narrative assumes an additional dimension—the aim of persuading the anticipated reader.

This form of writing relies on persuasive strategies designed to convince the reader that the events described in the judgement genuinely occurred as presented. While the goal is to represent past occurrences with maximum fidelity, there is also an inherent effort to assure the reader of this equivalence, sometimes implying complete accuracy. This approach risks constructing arguments that appeal more to persuasion than to proof established during the proceedings. As Cordero notes, ideally, no motivation should serve as an "exercise in persuasion" or reflect self-justifying intentions that promote argumentative tactics; rather, it is preferable to clearly articulate the reasons behind a particular decision, using language that is accessible and transparent (Cordero 1986: 366).

Conversely, some scholars choose not to address this matter. I wish to reiterate—one final time—my divergence from Taruffo's perspective. Taruffo contends that narratives are deliberately constructed to impart coherence to a collection of fragmented discursive elements (Taruffo 2010: 79). Nonetheless, he asserts that judges are neither intent on persuasion nor guided by any predetermined thesis; from his standpoint, a judge's role is to justify their decision, and the reasoning within a judgement serves no persuasive purpose (Taruffo 2010: 232). My disagreement persists, as I maintain that persuasion is inherently embedded in narrative construction. Furthermore, it is essential to remain vigilant regarding narrative's potential to distort, particularly when interpretation forces harmony where discord exists, shaping the undefined into form; such actions can only be interpreted as products of interpretive violence (Ricoeur 1994: 112).

The risk of distortion is amplified within judicial judgements compared to historiographical studies, as the latter typically pursue broader explanatory goals and attempt to encompass phenomena on a larger scale. This ambition can often render the truth value of the historian's narrative less apparent. Conversely, in judicial judgements, narrators exercise more structural control over the text, enabling them to impose order and potentially construct an argument that creates an illusory coherence. In this setting, any imposed continuity may be interpreted as a form of violence, wherein decisionism risks obscuring the distinction between historical and fictional narratives—a concern particularly relevant for regulated structures intended to contain punitive authority.

Advocates of "free motivated conviction" frequently overlook this issue. It is important to highlight the significant potential for harm inherent in narrative construction, even when it is substantiated by analogical traces referring to the past. According to Ricoeur, all narratives are inherently fictional and rooted in lived experience. The author intentionally aligns historical narrative with literary narrative, asserting that every text must demonstrate its truthfulness in some manner; however, he differentiates historical texts from literary narratives in their respective truth criteria. Regarding historiography, it is accurate to maintain that past events—regardless of their absence from current perception—should continue to inform historical intentionality and impart a realist aspect that no literary work, regardless of its "realist" aspirations, can achieve (Ricoeur 1994: 125). Historical narrative uniquely claims reference rooted in empirical reality, as historical intent targets actual events accessed indirectly through traces, thereby precluding absolute interpretation under the sign of the *Other* (Ricoeur 1994: 125).

In contrast to fiction, historical narrative is required to interpret actual periods and events with a level of accuracy; however, true correspondence to the past remains unattainable. The historian relies on traces that merely suggest previous occurrences, so narrative inherently conveys fragmented knowledge, capturing only portions of a broader context. While this knowledge cannot fully correspond to historical reality, it differs from literary narrative through its analogical reference enabled by surviving traces of the past.

This phenomenon reduces the metaphorical significance of other narratives, since within those frameworks, the past is reconstructed only through imagination. As previously outlined, misunderstanding this foundational concept can result in a referential illusion characterised by the sign of the *Same*, which enables such narratives to be perceived as true—an epistemic excess. Marrou observes that historians are not tasked (nor is it necessarily feasible without contradiction) with reanimating or reviving the past; these actions are merely metaphoric. Although historians may restore some aspect of the past to present existence—something that has become past and ceased to be—in being transformed into "history" and made known, the past is not simply replicated as it existed during its own present (Marrou 1978: 36–37). This brings forth the tension between the signs of the *Same* and the *Other*, a dynamic previously discussed and addressed through the concept of the *Analogous*. The ability to reconfigure temporal dimensions introduces the issue of truth as it pertains to elapsed time. It is important to note that even if the lived past were directly accessible, rather than accessible only via traces, it would still not constitute absolutely true knowledge—truth that corresponds fully to reality. This is because the past, when present, was marked by complexity, diversity, and lack of clarity, much like our current experience. According to Marrou, the past, when it was "real", was entirely different for its participants, who experienced it as their present—a convergence of forces shaping an unpredictable moment, full of motion and becoming (Marrou 1978: 37).

Although knowledge derived from traces may lack an immediate corresponding sense, its indicative meaning relies on reference to proof, thereby enabling the grounding of knowledge within the domains of *Being-as* and *Not-being*, or the *Analogous*. This standard is especially critical in criminal proceedings, where the mechanisms for exercising punitive authority necessitate an even more rigorous control over the recognition of evidence as traces from the past than is required by historiographical narrative—where both epistemological and ethical criteria are uniquely tied to the historian's methodology. For this reason, it is essential to underscore the importance of referential distinction; a judicial sentence must be anchored in traces that are analogous to the period they represent, which can only be sufficiently ensured through a structure designed to constrain the hallucinatory character of evidence.

Unrestrained conviction coupled with a relentless pursuit of truth risks undermining the integrity of a rights-based criminal procedure. Judgements that rely on uncorrected or unverified evidence risk becoming indistinguishable from literary narratives, as they fail to establish the requisite indicative reference to past events through verified traces.

Insistence on correspondence to truth does not necessarily enhance the validity of the decision-making narrative; rather, it often increases the likelihood that such narratives are grounded in speculative assumptions, thus distancing them from objective truth and potentially serving as rhetorical justification for authoritarian outcomes.

This analysis does not suggest that all judicial sentences are unfounded, nor does it presume that adopting an accusatory epistemology designed to curb punitive authority would eliminate the possibility of judicial error. While a judge may pursue absolute truth in criminal proceedings, and such convictions may align with the defendant's guilt, this method does not necessarily promote harm reduction; rather, it can heighten the risk of wrongful convictions. Conversely, adherence to due process increases the likelihood that verdicts are grounded in proof, thereby supporting harm reduction efforts. Nevertheless, judicial narratives are analogically constructed, emphasising the contingent nature of truth and the inherent challenges within judicial decision-making—ultimately, representance persists.

The influence of the narrator becomes evident in this context. While there may be an intention to depict past events accurately, the organisation of traces into a narrative inherently subjects them to the narrator's argumentative authority. Consequently, when it comes to decision-making processes, it is essential to implement mechanisms that regulate this influence and mitigate the risk of arbitrariness. This observation further underscores that assigning the judge the role of "seeking the truth" can amplify potential harm within the system; the resulting truth, shaped solely by this perspective, may not even approximate analogy, but instead could reflect bias or distortion, diverging substantially from the actual event and potentially leading to wrongful convictions.

Arbitrariness occurs when discourse prioritises persuasive appeal over proof, yet is presented as an unequivocal representation of reality, thereby ascribing a level of truth to the narrative that is not justified nor plausible. Drawing on Certeau's framework, this dynamic reveals a paradoxical process: a gesture that combines elements of myth and ritual in the act of writing (Certeau 1982). Such narratives exemplify how absence and production are articulated simultaneously within the same context. Notably, absence is rendered "present" through artificially constructed arguments that produce an effect of truth regarding the past, while the actual site of narrative construction is intentionally obscured and appears to originate from an indeterminate source. As a result, the mechanism by which discourse creates seemingly coherent and credible scenarios about the past becomes concealed, diminishing awareness of its constructed nature.

The judicial sentence can introduce a degree of separation by obscuring the origins of its discourse, which may be concealed behind claimed neutrality and ostensible detachment from the subject matter. It is frequently presented as a straightforward application of legal principles or as the fulfilment of an epistemic function aimed at discovering truth. However, such positions, as previously indicated, can result in significant negative consequences. Despite the continued influence of this reductionist approach, it is important to recognise that all writing originates beyond purely rational frameworks. Its formation is shaped by context, specific conditions, constraints, associated privileges, and particularities that ultimately determine the characteristics of its methodology (Certeau 1982: 66).

The judge operates within an environment of considerable tension: while vested with authority, the judge remains subject to external forces. On one side is the institutional authority of criminal justice, which expects adherence to its prevailing directives and can render the individual judge a functional part of a larger system; on the other, there are social influences, including media scrutiny and public opinion shaped by such coverage, which foster a punitive culture (Prado 2006: 110; Martins 2010: 66–68). Consequently, issues such as privileging hypotheses over factual evidence represent only one of several potential challenges facing the judiciary. This context underscores the risk that a judicial narrative may serve, perhaps inadvertently, as a further mechanism for arbitrary exercise of judicial power.

When this situation arises, the judicial sentence becomes the complex outcome of an illegitimate process of collective fabrication, rather than the result of an independent judge striving to reach a fair verdict about past events. The judge is effectively deprived of the ability to form an autonomous conviction and to gain understanding through practical experience; instead, practice becomes a source of frustration. The environment thus performs a dual role, permitting and prohibiting as it determines what may or may not be expressed. Linking discourse to practice is essential for meaningful interpretation, and it allows the identification of the practical consequences that arise from a distorted discourse. This approach can help establish practices that align with a discourse intended to restrain punitive authority. Ultimately, the interaction between practice and discourse reveals the degree to which the original purpose of the discourse has been altered. Although judicial independence remains a central principle, its practical application often differs significantly from theoretical intent—sometimes in ways that even proponents of the search for absolute truth would hesitate to endorse in judicial settings.

Addressing and rectifying this cycle is essential. Genuine realisation of judicial independence requires a departure from the inquisitorial, positivist and rationalist epistemologies that emphasise aggressive fact-finding and the relentless pursuit of the accused, who is often objectified and perceived as a societal enemy. In contrast, the accusatorial system's discourse of problematic truth promotes respect for judicial independence and fosters impartiality. It is important to examine the mechanisms by which the truth is produced, in order to delineate acceptable parameters and prevent acquiescence to illegitimate demands for increased punitive measures.

The concepts of production and fabrication are central here, as they elucidate that truth within a narrative is defined less by overt appearances and more by the way in which it is constructed narratively (Certeau 1982: 33). From this perspective, judgement extends beyond mere narration; it constitutes a written fabrication. Of particular concern is the possibility that argumentative discourse, when utilised without transparency, may obscure its own construction, thereby promoting uniformity at the expense of diversity. This process suppresses difference on two levels: first, by constraining judicial independence through adherence to prevailing views, and second, by intentionally shaping the narrative to this effect, often overlooking the necessity for a substantiated probatory foundation. Such practices could aptly be described as embodying a "falsification function". Consequently, as previously indicated, the role of the report within the judicial sentence remains crucial.

This analysis demonstrates that, beyond the trace providing only an analogical reference to past events, it is essential to implement mechanisms that guide the formation of conviction and the narrative productive of truth. Persuasion should not be unrestricted, as subjectivity in this regard is inappropriate, and its translation into narrative must be carefully managed. The notion of pursuing absolute truth should be set aside. Allowing the narrator unilateral authority to construct the entire account risks producing a monologic narrative—one shaped by impermissible ambitions for truth—which ultimately echoes Eymerich's discourse.

To satisfy the requirement of appearing analogically true, a conviction must be firmly based on proof obtained through disclosure in an adversarial context, where prosecutorial assertions have undergone rigorous scrutiny. This approach reflects an epistemology that upholds a stringent probatory threshold for representations of the past with condemnatory implications. It distinctly diverges from the modern reformulation of inquisitorial epistemology—a perspective still held by many rationalist scholars—which inadvertently perpetuates the misconception of truth-seeking within legal proceedings.

According to Lopes Jr., a cultural transformation is necessary to move away from the persistent inquisitorial mindset. Judges are not intended to act as inquisitors with responsibilities for "social cleansing" despite common perceptions (Lopes Jr 2010). The author advises: "Reject this 'ambition for truth.' Adjudicate objectively, relying solely on evidence presented during proceedings, and acquit without reservation where appropriate. Conversely, convict when the evidence provided is comprehensive and conviction is warranted" (Lopes Jr 2010: 546). Consequently, judges should refrain from constructing narratives that emulate monological police discourse or conceal the lack of evidentiary foundation in order to facilitate conviction and reiterate criminal selectivity. As Lopes Jr. notes, "Uncertainty should lead to acquittal, not distress. Those unable to accept this principle may be unsuited for their role" (Lopes Jr 2010: 546).

In this context, it is advisable for legal scholars to adopt approaches that transcend outdated methodologies and unexamined societal influences. Addressing the persistent silences inherent in evidentiary rationalism is imperative. Re-envisioning the criminal justice system calls for both conceptual reassessment and practical transformation, alongside a shift in perspective, thereby enabling meaningful reform within an environment fundamentally shaped by its participants.

When a judge presumes that a pre-existing past is accurately reflected in his narrative, he may overlook the fact that, fundamentally, he is creating something new through his writing—a point which warrants careful consideration.

The judge's written narrative, therefore, is not merely a passive recounting of facts but an active construction, shaped by the interplay of institutional pressures and subjective influences. Recognising these dynamics is crucial for maintaining the integrity of judicial reasoning and ensuring that the narrative remains anchored to proof rather than becoming an instrument of arbitrary authority.

A narrative framework must be developed that adequately addresses the complexities posed by historical events, while also acknowledging the inherent limitations of any such model: achieving an absolute and corresponding truth remains unattainable, and assigning to the judiciary the task of seeking this truth is fundamentally misguided. It is essential to re-evaluate certain procedures and challenge established epistemological traditions; otherwise, there is a persistent risk of perpetuating authoritarian tendencies within the criminal justice system.

The sentence should be rigorously scrutinised to prevent it from becoming a narrative fabrication unanchored from proof and justified solely by rhetorical appeals to free conviction. Granting the judge additional powers to independently seek the absolute truth does not appear to support this objective of oversight; rather, it may promote the development of a single-perspective narrative—one that favours wrongful convictions.

Accordingly, it is essential to acknowledge that judgement represents both presence and absence. On one hand, it conveys the lived experience and the perspective from which it is articulated; on the other, it reflects what is missing—the past it aims to depict. Consequently, truth may only be understood as being produced analogically through narrative form.

When critically evaluating the implications of a sentence, it becomes evident that narrative construction often seeks to establish a logical sequence among observed phenomena, irrespective of whether such coherence is firmly supported by proof—a concern previously highlighted as a problematic focus on attaining punishment within criminal law. This inclination aligns with Certeau's observation of "the almost obsessive suffering of filling the gaps" (Certeau 1982: 23). As Lyotard notes,

> There are various ways of telling a story, but narrative as such can be considered a technical device, which gives a people the means to store, order, and recall units of information, that is, events. More precisely, narratives are like temporal filters whose function is to transform the emotional charge attached to an event into sequences of units of information capable, ultimately, of generating something akin to meaning. (Lyotard 1997: 70)

Lyotard's concept can be interpreted as narrative sensibility. Genuine narrative sensibility is demonstrated when complexity is acknowledged, and discontinuity is not eliminated through the imposition of structure upon the formless, simply to achieve a persuasive effect. Conversely, this sensibility is absent when complexity is either oversimplified or artificially manipulated to construct a conviction narrative. All written work necessarily involves choices and selections; thus, it is essential to recognise the inherent distinction between narrative representations and actual historical events—between "what once was and is no longer" and the discourses that replace them, to favour a harm reduction programme.

This brings into focus the significance of the concept of place of production and the potential distortions it introduces—an essential consideration for rethinking how convictions transition from evidentiary foundations to narrative construction. The narrative is not generated in isolation; it is neither merely the product of residual evidentiary content following adversarial proceedings, nor simply derived from the author's imagination and existential context. Instead, it represents the complex outcome of an interaction between these elements.

Merely listing proof does not suffice; the sentence must validate traces of the past by constructing a logically consistent narrative grounded in legal significance. This procedure requires careful application of interpretative reasoning and involves considerable complexity.

In this context, the term "fabrication" should not be interpreted as indicating outright falsehood, as such an assumption fails to account for the nuanced role of trace as a substitute of past events. The application of proof distinguishes historical narratives from fiction. However, proof alone does not constitute a guilty verdict, even when acquired through legitimate legal procedures. It is imperative to construct a coherent narrative utilising the available proof to achieve logical consistency and cohesion.

Recognising the inventive nature inherent in judicial fabrication presents two possibilities: first, it offers a means to transcend solitary truth-seeking when the judge adopts an appropriate disposition; second, it permits, through deliberate intention and reliance on "free motivated conviction" the potential for the judge to determine the outcome according to personal objectives, reminiscent of historical inquisitorial practices that predetermine results. To address these dynamics constructively and prevent arbitrary interpretations of truth, it is essential to shift focus away from assuming reality is fully or partially revealed. Instead, emphasis should be placed on analysing the interpretative choices involved in the production of truth within judicial processes. This approach allows for a transformation in how we relate to both historical realities and the narratives generated, moving beyond the pursuit of absolute truth.

Given the added significance attributed to life events, it follows that historical narratives—whether historiographical or judicial—cannot be governed by a strict logic of correspondence, even in a relative or approximate manner. The remnants of the past are fragmented and serve merely as indicators, choices must be made from this incomplete record, and causal links are often assigned where none existed or are oversimplified. Additionally, the limitations imposed by adherence to a particular narrative framework are challenging to transcend, as an individual's perspective as a being-in-the-world invariably restricts what can be conceived, even when based on traces that analogically point to the past.

Following the narrative transcription of a judicial conviction, absolute truth remains unattainable. As a result, uncertainty persists even after the final judgement: in criminal proceedings, truth is produced analogically, based on traces of past occurrences. The truth produced through narrative methods is inherently contingent. Ultimately, only representance remains, emphasising the significance of procedural integrity and the ritualised restriction of punitive power through due process.

The persistent uncertainty inherent in criminal proceedings highlights the limits of narrative truth, underlining the necessity of procedural safeguards that ensure fairness and respect for human dignity. Rather than striving for unattainable absolute truth, the criminal justice system should prioritise the ethical management of doubt and the careful consideration of interpretative choices, to prevent objectifying judicial practices. This paradigm shift supports a more humane approach, recognising the provisional nature of knowledge and the importance of protecting human rights, rejecting the search for absolute truth in criminal proceedings.

CHAPTER 10

A Reimagined Criminal Justice System Freed from the Pursuit of Truth

The arguments presented in this book reflect a specific political and epistemological perspective. They are shaped by intellectual traditions that inform my interpretive framework, outlining both the scope and boundaries of my understanding. As such, this work was not written from an abstract or detached position; rather, it demonstrates engagement and commitment to these identifiable horizons throughout the text and represents a counterpoint to inquisitorial, positivist and rationalist epistemologies.

It is important to clarify that I do not purport to resolve the complex issue of truth in criminal proceedings, which exceeds both my capacity and the scope of this work. Nor do I seek to present an ultimate theory capable of definitively addressing the matter—a pursuit inconsistent with the intellectual tradition to which I subscribe, one that acknowledges the provisional and metaphorical nature of our understanding of reality. Rather, the arguments advanced herein represent a hypothesis, substantiated by extensive bibliographical research and shaped by the theoretical framework applied. No claim is made to establish any absolute truth regarding the research problem under discussion. Instead, the objective is to lay the groundwork for reimagining the criminal justice system, emphasising the protection of human rights rather than the pursuit of absolute truth.

S. H. Khaled Jr., *Reimagining Criminal Justice, Search for Truth and Human Rights*, https://doi.org/10.1007/978-3-032-27227-0_10

Having established the range of possibilities attributable to the results obtained, I am now able to synthesise several key conclusions emerging from this research.

As outlined in chapter one, my analytical effort aimed to discuss the production of truth in criminal proceedings beyond the epistemic excess that characterises the notion of corresponding truth, whether in its absolute or relative form—a requirement for a reimagined criminal justice system committed to the defence of human rights.

In this analysis, I have examined a range of issues pertaining to the cognitive framework of criminal procedure, with the intention of adequately addressing its inherent complexity. This approach has facilitated a departure from the dominant monologic and coercive method of knowledge construction and imposition of truth in criminal proceedings. Historically, this authoritarian approach harkens back to Ancient Rome and was truly introduced to its full extent in the centuries of the Inquisition's heyday. This persecutory epistemology was motivated by an unwavering pursuit of truth and was later adopted by secular courts in Continental Europe. This ambition for truth established a system wherein the primary concern was securing convictions against perceived societal enemies. Inquisitorial procedure transformed truth into an instrument of domination by concentrating evidentiary power in the hands of the judge, objectifying the accused, and legitimising coercive techniques such as secrecy, confession, and torture. Notably, this epistemological and political stance persisted into modernity. With the introduction of a mixed procedural system, the ambition for truth became further entrenched through discourses of scientific rationality (Gauer). Utilising Cartesian principles, this perspective enabled the continuation of inquisitorial practices in modern criminal justice and reinvigorated the search for truth (Coutinho). I argued that rather than viewing defendants as enemies of society, we should critically examine and resist the penal system's selective targeting of poor, marginalised, and racialised groups (Zaffaroni). Historically, criminal justice has not empowered the underprivileged against authoritarian power; instead, it has reinforced police selectivity, mass incarceration, and hierarchies of class, race, gender, sexuality, and spirituality.

The search for truth is not a neutral epistemic objective, but a historically situated practice shaped by political authority, legal culture, and changing conceptions of knowledge. The distinction between proponents of evidentiary positivism—so-called real truth—and those advocating its relative or approximate form—evidentiary rationalism—is of minimal significance; both approaches uphold the corresponding truth model, thereby perpetuating the established discourse and myth surrounding the pursuit of absolute truth. Even relativised versions of correspondence truth, such as those advanced by evidentiary rationalism, preserve an epistemological and political structure that privileges punitive power over human rights. By revisiting Alfred Tarski's semantic conception of truth, the legacy of modern scientific thought, and the positivist ideal of judicial fact-finding, I demonstrated the inadequacy of these frameworks for addressing the complexity, uncertainty, and interpretive plurality inherent in criminal proceedings. In direct contrast to this prevailing view, I have drawn from a diverse range of intellectual traditions to propose an alternative framework: the epistemology of pastness. This approach fundamentally challenges the corresponding truth model without completely rejecting the notion of truth (Cunha Martins), while deliberately discarding the premise that truth must be actively pursued (Lopes Jr.), a perspective that privileges the value of hypotheses over facts (Cordero).

Initially, I established a distinction between facts and events and recognised that the event subject to judicial determination existed within an intricate web of life that cannot be comprehensively understood. I highlighted that the proceedings concern statements regarding events rather than the actual events themselves, noting that the normative framework shaping the legal-penal response to criminalised behaviour increases this separation. I argued that the persistence of truth-seeking models centred on judicial epistemic authority risks reinforcing inquisitorial tendencies, weakening procedural safeguards, and increasing the possibility of wrongful convictions. In contrast, I defended an approach grounded in accusatorial procedure, the presumption of innocence, and the recognition of uncertainty as intrinsic to the interpretation of the past. Furthermore, I observed that normative construction simplifies the complexity of criminalised performances, though it does not eliminate it entirely, as the array of inquiries directed towards these phenomena still surpasses what is typically addressed by modern scientific standards. By revisiting the traditional analogy between judge and historian, I argued that although both engage in retrospective reconstruction, the judge must operate under stricter institutional limits because criminal adjudication directly affects liberty, punitive power, and human rights.

Building on my initial arguments, I advanced to the concept of traces from the past, conceptualised as cognitive connectors that provide, to a certain extent, relevant—though incomplete—knowledge about historical events. This understanding of the trace originates with Heidegger and was further elaborated through the analyses of Ricoeur.

Traces are defined by their indirect reference, setting boundaries and conditions for the acquisition of knowledge regarding events from the past. They represent both presence and absence simultaneously. A trace encapsulates the paradox inherent to the past: while the past is irretrievable and cannot be altered, it nonetheless persists insofar as it is preserved through traces that point back to it. These traces facilitate the formation of meaningful substitutions or representations, thereby sustaining a possible epistemological connection to what has transpired.

It appears that a misapprehension regarding the distinct characteristics of the trace and its cognitive capacities underpins two perspectives I regard as erroneous: the conviction that absolute truth can be achieved and the outright dismissal of truth. These viewpoints align with the categories I identified as *Same* and *Other*, which embody the inherent difficulty in addressing the pastness of the past.

Confronted with the paradox inherent in categorising the possibilities of knowing the past, I examined this longstanding aporia, which has historically remained unresolved regarding the issue of truth in criminal proceedings. On one side, the concept of the *Same* signifies an epistemic excess, as it eliminates temporal distance and, consequently, sacrifices an essential characteristic of the event under judicial scrutiny—its pastness, which is ontologically fundamental and cannot be transcended by any epistemological approach. Conversely, I also noted that when the past is partially retained through traces, it cannot be defined solely as an *Other*, since a form of presence persists, signifying that it continues to exist in some capacity. This ongoing presence precludes the complete exclusion of truth from knowledge constructed on remnants of the past. This is the epistemological barrier I sought to overcome in reimagining criminal justice as a system grounded in the protection of human rights and the reduction of harm.

As has been observed, various scholars have recognised this tension and addressed it by refining the notion of correspondence truth, which subsequently became viewed as relative or approximate. Notwithstanding these adjustments, the redefinition of correspondence truth continued to uphold the ideal of pursuing absolute truth, thereby sustaining the dominance of a prosecutorial epistemology—a framework I aimed to challenge in reconsidering criminal justice. Whether intentionally or otherwise, such scholars remained attached to the paradigm of the *Same*, which exemplifies epistemic excess and leads to confirmation bias. Criminal justice should serve as a safeguard against the selective nature of primary criminalisation, rather than reinforcing this enduring authoritarian pattern.

From the beginning, my objective was to identify an alternative that could resolve the identified aporia and facilitate the development of a concept of truth suited to the context of historical pastness. This approach highlights the ritualised, regulated aspect of punitive power, emphasising the procedural framework necessary for upholding human rights. Consequently, I intentionally pursued an epistemological break as articulated by Bachelard.

In addressing this issue, I contended that the resolution of the enigma resides in the concept of trace, which inherently leads to representance (as discussed by Ricoeur). This notion entails an acknowledgement of an irreconcilable debt to the past, since any narrative representation of a historical event functions as a substitute—serving *as if it were* the original event—rather than as its equivalent or direct counterpart. Although traces facilitate cognitive connections to the past, their representative function is necessarily substitutive rather than truly correspondent.

Accordingly, I posit that the past, as preserved through traces and narratively reconstructed, should not be confined exclusively to the domains of the *Same* or the *Other*. The narrative contained in a conviction is best situated within a third ontological category: the *Analogue*, which reframes rather than eliminates the relevance of the other two spheres. The concept of *Analogue* here encompasses both *Being-as* and *Not-being*; it describes a truth produced amidst continual tension between revelation and concealment, ultimately manifesting as a narrative artefact fashioned by the judge from remnants of the past. In this view, such truth is analogically produced in narrative form, serving as a criterion for truth based on the analogical (re)production of history, rather than on absolute or relative correspondence with events of a previous era.

By repositioning truth rather than rejecting it entirely, I removed its canonical status. The conception of truth as *Analogue* promotes careful consideration and harm reduction, in contrast to the correspondence notion of the *Same*, which often leads to assumptions of oppressive omnipotence motivated by an unyielding ambition for truth.

Based on the sign of the *Analogue*, I presented a relevant inquiry regarding criminal law: if the character of criminal proceedings depends on the substantive law to which it is attached, then recognising that the regime of truth in criminal proceedings is structured by the sign of the *Analogue* yields notable implications. This is particularly significant given that criminal law prohibits analogy—except *in bonam partem*.

As noted in chapter one, it is not solely the need to limit punitive authority that necessitates moving away from a truth-centric view of criminal proceedings. Rather, the inherent impossibility of achieving an absolute or even approximate truth serves as a compelling justification for prioritising procedural safeguards over the pursuit of truth, since ultimately only representance endures— the judge will always be an insolvent debtor of the past event that he seeks to represent narratively in the sentence. Accordingly, I contend that truth should be regarded as contingent at best, and that a conviction is legitimate only when due process is rigorously upheld. Such adherence is essential for prioritising the reduction of harm resulting from wrongful convictions.

Whether this represents a comprehensive theory of truth, as Ferrajoli considers necessary to prevent the procedural structure from devolving into a ritualistic exercise of hierarchical punitive authority, remains subject to analysis. Nevertheless, as previously indicated, I do not claim to have produced such a theory and instead regard this study as my contribution to a re-envisioned model of criminal justice that upholds human rights, consistent with the interpretative framework to which I adhere.

Accordingly, I reject the concept of an all-encompassing theory of truth, as I do not seek to assume such a discursive position. In this regard, I maintain my resistance to the persistent inclination towards conceptual unification, even with respect to concepts articulated herein. Consequently, no comprehensive theory of truth in criminal proceedings has been proposed throughout this work, nor is such a theory advanced here; any formulation with exhaustive ambitions would inevitably oversimplify the issue. As Ricoeur aptly observes, "The trace, we said, signifies without making appear. It is at this point that the analysis of representation comes into play; the aporia of the trace as 'standing for' the past finds in the 'seeing-as' a partial solution" (Ricoeur 1997: 261). This study builds upon this partial solution, contributing additional interpretation beyond Ricoeur's proposal, by attributing to it a narratively constructed character of truth, whose status must be anchored within the domain of the *Analogous*: *Being-as* and *Non-being*.

Nonetheless, my modest proposal has prompted significant reflections that contribute to and enhance the ongoing, broader discourse of defence of human rights. The aim remains the strengthening of safeguards against punitive authority (Zaffaroni), in line with the standards prescribed by the accusatorial model grounded in democratic-constitutional principles (Coutinho, Lopes Jr., Prado, Morais da Rosa, and Cunha Martins).

By examining the hallucinatory qualities of evidence (Gil and Cunha Martins), this analysis demonstrates that only a ritualised framework for regulating punitive authority and addressing evidentiary contamination can, to some degree, maintain the analogical nature of traces and enhance the probability that convictions are at least substantiated by the sign of the *Analogous*. Accepting anything less legitimises decisionism through the "free motivated conviction" discourse fallacy, which purports to pursue truth under the guise of the sign of the *Same*, yet ultimately engenders a violent form of truth reflective solely of itself. Consequently, evidence may inappropriately supplant traces, leading to convictions that are phantasmagorical in nature, paradoxically invoking the sign of the *Other* and representing a substantive form of judicial violence.

I have indicated that evidentiary activity should not be interpreted solely as demonstrative of the truth (the sign of the *Same*), nor simply as a formal establishment of facts or as argumentative rhetoric (the sign of the *Other*). Instead, it is best understood as a dialogical process wherein, through regulated procedural means, evidence is introduced with the purpose of persuading the judge—by psychological means—that these constitute analogical traces of past events (thus emphasising once again the sign of the *Analogous*).

By recognising the judge as the primary recipient of evidentiary activity, I established a framework to explore the inherent uncertainty in judicial decision-making, referencing the insights of Einstein, Morin, and Prigogine. This uncertainty arises from the complex interplay between belief and conviction, extending beyond the modern pursuit of absolute certainty. Additionally, I highlighted the opacity of consciousness, drawing on Coutinho and Morais da Rosa, and addressed the ontological dimension of the judge's perspective—considering Heidegger's concept of being-in-the-world and the influence of tradition as discussed by Heidegger and Gadamer—which further underscores the fundamentally analogical nature I intended to emphasise.

I also examined the dynamics of risk and uncertainty inherent to criminal proceedings, where competing narrative representations, each driven by narrative purpose, aim to influence the judge's perception. Their objective is to secure agreement that the evidence presented serves as analogical indicators of past events. I concluded that this distinctive cognitive framework differs fundamentally from the "laboratory of history" model, which is characteristic of modern reasoning based on objective truth and epistemic certainty.

In addressing the lived experience of evidentiary procedures, I examined the procedural frameworks advanced by Bülow and Goldschmidt. My analysis led to the conclusion that the requisite departure from traditional civil procedure categories (as articulated by Coutinho), along with the associated notions of security and stability, necessarily supports the adoption of Goldschmidt's model, which is better suited to the nuances of criminal procedure. Accordingly, I underscored that the burden of proof rests with the prosecutor, while the defendant is subject to considerations of risk. The act of seizing an opportunity equates to fulfilling a burden or mitigating a risk, with the judge regarding the submitted evidence as an analogue of historical events. Within this paradigm, I noted that the judge's function remains essentially receptive, devoid of any probative responsibilities, as such involvement would compromise the integrity and effectiveness of the adversarial process that should fundamentally underpin the proceedings (Fazzalari).

Accordingly, within an accusatorial epistemology that operates under democratic principles, the judge's conviction is developed through dialogue (as described by Ricoeur). It is the responsibility of the parties to present and narratively articulate the evidence, as well as to manage its presentation. The judge's primary role is to ensure due process and to establish a conviction based on elements that have survived rigorous dialogical scrutiny, thereby confirming their status beyond mere evidentiary value.

I noted that, through such proofs, a judge can analogically produce the truth, narratively articulating a conviction developed from traces of past events. Accordingly, I proposed a framework designed to contain punitive authority, with the objective of minimising harm to human rights and limiting judicial discretion. This approach aims to address and mitigate the frequent abuses of decisionism, which are common within epistemologies focused on uncovering the truth—specifically, those that prioritise the conviction of the defendant, who is often perceived as a societal enemy (Lopes Jr.).

This analysis examined the complexities of the lat modern era, exploring concepts such as acceleration and speed (Virilio), risk (Beck), and rules of the game (Calamandrei), demonstrating that even regulated structures intended for harm reduction must acknowledge the existence of uncertainty. It is through embracing risk and discarding misguided notions of absolute security and predictability that the potential for mitigating harm emerges. Consequently, it is recognised that within procedural legal contexts and their inherent dynamism (Goldschmidt), risks are pervasive, requiring emphasis on safeguards. However, the epistemology proposed herein cannot entirely remove belief as a foundational aspect of conviction; it can only decrease the potential harm resulting from this interaction (Cunha Martins).

Despite my initial optimism regarding harm reduction, I found that the reliance placed on testimony within criminal proceedings was significantly limited by inherent challenges associated with perception, memory, and the fiduciary nature of testimonial evidence (Ricoeur). After considering these complexities, I proceeded to critically examine the myth of absolute truth in criminal proceedings. Referencing multiple scholars, I questioned the discursive authority typically afforded to judges by this myth, thereby paving the way for a reconsideration and redefinition of their role within an evolving criminal justice framework.

After addressing the myth, I examined the hermeneutics of facticity and provided an analysis of the judge as being-in-the-world (Heidegger), along with the pressing necessity for judicial desubstantialisation (Morais da Rosa). This approach highlights the limitations of forming conviction strictly within the correspondence model of truth based on the subject/object dichotomy characteristic of modern rationality. My argument situates understanding and interpretation within the process of disclosure and concealment (Heidegger), proposing that truth is best understood as encompassing both revelation and concealment. This framework more accurately reflects the interplay between belief and conviction (Martins) and aligns with the inherent uncertainty of procedural legal contexts and the narrative constructs presented by the parties in adversarial proceedings (Fazzalari), framed within the dynamics of procedural warfare (Goldschmidt).

When reflecting on the unavoidable connection to tradition (Heidegger), I noted that some traditions are open to engaging with objects and embracing their complexity, while others are defined by the domination of objects, representing what Nietzsche termed the malice of knowledge. I further observed that while all concepts are inherently metaphorical, certain concepts recognise the richness of reality and possess substance, whereas others merely create distance from the subject matter. Historically, the latter type of concept has prevailed in criminal proceedings, which underscores the need for a significant discursive shift to re-envision contemporary criminal justice.

It is asserted that adherence to tradition requires the judge to be cognisant of their own preconceptions (Heidegger), thereby enabling partial regulation of those biases and the formulation of hypotheses that critically engage with external realities rather than imposing self-referential explanatory models. Consequently, the principle that the interpreter operates within the hermeneutic circle (Heidegger and Gadamer) supports the receptive position (Goldschmidt) expected of the judge, while simultaneously underscoring the role of creative imagination (Gadamer) in contributing novel insights during the process of understanding.

It can be concluded that when a judge reaches a conviction and articulates it in the judgement, this epistemological process generates something fundamentally new—transcending a simple correspondence theory of truth. Truth, in this context, is not merely an alignment between the subject's judgement and its object, as such a binary is inadequate given that the judge operates as a being-in-the-world, influenced by a comprehensive legal-criminal tradition that informs their interpretative framework. This is further complemented by creative imagination, resulting in the formulation of genuinely novel hypotheses, even when these are contrasted with remnants of past events. Consequently, truth should primarily be viewed as something produced (sign of the *Analogue*) rather than merely discovered or corresponding to external realities, even in a relative sense (sign of the *Same*).

By centring the analysis on the notion of freely motivated conviction, I argued that this principle may, at times, function as a hermeneutical device enabling judges to make a decision prior to evaluating evidence, subsequently seeking justification for their predetermined conclusion(Streck). In this context, I highlighted that if the aim of motivation is to regulate discretion, it is unclear how granting unrestricted authority to the narrator to fulfil an "epistemic function of truth" (Taruffo) would accomplish this goal; indeed, such a measure may undermine it. The principle of freely motivated conviction does not address this concern and often acts as a rhetorical pretext for judicial intervention in evidence management. Consequently, the deconstruction (Cunha Martins) of this monologically imposed approach should inevitably lead to its dissolution, given that it that conflicts with democratic-constitutional principles.

In the final section, I examined the narrative production of the sentence, drawing on the works of Ricoeur and Certeau. This epistemological process is inherently influenced by areas of discretion that can encourage decisionism; thus, it is crucial to regulate these discretionary spaces to limit the narrator's autonomy. By analysing the narrative context underpinning judgements, I introduced the last component necessary to support the argument that truth is produced analogically through narrative, rather than uncovered as mere correspondence during proceedings.

Upon concluding this comprehensive analysis, it can be stated that the historical narrative reflected in the guilty verdict represents a precarious substitute for an event gone by, derived analogically from remnants of the past, and cannot be interpreted through corresponding theory of truth. Ultimately, representance prevails, rendering truth contingent and necessitating that criminal proceedings are legitimised primarily as structured processes to minimise the risks of wrongful convictions. Assigning judges the pursuit of absolute truth does not resolve the inherent challenges associated with upholding human rights or the uncertainty of past events; rather, it underestimates these complexities and facilitates objectifying judicial practices. Therefore, it is essential to move beyond the illusion of certainty (Bachelard), the fallacies of modern certainty (Morin and Prigogine), and inquisitorial epistemologies (Lopes Jr.).

To advance criminal justice reform, the presumption of innocence should be recognised as a fundamental and structuring principle in criminal proceedings, in alignment with democratic and constitutional standards. This approach applies to all aspects, including the role and responsibilities of the judge. Emphasising this principle allows for a departure from inquisitorial, positivist and rationalist epistemologies underpinned by the ambition for truth and focused on punishing perceived societal enemies.

In summary, given that the truth produced during proceedings is inherently contingent, strict adherence to procedural rules remains the most effective means of limiting the potential arbitrariness of punitive power within a criminal justice system committed to upholding human rights.

Ultimately, there exists only one representation of truth: the perspective that challenges injustice. The deconstruction presented here highlights the fundamental potential for justice, to the extent that it may converge with its very concept. However, further analysis is required before addressing this issue in greater detail; at present, I acknowledge the direction taken and recognise, above all, the essential role of absence.

References

ALCALÁ-ZAMORA Y CASTILLO, Niceto. Estudios de teoria general y historia del proceso: Tomo II. México: UNAM, 1992.

ALMEIDA PRADO, Lídia Reis. O juiz e a emoção: aspectos da lógica da decisão judicial. Campinas: Millenium, 2003.

AMBOS, Kai. O principio acusatorio e o proceso acusatorio: un intento de comprender su significado atual desde la perspectiva histórica. In: BACH-MAIER WINTER, Lorena (Org.). Proceso penal y sistemas acusatorios. Madrid: Marcial Pons, 2008.

ANDRADE, Vera Regina Pereira. A ilusão de segurança jurídica. Porto Alegre: Livraria do Advogado, 2003.

ANDRADE, Vera Regina Pereira de. Pelas mãos da criminologia. Rio de Janeiro: Revan, 2012.

ANKARLOO, Bengt; CLARK, Stuart; MONTER, William. Witchcraft and Magic in Europe: the period of witch trials. London: Athlone Press, 2002.

APPADURAI, Arjun. Modernity at large: cultural dimensions of globalization. Minneapolis: University of Minnesota Press, 1996.

ARAGONESES ALONSO, Pedro. Instituciones de derecho procesal penal. Madrid: Rubi Arts Graficas, 1986.

ARAGONESES ALONSO. Proceso y derecho procesal: introduccion. Madrid: Editoriales de Derecho Reunidas, 1986.

ARIÈS, Philippe. O tempo da história. Rio de Janeiro: Francisco Alves, 1989.

ARISTÓTELES. Arte retórica e arte poética. Rio de Janeiro: Ediouro, 2000.

ARISTÓTELES. Ética a Nicômaco. São Paulo: Martin Claret, 2002. p. 126.

ARMENTA DEU, Teresa. Principio acusatorio y derecho penal. Barcelona: JM Bosch, 1995.

S. H. Khaled Jr., *Reimagining Criminal Justice, Search for Truth and Human Rights*, https://doi.org/10.1007/978-3-032-27227-0

BACHELARD, Gaston. A poética do espaço. Rio de Janeiro: Livraria Eldorado Tijuca, 1960.
BACHMAIER WINTER, Lorena. Acusatorio *versus* inquisitivo. Reflexiones acerca del proceso penal. In: BACHMAIER WINTER, Lorena (Org.). Proceso penal y sistemas acusatorios. Madrid: Marcial Pons, 2008.
BADARÓ, Gustavo Henrique Righi Ivahy. Direito processual penal: Tomo I. Rio de Janeiro: Elsevier, 2008.
BADARÓ, Gustavo Henrique Righi Ivahy. Ônus da prova no processo penal. São Paulo: Revista dos Tribunais, 2003.
BADARÓ, Gustavo Henrique Righi Ivahy. Epistemologia judiciária e prova penal. São Paulo: RT, 2019.
BANN, Stephen. As invenções da história: ensaios sobre a representação do passado. São Paulo: Unesp, 1994.
BAPTISTA, Francisco das neves. O mito da verdade real na dogmática do processo penal. Rio de Janeiro: Renovar, 2001.
BATISTA, Nilo. Apontamentos para uma história da legislação penal brasileira. Rio de Janeiro: Editora Revan, 2016.
BATISTA, Vera Malaguti. Introdução crítica à criminologia brasileira. Rio de Janeiro: Revan, 2011.
BAR, Ludwig Von. A history of continental criminal law. New Jersey: The Lawbook Exchange, 2007.
BARTLETT, Robert. Trial by Fire and Water: the medieval judicial ordeal. Oxford: Clarendon Press, 1986.
BAUMER, Franklin L. O pensamento europeu moderno: volume I: séculos XVII e XVIII. Lisboa: Edições 70, 1977.
BECCARIA, Cesare. Dos delitos e das penas. São Paulo: Martin Claret, 2003.
BECK, Ulrich. La sociedad del riesgo: hacia una nueva modernidad. Barcelona: Paidós, 2002.
BENTHAM, Jeremy. Tratado de las provas judiciales: tomo I. Buenos Aires: EJEA, 1959.
BENTHAM, Jeremy. Anarchical Fallacies: The Works of Jeremy Bentham. Edimburgh: John Bowring Editor, 1843.
BENTHAM, Jeremy. An Introductory View of the Rationale of Evidence: for the use of non-lawyers as well as lawyers. Edinburgh: Bowring and Mill, 1812.
BENTHAM, Jeremy. A Treatise in Judicial Evidence. London: Baldwin, Cradock and Joy, 1825.
BENTHAM, Jeremy. Principles of Judicial Procedure, With the Outlines of a Procedure Code. In: The Works of Jeremy Bentham. v. II. Edinburgh: William Tait, 1843.
BENTHAM, Jeremy. Rationale of Judicial Evidence. v. 1. London: Hunt & Clarke, 1827.
BENTHAM, Jeremy. Tratado de las provas judiciales. Buenos Aires: EJEA, 1971.

BERGSON, Henry. Matéria e memória. São Paulo: Martins Fontes, 1999.
BETTIOL, Giuseppe. Instituciones de derecho penal y procesal. Barcelona: Bosch, 1973.
BITENCOURT, Cezar Roberto. Tratado de direito penal, volume 1: parte geral. São Paulo: Saraiva, 2009.
BLOCH, Marc. Apologia da história ou o ofício do historiador. Rio de Janeiro: Jorge Zahar, 2001.
BOBBIO, Norberto. O positivismo jurídico: lições de filosofia do direito. São Paulo: Ícone, 1999.
BOSWORTH, Mary. Introduction: reinventing penal parsimony. Theoretical criminology. Vol. 14(3): 251–256.
BRASIL. Códigos penal, processo penal e constituição federal. São Paulo: Saraiva, 2010.
BÜLOW, Oskar Von. La teoria das excepciones procesales y presupuestos procesales. Buenos Aires: EJEA, 1964.
CALAMANDREI, Piero. Direito processual: volume III. Campinas: Bookseller, 1999.
CALAMANDREI, Piero. Eles, os juízes, vistos por um advogado. São Paulo: Martins Fontes, 1996.
CALAMANDREI, Piero. Estudios sobre el proceso civil. Buenos Aires: EJEA, 1973.
CARNELUTTI, Francesco. Arte do direito: seis meditações sobre o direito. Campinas: Bookseller, 2001.
CARNELUTTI, Francesco. Las miserias del proceso penal. México: Cajica, 1965.
CARNELUTTI, Francesco. Lições sobre o processo penal: tomo I. Campinas: Bookseller, 2004.
CARVALHO, Amilton Bueno de. Garantismo penal aplicado. Rio de Janeiro: Lumen Juris, 2003.
CARVALHO, Salo de. Antimanual de criminologia. Rio de Janeiro: Lumen Juris, 2008.
CARVALHO, Salo de. Criminologia e transdisciplinaridade. In: GAUER, Ruth Maria Chittó (Ed.). Sistema penal e violência. Rio de Janeiro: Lumen Juris, 2006.
CARVALHO, Salo de. Pena e garantias. Rio de Janeiro: Lumen Juris, 2003.
CARVALHO, Salo de. Antimanual de criminologia. São Paulo, SaraivaJur, 2022.
CASARA, Rubens R R. *O Estado pós-democrático*: neo-obscurantismo e gestão dos indesejáveis. Rio de Janeiro: Civilização Brasileira, 2017.
CASARA, Rubens R.R. Processo penal do espetáculo: ensaios sobre o poder penal, a dogmática e o autoritarismo na sociedade brasileira. Florianópolis: Empório do Direito, 2015.

CATROGA, Fernando. Memória e história. In: PESAVENTO, Sandra Jatahy (Org.). Fronteiras do milênio. Porto Alegre: Editora da Universidade/ UFRGS, 2001.

CAVALLONE, Bruno. En Defensa de la Verifobia: consideraciones amigablemente polémicas sobre un reciente libro de Michele Taruffo. In: CAVALLONE, Bruno; TARUFFO, Michele. Verifobia: un diálogo sobre prueba y verdad. Lima: Palestra Editores, 2012.

CERTEAU, Michel de. A escrita da história. Rio de Janeiro: Forense, 1982.

CHARTIER. Roger. À beira da falésia: a história entre certezas e inquietude. Porto Alegre: Editora da Universidade/UFRGS, 2002.

CHARTIER, Roger. Uma crise da história? A história entre narração e conhecimento. In: PESAVENTO, Sandra Jatahy (Org.). Fronteiras do milênio. Porto Alegre: Editora da Universidade/UFRGS, 2001.

CHAUI, Marilena. Brasil: mito fundador e sociedade autoritária. São Paulo: Fundação Perseu Abramo, 2001.

CHIESA, Luis E. Beyond Torture: the nemo tenetur principle in borderline cases. In Boston College Third World Law Journal. v. 30, 2010.

CHIOVENDA, Giuseppe. Instituições de direito processual civil. Campinas: Bookseller, 1998.

CHIOVENDA, Giuseppe. La acción en el sistema de los derechos. Bogotá: Temis, 1986.

COHN, Gabriel. Weber: sociologia. São Paulo: Ática, 1997.

COMTE-SPONVILLE, André. O ser-tempo: algumas reflexões sobre o tempo da consciência. São Paulo: Martins Fontes, 2000.

CORDERO, Franco. Guida alla procedura penale. Torino: UTET, 1986.

CORDERO, Franco. Procedimiento penal: Tomo I. Bogotá: Temis, 2000.

CORDERO, Franco. Procedimiento penal: Tomo II. Bogotá: Temis, 2000.

CORDERO, Franco. Riti e Sapienza del Diritto. Bari: Laterza, 1981

COSTA, Thaís Tanure de Oliveira. Nas terras remotas o diabo anda solto: degredo, inquisição e escravidão no mundo atlântico português (séculos XVI a XVIII). Dissertação (mestrado). Universidade Federal de Minas Gerais, Faculdade de Filosofia e Ciências Humanas. 2018.

COUTINHO, Jacinto Nelson de Miranda. A lide e o conteúdo do processo penal. Curitiba: Juruá, 1998.

COUTINHO, Jacinto Nelson de Miranda. O papel do novo juiz no processo penal. In: COUTINHO, Jacinto Nelson de Miranda. Observações sobre os sistemas processuais penais. Curitiba: Observatório da Mentalidade Inquisitória, 2018.

COUTINHO, Jacinto Nelson de Miranda. Verdade e Fake News. Revista Brasileira de Ciências Criminais n. 198. 2023.

COUTINHO, Jacinto Nelson de Miranda. Barbárie do processo penal não pode ser enfrentada apenas com retórica. Em: < https://www.conjur.com.br/2015-set-25/limite-penal-barbarie-processo-penal-nao->

COUTINHO, Jacinto Nelson de Miranda. Por que sustentar a democracia do sistema processual penal brasileiro. R. do Instituto de Hermenêutica Jur. – RIHJ | Belo Horizonte, ano 11, n. 14, p. 145–152, jul./dez. 2013.

COUTINHO, Jacinto Nelson de Miranda. Glosas ao verdade, dúvida e certeza, de Francesco Carnelutti, para os operadores do Direito. In: Anuário Ibero-americano de direitos humanos. Rio de Janeiro: Lumen Juris, 2002.

COUTINHO, Jacinto Nelson de Miranda. Introdução aos princípios gerais do processo penal brasileiro. Revista de estudos criminais n. 1. Porto Alegre: Notadez, 2001.

COUTINHO, Jacinto Nelson de Miranda. O papel do juiz no processo penal. In: COUTINHO, Jacinto Nelson de Miranda (Coord.). Crítica à teoria geral do direito processual penal. Rio de Janeiro: Renovar, 2001.

CUNHA MARTINS, Rui; GIL, Fernando. Modos da verdade. Revista de História das Idéias. Instituto de História e Teoria das Idéias da Faculdade de Letras da Universidade de Coimbra, v. 23, 2002.

CUNHA MARTINS, Rui. O ponto cego do direito: the Brazilian lessons. Rio de Janeiro: Lumen Juris, 2010.

CUNHA MARTINS, Rui. A hora dos cadáveres adiados: corrupção, expectativa e processo penal. São Paulo: Atlas, 2013.

CUNHA MARTINS, Rui. Contra-intuição e processo penal. In: KHALED JR., Salah H. (Oorg.) Sistema penal e poder punitivo: estudos em homenagem ao prof. Aury Lopes Jr. Belo Horizonte: Letramento, 2020.

DESCARTES, René. Discurso do método/meditações. São Paulo: Martin Claret, 2008.

DÖHRING, Erich. La investigacion del estado de los hechos en el proceso: la prueba su pratica y apreciacion. Buenos Aires: EJEA, 19XX.

DUCLERC, Elmir. Prova penal e garantismo: uma investigação crítica sobre a verdade fática construída através do processo. Rio de Janeiro: Lumen Juris, 2004.

DUSSEL, Enrique. Europa, modernidade e Eurocentrismo. In: A colonialidade do saber: eurocentrismo e ciências sociais. Perspectivas latino-americanas. Buenos Aires: CLACSO, 2005.

DRAY, William. Filosofia da história. Rio de Janeiro: Zahar, 1977.

EINSTEIN. Vida e pensamentos. São Paulo: Martin Claret, 2002.

ELIADE, Mircea. Mito e realidade. São Paulo: Perspectiva, 2002.

FAZZALARI, Elio. Instituições de direito processual. Campinas: Bookseller, 2006.

FEBVRE, Lucien. História. São Paulo: Ática, 1978.

FEDERICI, Silvia. Calibã e a Bruxa: mulheres, corpo e acumulação primitiva. São Paulo: Elefante, 2017.
FEDERICI, Silvia. Mulheres e Caça às Bruxas. São Paulo: Boitempo, 2019.
FEITLER, Bruno. Nas Malhas da Consciência: igreja e inquisição no Brasil nordeste 1640–1750. 2 ed. São Paulo: Unifesp, 2019.
FERRAJOLI, Luigi. Direito e razão: teoria do garantismo penal. São Paulo: Revista dos Tribunais, 2002.
FERRAJOLI, Luigi. Derecho y Razón: teoria del garantismo penal. 6 ed. Madrid: Trotta, 2004.
FERRELL, Jeff; HAYWARD, Keith; YOUNG, Jock. Criminologia cultural: um convite. Belo Horizonte: Letramento, 2019.
FERRER BELTRÁN, Jordi. La valoración racional de la prueba. Madrid: Marcial Pons, 2007.
FERRER BELTRÁN, Jordi. Prueba y verdad en el derecho. Madrid: Marcial Pons, 2005.
FERRER, Luiz Alfredo Brodermann. Relación Jurídica Procesal, Alegatos, México, n. 62, en./abr. 2006.
FERRER BELTRÁN, Jordi. La Prueba es Libertad, Pero no Tanto: una teoria de la prueba cuasi-benthamiana. In Revista Jurídica Mario Alario D'"Fillippo,. v. IX. n. 18, 2017.
FERRER BELTRÁN, Jordi. Prueba sin Convicción: estândares de prueba y debido proceso. Madrid: Marcial Pons, 2021.
FERRER BELTRÁN, Jordi. Valoração Racional da Prova. São Paulo: JusPodium, 2023.
FIGUEIREDO DIAS, Jorge. Direito processual penal. Coimbra: Coimbra Editores, 2004.
FOUCAULT, Michel. A verdade e as formas jurídicas. Rio de Janeiro: Nau, 2003.
FOUCAULT, Michel. Em defesa da sociedade: curso no Collège de France (1975–1976). São Paulo: Martins Fontes, 2005.
FOUCAULT, Michel. História da sexualidade I: a vontade de saber. Rio de Janeiro: Graal, 1998.
FOUCAULT, Michel. Microfísica do poder. Rio de Janeiro: Graal, 2002.
FOUCAULT, Michel. Vigiar e punir: nascimento da prisão. Petrópolis: Vozes, 2008.
FRAHER, Richard. Conviction According to Conscience: the medieval jurists' debate concerning judicial discretion and the law of proof. Law and History Review. v. 7. n. 1, 1989.
FRAHER, Richard. The Theoretical Justification for the New Criminal Law of the High Middle Ages: "*rei publicae interest, ne crimina remaneant*". University of Illinois Law Review. n. 3, 1984.
FURET, François. A oficina da história. Lisboa: Gradiva, 1979.

GADAMER, Hans-Georg. Verdad y método: fundamentos de una hermenéutica filosófica. Salamanca: Sígueme, 1984.

GADAMER, Hans-Georg. Verdad y método II. Salamanca: Sígueme, 1992.

GARAPON, Antoine. Bem julgar: ensaio sobre ritual judiciário. Lisboa: Piaget, 1997.

GARAPON, Antoine; PAPAPOULOS, Ioannis. Julgar nos Estados Unidos e na França: cultura jurídica francesa e Common Law em uma perspectiva comparada. Rio de Janeiro: Lumen Juris, 2008.

GAUER, Ruth M. Chittó; TIMM DE SOUZA, Ricardo. Apresentação. In: GAUER, Ruth M. Chittó (Org.). A qualidade do tempo: para além das experiências históricas. Rio de Janeiro: Lumen Juris, 2004.

GAUER, Ruth M. Chittó. A fundação da norma: para além da racionalidade histórica. Porto Alegre: EDIPUCRS, 2009.

GAUER, Ruth M. Chittó. A ilusão totalizadora e a violência da fragmentação. In: GAUER, Ruth Maria Chittó (Coord.). Sistema penal e violência. Rio de Janeiro: Lumen Juris, 2006.

GAUER, Ruth M. Chittó. Conhecimento e aceleração (mito, verdade, tempo). In: GAUER, Ruth M. Chittó (Org.). A qualidade do tempo: para além das aparências históricas. Rio de Janeiro: Lumen Juris, 2004.

GAUER, Ruth M. Chittó. Falar em tempo, viver o tempo! In: GAUER, Ruth M. Chittó (Coord.); DA SILVA, Mozart Linhares (Org.). Tempo/história. Porto Alegre: EDIPUCRS, 1998.

GAUER, Ruth M. Chittó. O reino da estupidez e o reino da razão. Rio de Janeiro: Lumen Juris, 2006.

GAY, Peter. O estilo na história. São Paulo: Companhia das Letras, 1990.

GEERTZ, Clifford. A interpretação das culturas. Rio de Janeiro: LCT, 1989.

GERBER, Daniel. Breves considerações sobre o flagrante. In: CARVALHO, Salo de (Org.). Leituras constitucionais do sistema penal contemporâneo. Rio de Janeiro: Lumen Juris, 2004.

GIACOMOLLI, Nereu José. Atividade do juiz criminal frente à constituição: deveres e limites em face do princípio acusatório. In: GAUER, Ruth Maria Chittó (Coord.). Sistema penal e violência. Rio de Janeiro: Lumen Juris, 2006.

GIMENO SENDRA, Vicente. Fundamentos del derecho procesal. Madrid: Civitas, 1981.

GINZBURG, Carlo. Micro-história e outros ensaios. Rio de Janeiro: Bertrand, 1989.

GINZBURG, Carlo. Olhos de madeira: nove reflexões sobre a distância. São Paulo: Companhia das Letras, 2001.

GINZBURG, Carlo. Relações de força. História, retórica, prova. São Paulo: Companhia das Letras, 2002.

GOLDSCHMIDT, James. Problemas jurídicos y políticos del proceso penal. In: GOLDSCHMIDT, James. Derecho, derecho penal y proceso I: problemas fundamentales del derecho. Madrid: Marcial Pons, 2010.
GOLDSCHMIDT, James. Teoría general del proceso. In: GOLDSCHMIDT, James. Derecho, derecho penal y proceso I: problemas fundamentales del derecho. Madrid: Marcial Pons, 2010.
GOMES FILHO, Antônio Magalhães. Direito à prova no processo penal. São Paulo: Revista dos Tribunais, 1997.
GOMES FILHO, Antônio Magalhães. A motivação das decisões penais. São Paulo: Revista dos Tribunais, 2001.
GÓMEZ ORBANEJA, Emilio. Comentarios a la ley de enjuiciamento criminal. Barcelona: Bosch, 1947.
GÓMEZ ORBANEJA, Emilio; HERCE QUEMADA, Vicente. Derecho procesal: Vol II: Derecho procesal penal. Madrid: EGESA, 1997.
GÖSSEL, Karl H. El principio de estado de derecho en su significado para el procedimiento penal. In: El derecho procesal penal en el estado de derecho: obras completas. Santa Fé: Rubinal-Culzoni, 2007.
GÖSSEL, Karl H. La verdad en el proceso penal: es encontrada o construída? In: El derecho procesal penal en el estado de derecho: obras completas. Santa Fé: Rubinal-Culzoni, 2007.
GRAHAM JR, Kenneth W. "There'll Always be an England: the instrumental ideology of evidence. Michigan Law Review. v. 85, 1987.
GRINOVER, Ada Pellegrini. A iniciativa instrutória do juiz no processo penal acusatório. Revista Brasileira de Ciências Criminais. São Paulo: Revista dos Tribunais, ano 7, n. 27.
GRINOVER, Ada Pellegrini; SCARANCE FERNANDES, Antonio; GOMES FILHO, Antonio Magalhães. As nulidades no processo penal. São Paulo: Revista dos Tribunais, 2004.
GUASP, Jaime. Estudios jurídicos. Madrid: Civitas, 1996.
GUASP, Jaime; ARAGONESES ALONSO, Pedro. Derecho procesal civil: tomo primero. Madrid: Civitas, 1998.
HALBWACHS, Maurice. A memória coletiva. São Paulo: Vértice, 1990.
HARTOG, François. A testemunha e o historiador. In: PESAVENTO, Sandra Jatahy (Org.). Fronteiras do milênio. Porto Alegre: Editora da Universidade/ UFRGS, 2001.
HAYWARD, Keith.; FERRELL, Jeff. Possibilidades insurgentes: as políticas da criminologia cultural. *Sistema Penal & Violência*. Porto Alegre, v. 4, n. 2, p. 206–218, jul./dez. 2012.
HAYWARD, Keith; YOUNG, Jock. Cultural criminology: some notes on the script. In: Theoretical Criminology, v. 8, n. 3, 2012. p. 259-285.
HEIDEGGER, Martin. Ser e tempo Parte I. Petrópolis: Vozes, 2005.
HEIDEGGER, Martin. Ser e tempo Parte II. Petrópolis: Vozes, 2005.

HELLER, Agnes. Uma teoria da história. Rio de Janeiro: Civilização Brasileira, 1993.

HOBSBAWM, Eric J. Sobre história. São Paulo: Companhia das Letras, 2001.

HUERTAS MARTIN, M. Isabel. El sujeto pasivo del proceso penal como objeto de prueba. Barcelona: Bosch, 1999.

IBÁÑEZ, Perfecto Andrés. Los 'hechos' en la sentencia penal. México: Fontamara, 2005.

JAKOBS, Gunther. MELIA, Cancio. Derecho penal del enemigo. Madrid: Civitas, 2003.

KOSELLECK, Reinhart. Futuro passado. Rio de Janeiro: Contraponto, 2006.

KELSEN, Hans. Teoria pura do direito. São Paulo: Revista dos Tribunais, 2003.

KHALED JR, Salah H; MORRISON, Wayne J. Curso de criminologia crítica e cultural decolonial: Volume I – fundamentos, classicismo e positivismo. Belo Horizonte: Letramento, 2024.

KHALED JR, Salah H. Discurso de Ódio e Sistema Penal: Tradição Inquisitória, Tentação Autoritária e Racionalidade Binária. Belo Horizonte: Letramento: 2021.

KHALED JR, Salah H. Direito Penal e Liberdade: Ensaios sobre Castigo, Culpabilidade e Poder Punitivo. Rio de Janeiro: Lumen Juris, 2026.

KHALED JR, Salah H; GLOECKNER, Ricardo Jacobsen. Prova e verdade no processo penal: fundamentos para uma epistemologia decolonial. Florianópolis: Tirant Lo Blanch, 2026.

LANGBEIN, John. Torture and the Law of Proof: Europe and England in the Ancien Régime. Chicago: Chicago University Press, 2006.

LAUDAN, Larry. Strange Bedfellows: inference to the best explanation and the criminal standard of proof. In The University of Texas School of Law, n. 143, 2008.

LAUDAN, Larry. Verdad, Error y Proceso Penal. Madrid: Marcial Pons, 2013.

LAUDAN, Larry; ALLEN, Ronald J. The Devastating Impact of Prior Crimes Evidence and Other Myths of the Criminal Justice Process. In The Journal of Criminal Law & Criminology. v. 101,. n. 2, 2011.

LEENHARDT, Maurice. O mito. In: Religião e sociedade. Rio de Janeiro: Iser, n. 14, p. 87–98, mar. 1987.

LEONE. Giovanni. Tratado de derecho procesal penal: tomo II. Buenos Aires: EJEA, 1963.

LÉVY-BRUHL, Henry. La Preuve Judiciaire: etude de sociologie juridique. Paris: Marcel Rivière, 1964.

LIMA, Roberto Kant de. Cultura Jurídica e Práticas Policiais: a Tradição Inquisitorial no Brasil. Revista Brasileira de Ciências Sociais. Rio de Janeiro, v.4, n.10. 1989.

LOPES JR., Aury; BADARÓ, Gustavo Henrique Righi Ivahy. Direito ao processo penal no prazo razoável. Rio de Janeiro: Lumen Juris, 2006.

LOPES JR., Aury; MORAIS DA ROSA, Alexandre. Processo penal no limite. Florianópolis: Empório do Direito, 2015.

LOPES JR., Aury. Direito Processual Penal. São Paulo: Saraiva, 2014.

LOPES JR., Aury. Direito processual penal e sua conformidade constitucional. Rio de Janeiro: Lumen Juris, 2007.

LOPES JR., Aury. Direito processual penal e sua conformidade constitucional. Rio de Janeiro: Lumen Juris, 2008.

LOPES JR., Aury. Direito processual penal e sua conformidade constitucional. Rio de Janeiro: Lumen Juris, 2009.

LOPES JR., Aury. Direito processual penal e sua conformidade constitucional. Rio de Janeiro: Lumen Juris, 2010.

LOPES JR., Aury. Direito processual penal e sua conformidade constitucional: volume II. Rio de Janeiro: Lumen Juris, 2010.

LOPES JR., Aury. Introdução crítica ao processo penal: fundamentos da instrumentalidade garantista. Rio de Janeiro: Lumen Juris, 2005.

LOVEJOY, Arthur O. A grande cadeia do ser. São Paulo: Palíndromo, 2005.

LYOTARD, Jean-François. O inumano. Lisboa: Estampa, 1997.

MAFFESOLI, Michel. O instante eterno: o retorno do trágico nas sociedades pós-modernas. São Paulo: Zouk, 2003.

MAIER, Julio B. J. Derecho procesal penal I: fundamentos. Buenos Aires: Editores del Puerto, 2006.

MANZINI, Vicenzo. Tratado de derecho procesal penal: tomo I. Buenos Aires: EJEA, 1951.

MARAT, Jean-Paul. Plano de legislação criminal. São Paulo: Quartier Latin, 2008.

MARCHETTI, Paolo. Testis Contra Se: l'imputato come fonte di prova nel processo penale dell'età moderna. Milano: Giuffrè, 1994.

MATZA, David. SYKES, Gresham. Techniques of neutralization: a theory of delinquency. American sociological review. V.22, No. 6 (Dec.1957).

MERLEAU-PONTY, Maurice. O olho e o espírito. Rio de Janeiro: Grifo, 1969.

MARROU, Henri-Irenée. Sobre o conhecimento histórico. Rio de Janeiro: Zahar, 1978.

MAUSS, Marcel. A prece. In: OLIVEIRA, Roberto Cardoso de (Org.). Mauss. São Paulo: Ática, 1979.

MIRABETE, Julio Fabbrini. Processo penal. São Paulo: Atlas, 2002.

MISSE, Michel. Sobre a construção social do crime no Brasil: esboços de uma interpretação. In: MISSE, Michel (Org.). Acusados e acusadores: estudos sobre ofensas, acusações e incriminações. Rio de Janeiro: Revan, 2007.

MONTESQUIEU, Charles de Secondat, Baron de. O espírito das leis. São Paulo: Martins Fontes, 1996.

MONTERO AROCA, Juan. Principios del proceso penal. Valencia: Tirant Lo Blanch, 1997.

MONTERO AROCA, Juan. Proceso y garantia (civil y penal): el proceso como garantia de libertad y de responsabilidad. Valencia: Tirant Lo Blanch, 2006.
MORA, Luis Paulino. La prueba como derecho fundamental. In: GONZÁLEZ-CUÉLLAR SERRANO, Nicolás (Dir.); SANZ HERMIDA, Ágata (Coord.). Investigación y prueba en el proceso penal. Madrid: Colex, 2006.
MORAIS DA ROSA, Alexandre. Decisão penal: a bricolage de significantes. Rio de Janeiro: Lumen Juris, 2006.
MORAIS DA ROSA, Alexandre. Guia Compacto do Processo Penal conforme a Teoria dos Jogos. 2ª Edição. Rio de Janeiro: Lumen Juris, 2014
MORIN, Edgar. Complexidade e liberdade. In: MORIN, Edgar; PRIGOGINE, Ilya (Org.). A sociedade em busca de valores: para fugir à alternativa entre o cepticismo e o dogmatismo. Lisboa: Instituto Piaget, 1996.
MORIN, Edgar. Introdução ao pensamento complexo. Porto Alegre: Sulina, 2005.
MORRIS, Judicium Dei: the social and political significance of the ordeal in the eleventh century. Studies in Church History. n. 12, 1975.
MOURA, Maria Thereza Rocha de Assis. A prova por indícios no processo penal. São Paulo: Saraiva, 1994.
MUÑOZ CONDE, Francisco. Edmund Mezger e o direito penal de seu tempo: estudos sobre o direito penal no nacional-socialismo. Rio de Janeiro: Lumen Juris, 2005.
MUÑOZ CONDE, Francisco. Introduccion al derecho penal. Buenos Aires: BdeF, 2001.
MUÑOZ CONDE, Francisco. La búsqueda de la verdad en el proceso penal. Buenos Aires: Hammurabi, 2003.
MUNSLOW, Alan. Deconstructing history. London: Routledge, 1997.
NASSIF, Aramis. Sentença penal: o desvendar de themis. Rio de Janeiro: Lumen Juris, 2005.
———. Reflexões crítico-fragmentárias sobre a sentença penal. In: CARVALHO, Salo de. (Org.) Leituras constitucionais do sistema penal contemporâneo. Rio de Janeiro: Lumen Juris, 2004.
NIETZSCHE, Friedrich Wilhelm. Sobre verdade e mentira no sentido extra-moral. In: ———. Wilhelm. Obras incompletas. São Paulo: Abril Cultural, 1983.
NUCCI, Guilherme de Souza. Código de Processo Penal comentado. São Paulo: Revista dos Tribunais, 2005.
OLIVEIRA, Eugênio Pacelli de. Curso de processo penal. Belo Horizonte: Del Rey, 2005.
OST, François. O tempo do direito. Lisboa: Instituto Piaget, 2001.
OUTHWAITE, William. Hans-Georg Gadamer. In: The return of grand theory in the Human Sciences. SKINNER, Q. (Org.). Cambridge: Cambridge University Press, 1985.

PALMER, Richard E. Hermenêutica. Lisboa: Edições 70, 1997.
PARINETTO, Luciano. Streghe e Potere: il capitale e la persecuzioni dei diversi. Milano: Rusconi, 1998.
PATETTA, Federico. Le Ordalie: studio del diritto e scienza del diritto comparato. Torino: Fratelli Bocca, 1890.
PAULA, Leonardo Costa de; BARROS, Vinícius Diniz Monteiro de; SANTIAGO NETO, José de. Assis. Entre o topoi e a prova tarifada: sistemas processuais, direito comparado e a impossibilidade de aplicação dos standards de prova no processo penal brasileiro. Revista Brasileira de Ciências Criminais. vol. 199. ano 31. p. 119–152.
PAZ, Octavio. Claude Lévi-Strauss, ou o Novo Festim de Esopo. São Paulo: Perspectiva: 1977.
PESSIS-PASTERNAK, Guitta. Do caos à inteligência artificial: quando os cientistas se interrogam. São Paulo: UNESP, 1992.
POSNER, Richard. Not a Suicide Pact: the Constitution in a time of national emergency. New York: Oxfordf University Press, 2006.
POPPER, Karl R. Um mundo de propensões. Lisboa: Fragmentos, 1991.
POZZEBON, Fabrício Dreyer de Ávila. A crise do conhecimento moderno e a motivação das decisões judiciais como garantia fundamental. In: GAUER, Ruth Maria Chittó (Coord.). Sistema penal e violência. Rio de Janeiro: Lumen Juris, 2006.
PRADO, Geraldo. Prova penal e sistema de controles epistêmicos. São Paulo: Marcial Pons, 2014.p.19.
PRADO, Geraldo. Sistema acusatório: a conformidade constitucional das leis processuais penais. Rio de Janeiro: Lumen Juris, 2006.
PRIGOGINE, Ilya. O reencantamento do mundo. In: MORIN, Edgar; PRIGOGINE, Ilya (Org.). A sociedade em busca de valores: para fugir à alternativa entre o cepticismo e o dogmatismo. Lisboa: Instituto Piaget, 1996.
PRONER, Carol; CITTADINO, Gisele; TENENBAUM, Marcio; RAMOS FILHO, Wilson (Org.). A Resistência ao Golpe de 2016. Bauru: Canal 6; Projeto Editorial Praxis, 2016.
PRONER, Carol; CITTADINO, Gisele; RICOBOM, Gisele; DORNELLES, João Ricardo. (Org.). Comentários a uma sentença anunciada: o processo Lula. Bauru: Canal 6; Projeto Editorial Praxis, 2017.
PUTNAM, Hilary. Do true assertions correspond to reality? In: PUTNAM, Hilary. Mind, language and reality. Cambridge: Cambridge University Press, 1975.
PUTNAM, Hilary. A comparison of something with something else. New Literary History, Vol. 17, No. 1, Philosophy of Science and Literary Theory (Autumn, 1985).
RAMONET, Ignacio. A tirania da comunicação. Petrópolis: Vozes, 2001.

RICOEUR, Paul. Arquitetura e narratividade. Urbanisme, Paris, n. 303, nov./déc. 1998.

RICOEUR, Paul. La memória, la historia, el olvido. Madrid: Trotta, 2003.

RICOEUR, Paul. O justo ou a essência da justiça. Lisboa: Instituto Piaget, 1995.

RICOEUR, Paul. Tempo e narrativa, tomo I. Campinas: Papirus, 1994.

RICOEUR, Paul. Tempo e narrativa, tomo III. Campinas: Papirus, 1997.

RICOEUR, Paul. Verdade e história. Rio de Janeiro: Forense, 1968.

ROXIN, Claus. Derecho procesal penal. Buenos Aires: Editores del Puerto, 2003.

SAMPAIO, Denis. A verdade no processo penal: a permanência do sistema inquisitorial através do discurso sobre a verdade real. Rio de Janeiro: Lumen Juris, 2010.

SANTOS, Myrian Sepúlveda. Memória coletiva e teoria social. São Paulo: Annablume, 2003.

SBRICCOLI, Mario. Justiça Penal. Discursos Sediciosos. n. 17/18, 2011.

SENDRA, Vicente Gimeno; MORENO CATENA, Victor; CORTÉS DOMÍNGUEZ, Valentín. Derecho procesal penal. Madrid: Colex, 1996.

SENTIS MELENDO, Santiago. El proceso civil: Tomo I. Buenos Aires: EJEA, 1959.

SEIXAS, Jacy Alves de. Halbwachs e a memória reconstrução do passado: memória coletiva e história. In: História. São Paulo: EDUNESP, n. 20, 2002.

SOARES, Luis Eduardo. Hermenêutica e ciências humanas. In: GAUER, Ruth M. (Org.). A qualidade do tempo: para além das experiências históricas. Rio de Janeiro: Lumen Juris, 2004.

STRECK, Lenio Luiz. O que é isto – decido conforme minha consciência? Porto Alegre: Livraria do Advogado, 2010.

STRECK, Lenio Luiz. Dicionário de hermenêutica: 50 verbetes fundamentais da teoria do direito à luz da crítica hermenêutica do direito. Belo Horizonte: Letramento, 2020.

STRECK, Lenio Luiz. Processo Judicial Como Espelho da Realidade? Notas Hermenêuticas à Teoria da Verdade em Michele Taruffo. Sequência. n. 74, 2016.

STRECK, Lenio Luiz. Um manifesto antirrelativista: só há interpretações porque existem fatos, regras e princípios a serem interpretados. Revista Brasileira de Ciências Criminais. vol. 199. ano 31.

STRECK, Lenio Luiz. O que é decidir por princípios? A diferença entre a vida e a morte. Em: < https://www.conjur.com.br/2015-ago-06/senso-incomum-decidir-principios-diferenca-entre-vida-morte>

TARSKI, Alfred. The Concept of Truth in Formalized Languages. In: TARSKI, Alfred. Logic, Semantics Metamathematics. Oxford: Oxford University Press, 1936.

TARSKI, Alfred. The Semantic Conception of Truth: and the foundations of semantics. Philosophy and Phenomenological Research, v. 4, 1944.
TARUFFO, Michele. La prueba de los hechos. Madrid: Trotta, 2005.
TARUFFO, Michele. Simplemente la verdad: el juez e la construcción de los hechos. Madrid: Marcial Pons, 2010.
TARUFFO, Michele. A prova. São Paulo: Marcial Pons, 2014.
TARUFFO, Michele. A Prova dos Fatos Jurídicos: noções gerais. São Paulo: JusPodium, 2025.
TARUFFO, Michele. Contribución al Estudio de las Máximas de Experiencia. Madrid: Marcial Pons, 2023.
TARUFFO, Michele. Senso Comum, Experiência e Ciência do Raciocínio do Juiz. In Revista da Escola Paulista de Magistratura. v.2. n.2, 2001.
TARUFFO, Michele. Uma Simples Verdade: o juiz e a construção dos fatos. São Paulo: Marcial Pons, 2012.
THOMPSON, E. P. Costumes em comum: estudos sobre a cultura popular tradicional. São Paulo: Companhia das Letras, 1998.
THUMS, Gilberto. Sistemas processuais penais: tempo, tecnologia, dromologia e garantismo. Rio de Janeiro: Lumen Juris, 2006.
TIMM DE SOUZA, Ricardo. Justiça em seus termos: dignidade humana, dignidade do mundo. Rio de janeiro: Lumen Juris, 2010.
TIMM DE SOUZA, Ricardo. Razões plurais: itinerários da racionalidade ética no século XX: Adorno, Bergson, Derrida, Levinas, Rosenzweig. Porto Alegre: EDIPUCRS, 2004.
TIMM DE SOUZA, Ricardo. Sobre as origens das filosofias do diálogo: algumas aproximações iniciais. In: GAUER, Ruth Maria Chittó (Coord.). Sistema penal e violência. Rio de Janeiro: Lumen Juris, 2006.
TUCCI, Rogério Lauria. Teoria do direito processual penal. São Paulo: Revista dos Tribunais, 2002
TWINNING, William. Rethinkink Evidence: exploratory essays. 2 ed. New York: Cambridge University Press, 2006.
TWINNING, W. L; TWINNING, P. E. Bentham on Torture. In Northern Ireland Legal Quarterly. v. 24. n.3, 1973.
VATIMO, Giani. As aventuras da diferença. Lisboa: Edições 70, 1980.
VEGAS TORRES, Jaime. Presunción de inocencia en el proceso penal. Madrid: La Ley, 1993.
VERNANT, Jean Pierre. Mito e sociedade na Grécia Antiga. Rio de Janeiro: José Olympio, 1992.
VERRI, Pietro. Observações sobre a tortura. São Paulo: Martins Fontes, 2000.
VIERA, Antonio; QUEIROZ, Paulo. Sobre a relação entre o direito penal e direito processual penal. In: MOREIRA, Rômulo (Org.). Leituras complementares de processo penal. Salvador: JusPodivm, 2008.
VIRILIO, Paul. Cibermundo: a política do pior. Lisboa: Teorema, 2000.

VIRILIO, Paul. Velocidade e política. São Paulo: Estação Liberdade, 1996.
VOGLER, Richard. El sistema acusatório en los procesos penales en Inglaterra y en Europa continental. In: BACHMAIER WINTER, Lorena (Org.). Proceso penal y sistemas acusatorios. Madrid: Marcial Pons, 2008.
WHITMAN, James Q. The Origins of Reasonable Doubt: theological roots of the criminal trial. New Haven: London: Yale University Press, 2008.
WINDSCHEID, Bernard; MUTHER, Theodor. Polemica sobre la "Actio". Buenos Aires: Ediciones Juridicas Europa-America, 1974.
YAR, Majid. Cesare Beccaria (1738–94). In: HAYWARD, Keith; MARUNA, Shadd; MOONEY, Jayne. 50 key thinkers in criminology. London: Routeledge, 2010.
YOUNG, Jock. A sociedade excludente. Rio de Janeiro: Revan, 2002.
ZAFFARONI, Eugenio Raúl. Colonialismo y derechos humanos: apuntes para una historia criminal del mundo. Buenos Aires: Taurus, 2022.
ZAFFARONI, Eugenio Raúl; SLOKAR, Alejandro; ALAGIA, Alejandro. Derecho Penal: parte general. Buenos Aires: Ediar, 2002.
ZAFFARONI, Eugenio Raúl; BATISTA, Nilo; ALAGIA, Alejandro; SLOKAR, Alejandro. Direito penal brasileiro – I. Rio de Janeiro: Revan, 2003.
ZAFFARONI, Eugenio Raúl. O inimigo no direito penal. Rio de Janeiro: Revan, 2007.
ZILLI, Marcos Alexandre Coelho. A iniciativa instrutória do juiz no processo penal. São Paulo: Revista dos Tribunais, 2003.

The manufacturer's authorised representative in the EU is Springer Nature Customer Service Centre GmbH, Europaplatz 3, 69115 Heidelberg, Germany. If you have any concerns regarding our products, please contact ProductSafety@springernature.com

Printed and bound by CPI Group (UK) Ltd, Croydon, CR0 4YY
20/09/2026
02219628-0001